YONDER THE BRIDGE

The Story of an Impossible Courtship

YONDER THE BRIDGE*
The Story of an Impossible Courtship

Eva Berck

*Original title: *Letters to My Granddaughters*

Somerset House Publishing   *Somerset PA*

Printed in the United States of America.
Second printing October, 1991.

ISBN 0-9629937-0-0
ISBN 0-9629937-1-9 (paperback)

This book is printed on acid-free, recycled paper.

Jacket Design by Karl Steinbrenner
Author photo © 1991 by Chris Hay Photography

SOMERSET HOUSE PUBLISHING

In Memoriam:

Peter

*To **Clarinda**, who listened,*

*To **Susie**, who cheered,*

*And to **Bob** and his indefatigable pencil,*
for 496 reasons

CONTENTS

Rudolf Presber and his daughter, Eva, 1927.

PART I

1945

Thuringia, Germany

In May, 1945, after five and a half years of bitterly fought war, Germany surrendered to the Allied Forces. American tanks had thundered into our small town in the midst of the Thuringia Forest, stopped briefly, and rolled on eastward. A smaller unit of American troops, less formidable than the first, followed and officially took possession of the town.

On a mild and cloudless May morning I opened the house door to a timid knock to find two women facing me, each gripping half a handle of a small wooden wagon. Tightly wrapped bundles and a few household goods filled the wagon and in a crack between the bundles sat a small girl of about four years. The women did not explain their appearance nor was there any need for it; they were refugees from the western provinces on their way home. They came straight to the problem. Would I, the older woman asked, accompany them to the town commandantur? They were on their way west and had two days' marching behind them already without interference; but, leaving town that morning, they had been stopped by an American patrol car and made to understand that they were not permitted to continue unless they had special permission—a pass that entitled them to use the open road.

Neither of them spoke any English so they had looked around and asked the first person they saw for assistance. It was an elderly man who told them that he himself was unable to help them. He thought, however, that in the old inn they called the Rock Cellar a family of "big city" refugees were staying and that the girl, most likely would speak some English.

Would I come with them?

Well, of course I would.

* * * * * * * * * * * * * *

My English was woefully inadequate. My vocabulary was very restricted. As I was gradually discovering, however, what it lacked in quantity it made up for in quality.

My first English teacher had been an exceedingly tall young woman on the verge of spinsterhood. Undaunted by this possibility, the spirited lady pressed her wire rimmed glasses firmly on her long, thin nose and set out to make learning English a fun experience for her pupils. In this she was very much ahead of her time. To the best of my recollections, none of my other teachers were ever concerned in the slightest with any of us having fun. I remember Fräulein Mueller unrolling (with a triumphant little smile) a large scroll hanging from the blackboard that revealed numerous drawings of jolly little men, women and animals. Tapping each picture energetically with a long pointer in her left hand, and beating the rhythm in the air with her right, she led the way and we followed enthusiastically. Through the open classroom windows of the second floor, over the tops of the chestnut trees, bouncing off the cobblestones below and across the sleepy canal toward the great Frederic's Garrison church, our joyful chant could be heard:

"This is the man, all tattered and torn,
Who kissed the maiden, all forlorn,
Who milked the cow with the crooked horn,
Who kicked the priest, all shaven and shorn,
Who dwelled in the cottage . . . " whatever . . .

I may have gotten it turned around a bit, but that's all I remembered of my first year of English, now and then.

My second-year English teacher was not verging on anything; she was the finished product: an upper-middle class Potsdamer spinster lady, straight-backed, impeccably mannered and in perpetual mourning for some relative. In those days, the departure of a loved one required a lady of her principles and position to wear black clothes for a minimum of one year. I never saw her in anything but black—dresses, stockings and shoes. Her hair was snow white and her face very pink. She was, really, a rather kind person but she had her standards and she was hellbent on erasing in us all deplorable notions that English was a fun language. In this endeavor she was relentlessly supported by the textbook we had to use. The only English I remembered of this second, uncompromising year was a sentence out of this book which I failed to translate properly during the course of our assigned homework:

Im Jahre 1861 wurde Koenigin Victoria ihres edlen Gemahls durch den Tod beraubt.

"In the year 1861, Queen Victoria was bereft by the death of her noble consort."

There is no doubt that we were being taught the "King's English." We just had the wrong king.

To this "Treasury of the English Language" one more sentence had been added by courtesy of my brother, Peter. He used to sing once in a while: "What shall we do with the drunken sailor so early in the morn?"

I wasn't sure how much of this could be used on my errand that morning, but I trusted that I would get together enough words to ask for a pass for the two women.

"I don't think much of your waltzing off before the beds are made," my mother said testily when I told her where I was going.

"Well, I promised," I said, and I waltzed off.

* * * * * * * * * * * * * *

The town, as usual, seemed all but abandoned. I walked alongside the two women who were pulling the wagon. The unsteady wheels clattered over the cobblestones of the market square, shaking the little girl on top of the bundles so roughly that her pigtails flew about her ears. Unprotesting, the child held on tightly to the sides of the wagon, her eyes fixed on the back of the two women, as if she knew that this could not be helped and would have to be endured yet for a very long time.

In front of the tavern at the far corner of the marketplace, the women hesitated. The younger one lifted the child out of the wagon and took the girl's hand protectively into hers.

"It's here where they told us to go," said the older woman in a hushed voice. They looked timorously at the carved old tavern door.

"Let's go, then," I said, more jauntily than I felt and, taking the child's other hand in mine, I marched up the few steps.

The room had been converted into a primitive office. Three of the wooden tables, their tops scrubbed almost white over the years, had been moved to the middle of the room to serve as desks. Two of those desks were occupied; a third chair was empty. A coat of undisturbed dust covered the bar along the far side of the room.

The two soldiers sitting at the tables were, so to speak, my first "indoor" Americans. We all had heard by now that Americans liked to chew some sort of gummy substance for several hours each day and that, when at leisure, they usually put their feet on a table. I suppressed a quick smile when we entered the room: Both soldiers had their chairs tilted way back, their feet were resting on the tables, and their jaws moved rhythmically from side to side. As far as I could see, they had been doing nothing else.

As our little group straggled through the door, they leaned forward and began to shuffle through some papers. The one with more stripes, a corporal, I supposed, looked up with a preoccupied air, "discovered" us, and tilted his chair back again until it was balanced at an accident-defying angle.

"Oh, hello there," he said pleasantly. "Can we help you?"

My charges were scrambling behind my back, which was not broad enough to hide all three of them. I began to explain our errand which I had carefully rehearsed in advance.

"They . . ." I pointed to the women behind me, "desire to return to their home."

"Yeah, why don't they?" said the soldier beside the corporal, nodding amiably in their direction. "And you stay here and talk to us."

I could see that we were on the wrong track.

"Their home is on the Rhine River," I clarified the issue.

"Ah, so," said the corporal, straightening his chair a bit. "Well tell them that they can't. No busses, no trains, nix. Not for weeks yet, anyway. Everything kaput. Versteh? They will have to wait."

I turned the answer over in my head, trying to get the gist of it. The older woman pulled my sleeve.

"What did he say?" she whispered.

I shook my head to silence her. I was formulating my next sentence.

"They wish to walk."

"Walk!?" yelled the soldier. "This old dame and the kid? Why, it's a couple hundred miles . . ."

"No walking!" said the corporal firmly. "Tell your friends they cannot walk along any road without a special permit."

He had said the magic word.

"They wish to have the permit," I said. "Please," I added politely.

The corporal weighed the matter in his mind. "Well," he said at length, "you'll have to see the lieutenant about it," and, as I looked doubtful, he turned his face fully toward the two women and repeated loudly:

"You must wait for the lieutenant. Versteh?"

He obviously shared the sanguine belief of most Americans that everybody would understand at least a little English if one just hollered it loud enough. He motioned toward the bench along the wall.

"Sit down. It won't be long."

The younger woman held the child on her lap, rocking it back and forth. The older one shook my arm more urgently and would not be denied. I explained the conversation to her while the two soldiers watched.

"Tell her not to be scared," said the corporal, seeing the fear in the old woman's face. "The lieutenant won't bite her."

I tried to put the women more at ease and gradually they relaxed a little. There was nothing at all scary about the two soldiers. They regarded us with friendly curiosity. I would have liked to make conversation, but what could I say?

I looked at the corporal, who looked positively encouraging. Did he have a family in America? Was he married? I didn't know the word for married.

"I trust your noble consort is alive and well?" I pictured his face if I would ask him that. It wouldn't work.

8

"Perchance, it was the priest who kicked the cow?" He probably never even heard of the poem. Himmel! What did they have in mind when they taught us that stuff?

But now the corporal took the initiative.

"Where d'you live?" he asked pleasantly.

This was unexpected. He knew where I lived. Why did he ask me that? I looked at him silently, at a loss for an answer.

"Where do you live?" the corporal said, raising his voice.

Now I knew he was teasing me. I decided to go along with his little joke.

"I live in Germany," I said, a bit stiffly.

This, apparently, was not the right answer.

"No, no," said the corporal, shaking his head, "I mean: Where do you live? You know: eat, sleep . . . stay?"

Comprehension dawned on me. I almost laughed with relief. Turning around, I pointed through the window toward the green hills.

"I dwell in the last house yonder the bridge."

The two men looked totally nonplussed. What had I said that startled them so? They must have gone by our Rock Cellar and taken it for a pub.

"We do not sell inebriating matter," I added hastily.

(I had looked this up in the dictionary during the first days of occupation when many soldiers thought we were a pub.)

"Brother!" said the younger soldier, visibly impressed.

"Well . . .!" said the corporal, trying to get on top of that one.

Just then the door opened and the lieutenant strode into the room.

* * * * * * * * * * * * * * *

I have described the room. The scene is set. The young woman who had been so unceremoniously cast into the role of interpreter is wearing a blue and white checkered Dirndl dress with a blue apron tied around her waist. A light blue scarf is holding back her hair that in those days was brown and plentiful. She is, at the moment, too busy rehearsing her lines to be worried.

The young man is of medium height. He is wearing the uniform and insignia of a first lieutenant of the United States Army. He has a full face and very dark hair which is already thinning (if almost imperceptibly) at the crown. On a long, straight nose he wears steel-rimmed glasses that hide large brown eyes (a little sad I thought) and the most beautiful long curved eyelashes imaginable. He has strong, even teeth and a marvelous smile, but since none was directed that morning toward the hapless little group on the wooden bench the young lady did not discover this smile until a later date.

I don't think I have forgotten a single moment of this brief meeting. It certainly was anything but jolly. The lieutenant saw to that. Looking at his bland, unsmiling face I was growing restless and uneasy.

"Three women here to see you, Sir," said the corporal, remembering his lines.

"Do they speak English?" asked the lieutenant, not looking at us.

"No, Sir. That is—yes. Two don't say nothing, and the girl speaks some." The corporal grinned expectantly in my direction.

But the lieutenant was not in a playful mood. He did not like the war, although he believed in it. He did not care for the town or the job he was supposed to be doing in it. ("I was running the town jail," he was to put it at a later date.) His request for transfer to the Pacific, where the war was still raging, was still pending. He found nothing amusing in the sight of three German women who came to his office with requests of their own. It was the lieutenant's unspoken but fervent opinion that they should be thanking their God—if they had one—on their knees for being still alive and should try to keep out of sight as much as possible.

The corporal explained briefly the reason for our presence.

"Well, what do you want?" The lieutenant indicated with a curt nod that he was addressing me now.

I had not taken my eyes off him since he entered. The two soldiers had been friendly and good natured, even if they seemed to make fun of us. But with the lieutenant, a new and hostile element had entered the room. My initial apprehension turned to a kind of stubbornness in the face of this condemnation without a hearing. His question hardly registered.

"You do not like us," I said, staring straight at this unfriendly man who would not even look at us. "You do not like the German people."

"I hate them," said the lieutenant flatly, talking to the wall in front of him.

I could not let that ride. Not for all the road-permits-to-the-Rhine he might be carrying in his bulging back pockets! A long and passionate speech of defense rose in me, unfortunately, all of it in German. In English, it boiled down to one scanty sentence, but spoken rather warmly:

"They are not bad, they are only a little stupid . . ." Politically, I wanted to say, but could not pronounce the word.

"Then I hate their stupidity," said the lieutenant showing a solid streak of stubbornness himself.

* * * * * * * * * * * * * *

With his last forceful statement the lieutenant might have cleared the air, but nobody felt the better for it. The soldiers, embarrassed, shuffled through their papers. The two women looked highly alarmed. The little girl hid her face on her mother's shoulder. They did not understand a word, but hostility as well as kindness need not be understood; it is discerned. It permeates the air.

I was at a loss on how to proceed with this conversation. The lieutenant seemed to find himself in a similar position. By nature a quiet and temperate man, it was beyond his comprehension how he had managed, in record time, to bully two women and a child into speechless terror.

He suddenly addressed the women in German. He spoke it slowly and with a heavy accent, and it cost him a great deal of effort, but it was German, nevertheless, and his voice did not sound unfriendly. The women, who had probably never heard an American speak German just stared at him and huddled closer together. So he turned to me again and fell back into English. From then on whenever the one language failed us, we tried the other.

He told me that he was not authorized to give such a pass as the women needed and that they would have to apply at the next bigger city. He said that he had business there himself that morning and that he would take the women and the child along in his jeep. When I translated this to the women they burst into tears.

"They think that you will arrest them," I explained.

"I am just giving them a ride; how else would they get there?" said the lieutenant reasonably. "Why don't you get into the jeep, too, if it reassures them? I'll drop . . . I'll take you to your house. Where do you live?"

"She dwells in the last house yonder the bridge, Sir," said the corporal, deadpan.

I gave him a gratified little smile. I knew I had said that right.

* * * * * * * * * * * * * *

The day after my memorable visit to the town commandantur the grim lieutenant appeared at our house. I was carrying a basket of wet clothes and had started up the steps to the back yard when he was about to knock at the front door. The sudden meeting took us both by surprise and we both blushed. The lieutenant immediately recovered and assumed a businesslike manner. He asked if I knew where the two women had gone. I didn't know, I said. I really didn't. I had last seen them in the army jeep, only partly reassured, driving off with him toward the city.

The lieutenant said that their request had been denied and that he had brought them back to our town. And now they had disappeared. He tried to look severe, gave up, glanced around leisurely and took in my full laundry basket.

"Let me," he said. He took it out of my hands and ran up the stone steps with it while I panted after him.

The lieutenant set down the basket beside the clothes line and began handing me the wet clothes, one piece at a time—diapers, little shirts, sheets, and kitchen towels—in the most matter-of-fact way as if he had come for this purpose and had done it all his life. We were talking while we were doing this and when the basket was empty we sat down in the grass and talked some more.

When it was time for the baby to be picked up after his nap, we walked down toward the house together. At the door I turned toward him and stretched out my hand to say goodbye. The hand I meant to reach hesitated for a split second then disappeared behind the young man's back.

"No fraternization. We don't shake hands with Germans," said the lieutenant. He turned and walked into the sunset, leaving me in stunned consternation at the door.

I ran upstairs, cheeks burning with humiliation, and slammed the apartment door shut. To my perplexed mother I announced my irrevocable decision:

"I don't ever want to see that man again!"

At five o'clock the next afternoon I opened the door to a modest knock and stared into the face of my nonfraternizing acquaintance of yesterday.

"Will you teach me German?" asked the lieutenant.

* * * * * * * * * * * * * *

He came in the afternoons when his duties were finished. He would carry Bertel or the laundry basket, and sometimes both, up the steps to the back yard and we would settle down in the grass, the baby beside us on a blanket, and proceed with our lessons. Often Katja, our white-Russian refugee friend, would be sitting in her garden chair, a little way off, knitting, nodding and smiling. Bees hummed behind us in the raspberry bushes where tight little green berries were beginning to show the first pink glow. The windmill across the dale waved at us benignly and rheumatically with its four old, gray arms.

How many subjects we covered with those few words we knew in each other's language! We often abandoned the intricacies of the German grammar to discuss more important things like war and peace, God and country, and, the most weighty subject of all, ourselves. We had to catch up on the twenty-three years we had lived without knowing of each other's existence.

I remember one afternoon when I tried to teach my pupil the meaning of the word *doch*. He always arrived with a dictionary and a pad on which he had written a few German words he had heard frequently and whose usage he did not understand. There are words in each language to which one has to be born, I think. They are often simple, much in use and almost impossible to explain to a foreigner. *Doch* is such a word. But I gave it a sporting try.

"If I say to Bertel: 'Do not put your hand into the pot of marmalade, it will not please your mama,' but he does it, nevertheless, that's *doch*!"

"If I tell my friend: 'Do not carry both the baby *and* the laundry basket up those bad steps at the same time,' but he does it anyway, that's *doch*!"

"If your rules say: You must not shake hands with Germans, but you shake my hand in spite of it, that's *doch*!"

"*Doch*" is nevertheless, in spite of, anyway. Versteh?"

"Hmm," said the lieutenant.

* * * * * * * * * * * * * *

The lieutenant was no longer our only American visitor. The search parties had ended for the time being. Whoever knocked at our door came on a peaceful mission. Other soldiers found their way to the Rock Cellar with polite requests: Would I iron their shirt? Fasten buttons? Mend a tear?

"How can I pay you?" they asked. "What would you like?"

And, breathless with the possibilities of choice, I would, nevertheless, unhesitatingly answer "Soap."

* * * * * * * * * * * * * *

The fair weather continued all through the month. Day after day a story-book blue sky stretched over our little town and the green hills around us. The air was mild and sweet with the scent of a thousand blossoms. It seemed as if heaven were saying: "I will not add to all this misery by sending rain storms and sleet and cold winds upon the heads of the homeless."

The people who did have a roof over their heads were spared only a few of the hardships. The bombs had ceased to fall; a different battle of survival had begun. Food rations grew steadily smaller. Gas had been shut off for weeks. Wood was rationed and, with careful usage, was just enough to cook one warm meal a day. Even the waterworks had closed down temporarily. (Once again we had reason to be grateful for our outhouse. We were far less incommoded during that time than most of the town's people. And, twice so far, our outhouse had saved us from being evicted.) For our drinking, washing, and cooking water we went down to the creek where a small spring had been cleared. I would push my bucket and pitchers under the thin, clear trickle and lie back in the weeds waiting for them to fill, then haul them up the embankment, one at a time, and carry them across the road to the house.

Why did I ask for soap and not for bread that spring? The answer must be that we were not yet that hungry. The gnawing, hurting hunger that did not leave us day or night was still ahead of us. We had cabbage and carrots and potatoes. We had our weekly bread allowance and our tiny meat ration, which we often took out in wurst to spread on the bread. Using our combined sugar rations, my mother had cooked the berries to marmalade. She had packed grated white cabbage into a large stone crock, adding a handful of salt and covering it with a cloth and a brick, where, undisturbed, it fermented into the devilish smelling but nutritious mess called sauerkraut. And there were still some mealy apples left in the storage room. We had all of that, but we had no soap. I had washed my baby with gray clay from the day I brought him home. Soap was the first thing that rushed to my mind when I was asked what I wanted.

One day the lieutenant came walking up to the door just as I returned a neatly folded and mended shirt to a young officer who, in exchange, handed me a small parcel.

"What is that?" the lieutenant demanded, glaring first at the innocent back of my departing customer and then at the little package in my hand.

"Soap. I mended his shirt and he brought me soap."

"Why didn't you tell me that you needed soap?" The lieutenant's face was like a thundercloud.

For the first time my heart skipped a beat. He is jealous, I thought, delighted. He is truly jealous!

The lieutenant wanted an answer.

"You did not ask," I defended myself.

It was true, he had never asked. My friend and pupil who came almost daily and helped and learned so willingly had been blissfully oblivious of the way we lived.

One day, a week or so before this incident, my mother, who had been anxious to sort out some business and make inquiries, got a chance to ride to the county seat with the milk truck. She was to return with the same truck on the next day. That evening, after we had finished our lesson on the hill, the lieutenant, as he often did, carried the baby upstairs to the kitchen. Since my mother was not there, he sat down on the kitchen stool and prepared to be companionable. He watched me as I got Bertel's "Wurstbrot" ready, a slice of dark bread spread with soft sausage.

"We don't feed that to our babies," he remarked, astonished.

Sitting on the kitchen chair across the little table from him, I, too, was watching Bertel eat and getting more and more hungry myself. It had been a long time since the noon meal, which had consisted of little more than carrots and potatoes and had not exactly stuck to the ribs. The lieutenant made no preparations to leave. I could not very well invite him to join me for supper; there was nothing on the menu he would care to try.

The lieutenant, at this point, was looking closely for possible ill-effects that the wurstbrot might have had on the baby. Bertel showed none, but I was getting lightheaded from the lack of food. Finally I got up, stirred the spark in the stove and piled some twigs on top of it. When the twigs began to crackle I put the skillet on the open burner and began to slice some cold boiled potatoes into it. In a pitcher near the stove we kept the rest of the Ersatzkaffee. I poured a little at a time over the potato slices. It gave them a comforting brownish color and kept them from burning. The lieutenant had ceased observing Bertel and seemed mesmerized by my activities.

"What are you doing?" he finally asked.

"I am frying potatoes."

"We use fat for that in America" said the lieutenant as if he had witnessed a strange native ritual and was now explaining his own country's customs. I could think of no answer that would not have sounded melodramatic. I pulled the skillet off the stove and emptied it on to a plate.

"May I eat? Will you excuse me?" I asked.

"Oh, certainly," said the lieutenant kindly.

"We would eat meat with this," he said, announcing another one of his country's different customs to me.

"Yes. We do, too . . . sometimes . . ." when we have some, I wanted to add but swallowed it together with the steaming potatoes.

It took all of three minutes to clean up after this meal. I took off my apron and sat down again on the kitchen chair. The lieutenant still showed no sign of departure.

Houses in small towns are not built of brick or wood; they are surely made of glass. By noon tomorrow everybody in town would know that my mother had left for two days and that the American officer, who supposedly took German lessons at the Rock Cellar, had not left until after dark. I was racking my brain for a subtle way to let him know that he simply had to leave; but I could think of nothing at all.

My visitor, inspired by earlier reminiscing of native habits, was now telling me how many of the city streets in his country had numbers rather than names. That way, he said, nobody could possibly get lost. Having arrived at a desperate decision, I got up, picked up his helmet, and wordlessly held it out to him.

The lieutenant looked rather startled. For a second he seemed to think that I had taken a remarkable exception to the numbering of streets. Then enlightenment dawned.

"Oh. Yes. Right," he said, blushing a bit. He grabbed the helmet, planted it on his head and hastily took his leave.

Downstairs the heavy front door slammed shut and I winced.

"I wonder if he is mad at us?" I was looking at my little son for comfort. But Bertel, making the most of the few golden moments of unsupervised freedom, had found the coal bin and could not be bothered just then.

* * * * * * * * * * * * * *

It happened on an early June evening. Our lesson was finished. My pupil was rolling in the grass rough-housing with the delightedly squealing baby. I was picking raspberries. Those first red ripe berries between the still spring fresh green of the bushes looked so lovely that I left them on the stem and was gathering a little bouquet of them when I heard my mother calling me from the house. Her voice sounded so urgent that I threw my little bouquet in the grass and hurried down the steps, somewhat hampered by a tight, white skirt. (I often happened to wear one of my two very best outfits for our afternoon lessons; this skirt predated the war and was my pride and joy.) My mother was standing outside the door, her face vivid with emotion. She whispered rather than talked in a normal voice, as if she were afraid that whatever she had to say to me might evaporate if proclaimed too loudly.

"They let the young Lehmann boy go . . ." ("They" at that time were always the Americans, as opposed to "we," just as later on "they" would be the Russians.)

"He has lost an arm, and they released him early from prison camp. He told his parents that there was a soldier in camp with him who told him that his mother and sister were refugees in this town and lived in an old Inn, he thought." My mother and I looked at each other not daring to voice our thought.

"What else did he say?" I, too, spoke in a hushed voice. "Did he say what the soldier looked like?"

"I don't know," said my mother miserably. "Herr Bossier sent his girl up to tell us and that's all she knew. She had to run back not to be caught in the curfew."

A strict six o'clock curfew was imposed on our town. People who were caught afterward had been exposed to some rough penalties.

"You mean we have to wait till tomorrow at eight?!"

"What else can we do?" said my mother, trying to get control of her emotions. Abruptly she turned and walked back into the house.

I flew up the stone steps, trembling with excitement. The lieutenant was sitting in the grass, Bertel on his lap. I sank down beside them, pouring out the frustrating news.

"Fourteen hours!" I said wildly. "Imagine waiting fourteen hours to find out if my youngest brother is alive or if it was just a cruel coincidence! It would have been better if we had not heard about it just yet."

The lieutenant put Bertel beside me in the grass and got up.

"I'll go and talk to the young man," he said. "Tell me where he lives and what I should ask him."

My mother and I waited together, not talking, scarcely moving, until the lieutenant appeared again.

It seemed the soldier back in prison camp (whose name the Lehmann son did not know) was big and bony and very young. He had blue eyes and was always hungry and sometimes managed to sneak into the same food line twice which was risking a great deal of grief; but he seemed quite cheerful about it . . .

Now my mother's and my eyes were brimming with tears: we knew a boy like that! He would come home now, one day. Our youngest would come home!

It was not until I bent down to put Bertel to bed that my mother exclaimed: "For heaven sakes, what happened to your skirt?!"

When I had run up to tell the lieutenant the news I had sat down, dead center, on the little bouquet of raspberries. In all those years since I have never picked raspberries without thinking of my youngest brother's homecoming, of the lieutenant's errand of mercy, and of the demise of that pretty white skirt. And to be perfectly honest, not always in that order.

* * * * * * * * * * * * * *

Around ten o'clock one morning my mother was feeding Bertel and I was cleaning the ashes out of the stove when suddenly the lieutenant was standing in the door of the kitchen. Never before had he come at this hour. We could see that he was deeply disturbed. Bad tidings were written all over his face.

"It is true," he said without any introduction. "We are leaving. The first units are getting ready to leave now and in three days we will all be gone."

"How do you know that?" I asked, incredulous. There was always the faint hope of an error.

"I overheard it at headquarters just now," he said simply.

"What will happen to our town?!"

The lieutenant had trouble with an answer.

"The Russians are coming," he said, not very distinctly.

"Why? Why?" I yelled; and the lieutenant shrugged his shoulders and looked as bewildered as we.

"The Allies have reached an agreement. The Russians will occupy this part of Germany. Our troops will withdraw from Thuringia."

He had to leave us with this devastating news, and he did not return that afternoon nor the following day.

That the Americans were departing was soon apparent to the whole town. But that their beautiful Thuringia had been surrendered to the Red Armies the people refused to believe. You must remember that there had been no newspapers, no mail, no German news on the radio for months now. Everything was by word of mouth. And word of mouth from the East had not exactly been rosy.

On the third day, just as he had said, the last of the big U.S. Army trucks and jeeps were heading out of town toward the West. And still I had not seen the lieutenant since he brought us the gloomy news. I could not believe that he would go without saying goodbye; yet, by eleven that morning the last of the soldiers had left. My mother announced that she would take Bertel and walk into town to see what was happening.

"They are all gone now," she said, busying herself with the baby and not looking up. But I only shook my head.

I watched her from the window bouncing the buggy down the road. I had waited for two days now and I sat quietly down on the kitchen chair, prepared to go on waiting. There was a dogged faith in me that I could not have been that wrong.

When I finally heard the familiar steps running up the stairs the first rush of feelings was one of joyful confirmation before the misery of parting really took hold.

When the lieutenant came in he wore full dress uniform. I had seen him only once before in it, on some special occasion, and it had taken me by surprise.

"You are very pretty!" I had exclaimed.

"Men are not pretty," he told me. "Men are handsome. And I am not handsome."

You are beautiful to me, I wanted to say, but, as so often, I did not know how to say it. That was after he had gotten our frightened Katja into the West camp for political refugees. And after he had gone into town that night to inquire about my brother. After he had made a devoted friend of Bertel and had carried countless laundry baskets up the stone steps and helped me hang up innumerable diapers. And after his colonel (who really wasn't such a bad old guy) had said to him he felt he should remind him of the nonfraternization rules. And the lieutenant had said "Yes, Sir," and had gotten that obstinate look about him that I knew so well by now and staunchly continued to appear at the same hour as always at our doorstep. And after he told me about his first visit to the Rock Cellar when he had come to inquire after the whereabouts of the two women. He had quite believed me when I said that I didn't know, he told me, because he knew! He had seen them very early that morning, walking across the fields, pulling their little wagon with the child, unmistakably heading west.

And now he was heading west himself, in full dress uniform, and Stalin's armies were going to move in. He didn't know the destination of his unit. The war with Japan was still raging. There was no mail service and no telephone. We were standing in the little cramped kitchen looking at each other in wordless dismay. We had never talked about love, never about the future. And all we had left now were three minutes. His driver kept the jeep running outside the house; I could hear the motor growling.

"My good friend," I finally said, helplessly.

"My good friend," the lieutenant repeated. And then he took me in his arms and it was just as well that the colonel with his nonfraternizing rules was already thirty miles out of town rolling toward the Rhine.

"I will come back for you and Bertel," said the lieutenant in one breathless rush, "I will get you both out of here and you will love my town and Bertel will love the woods and fields and you will see it is a marvelous place for our children to grow up and you will be very happy there . . ."

My head was spinning. I knew what he was saying but he might as well have asked me if I wanted to ride with him to the moon.

"This is what you think and what you hope," I said, trying to face the desolate reality with some shred of composure, "but you will see that it cannot be done."

"*Doch!*" said the lieutenant and that wonderful stubborn look came over his dear face. And then he was out of the door and I ran to the window and watched him jump into the seat beside the driver, pushing his helmet over his head as the jeep roared down the hill.

* * * * * * * * * * * * * * *

My mother had walked down the road to discuss the worrisome new situation with our neighbors. I was sitting in the kitchen, holding the baby on my lap, staring morosely into the purple twilight beyond the window. Those were the longest days of the year and dusk was lingering. Bertel stirred on my lap and yawned. It was long past his bedtime. Unable to rouse myself, I buried my face in his hair. It smelled of sunshine and grass and lovely American soap.

"Do you think he will come back?" I murmured.

In answer Bertel poked his grimy little fingers amiably into my ear. He definitely thought so.

PART II

The Early Years

Chapter 1

My grandmother Caroline was born some time in the late eighteen fifties. She was one of a large family of bright youngsters in which the females in particular seemed to have been blessed with a quick mind and an impatient curiosity. If she had been born a century later, Caroline would have gone far. As it was, she finished school at fifteen and stayed home, learning all the domestic skills required in her time. In her early twenties she married a young, mild-mannered stone mason and, being at all times two steps ahead of him, she led him a merry chase through the next forty-five years. The young mason took his bride to Berlin, which was just then bustling with the pride and growth of the newly founded empire. She bore him, in quick succession, two children, a girl named Frieda, and a boy, Robert. Caroline considered this a satisfactory family and the end of her childbearing; the more so as the boy showed a quick intelligence and the girl, who had inherited the best features of each parent, promised to grow into a classical beauty.

When Frieda was fourteen and Robert twelve and my grandmother was approaching midlife, she found herself, much to her consternation, once more with child.

On a few occasions, when something had greatly displeased her or her family had seemed to her more intractable than necessary, she had taken a long kitchen knife and locked herself into the food pantry. It never failed to drive her family frantic and promptly have them see things her way. In the present situation, however, Caroline — being of a practical mind — realized that such high dramatics would serve no purpose; it would change nothing and only waste everybody's time. Her second daughter, my mother, was born in the middle of August, 1895. Caroline resigned herself to the inevitable and turned to the task at hand, raising little Lucie with a mixture of love, exasperation, and common sense.

Her husband's feelings were different. He was devoted to the cheerful little girl who returned his unconditional love with a stormy affection of her own. Lucie was not as beautiful as her older sister nor did she possess her brother's sharp intelligence, but she was pretty and quick and had the wide-eyed curiosity of her mother's family, completely lacking in her beautiful sister.

Frieda was married young to a man of property. Older than his beautiful, passive bride by some fifteen years, he tried to play Pygmalion to her reluctant Galathea. It was a dismal failure and the marriage ended in divorce. My aunt never remarried, never held a job, and she raised her only son with the single-mindedness of the otherwise unoccupied.

When I was born, my grandmother came to visit. After a benign look into the cradle she turned to my mother and said:

"It's nice that you have a daughter, Luciechen." And with a wistful little sigh she added:

"Wouldn't it have been lovely if it had been Frieda's little girl."

This remark signified nothing to me when I was told of it; I was quite indifferent to it. My mother was not, I know, for she told it to me more than once.

I remember my Aunt Frieda as handsome rather than beautiful. Her face, when I knew her, had already taken on a faintly pinched, discontented look, and her voice dragged as the voices of women do who see themselves perpetually wronged by life. At that time my mother had not seen her sister for almost ten years, but once in a while I was taken along by my grandmother to a tea party at my aunt's apartment.

* * * * * * * * * * * * * *

When Lucie was seventeen, her father retired from his trade and bought a small farm about an hour's train ride north of the city. Lucie stayed on with her sister in Berlin while attending a commercial school. On graduation, she quickly found a job and a place of her own to live.

In the days before the first world war there were few official state-supervised social agencies. The courts, except in extreme cases, kept out of such matters and most of the welfare and charity work was done and dispensed by private organizations with very little interference from the outside. It was for such an organization that Lucie went to work, bringing with her a satisfactory knowledge of shorthand and typing and a great deal of enthusiasm.

During her first year there, on the day before an Easter weekend, the Anna incident happened. Everybody at the agency had gone, having made their own plans for the long holiday. There was only one task left to be done — one that everyone considered to be quite disagreeable, and it therefore fell to the youngest member of the staff, my mother.

The agency had been in contact with a childless, middle-aged couple who had shown an interest in adopting a well-mannered little girl. The agency thought they had just the child for them, Anna, a four-year-old who lived with a family whom the agency had come to regard as unsatisfactory. During the lengthy negotiations these foster parents became increasingly difficult and uncooperative. They were accustomed to having the child around and they did not want to lose the monthly support check. So the agency simply and firmly set a day and hour when the child was to be packed and ready to be taken to her new home. This was what the eighteen-year-old Lucie set out to do on that particular afternoon.

When she arrived at the foster parents' apartment, the child had indeed been prepared for leaving but in rather unexpected ways. She was wearing absurd, ill-fitting clothes and apparently had been crying for hours; her nose and eyes were red and inflamed. Her rather prominent ears were sticking out from a head that showed not a single hair. The foster parents, in a last act of defiance, had shaved her head down to the scalp. The child was completely bald. My mother, unwarned and unprepared, gazed at her in stunned disbelief.

The foster parents had removed themselves from the scene. My mother pulled a cap low over little Anna's ears and forehead. She wiped the child's nose and face with her own handkerchief, gripped her sticky little fingers with one hand and the small cardboard suitcase with the other and, with the direst forebodings, headed for the child's new home.

It was over very quickly. The stately, elderly couple, who had greeted them with pleasurable anticipation, took one horrified look at the monstrous little thing on my mother's hand and — pressing her handkerchief to her mouth — the lady fled from the room. The husband, in an admirably controlled voice, told my mother to leave as quickly and quietly as possible in order not to upset his wife any further. Any dealings with her agency, he said coldly, would thereafter be out of the question.

My mother found herself back on the street with little Anna hanging on to her skirt, whimpering and wiping ever more grime into her eyes. It was late afternoon. The lady in charge of the agency had gone out of town for the holidays. The child's former and future homes were permanently closed to her.

It took Lucie no more than a minute or two to come to a decision. Taking hold of the child and the suitcase, she marched to the nearest northbound railroad station. She would take Anna to her mother.

It did not occur to her to announce her coming. Her parents had no telephone and, anyway, this was nothing for which one could properly prepare anybody. They took the first train out. Little Anna, at long last, had stemmed her tears, much comforted by some sweets and the promise of meeting very soon a kitty, five brown chickens, and some real live piglets.

When my grandmother opened the door, my mother took the child's cap off. It was dark by now but the lamp in the doorway was quite enough for my grandmother to take in the wretched, bald-headed little figure at the threshold, nor did she miss the shabby little suitcase.

"Ach du Lieber Gott!" was all she said. Then she went to heat some soup and make up a bed for the child.

Anna stayed with my grandparents for six years. At that time her natural mother had gotten herself sufficiently on her feet to be able to take her child back.

* * * * * * * * * * * * * *

Two or three times a year and sometimes the day before a holiday I would accompany my mother on her visit to the old lady. When we entered the elevated train that cut right through the heart of Berlin, I eagerly looked for a window seat. My parents never took us to those parts of the city and everything out there was unfamiliar and exciting to me. As the train approached the city center, the streets took on a neglected appearance and the storefronts looked dingy. The sunless courtyards were paved and showed at the most a few straggling shrubs. As the houses on both sides pressed closer to the tracks I caught glimpses of the rooms inside. On warm sum-

mer days women in carelessly buttoned blouses, tight yellow curles clinging to their ears and forehead, were leaning out of the windows, their
plump arms resting on cushions placed on the windowsill. If I looked quickly enough I could make out beyond them a black-iron stove with an old-
fashioned coffee pot on it, or some men in shirtsleeves playing cards around
a kitchen table, or maybe a cluttered bedroom with a narrow wooden
washstand. Sometimes a big gray cat would be sunning itself beside a flower
box that half-heartedly sported a few anemic geraniums.

This was my favorite part of the trip and when we were past it my interest waned. The streets became tree-lined again and the houses looked
like old dowagers in their faded and outmoded finery left behind at a party
that was long over. It was there that we would get off the train and walk
the five minutes to the large yellow brick building where the old lady lived.

Our steps might have echoed as in a cathedral through the high deserted
stone hall but for the thick, brown linoleum under our feet. We stopped
in front of the seventh door from the stairs (I always counted them); my
mother tapped her fingertips lightly against the wood and opened the door
without waiting for an answer.

In those days the residents of the city's homes for the aged were encouraged to bring as many of their belongings with them as they wished
and found space for. The room we entered was so crammed with dark furniture that it always took me a second before I located the old lady. She
was then already shorter than I, having shrunk during the last years while
I had grown. Her iron-gray hair was caught in one of those invisible nets
that allowed no strand to escape. She walked with a pronounced limp and
used a rubber-tipped cane to steady herself. Inevitably, she wore a solemn
black dress and a cameo brooch at her throat.

We were expected. Spread over the dark green cloth that covered the
large round table in front of the sofa was a white doily of handmade lace
on which three dessert plates, napkins and spoons were laid, but only two
cups and saucers. An odor of freshly brewed coffee filled the room. The
pot itself was hidden under an oversized flowered coffee-cozy. In the little blue enamel pan on the spirit burner was the hot cocoa that would be
served to me.

My mother's lips brushed quickly over the wrinkled cheek offered to
her and then I bent down and kissed a spot near the hairline where the
skin was drawn paper thin over the high cheekbone, as far away from the
dry, bluish lips as I dared.

The old lady smiled at me and limped to a small china closet at the far corner of the room. There on the top shelf, in the midst of various knickknacks (which included my brothers' cups and saucers) would be my very own cup. Nobody else was permitted to drink from it. It was bell shaped, made of heavy porcelain and decorated with broad gold trim. Over the years the gold had paled and a little of it had washed off; this only enhanced its charm in my eyes. The grandest part, though, was the handle. It was very thin and formed a high arch that descended into a number of curlicues making it difficult to lift the cup when filled. The porcelain was heavy, and so was the hot chocolate, and a sharp curlicue buried itself into the side of my middle finger leaving a deep, red imprint. Not only was I prepared for it, I was looking forward to it. Experimenting with this mysterious imprint, wondering if it was deeper this time than the last, waiting for it to disappear and trying to recreate it on another finger was my main entertainment during the next hour and a half.

There was very little else to distract me. My mother did not speak much and when she spoke it was in a low, colorless tone, very unlike the way she usually talked. I don't remember her ever laughing during one of these visits. Once in a while, when the old lady had talked long and comma-less in her thin old voice, two red spots would appear on my mother's cheekbones which were much like the old lady's but for the fact that my mother's skin was smooth and vibrant.

"Why don't you at least try Luciechen," said the old lady. (Nobody else called my mother that.) "What is the matter with you? But you were always headstrong. When have you tried the last time? I asked Friedchen what she would do if you came one day unexpectedly and she said she certainly would not put a chair out in the hall for you; she would be nice about it. It's all so long ago what is the matter with you. But you always wanted it your own way Luciechen, you never did listen . . ."

My mother began talking about the weather. She asked if the nurse had done anything about the old lady's rash. Could it be that the sheets were not rinsed properly? And I turned my attention back to my tormented finger. Before we left my mother unobtrusively placed an envelope under the little reading lamp with the painted rose on the glass globe. She did this every time. I knew that there was money inside because I had seen her put it in once before we left home. We put on our coats and hats and I dutifully kissed the old lady someplace above the ear and thanked her for the nice time.

"Goodbye, Mama," said my mother when she walked out of the door. I never got over the wonder of it.

* * * * * * * * * * * * * *

I never got over the wonder of it that she was my mother's mother. We children called her Oma. When we were still living in the big house in the country, Oma came to stay with us a few times. Once, when she came out of the hospital after she had broken her hip, she stayed with us for weeks. She slept in the little guest room at the end of the hall. She rested a great deal and I would go in there at times and visit with her. I would tell her some mischief we had done in school, which I would not tell my parents because I was not sure they would think it funny. Oma always laughed. Once I asked her to tell me a story. I had read somewhere that grandmothers were supposed to tell stories. She looked surprised and seemed to think about it for a while. Then, with a grim little smile, she began: "There was a young boy once who was very smart. In school he did arithmetic faster than the teacher and he always brought prizes home in geography and history. He could have gone on to a university. He could have done anything at all in life. But he grew up and married a very stupid woman. And that was the end of it."

That, also, seemed to be the end of the story. Oma leaned back, closed her eyes, and rested some more.

I thought about the story for a few days. I was wondering if she had been talking about my Uncle Robert. I had only been to his house a few times. He was married to a large woman with yellow hair who kept filling our plates with thick slices of raisin cake. She wore a ruffled apron which she never took off, not even when she sat down with us at the dinner table. When I saw my mother sorting her linen closet one morning and looking quite cheerful with it, it seemed like a good time to ask.

"Is Aunt Hedwig stupid, Mutti?"

My mother turned around and stared at me for a while with that absent look she had when she was not sure about something.

"Well," she finally said, "she does some lovely embroidery." And that was all the answer I got.

In 1940, during the first year of the war, my mother went to the southern part of Germany, into the Bavarian mountains, to look for an apartment. She hoped to find one where she could spend the summer months and offer my brothers and me a vacation place when the time came. She could not find a small apartment she liked and could afford, so she rented a very large one that was surrounded by a park and had a lake front. She rented out all the rooms but two and with no obligations other than a few hours of work a day, my brothers and I spent some enjoyable vacation weeks there.

My grandmother died during that summer. My mother did not go north for the funeral. Traveling was difficult, all the rooms at the apartment were filled and she did not feel well that week, my mother wrote in her letter to me, informing me of my grandmother's death.

* * * * * * * * * * * * * * *

Paul Schulz was one of the urchins who lived in the dilapidated houses near the river – the only one who was old enough to come to my father's funeral. He didn't actually attend it, but he did pedal up to the Potsdamer cemetery chapel, and during the services he leaned against his bike outside on the graveled path and peered through the open doors into the dim stone vestibule and the long aisle toward the flower-covered casket.

The other boys from down the river were just hanging around the bakery that afternoon in a listless sort of way, looking up the street toward our house out of sheer habit and, eventually, drifting off, one at a time: Gustave and Gerhard, Jörgen and Jürgen, whatever their names were, and, of course, the twins. The twins I remember best; they both had the same red hair and slightly crossed eyes and the same unwashed, freckled faces. But nobody ever got them mixed up because one of them was crippled. His short, matchstick legs would carry his weight but could not move him and he propelled himself forward by pushing a sturdy little stick between them and jumping, leap-frog style, over it. He was quite good at it, really.

Those kids were younger than Paul by three or four years and they always hung around the bakery corner in the afternoons. There they would stand and shove one another about or crouch on the dusty sidewalk and cheat each other at marbles. After a good rainfall they would stomp around in the big puddle that formed in the empty lot next door. On wintry afternoons, when there was no puddle and no marble games they would hide behind the telephone booth at the corner and throw snowballs at the bakery window. In the end, the baker always obliged and came running out of the shop, his face even redder than usual over his white floured apron, swearing and shaking his fist at them while they would fly down the street in mock terror, the leap frog as fast as the best of them.

It was not long after we had moved to this small country community that my father, who was taking our dogs for their afternoon walk, happened upon this scene. The baker apologized. There was no getting rid of those pesky kids, he said; one of these days he would get the constable after them.

My father contemplated the feisty little mob who had returned and huddled together at a cautious distance. It occurred to him that one might conceivably turn those pint-sized loiterers into potential customers to the mutual satisfaction of all parties concerned. He entered the bakery and bought a number of flat, round cakes (for inexplicable reasons called "Amerikaner" by everybody); they were about the size of a small saucer and were covered with a thick sugar icing. He already had the doorknob in his hand when he noticed through the glass door the boy with the stick.

He turned back to the counter and bought one more. Once outside, the first small, cold hand stretched hesitantly out toward him, followed in quick succession by all the others. Into each hand, my father deposited one "Amerikaner;" the leap frog got two. A tradition was born.

From that day on every afternoon at roughly the same hour my father would enter the bakery and anybody present at the street corner would receive an "Amerikaner." No conversation of any importance ever took place except for the time when my father inquired about the absence of the crippled boy. He was informed by the twin that his brother had the measles. My father left the bag with the two remaining cakes in his care, severely admonishing him not to eat them himself.

Yes, that is the way I remember it: everybody got one round, iced cake except for the boy with the red hair and the dirty face who now had the measles and who could not walk even when he was up and about but had to hop over a stick between his legs. He always got two. It was that simple. Nobody ever wondered or questioned it.

Paul Schulz was rarely around on those afternoons. Although he lived in the same neighborhood at the river, he was now too old and too proud to hang out with the small fries. Besides, he could boast of an earlier and more personal acquaintance with my father.

We had only recently moved out of Berlin and into the small commuter community just outside an old, sandy farm village. My oldest brother, Wolfgang, going on eleven, set out every morning to pedal the seven kilometers to a Potsdamer high school for boys. My youngest brother, Dolfi, not yet five, was still at home. Being a child of great resources, he had no particular trouble amusing himself. He spent much time lying on his stomach teasing the frogs which were squatting around our pond. With a long blade of grass he would tickle their short, bloated necks or hasten their return to their natural habitat with the help of a wooden kitchen spoon. On rainy days he tried his hand at giving the dogs a haircut, an experiment that was frowned upon by the dogs and my father alike. He would lie on his bed and study for hours the great world atlas (later, when he could read, he added the encyclopedia to those studies). He was under foot in the kitchen and on Thursdays he kept an eye on Herr Platt.

Herr Platt, a small, elderly man with a skull-like head and no noticeable flesh on his bones, came every Thursday to pump out the septic tank. This was during the depression and in addition to his wages Herr Platt would appear in the kitchen after his work where the cook would serve him a hot meal. It was this meal that held the family's general interest. On any given Thursday Herr Platt would eat about as much as two coal miners after a ten-hour work day, never gaining an ounce. We children had heard our parents discuss the possibility that the man hosted a tapeworm. After this we regarded him with the greatest fascination, and Dolfi, the only one at home, was ordered to observe him for possible signs of an escaping tapeworm. My brother Peter, ever the future scientist, was all for Dolfi having a glass jar ready for the occasion, but Dolfi balked at this.

At that time Peter and Dolfi, among their other enterprises, were in the business of selling postcards. That is, Peter would buy a number of stamped, blank postcards at the post office at three cents each on which he would draw rather surrealistic pictures of houses, trees, and little people with large round smiles, no noses, and wide-apart stick fingers. Dolfi was commissioned to sell those cards at ten cents a piece, a net profit of better than two hundred percent. When the neighborhood began to show strong symptoms of saturation, the artist instructed Dolfi to try a certain street corner. Sales had just begun to pick up when my father and the dogs rounded this particular corner one day at an unexpected hour. The joyful greetings of the dogs prevented a successful retreat over the nearest fence, and Simple Simon and his wares were speedily and permanently removed from their place of business.

With Wolfgang pedaling off to Potsdam and Dolfi being usefully employed at home, Peter and I were dispatched to the village school. When we moved to the country my mother saw no reason to buy us children a new wardrobe. After all, we had moved out of the big city to get away from all the emphasis on private schools, new clothes, and taxi cabs. I honestly don't remember what Peter was made to wear, but I was splendidly attired in a gray little coat with collar and cuffs of Persian lamb. Around my neck hung a matching little muff and I wore a gray hat with a broad round rim. Two ribbons streamed down from it over the polished leather book satchel on my back. My mother regarded this outfit as very pleasing, an opinion that was enthusiastically shared by every village boy between six and twelve. They had not had so much fun since the firemen's fair.

My greatest tormentor was Paul Schulz. He was two years older and half a head taller than I. He also, most unfortunately, shared the same way home with me, the river settlement being on the far side of our community. We soon became something of a regular sideshow. I would cautiously walk on the other side of the street, away from the rest of the children, but sooner or later Paul would cross over and walk on my side. He would not really walk, he would hop on one leg around me and pretend to stumble or he would walk directly in front of me and suddenly stop dead in his tracks scanning the air for a non-existing airplane, or else he would grab his book satchel by its torn leather strap and swing it in a wide circle around him — one way or another he would make me fall into the ditch along the road. The ditch was soft and moist and full of nettles; my legs were protected by thick cotton stockings, but I often burned my fingers trying to scramble back onto the road. In addition, my pride was bruised; I was slowly turning to ashes right there in front of a cheering audience.

Emotional upheavals in children were not encouraged in those days; certainly nothing much was done about them unless they began to discommode their elders. We usually tried to muddle through on our own. But this daily ordeal was more than I could handle and after a week I tearfully told my parents about it. My father listened, his face like a thundercloud. Nobody was going to do this to his little girl! He would meet me after school the next day. He would see about *that*!

I was walking on my solitary side of the road when I saw my father and the dogs coming toward me. When he caught up with me I pressed my face into his comforting overcoat.

"That one over there," I whispered fiercely," the tall one with the brown jacket and no cap." And my father was on his way. No Roman matron in the ancient colosseum could have watched more eagerly the march of the lions toward the Christians than I watched my father's progress across the street. He was a big man and he was swinging his silver-ringed walking stick, and holding the two shepherd dogs on a short leash, and his face must have shown all the called-for parental wrath. While the rest of the children scattered in every direction, he firmly anchored my tormentor to the road. The ensuing conversation took all of five seconds; then my father turned on his heels and marched down the street with Paul trotting beside him. To my speechless consternation the two of them disappeared into the dairy store at the next corner. When they emerged again, Paul was busy digging into a brown paper bag before loping off in the direction of the river.

My father crossed the street swinging his walking stick more jauntily than ever and looking so grandly unconcerned that—young as I was—I sensed that he was embarrassed. He talked about school, he talked about the dogs, my brothers, and the weather, anything but what had happened over there.

"He bought him three candy bars! I saw them!" I protested indignantly to my mother that evening.

"Weelll . . .," said my mother, who sympathized a little with my frustration. "You see, this is what happened . . ." And she told me.

My father had cornered Paul with all the necessary determination.

"You are obviously a very naughty and mischievous boy," he told him. "I shall certainly talk to your father about you. What is your father's name?"

"My father is dead," stammered the boy.

This had all the effect of an overhead thunderclap on my father. Suddenly he took in the frightened blue eyes staring into his own, the red chapped cheeks, the much-mended pants, the scruffy book satchel, the jacket with sleeves that were inches too short and exposed thin, childish wrists.

"Well, come along, then," he said, clearing his throat, and without another word from either of them, they were off to the dairy store.

Nobody pushed me into the nettles again. I suspect Paul saw to that. I eventually outgrew the Persian lamb coat and the hat with the ribbons and got school clothes like everybody else's. My brothers and I settled down, made our own friends and enemies and forgot all about big city ways just as our parents had intended us to.

It was five and a half years later in the fall of 1935 that Paul took his bike and rode to my father's funeral in Potsdam. I saw him out of the corner of my eye when my mother walked into the chapel with my brothers and me. It was one more familiar face among so many unknown ones that filled the chapel like a dark sea. Although my father had not been in the habit of going to church, my mother wanted him to have a Christian funeral. To her mind and the way she understood her religion, he was the best Christian she ever knew. She did not want a prominent city pastor who had never laid eyes on my father, so she asked the village pastor to hold the service.

"Say what your heart dictates," she told him, "but be short."

The pastor's mild, watery eyes looked much chagrined behind his thick glasses. This was a chance of a lifetime, he felt, and she wanted him to be short.

But my mother was adamant.

"Short," she said firmly, "and nothing about the blood of the lamb."

There were many speeches that day while my brothers and I, in our stiff, black clothes, sat quietly beside my mother in the first row; but I only remember one sentence. It was spoken by an old, white-haired gentleman with fierce blue eyes, a well-known playwright who had collaborated with my father in a number of successful plays.

He was standing on the altar steps and his sharp blue eyes swept over the crowded hall, taking in the friends and family, neighbors and trades-men, artists and aristocrats, writers, publishers, the famous and the un-known, two princes of the blood, sons of the last German Kaiser, and perhaps the skinny boy peering through the open chapel doors.

"It is right that we should mourn today," said the old man, his hand resting heavy on the coffin, "for we are here to bid goodbye to the last of the true noblemen."

I never saw Paul Schulz again. But we had been a tight little crowd growing up together, and there was always somebody who kept track of the others. He didn't return to the village when he came home from the war, I was told. He went to live in Hamburg and he made something of himself.

* * * * * * * * * * * * * *

Bicycles, when I was young, were not just the means of toning one's muscles or entering competitive events. They were a way of life. We would have sooner gotten through a meal without a spoon or fork as through an ordinary day without a bike. It took us to school which, after we entered high school in Potsdam, was a round trip of fourteen kilometers, and to the grocery store at the next corner. It carried us to a birthday party and to the dentist, to a swim in the stream and to the Turnverein and, for two years, to the village church for confirmation lessons. We accepted our first proposal to go "steady" while pushing our bikes through the fields, side by side, with the boy of our dreams, and we were leaning against our bicycles, arms crossed over the chest and pretending not to care when the same despicable boy "broke up" with us.

The one bike you owned had to last all the years of your childhood. You took very good care of it, because if you didn't, you walked. There was a man in the village, Herr Lindemann, who made a respectable living doing nothing but repairing bikes.

When I was twelve, I began riding my bike to the B.D.M. meetings. The B.D.M., which stood for "Bund Deutscher Mädchen" (Federation of German Girls), was the girls' branch of the Hitler Youth. Getting permission to join had not been easy. The village group had been organized by a young woman named Waltraut. I never had a real conversation with her, nor do I remember the exchange of a single personal sentence, but I could paint her still in every detail. She was buxomy rather than plump with a round, doughy face and very dark hair, but there was nothing either sexy or flabby about her. Her mouth was firmly set; her dark eyes were hooded and brooding. Waltraut carried three torches in her regal bosom—for her parents, her country, and her Führer—all three burning with a searing flame.

She had founded the local B.D.M. charter group before Hitler came to power but few of us knew that it existed then. After the Nazi takeover in 1933 the arm of the new government quickly made itself felt, even in such a small community as ours. The new broom cut a mighty swath, it swept away all of the other existing youth groups in the country including the "Wandervögel," a group dedicated to long hikes, guitar playing and preserving of folk songs. The new rulers did not abolish those activities; on the contrary, they were eager to adopt and control them. This they achieved by sweeping out the old and established and forming a new organization under the auspices of the government. This organization, of course, had political overtones and was called the Hitler Youth.

With Hitler's rise to power, Waltraut came into her own. She was tireless in her efforts to gather all girls between eight and eighteen into a group structured and guided by her. Parents finding themselves besieged by their children for consent to join offered little resistance. Membership grew rapidly and Waltraut selected a few sub-leaders to head small peer groups at their weekly meetings. A wealth of activities was offered: singing and marching, playing a musical instrument, hiking, group games, competitive sports events, and square dancing. Nothing like it had ever been offered before in our community. Our village school, which began at 7 a.m. and ended at noon, concentrated almost solely on the three R's.

When the last of my friends began going to the meetings, I asked my mother for permission to join. My mother looked absent-mindedly over my shoulder, which meant that she was not about to make a decision. She told me to ask my father. This seemed odd, since she usually settled such matters herself. I waited for an opportune moment, which most often presented itself during the afternoon coffee hour. By now I had a pretty good hunch that, for reasons that were not clear to me, this would not be as simple as I had thought and I had my case well prepared. When I saw my father frown and look doubtful, I pulled out all the stops.

Everybody was going, I implored him, all my friends! I was the only one left. I would not be able to go on bicycle trips with them! I could not join in certain sport events; at the May dance I would be doomed to be a wallflower instead of a participant. My father, who generally found it difficult to say no to me, began to look uncertain and I quickly pressed my advantage.

"It will be so much fun, Papa. And I promise not to be a nuisance!"

The last was a touch of inspired diplomacy. Whenever we children wanted to do something or go somewhere out of the usual and had wangled permission from our parents, my father always added one last admonition: ". . . and don't make a nuisance of yourself."

Hearing his own words repeated to him, my father smiled and I knew my cause was won.

Being eleven at the time, I was assigned to the children's group of the B.D.M. which meant I went once a week to an afternoon meeting wearing a starched white blouse, a black scarf held together by a leather ring, and a dark blue skirt which was buttoned onto the blouse with a number of large mother-of-pearl buttons. Those buttons were a source of considerable grief to my friends and me. It meant that we were too young to wear skirts with belts. Translated into our own world of values, this meant that we did not have enough hips yet to hold up a skirt. We could hardly wait to graduate into the buttonless skirts which great event took place when we were fourteen, old enough to be taken into the senior group.

The meetings now were in the early evenings and took place in a barn in a room above the solitary village fire engine. Our group consisted of about ten girls, all more or less the same age, led by Ellen, a girl who had won our secret admiration by wearing red fingernail polish in the face of formidable opposition and admitting that she had been kissed already by three different boys. Our activities were as colorful as our leader. We made plans for weekends and sporting events, we practiced square dancing. We played games – the most popular being a game called "Drei Fragen auf Ehre und Gewissen." Roughly translated it meant that one had to answer three questions absolutely truthful, "cross my heart and hope to die." That's how we found out about Ellen's kissing. And we did battle with the boys. This last activity was the most fun. There was no way a dozen young girls could meet in a country barn without some interference from the young village males. Victory was always temporary – a matter of which party managed to be sneakier that evening. The boys crept up on the barn and let the air out of the tires of our bikes. We hid the bikes. They found them. We placed the bikes carelessly under the window of our upstairs meeting room and when the boys were busy with them we poured buckets of cold water on them. We hid behind the barn and when the boys went looking for our bikes we let the air out of their tires.

When we were not playing, planning, or battling, we sang. We must have known a hundred songs, Wanderlieder, folk songs, evensongs and lullabies, and songs of the fatherland, some of the last dating as far back as Napoleonic times. We liked those patriotic songs and sang them with an innocent pride that was not very different, I suppose, from the emotion with which English teenagers in those days sang "Britannia, Rule the Waves," or, across the border from us, French fourteen-year-olds chanted their rousing "Marseillaise." We liked them because they made us feel proud, but we did not sing them nearly as often as we did the wander-and-marching songs, which were less solemn and more fun. Some of the girls played a recorder or mouth organ; two or three of them were true virtuosos on these instruments.

Once a month—less frequently as she got busier—Waltraut would appear at a meeting. She always came with a folder of important-looking papers under her arm; she was pleasant, earnest and intent. The papers contained organizational rules and instructions and, more often than not, new lofty goals for us. Eventually, we got our own little flag and Waltraut had to designate a flag bearer. This would be a great honor, she said, and must not be taken lightly. It was apparent that none of us qualified, and she finally selected a girl named Gerta who was younger than we by two years. Gerta, the only child of elderly parents, was small, anemic looking, and rather pretty. She also was without a shred of humor and so was eminently suited for the job.

At the end of the meeting Waltraut would sometimes teach us a new song which she accompanied on the flute. Those songs, always political, were often written by the leader of our entire organization, the head of the Hitler Youth, Baldur von Schirach. This man had two things going for him: he had a bottomless capacity for enthusiasm, and he was genuinely stupid. As far back as I can remember I have loved poetry, and the lyrics of those songs used to tie my stomach in knots. He thought nothing of rhyming something like "sham" with "wham," and if "wham" was not a word, he deigned it to be one. The tunes were equally appalling. Waltraut taught them to us unflinchingly and with the same earnest dedication with which she did everything, but she never insisted on our singing them afterward. She had a fine musical ear and maybe those tunes were more than her own stomach could tolerate.

Waltraut was not dumb and I used to wonder if she did not see how silly some of the things were that she had to teach us. As I grew older I came to realize that people who are hooked on an issue tend to lose not only their perspective, but also their sense of humor, no matter if the subject is love or religion, politics, living vegetarian style, or an abhorrence of white sugar and ethnic jokes.

Any extensive plans made by our group had to have Waltraut's approval. When we went on overnight bicycle trips she sometimes accompanied us.

It was on the second day of such a trip that we passed a sign in a cemetery. It was nailed to a tree near the cemetery wall so that it could be more easily read from the street. At that time, most of us had already seen "Jews not wanted" signs posted at public places or hotels. The sign at the cemetery was different. It said "Jews wanted here." It staggered me.

I pedaled my bike closer to Hanne, who was my best friend.

"Did you see that?" I whispered furiously. "Can you imagine anything so tactless? What if some Jewish people come by here and read that!?"

"It's worse than tactless," said Hanne rather loudly. "It's vulgar! But what do you expect from them!"

"They" and "them" in those days were active party members (there were a great many more inactive ones) and "vulgar" happened to be the bottom word of Hanne's vocabulary at the moment. It meant "the pits."

"You mean the sign at the cemetery?" said a girl riding behind us. "I read that, too. Pretty bad!"

Waltraut, who was riding at the head of the group, slowed down and steered her bike alongside us.

Our conversation stopped immediately. We studied the countryside.

"Did you know," said Waltraut pleasantly, "that Clemençeau has said that there are twenty million Germans too many in this world?"

Hanne and I did not answer, momentarily struck down by this reminder.

"That's terrible!" exclaimed the girl behind us, sincerely shocked. "What did people say to that?"

"I imagine that most of the world thought that it was rather clever of him," said Waltraut calmly, "and the rest ignored it. All but a few people in this country," she added.

She gave her pedals a strong push and took her place at the head of the group again.

"Who is Clemençeau?" asked Gerta, our flag carrier, in her high, querulous voice. Nobody bothered to answer.

As we rode on in silence I thought of my father whom I had loved more than anybody else in the world. What would have happened if he had come upon a sign like that? It didn't bear thinking. My father who had taken out his black suit more frequently after January 1933 and gone to talk at the graveside of old Jewish friends. There were more such occasions now, it seemed. Broken hearts or suicides; we children were left in the dark. Years later my mother told me that she had begged him not to go or, at the very least, not to speak at the grave. "They will not forget. There will be repercussions," she had warned. My father only shook his head. If he could not do his friends this last honor, he said, he did not wish to go on living himself.

He died a few months later in the fall of 1935, succumbing to a lung embolism, and when the predicted repercussions came they diminished the family income, but they could not hurt my father any more.

On those weekend trips we stayed either at a youth hostel or, if there was none nearby, in a barn. For fifty cents a head the farmer would let us have the hayloft for a night. Once again on this trip it was "barn night" and with as much noise and commotion as we could possibly manage, we climbed into the loft with our gear and staked out our sleeping niches. Hanne pushed me toward the corner near the ladder.

"This is a good place," she said, and then murmured under her breath "Let's get up in the night and go back to the cemetery."

"And take down the sign," I whispered delightedly. She and I were old hands at switching signs. But so far those signs had always simply indicated "Fresh paint!" or "Beware of the dog!" This plan was a bold step forward; it meant entering new dimensions.

At midnight! At the cemetery! What a lark! "Where are we going to put it?"

"In the creek," said Hanne, who was well organized when it came to mischief.

Before we went up to the loft to settle down for the night, Hanne and I took care to park our bikes against the farther side of the barn where they would not clank against the other bikes when we moved them later on.

The rustling, whispering, and giggling seemed to have no end that night. Hanne and I were too excited to fall asleep but we wished everybody else would. Finally, here and there, a gentle snoring could be heard. I pushed Hanne: "Now?" As if on cue a flashlight lit up at the other end of the loft. We closed our eyes and were breathing deeply and innocently when Waltraut made her last round to check on her charges. We would have to wait for her to settle down again and go to sleep.

The next thing I became aware of was somebody tapping her foot against mine: "Hey, get up! Breakfast time." The sun was sending brilliant slants through the cracks of the barn side. Hanne, buried deep into the hay beside me rolled on her back and squinted at the rafters above her.

"Oh, damn," she said after some lengthy meditation, "What happened?"

We took another road home that day and so did not pass the cemetery again and for some months afterward we pushed the whole thing out of our mind.

When we moved back to Berlin a year later I dropped out of the village group and did not register for the B.D.M. in our new district. Neither did I join anything else even faintly connected with the government. I was growing up and becoming increasingly skeptical.

Waltraut and her parents did not see the end of the war. Twenty-four hours before the Russians flooded into the village the old man said farewell to his wife and daughter, took out his World War I rifle and shot first the two women and then himself.

Ellen, our adventuresome leader with the pink nail polish, took a job as a secretary in Berlin where she roomed with a middle-aged lady who answered the front door at any time of the day wrapped in a large flowered kimono with a parrot perched on her shoulder. After some years Ellen married a penniless but stout-hearted aristocrat and studied happily ever after the Almanach de Gotha, an up-to-date register of European aristocracy of German descent.

Gerta, our solemn flag-bearer, grew into an anemic-looking, pretty young woman. On the eve of her marriage to the village plumber her parents told her that she was adopted and was in truth the secret daughter of a Baltic countess. Her subsequent prolonged crying fit was generally assumed to be caused by a combination of joyful shock and wedding nerves.

Chapter 2

"Everything I ever had, I earned with my right hand," my father once said. He had the advantage of starting out in life with a good name, a first-class education and no family fortune worth mentioning. His father had been a professor of literature at a junior college for girls in Frankfurt. His grandfather owned vineyards along the Rhine River and had been the mayor of Rüdesheim, a town famous for its good wines and scenic beauty. He came from a long line of "Magister und Pastoren" my father said in one of his poems. This background of scholarly learning, eloquence, and Rhine wine combined in my father's blood to a cheerful, generous and optimistic disposition. Cloudy skies were always quickly cleared by a short, stormy and quite harmless temper outburst, inevitably followed by a rueful effort to comfort anybody who might have been frightened by it.

There was one notable exception, a childhood memory as hazy as a pre-dawn dream. I see my father in his high, starched white collar and gray silk cravat — not young, not athletic, most assuredly not slim — rushing down the terrace steps of a seashore hotel. Down the road he stormed, brandishing his walking stick, in hot pursuit of a coachman who had driven by beating his horse unmercifully. I see my mother, left so unexpectedly at the table with three small children, sipping her coffee, gazing out at the sea, gallantly ignoring the gaping hotel guests around us.

My grandfather died while my father was still in high school. He left the family financially secure and my father spent five carefree student years at Heidelberg, one of Europe's oldest and finest universities. I have read Mark Twain's affectionate and hilarious description of his own stay in Heidelberg and I laughed so hard that I nearly fell out of bed. It must have been much like this when my father went there as a student some eight or nine years later. Twain's chapter on Heidelberg made me feel that I knew more now about my father than I had before.

On the day he finished his studies, successfully defending his Ph.D. thesis on Schopenhauer, my father proposed to the starry-eyed, pretty young daughter of an old Frankfurter family. He began his professional life as a journalist for a Frankfurter newspaper for which he was soon writing a weekly column. As the column grew in popularity, so grew my father's confidence in his craft and, still a young man, he moved his family to the country's capital to try his hand as a writer. By the time the first world war broke out my father was a rich man.

The marriage, contracted too young and unrealistic, did not survive this rapid rise. The young wife, feeling tied down and left out, took their four children and went to live in Wisconsin, which, just then, was receiving German immigrants with open arms. It was a hard and painful blow to my father. Over the years that followed, he and his first wife buried their bitterness and became what they had not been before, fast and loyal friends. My father offered her his house on Lake Lugano in Switzerland, but by then she had grown to love America and did not want to go back to live in Europe. Two of my half sisters came to live with my father for a while. My youngest half sister told me once that her mother had sometimes remarked: "The more I see of other men the better I like your father!"

My father's fortune was wiped out during the inflation that followed the first world war when people went shopping carrying their money in small suitcases, and an egg cost 2000 Marks and a loaf of bread 15,000. He went back to his desk and began all over again. He married my mother, twenty-six years his junior, and during the next eight years my three brothers and I were born. My father's work day was long; he kept two secretaries busy. Even during the grim depression years he could coax a smile out of his readers and laughter out of theater audiences. He treated his own and his fellow men's follies with wise and gentle humor and they identified with it and loved it.

When the banks closed in the early nineteen thirties, my father lost, once again, all his savings. He would have to start a third time. By now he was no longer young; he was weary and discouraged and it was harder to find humor in a society that was increasingly growing humorless. He had loved his country all his life with a deep and optimistic love that had its roots still in the romance of the nineteenth century, and he could not understand what was happening. He died, mercifully, before this love would have turned to utter despair.

My mother, left with four children between the ages of nine and sixteen, was eminently better equipped to deal with the situation. She dismissed the servants, divided the house into two apartments which she rented, and moved the family back to Berlin. She cut her hair and got her first permanent. She bought her first lipstick and had a tailor make her a few smart suits. She was ready to meet the world on new terms. There were long sessions with publishers and accountants during which she took stock of her circumstances. The picture was not rosy.

And yet, it had seemingly started so promising. When, many years later, well-meaning and genuinely puzzled friends asked me: "How could such civilized and intelligent people like the Germans fall for a man like Hitler?" I wanted to answer "How could they not?"

From the depth of my childhood I am, even now, able to conjure up pictures of city streets before Hitler's takeover. I remember beggars, one-armed, one-legged, or blind, victims of the first World War, rattling their pencils and tin cups in monotonous hopelessness. I remember large, political slogans and insults smeared over house walls and fences and the debris of street battles of the night before strewn over empty lots and bar entrances. I still have a picture in my mind after we moved to the country of dismal, hollow-cheeked men stopping at the kitchen door for a warm meal.

I remember jumping down our stairs one afternoon and catching a glimpse of the two daily newspapers on the hall table with unusually large headlines across the front page. I stopped for a second to inspect them. "REICHSKANZLER HITLER?" said one headline, and "HITLER REICHSKANZLER?" said the other. I thought that very funny, whatever it meant, and forgot it again at the next moment.

The world saw only the strutting, the big-mouthed oration, the shouting and mass acclaim. For the average jobless, despairing German, numbed by fourteen years of political strife and empty promises, something new and shining had appeared on the horizon: Hope. The new government addressed itself to the general misery in the country with such speed and impact, tackling cold, hunger, and homelessness so patently effective that it set everybody's head spinning. It silenced, for the moment, even the most dire predictions and the most doubtful cynics.

Within weeks of the takeover, the first great project, "Die Winterhilfe" (winter help), was not only under way, but working. Every German household was asked to serve once a week a one-course, one-pot meal, the famous *Eintopfgericht*, and give the savings, amounting to one or two marks, toward the Winterhilfe. Collection of the money was done by school children.

If people felt coerced, it was only moderately so. After all, it worked. Truckloads of coal and potatoes were distributed at every corner of the city. Nobody unemployed was left empty handed. The coal miners went back to work, the farmers sold their potatoes. Erzgebirge natives who had a century-old tradition of wood carving were asked to carve and paint hundreds of thousands of small Christmas tree decorations which the government bought from them. Every city, town, and village received their quota of those miniature toys which were sold at the street corners. This money was also used to pay for the coal and potatoes. Everybody, from the head of a family or a corporation to the youngster who still counted on his fingers, had to take a turn selling those little figures for an hour or two. Few people refused to buy; they were quality work.

People who had been running successful small businesses out of their basements or living rooms were told that they would have to show an official place of business or face an order to close down. Grumbling, they complied and began building sheds or small additions to their homes. It meant the immediate employment of a workman or two.

The government began to draw up plans for housing projects all over the country. These settlements shot up like mushrooms; not future slum districts, but one-family houses on fair-sized lots. They were government-owned and rent-controlled. The first families to be settled there were the World War I veterans and their families. Next in line were families with three or more children. The homeless disappeared from the streets; the vagrants ceased to knock at the back door. They were doing construction jobs now. Unemployment dropped from record highs to almost nothing. For the first time women teachers could get married without losing their jobs.

It was said about the German farmer during the depression that every single tile on his roof was mortgaged; they were drowning in debt. The state took over the mortgages, distributed seed and suspended payments until the next harvest. Young people who wanted to marry were offered "marriage loans" by the government at low interest. With every child, the interest rate would be lowered and with the arrival of a fourth child the loan would be canceled.

The cities and towns took on a new look. No beggars, no debris. The many parks looked cared for with new flower beds and playgrounds for children. Baby carriages appeared almost over night. Street crime ceased. A government branch was created for the sole purpose of taking care of the "recreation and well being" of the blue collar man and factory worker.

The man on the street now had a job, steady wages, a little house with a vegetable and flower garden, children with warm clothes, a wife who cooked and gardened, a vacation on a government-owned cruise ship to look forward to, and a great deal of pride in it all. He read his daily newspaper which was government-controlled and he listened to his radio which was government-owned. No other information was available to him, nor did he look for it.

"Has nobody read *Mein Kampf?*" my father used to say completely bewildered. *Mein Kampf* was the book in which Hitler had laid down his intentions and goals. But, of course, nobody had. The great disillusioning process did not begin until much later, and for some of the people it never came.

It was a different story with the intellectuals. Between them and Hitler there had been, from the very beginning, an unsurmountable dislike based on deep, mutual distrust. Hitler now wanted them to be effectively silenced. He selected a small, emaciated, fanatic little man, Joseph Goebbels, to be his Minister of Culture and Propaganda. Goebbels was the smartest and the most cunning of his disciples. His deep-set eyes were like coal burning with an unholy fire. His powers of persuasion were vast, his command of the language awesome. Hitler delegated him to deal with those troublesome intellectuals. And Goebbels dealt with them, with flattery and praise, enticement, bribes, threats, and, if all else failed, severe punishment. He had it all at his disposal.

It was with this man, Herr Kulturminister Goebbels, that my mother prepared to do battle.

My father was never officially persecuted. He died too early for that. A few zealous *Parteigenossen* in obscure places burned some of his books along with many others, but this had not been on official orders. There were subtler ways. My mother was notified that my father's plays would not be produced any more since a number of them had been written in collaboration with a Jewish playwright. My father's novels and short stories often had droll and likable Jewish characters in them; those books would not be printed any more. In other words, our income was threatened to be cut off.

My mother wrote a letter to the Ministerium for Culture and Propaganda in which she respectfully requested a reconsideration of this decision. There were no pensions for artists, she wrote. How was she to raise and educate four children if no royalties would be coming in? My father had been a good, staunch German. His books were humorous and non-political. His love for his country had been above question.

After five or six weeks she got an answer. The Ministerium for Culture and Propaganda wished to inform her that this was a matter for the Department of Theater and Visual Arts.

My mother wrote a second polite but urgent letter. This time almost two months passed before an answer arrived. The Department for Theater and Visual Arts was not in charge of this, they wrote, it was clearly a request to be directed to the Department for Authors and Playwrights. My mother wrote another letter. More weeks went by; she wrote again. The answer came: she had addressed herself to the wrong department. This was a matter for the Department of Racial Affairs. My mother delivered the next letter in person.

She had to wait more than an hour in an empty room before she could hand her letter personally over to the man who was (she hoped) finally in charge.

"I took Hitler's picture off the wall in the waiting room," she announced to me at her return.

"WHAT?"

"Well," said my mother grimly, "if they make me sit there for an hour in that awful place at least I didn't have that numbskull staring at me the entire time."

"What did you do with it?" I wasn't sure I wanted to know.

"I put it behind the radiator," said my mother considerably cheered by the recollection of it.

It was almost a year after the original letter had been sent when the answer came from the Department for Racial Affairs. This, it said, was not a departmental concern but a matter directly for the Ministerium for Culture and Propaganda.

That very evening my mother sat down and wrote another letter, to Herr Joseph Goebbels *himself*.

She was enclosing the entire correspondence, it was self-explanatory. "I won't be led around by the nose like this," wrote an enraged Lucie. "What is the matter with everybody? Is this the way the state intends to take care of its fatherless children? And don't tell me that, as a matter of principle, no Jewish authors will be put on the stage. The lyrics to *The Merry Widow* were written by two Jewish authors, and—correct me if I am wrong—our chancellor, Herr Hitler, attended no fewer than three performances of it last year."

She mailed the letter before she had time to get terrified.

No police appeared at our door. An answer came, eventually, bearing the seal of Goebbel's ministerium. Henceforth my father's plays would be permitted to be shown in provincial theaters but never in the capital. Heil Hitler!

The immovable object had met up with the irresistible force and it had moved over—just a little. That was still possible in 1936.

Ten years later when it had all ended in heaps of rubble, people were supposed to bring proof that they had not been ardent Nazis. It was a very naive request by the victors, the great and mysterious "denazification process," but if we wanted to make a new start we had to comply. So we all went around collecting testimony from everybody else that we had not been involved or actively supported the Nazi system. One of the friends whom my mother approached was an old gentleman who had been a publisher of plays long before the time of the Nazis.

"Dear friend," said the old man, genuinely distressed, "I would like very much to write such a letter for you, but I honestly do not remember what your political views were at the time."

For a moment my mother stared at him absolutely speechless. Then she spoke slowly and clearly:

"Do you remember when you and your sister came to visit me and my daughter at our vacation place at Tegernsee some time during the second and third year of the war?"

"I remember, I think," said the old man.

". . . and we walked along the lake, your sister and my daughter a few steps ahead of us, and you and I were discussing politics?"

"Well . . ." said the old publisher, frowning and thinking.

". . . and you suddenly stopped and turned to me and said: "Please, please, talk more softly! My sister is rather in favor of the government and she must not hear what you are saying!"

The old man's eyes became saucer-like; his hand went to his forehead.

"Oh my God," he said, "*THAT* I remember!"

* * * * * * * * * * * * * *

The little boy who entered the grocery store had innocent blue eyes, slightly crossed with which he looked trustingly up to the grocer.

"Rhade mal knoope te una pore?"

"What? What was that?"

"Rhade mal knore te upla porte?"

The grocer's clerk hurried over to aid his master. So did two ladies with shopping bags. They all stared at the friendly, confident little boy who smiled up at them.

"Don't you speak German?" asked the clerk.

"Rhade knoope upla?"

There was an exchange of perplexed looks and doubtful shaking of heads. Then the grocer had an inspired idea. The year was 1936.

"Are you with the Olympic Games? You know: O L Y M P I C S ?" He made a few Olympic motions with his plump arms, something between swimming, paddling, and shotput. The clerk and the two women nodded their emphatic support. The boy looked blank.

At that moment the shop door opened and an older boy entered. Blond hair, pink cheeks, definitely German. His eyes were, if possible, even more blue, even more innocent.

"Rhade upla pore itsu?" said the younger boy more urgently to the grown-ups around him. The older boy turned in obvious surprise toward the younger one, then questioningly to the grocer.

"Does he only speak Portuguese?"

"You know the language?" said the grocer astonished. "We don't know what he wants."

"Quo vadis domine?" said the older boy turning to the younger.

"Rhade una pore upla," said the younger boy who was rather stuck with variations of his opening statement.

"Ora et labora," said the older one benignly. Then he turned to the grocer and his clerk.

"The little boy wants to use your toilet" he said.

"No, I don't!" yelled the little boy indignantly. "You were supposed to say I want a candy bar!"

The grocer stared at the boys, then, visibly, enlightenment dawned on him. As he was preparing to come from behind his counter with the clerk, equally bent on revenge, close on his heels, the young "Portuguese" and his linguistic friend saw no reason to stick around any longer.

Another store had to be taken off my mother's list.

When we quit our rural domicile, my two younger brothers left behind them the undisputed distinction of being the best-known rascals for miles around. Whenever they appeared together, the village went automatically on alert. After any reported mischief, the constable, as a matter of routine, came first to our house. Experience had taught him that this tended to shorten the investigation. Things had become difficult in our small town even for two such resourceful entrepreneurs as my brothers. Here in the city where nobody knew us, surrounded by vast virgin grounds, the possibilities were limitless.

On rainy days it was the telephone. They would dial a number — any number would do.

"Ja, bei Neumanns."

"Herr Neumann?" Peter's voice was still unchanged; he had to be a female operator. That never presented a problem; he was a first-class mimic.

"Herr Neumann, sorry for the inconvenience. There have been disturbances reported on your line and we are working on it. But we need your cooperation. Would you be kind enough to hold the receiver about fifty centimeters away from your face and hum for us? Any tune will do. But, please, sir, keep it up for a while so we can locate the trouble."

It was incredible how many people obliged. They would hold the telephone stiffly at arm length and start humming whole songs, arias at times. Sometimes Peter would say: "Louder, please" and the humming would gain in volume. At the end Peter was full of praise.

"That was lovely, Herr Neumann, just lovely. Would you now hum something for my little brother? He likes nursery songs." At which point Dolfi would punch Peter and Peter, in order to punch back more efficiently, would drop the receiver to the floor. While my brothers settled their minor disagreement, muffled threats of calling the police emanated from the carpet. My mother's key could be heard in the front door; Herr Neumann would be picked off the floor and unceremoniously slammed back on the hook, and Diddledee and Diddledum would rush to the kitchen where they were supposed to be doing the dinner dishes.

My mother had no illusions about her situation. Education of my three brothers was at this time her primary concern. My oldest brother, Wolfgang, the quietest and least extroverted of us, had, through the intervention of a friend, been accepted into a boarding school in West Germany. This school, situated in one of Germany's most beautiful wooded mountain areas, had a reputation for its advanced teaching methods and its individual approach to each student's ability and character. It was the right school for a fast-growing, diffident, scholarly sixteen-year-old.

My younger brothers presented a different problem. For them my mother was looking for sterner stuff and more old-fashioned methods. She settled on Templin, a school two hours north of Berlin, which for some centuries now had been in the business of turning the feisty offspring of North Germany's "landed gentry" into scholars and gentlemen.

She wrote a short note to the headmaster, announcing her coming, donned a smart suit and—never meeting the trials of life unprepared—spruced up my brother Peter sufficiently to accompany her as exhibit number one and case-in-point. Sprucing up Peter was no small feat; having more important things on his mind, he had a tendency to wear his shirts inside out, his shoes unlaced, and socks of a different color.

The headmaster was familiar with my father's name. He received my mother with great courtesy at the door of his study and led her to the chair facing his desk. Peter, after a firm handshake, was told to take a stroll around the grounds. The headmaster would interview him later.

The Templiner school consisted of a number of ocher-colored two-story buildings spread amidst lawns and old trees bordering on the shore of a large lake. The headmaster's chair faced the grassy slopes toward the cool, gray expanse of water.

My mother did not waste any time. She wanted the school to take her two youngest boys, she said. For reasons she was sure needed no explaining, it would have to be on a full scholarship. She had gone over the list of possible schools and had selected the best of them, Templin. It was an honor to be educated at this school. (Here the headmaster bowed slight-ly, acknowledging the compliment.) My mother pressed on: by the same token, she said, it should be an honor to be asked to educate those two boys, not only for their father's sake, but because they were, in their own right, lively, promising, highly intelligent youngsters and a true challenge to any school.

My mother was prepared to go on in that vein for a while yet, but the headmaster's friendly gaze had moved past her face and over her shoulder. His eyes had taken on a slightly glazed expression and there suddenly seemed a distracted air about him.

"I didn't have to turn around," said my mother later, "I knew it was Peter!"

But she did turn around and discerned with some difficulty a small figure in a new winter coat sitting solemnly in a dilapidated dinghy without motor, oar, or paddle, drifting in the brisk March wind ever farther out onto the lake.

The headmaster's gaze returned to my mother's alarmed face.

"I see what you mean, Ma'am" he said, clearing his throat.

The school took them in. "Took them on," I should say. After their share of misdeeds and honorable spankings, they settled down to Shakespeare, Schiller and Moliere; they struggled with Caesar's campaigns and calculus and suffered in exquisite martyrdom through lessons in danc-ing and table manners. Peter graduated as valedictorian of his class, giving the commencement address in Latin. Dolfi followed a few years later in a graduation hastily advanced by the war.

* * * * * * * * * * * * * *

So far I have said very little about my oldest brother, Wolfgang. The reason for this is simple: Much of the time my two younger brothers oc-cupied the center of the stage. This was not always by choice—they often would have preferred a lot less attention—but simply because they generated a great deal of commotion. The spotlight had, they felt, a most unfortunate tendency to focus on them at very inconvenient moments. Thinking back, I suppose I was much like a courier between two different outposts, equally attracted to my oldest brother's low-key, reasonable mode of behavior and my two younger brothers' exciting and irreverent approach to life.

After my father's death in 1935 and our return to Berlin, we never again lived together as a family. My brothers came home for their school holidays, but that was not the same. As adolescents we lived in different parts of the country and as adults we lived on different continents. Miraculously, this premature separation did not estrange us. Our early years had forged a strong bond. The four of us in those years were as scrappy and squabbling as any batch of siblings anywhere, but out of our common memories grew a lasting affection and an almost fierce loyalty to each other.

In some ways, though, my oldest brother has always seemed closest to me, perhaps because he was there when the other two were not.

Out of the farthest, dimmest corner of my childhood, I conjure up a picture of a little girl sitting on a red chair at a small red nursery table. She would be about three years old. Across from her, on an identical chair, sits a boy, older and bigger than she by two years. He is as familiar to her as the roses on the nursery wallpaper or as Julchen, the stuffed doll in the corner of her crib. Which means: he is always there. He was there when she opened her eyes for the first time to take stock of her surroundings; he is there when she awakens in the mornings. He is tucked into bed at night right after she is tucked in, and he definitely is there now, across from her, at the little red table. A Person-of-Authority has just placed their noon meal in front of them. After admonishing them to empty the plate, the Person-of-Authority has left the room and they are staring in dismay at their plate, one large corner of which is taken up by a mixture of carrots and peas. They both know by now that vegetables are an inevitable part of life, and they are resigned to carrots. The peas, however, are a different matter. They are not as yet ready to accept peas as inevitable. The Person-of-Authority has ordained that the plates should be cleaned but she is not, at this point, any place near. Peas are *yakki*, but since they are supposed to disappear, they have to be dealt with. The solution is as simple as it is brilliant. It must have come from the five-year-old; no three-year-old is that clever. For the next few minutes the two children are totally absorbed in their task: the carrots go into the mouth, the peas are rolled under the table. One at a time. This not only solves the problem, it is also a great deal of fun.

Here ends the first image. I do not remember the Person-of-Authority returning, approving of the empty plates, praising the children, and shortly thereafter stepping on a pea that treacherously had rolled from under the table. The softly squashed item on the shoe sole is scrutinized and a more detailed inspection follows. The Person-of-Authority is not pleased. I don't remember who she was but all evidence points to my mother. No nursemaid would have dared to pronounce such astute and unsanitary punishment as was swiftly meted out to the culprits.

The next picture I see is that of two sorrowful children sitting under a little red table and slowly and tearfully eating a great many peas, one by one, off the worn brown nursery linoleum.

There is only one other person on earth who has the same pictures etched into his memory, brighter and clearer by two years, and filling me in on all the missing parts: my oldest brother, Wolfgang.

This notable event seems to be the beginning and solid base of all my early childhood memories, and Wolfgang played a part in each one of them. Peter was an infant and only slowly entering the conscious stage; and Dolfi, I suspect, was not even yet a possibility in my parents' minds. Neither of the two was present when, on cold winter nights, Wolfgang and I hopped out of bed, after "lights out" and my mother's footsteps had faded down the corridor, and climbed up on the window sill. Huddled into our long, warm flannel nightgowns we gazed down, five floors below us, onto an enchanted scene. Under glittering lights tiny people floated weightlessly and gracefully through the air to the strains of music that came from an invisible source. Muted snatches of waltzes and foxtrots found their way through the closed nursery windows. Tennis courts had been turned into an ice skating rink, but to the two children cowering on the window sill five stories up it was nothing short of a magic kingdom. And the two younger boys were not around when my mother decreed that Wolfgang and I henceforth were to spend one half hour every day stretched out on ironing boards thus insuring a future of wonderfully straight spines. Two ironing boards were put up, side by side, each on two chairs, in the middle of the nursery. We thought this rather a lark and entertained ourselves by making up little poems which we thought very clever and committed to our memory for all eternity—and forgot them again the minute we were permitted to get up. I don't remember how long this went on; it faded away (as all of these projects did) as soon as my mother stopped checking on it daily. There was a steady procession of nursemaids in our house, none of them was keen on dragging two ironing boards in and out of the nursery every afternoon.

Wolfgang graduated in 1937, a year ahead of his age group. The year thus saved he was to spend with our half-sister Else in America. Else was married to a man named Max who had been a fighter pilot in the Richthofen squadron in World War I. His plane had been shot down over France, but, unlike the unfortunate Red Baron, he had managed to free himself from the burning wreckage. He parachuted to a lopsided landing, sprained his ankle and was received by an old French lady who whacked him on the head a number of times with her sturdy umbrella.

In civilian life Max had been a chemical engineer, and after the war he emigrated to the United States where he eventually owned his own small chemical company. He and Else lived in a pleasant house on the shore of one of Wisconsin's lakes. They were childless and they invited Wolfgang to spend a year with them and attend a local college.

This plan needed the permission of the draft board, and, once again, my mother girded herself to tackle the powers-that-be. After innumerable battles with janitors, tenants, bill collectors, and the Ministerium of Culture and Propaganda, draft boards were small potatoes to her. It turned out to be even less difficult than she expected. The draft board was headed by a Lieutenant Colonel Koenig, a sensitive, intelligent man whom my mother in no time at all had wrapped around her little finger. (It was the same officer, by then a full colonel, who got me out of Switzerland a few years later.) So Wolfgang, seventeen years and still growing, journeyed to Wisconsin to spend a year there with our half-sister.

Else was an indomitable, high-strung wisp of a woman with hunched shoulders and fervent eyes who disliked housework and was much given to seeing specters and reading tea leaves. Wolfgang quickly learned to abhor both of those talents. He much preferred edible food on the plate in front of him to an apparition behind his chair, no matter how benignly it seemed to beckon, as Else assured him. Their relationship irrevocably collapsed when Wolfgang discovered that Else was, periodically, searching through his desk for open letters in order to ascertain if he was happy and thought well of her. He was not and he did not.

His memories of this American stay might have been permanently marred had it not been for a long summer vacation spent with our youngest half-sister and her husband, who were homesteading in the California Big Bear country. At the end of the year Wolfgang came home with a remarkable command of the English language, a love for the California mountains, and a life-long affection for his charming, good-natured sister Gaby. (He named his oldest daughter after her.)

On his return to Germany he was promptly drafted and swallowed up by the army barracks outside of Potsdam which rendered him all but invisible for the next six weeks. I remember my mother's joyful excitement at the prospect of his first home visit. Wolfgang had asked if he could bring a friend along and the two young soldiers appeared in the early afternoon. My mother had prepared a true feast for them and was busy carrying and fetching between kitchen and dining room. The friend turned out to be a skinny youngster with a large nose and guileless blue eyes who in civilian life was learning to be a baker. He was quiet and nice and very timid and his datives and accusatives tended to get mixed up a bit.

"Four hundred young men in the barracks," said my mother, exasperated, to me in the kitchen, refilling the gravy bowl, ". . . four hundred young men and he brings a baker's apprentice home!" But when she sat down in the dining room she was pleasant to the boy and tried to put him at ease.

When the two young men thanked her for the meal and prepared to go, my mother looked blank with astonishment.

"But you can't leave, Wolfgang," she exclaimed. "I have theater tickets for you and me!"

"Mutti," said Wolfgang patiently, "I explained to you on the phone; this is our first pass. We have to be back at the barracks at seven."

"Impossible," said my mother, "the play won't be over till ten thirty."

"I can't go to the play."

"Not go to the play?" said my mother, aghast. "The tickets are for *Venetian Velvet*! Do you realize how difficult it is to get tickets to that play?"

Wolfgang suppressed a sigh. "It does not make any difference, Mutti. *I HAVE* to be back by seven."

"That's ridiculous," said my mother. "How can you be at the barracks at seven if the play is not over until ten thirty?" And graciously turning to the future baker, she asked: "Would you be good enough to tell his sergeant that I had theater tickets for my son and that he will be back some time before midnight?"

At that point my brother got up and pushed his speechless friend ahead of him through the door. I think he was worried that my mother might coax the name of their sergeant out of his friend and place a person-to-person call to him at the Potsdamer barracks.

Chapter 3

When I was sixteen, my mother sent me up north to a small sandy farm, somewhere between Berlin and the Baltic Sea, to learn how to cook and to dust and to acquire various other nebulous skills of which she herself, being city born and bred, had only a rather vague notion. Most of all, I was to learn to appreciate my home and to love her better. It didn't work out that way. I don't think there is a case on record where a rebellious teenager was packed off on a penal mission of sorts and came home with a newly awakened love for the irate parent. But learn I did, quite a few skills, even though life never again called on me to milk twelve goats three times a day or feel the rear of a goose for her readiness to lay an egg.

The winter before this happened, my mother, widowed two years earlier, liquidated our house and household and returned to the big city. This meant moving from a large country house with lawns and trees and a lily pond inhabited by bold, sleek gold fish and timid little green frogs—from a household consisting of a husband and four children which my mother had ruled and run capriciously, but efficiently, with the help of a maid and a cook and a Kinderfraeulein, a twice-a-week seamstress, two secretaries, and a once-a-week yardman—to a small, crowded city apartment on the second floor of a pleasant, but unspectacular fifteen-apartment city house. It meant for my three brothers to be dispatched to various boarding schools, and for my mother and me it meant to be facing each other at the forlorn table for three meals a day, the lone survivors of the Camelot of my childhood.

The apartment was designed with a bit of black humor, I think. It had three very bright rooms and three very dark ones, connected by a long, narrow, pitch-dark corridor, which my mother divided by a dark velvet curtain, firmly separating the bright part of the apartment from the dark one. The dark rooms were the living room, dining room and bedroom, each having one window of northeast exposure and a large linden tree in front of each. The kitchen, bath, and narrow little "half-room" were southern exposure, bathed in light and, on sunny summer days, hot as an oven, melting everything in sight, particularly in the small food pantry which had its very own window, due south. No food could be stored there during spring and summer days. My mother furnished the living room and dining room with as much of my father's beautiful antique furniture as could be squeezed into them. The floors were covered with oriental rugs, one across the other. The last and best of them served as a table cover for the heavy black Friesian dining table. She lined the lower parts of the walls with bookshelves and hung ancestral oil paintings, shoulder to shoulder, on the upper parts. The front part of the velvet curtain-divided corridor she decorated with a small antique table, a gold framed antique mirror flanked by two electrical candles, and a number of original etchings. The general impression was that of a solemnly elegant, if slightly dramatic, stage setting, speaking mutely of culture, taste, tradition, and no money.

Those were the rooms my mother wished to "represent us" (a phrase she liked and often used), meaning that they would reflect by-gone status and lasting dignity which, indeed, they did. She rented the small, bright half-room to a divinity student, shrugged off the impossible pantry and enjoyed the sunny bathroom. A sleeping couch was placed for me in her bedroom. Thus we proceeded to start our new life, pursuing social contacts (both of us, but mostly I), seeking financial means to survive (my mother), doing our own cleaning (I), and getting on each other's nerves. While my mother put away her mourning clothes and got a new wardrobe together, in order to "represent us," and made the rounds at different publishing houses who had had the benefit of my father's diligent and successful writings, I scrubbed the kitchen and bathroom floors, dusted five hundred odd books, washed dishes, carried clothes to the laundry, and studied the marriage ads in the weekend papers hoping to find a tall, attractive, and wealthy man who would believe that I was over twenty and whom I could coax into marrying me and getting me out of the apartment, the shared bedroom, and the constant and overpowering presence of my mother.

By March I had managed to find two promising possibilities. One, alas, was limited to telephone conversations (where it is a great deal easier to lie about one's age). The other one had gone as far as two timid meetings in a café and a walk through the wintry park. The second candidate was certainly tall; I doubt that he was wealthy. He seemed smitten, which began to frighten me, and he made the fatal mistake of wearing earmuffs and a large wool scarf at the second meeting, which just about finished his chances for a long and happy marriage with me.

About that time my mother decided it was imperative to have life teach me a lesson and make me live without all those comforts which I seemed to take for granted. She was, in other words, at a complete loss of what to do with me. At a ladies' tea she heard about a farm up north, owned and run by a widow who was not a farm woman originally but had been a home economics teacher in the city when she married a farmer. Thus she was qualified to take in trainee girls who wanted to become home economics teachers and who had to serve as a prerequisite to their studies a practicum on a farm or in a large country household. It would be hard work, no doubt, but a wonderful opportunity for a young girl who, under the guidance of a firm, efficient, and understanding teacher, would be learning all the many household skills and virtues so highly esteemed in those pre-war years.

I do not remember my reaction when my mother informed me of her decision. I suppose I did not protest. The thought of other young girls cheered me and it probably seemed preferable to a man who wore earmuffs on a date.

I do remember the cold, clear noon in March when I arrived at the tiny country station that was nothing more than a short, sandy platform in the midst of nowhere. The train, having discarded me, rolled on and disappeared in the distance. I was standing there, my battered old suitcase beside me, shivering a little in the raw March air, when a woman approached me, spoke my name, not so much as a question as a reaffirmation, and shook my hand.

"I am Frau Schafer," she said, "I am a little late because I saw somebody off. Your predecessor." She gave me a hand with my suitcase and we started walking. "Oh God," she said, looking quite distraught and speaking much more to herself than to me, "I shall miss her! She was such an exceptional person!" My heart sank; I felt lamentably inadequate to fill the shoes of this departed paragon.

All the way to the farm Frau Schafer sang her praises. I sat on the narrow wooden seat of the open one-horse wagon, clinging to the thin iron side railing with numbed fingers, while we rattled at a leisurely gait over the bumpy country road. It was a cold ride and I tried not to shiver too obviously, particularly since this pearl of a young woman, who had just left, probably never got cold at all. She had gotten up before dawn, according to Frau Schafer, before anybody else; many of the morning tasks had been finished even before breakfast was on the table. She had been fast, competent, even-tempered, untiring; she had been everything I was not, and by the time we turned the last bend of the road, she had made me thoroughly miserable. Mothers' opinions notwithstanding, sixteen-year-old girls are not brimming with self confidence. Out of my misery rose one of my life's earliest resolutions: I would never do this to anybody. Not ever! And out of this resolution rose the first small flicker of puzzlement and doubt about my future hostess and teacher.

I remember the way I came to look on Frau Schafer in those days, without compassion, always curious, and at times vengeful. I see her now quite differently, knowing a great deal more, understanding more of her complex nature, her loneliness, her pride, her sense of inadequacy and insecurity, and her powerless rage against fate.

She was a woman in her mid thirties. Her thick black hair, which she wore in a bun at the nape of her neck, showed premature white streaks. She was short, not as tall as I; her face was thin and very fine, with bitter lines already drawn to the corners of her mouth. Her eyes were brown, with long, dark lashes, and her skin was the color of ivory. She had a pretty smile, but she seldom smiled. Her shoulders were narrow, but her hips were wide for such a small-boned woman, which made her walk all the more awkwardly. All her insecurity surfaced in that walk. A German farm woman is not known for her grace and litheness, but when she walks from her kitchen door to the hen house, the feeding bucket in her hand, her step is sure and composed and she might be Mother Earth herself. Frau Schafer always seemed to walk on alien ground, a displaced person, feeling observed and suspect. When she walked across the farm yard after having scolded us for some mistake or delay, she almost waddled in self-consciousness. Anyway, that was the way I thought of it when I was sufficiently mad at her.

One Sunday afternoon when we sat at the edge of the pond, enjoying a rare rest and warm sunshine, Elisabeth Schafer told me how she came to be a farm wife.

She was born and reared in Berlin, a single child who lost her father at an early age. While in high school she took part in a play to which, as was customary, all high schools in the area were invited. In the audience sat a boy, Herman Schafer, who had eyes only for the raven-haired girl on the stage. He found out her name and began writing her little notes. They had a few dates. Elisabeth went on to teachers' training; the young man went to college to study agriculture and husbandry. After graduation he took his modest inheritance and bought a small dirt farm to begin experiments in animal breeding. His goal was to breed sheep that would not only give wool but also milk acceptable for human consumption. After a few years he added cross-breeding experiments with goats. He kept two cows and some pigs and cultivated the land to make the farm self-supporting. He lived alone in the farm house and worked with one hired hand. "Every spring" said Frau Schafer, her face softening with the memory of it, "a letter would arrive: 'It's beautiful here now, the larks are singing, the hedge roses are in bloom, there are bluebells all around the house. Will you not come and walk with me, Elisabeth?'" But Elisabeth would not go and walk with him.

In time she passed her exams as home economics teacher and took a job in a city high school. She went on living with her mother, dated, went to dances, fell in love, fell out of love, hoped, lived, corrected papers, struggled with fallen soufflés, and graded skirts with crooked seams.

The years went by and the dates and the dances became fewer. And one spring day Elisabeth, now well over thirty, wrote to the young farmer up north: "If the hedge roses are blooming yet, I'll come and take a walk with you."

They were married six months later. Less than ten months later Elisabeth bore a little boy. They named him Herman after his father. And another ten months later, the big Herman was dead of pneumonia and Elisabeth, the little boy in her arms, was a widow.

Under any other circumstances, she would have sold the farm no matter at what loss and taken her child back to the city. Her mother would have cared for the little boy and Elisabeth would have gone back to teaching. But these were not normal circumstances. These were Hitler's times and Hitler's laws, and one of the laws forbade the sale of a farm if there was a male heir. If Elisabeth had borne a girl, her life would have run a very different course. But she had given life to a son and he was the chain that locked her to this poor little farm, to the half dozen sheep which she regarded as something of a sacred trust, and yet she could do nothing with them but loathe them from the bottom of her heart. It bound her to the goats and cows and pigs and the few acres of sandy soil, where potatoes, beets, and lupines struggled for survival. Elisabeth had received her life sentence. She petitioned the agencies; she protested to the powers that were that she knew nothing about farming; the state responded by sending her a young man, a second son of a farmer, to manage the farm for her.

This young man was called Herr Glauer. Surely he must have had a first name, but I never heard anybody call him by it. Herr Glauer was in his twenties, of more than medium height with broad shoulders, blond hair and blue eyes, with a hard, ruddy face. There was a primitive, almost brutal strength about the man; he was willful and, at times, cruel; he was a thorn in everybody's side, and he was Elisabeth Schafer's undoing.

When I joined the household on that distant March day in 1938, there were seven other people living at Rehbach ("Deerbrook Valley" as the young man had lovingly named his farm years ago): Frau Schafer and little Herman, who was three at the time; Herr Glauer; the milker and the shepherd boy, who slept in a small room in the barn; and two "trainees," Maria and Carla, each of them two years older than I.

The girls were dying to meet me. In time I discovered that they, too, had suffered from the eternal comparison to my inimitable predecessor. Now the replacement had arrived, a city girl, sixteen years old, knowing less than nothing about farming and animals. They planned to make the most of it. They informed me immediately that it was the duty of the youngest girl to keep the two buckets on the water bench in the kitchen filled from the pump in the barn, and to wash all vegetables used in the kitchen. The barn was across the farm yard and the water was carried in large pails over slippery cobblestones, mud puddles, and animal manure into the kitchen, a long and perilous journey. The vegetables were carried into the barn and washed straight under the pump, a highly unpopular job. All vegetables were home-grown and very sandy and it took a lot of pumping and water to clean them; the water came out of the pump only a few degrees above freezing and within seconds our hands began to turn blue. I don't remember how long it took me to catch on. When I finally protested the girls cheerfully admitted their joke. From then on the three of us took fair and square turns with the water and the vegetables as we did with all other chores we had to do.

The work day was long; the work was hard and ceaseless. I believe the reason that I do not remember my time in Rehbach as sheer hell is chiefly owing to the presence of those two girls. The three of us were absolutely united in moaning and conspiring, and in a hearty dislike of Frau Schafer and Herr Glauer. The girls themselves were very different. Maria was short and square with black hair combed back tightly into a bun; she had large, dark eyes, made larger by thick glasses, a generous mouth with strong white teeth and a wide smile, and a pink and white complexion. In her strong, healthy, earthy way, Maria was not unattractive.

Carla was the tallest of us, and the only one with short hair. Her features showed ancestors from the east — small, slanted blue eyes, high cheekbones, and a flat nose. She always wore a head scarf over her mousy, pale hair. Carla was not bright and sometimes she might have felt left out when Maria and I had whispering conferences, but our talk was never directed against her; we needed Carla as much as she needed us, and I do not remember a single fight among the three of us. We had a common enemy to bind us together.

I don't know if Frau Schafer had been a good teacher at one time. She had no way with young girls when I was there. I had been ready to like her, ready to adopt some sort of a mother substitute. Frau Schafer was no object for the affection of a sixteen-year-old in search of a mother figure. She was seldom cordial and often ungenerous and petty; she was erratic in her behavior, envious of our youth, quick to scold, and stingy with praise. She was, I think, the most frustrated woman I have met in my life. It made me think, in later years, about the girl whose leaving she so extensively mourned. Unlike the three of us, she had been a farm girl and knew farm work. She was quiet, responsible, and efficient, and she befriended the shy and lonely woman in a way which nobody had attempted in many years. Certainly the three of us never thought of it.

Our work day began at five. I slept in a tiny room off the master bedroom which I had to cross to get to the hall and stairs. The slanted roof was above my head so I could not sit up in it. There was just enough room for the bed and a crib, a chair, and a washstand. The little boy slept in the crib. It's surprising that I remember so little about the child. He was three years old, his name was Herman, like his father's. He was blond and nice looking. Perhaps his mother kept him too close or we worked too hard; I don't remember ever playing with him.

It was a very cold March when I arrived, and the little boy and I used to crawl deep under our featherbeds. We would fall asleep in seconds. There were many times when I planned to think something through at night in bed, but before even the first thought had clearly formulated itself I was fast asleep. Sometimes Frau Schafer would come in and bend over the sleeping child. She never knocked but the creaking of the door wakened me. She bent over the crib and talked in a low voice, not a whisper, very intensely, so that eventually the child would wake and become frightened. At that point she always turned and walked out, closing the door behind her and leaving me to climb out of my bed, shivering, teeth rattling with the shock of being roused from the first sleep and trying to calm down the whimpering child.

Frau Schafer wakened me every morning at a quarter to five by calling my name through the closed door. The first morning I jumped out of bed and ran to the washstand, only to stare at the frozen water in the wash basin. Very soon I didn't bother any more; with every icy dawn I would improve my getting-up technique till I had it down pat. At night I took all my clothes to bed with me and slept with them piled on my stomach. When Frau Schafer called, I simply grabbed them and sorted them by touch. They were as warm as toast. Dressing was no big problem; I got so good at it that the featherbed hardly moved. In those days, girls did not always wear bras, certainly no panty hose, no zippers to get stuck, everything was simple and uncomplicated; and in record time I would emerge more or less completely dressed. A quick combing and putting up the hair before the fingers got too stiff to manage the pins, and I would tiptoe through the master bedroom and down the steps into the kitchen, where the other two girls, who shared a room across the hall, were already waiting. We dipped the corner of a towel into the water bucket, rubbed our faces, dried them with the other corner, and the day had begun.

I feel that I should say something about this washing bit or lack thereof. We must have washed sometimes. Certainly we washed Saturday nights. We brushed our teeth in the evening before we jumped into bed. Sometimes during the week, when it seemed as if our arms and legs began to smell like the goats, we took warm water up to the bedroom and did some speedy soaping and rinsing. Eventually, spring came, it got warmer and we began to scrub ourselves down regularly. I know that when early summer arrived and the maneuvers began and the young soldiers took quarters in the next village, we were as clean and shiny as newly minted coins.

We took weekly turns with the different jobs. One girl was on kitchen duty while the two others donned heavy jackets, picked up their lanterns and disappeared into the chilly darkness in the direction of the goat and sheep stable. Some weeks later, after the hired hand quit in a huff and the shepherd boy ran away, one girl would go to the cow barn first.

The kitchen girl's first duty was to build a fire. The ashes have to be swept out of the stove, small sticks and larger wood pieces are strategically placed on top of each other, then a quick look and listen up the stairwell—nobody stirring yet—and the old kerosene bottle is whisked out of the corner. There is nothing like a shot of kerosene to get a fire going on a cold March morning, when your fingers will not bend and the sticks will not catch. Three rules must be observed religiously: Just the right amount, don't spill, and jump back instantly, just in case. The fire explodes, the flame shoots up toward the low ceiling, calms down, the sticks burn brightly. The rings over the burner are replaced; neither your hair nor your apron is on fire; the ceiling is only a very little bit blacker than the day before. The first task of the day has been satisfactorily accomplished, and not, if I may say so, without a certain amount of excitement. You are definitely wide awake now. The next fire that had to be built was in the big tile stove in the back room, the room with the long wooden table that served as a dining room and, in the evening, as a sitting room for the hands, of which I was one. This fire was more easily started. In the evening, a compressed piece of coal was wrapped tightly in newspapers and placed on top of the dying fire. With a little luck it would smolder there all night and, with some gentle poking in the morning, fall into pieces of glimmering cinders that readily started the fire for the day.

The kitchen girl began to prepare breakfast for the household: Homemade bread, homemade marmalade, butter and cheese made out of goat milk in that very kitchen, homemade lard, and freshly brewed coffee. Coffee, sugar, soap and kerosene were the only items ever bought in a store for daily use. Everything else was grown, raised, and prepared at the farm. Eggs or cow milk were seldom served; they were precious and were sold to the dairy and to the egg man. No fresh vegetables appeared till the garden yielded the first tender lettuce leaves.

The back room is swept, the table is set; the girls are back from the milking and the men come from the barn where they took care of the horses and pigs. Water is poured into a basin on the water bench, and all of us wash our hands. The water stays in the basin and will be used later to wash the sand off the potatoes before they are peeled for the midday meal. Only then is it hurled out of the back door and new water poured into the basin, which again will serve for many purposes until, at last, it will be used to scrub the kitchen floor after the supper dishes are done. I learned to appreciate this economy after dragging the first few buckets from the barn pump to the kitchen bench. Only the water that served to clean the centrifuge had to be absolutely pristine. The centrifuge — hand-operated by one of us every evening — separated the cream from the rest of the milk. The cream was poured into a stone jar and taken into the basement to be kept cool until it was churned into butter. The bluish-white, watery liquid that was left was used during the day's cooking. The centrifuge had two or three dozen parts to it which had to be taken apart and washed separately and thoroughly before being put together again. She was the *grand old dame* of all our hand-operated equipment, as difficult and capricious as a prima donna. She would not be hurried or taken lightly, and if we let our exasperation get the better of us, she spoiled the milk or simply ceased to function.

On Sundays the stable girls were free after the milking till the noon meal which the kitchen girl prepared. I soon learned that the main thing, then, was to look busy. Since the kitchen girl was not supposed to be *free* on Sundays, Frau Schafer always found some work for her if she found her dawdling. So I created all sorts of tasks for myself that made me look fully occupied whenever she glanced into the kitchen. For one thing, I weighed the pudding. Every Sunday we had pudding for dessert, and I was and still am a passionate pudding fan. Since my father, too, had liked it, we often had pudding at home. The pudding, beautifully molded, shiny and luscious, was placed in front of my mother, together with the small gold-rimmed, deep dessert dishes, and she airily and haphazardly slapped a few spoonfuls into each dish. This way the distribution was quite uneven, and my mother, noticing fleetingly herself that one dish was filled almost twice as much as another, invariable pushed those dishes towards my brothers, being of the firm opinion that boys should have the biggest portions of everything. I might have accepted that as inevitable, but it never seemed to happen with boiled white cabbage or brussels sprouts. When she noticed my long face, my mother would stop serving for a moment, look at me half laughing and half reproachful and remark that it seemed strange that a little girl should be so *"Futter neidisch"* (food envious). That was her expression. Yet it seems to me now that it was not so much the smaller portion of pudding but the constant and blatant unfairness of it that brought me close to tears.

Well, here in this quiet country kitchen, in charge of a whole delicious, wonderfully wiggly, red fruit pudding, was my golden opportunity to do better. The dessert dishes had no delicate little gold rim, they were sturdy and deep and, to the best of my judgment, all the same size. I got the kitchen scale and, for the next half hour or so, occupied myself by filling every dish with the exact same amount of pudding, down to the last tenth of an ounce. Nobody ever got more on my Pudding Sundays. Not even I. The only privilege I permitted myself was scraping the pot and licking the spoon at the end of this wonderfully absorbing and virtuous entertainment. That was about twenty-five years before I ever heard of star signs and even a few more years before I discovered that I was a Libra, born under the sign of the scales.

Stable duty was very different. On my first stable morning, Frau Schafer took me there and showed me how to milk the goats and sheep. A long narrow cement walk ran through the length of the stable, with small individual pens for each animal on both sides. Since the animals were not tied, the gate to each of those had to be firmly closed before the milking began. In other words, the animal, the bucket, and I were locked together into a tiny space and we had to make the best of it. For the first few mornings Frau Schafer appeared during or after the milking with a bucket of her own to spot check if the animals had been milked sloppily or were truly dry. After that I was on my own, with either Carla or Maria starting at the other end of the stable.

Goats have to be milked three times a day, not twice like cows. Young goats are difficult to milk; their nipples are tender and the goats are shy of the touch. But the older goats were quite agreeable; they had long, tough nipples and the milking was not hard. Not so the sheep. Those sheep, which had been the love of the late Herman Schafer's life, his interest, ambition, and ultimate goal, were without a doubt some of the most miserable creatures I have ever had the misfortune to come across. I am sure this was one sentiment Frau Schafer shared with me. I know Maria and Carla did. The moment we crouched down on our stool and touched their nipples, the sheep kicked. The moment we had pushed the bucket under them and started milking, they piddled. Not always were we successful in pulling the bucket away in time. And even if we got our buckets and hands out of the way, there was no room to draw back our feet. Their nipples were small and greasy and kept slipping out of our fingers. The sheep kept wiggling and moving and many times they stepped straight into the bucket so that straw and manure would swim on top of the milk. Often, just when we heaved a sigh of relief and began easing ourselves up from the low stool, they gave one last mighty kick, upsetting the whole bucket. We never left one of those sheep sties that our shoes were not wet and smelly with either sheep urine or milk, often both. Frau Schafer never really checked on the sheep milk. It had been her husband's idea that this milk might one day be used for human consumption. Her husband was dead and she was not about to drink milk mixed with sheep dirt. The milk was fed to the pigs or sometimes just thrown away. Nevertheless, we faithfully and punctually milked those awful creatures twice a day. The cleaning, feeding, and shearing were Herr Glauer's department and we had little to do with it.

Herr Glauer was surely a person of consequence. He might have been any age between twenty-five and thirty. His wavy hair was yellow rather than blond; he had cold blue eyes and his face was quite red. He was as strong as an ox and had emotions to match. There was no real intelligence but a lot of shrewdness in this man. Younger son of a farmer, a hopeless position the world over, he had accepted the job as manager of a farmerless farm. He quickly appraised the situation: A masterless farm, a neat little farmhouse, well-built stables, equipment in good repair, and a restless, unhappy woman. The poverty hardly struck him; he came from a farm no better, no richer than this. He took over the farm and the woman. And the woman let herself be taken by this young, strong, brutal man and hated herself for it; but neither could she stop herself.

Night after night the five of us—the troops—sat together in the back room around the long table, the lone kerosene lamp pushed closely toward

Maria and Carla to shed its soft light over the pages of the work diaries they had to fill every evening with details of their day's work; I, making the most of the dimmer light, was half-heartedly attempting to write letters to my mother, my brothers, and the various girl friends I had left behind when we moved to the city. The hired hand sat in the darkness at the far end of the table, barely outlined, whittling on a piece of wood; and the boy was asleep with his arms and head resting on the table which was still moist from the evening scrubbing. Frau Schafer and Herr Glauer had disappeared into the cozy little front room, behind a locked door, from which they never emerged until we had all gone to bed.

"What are they doing in there?" I asked Carla a few evenings after my arrival. "Farm accounts," she said, and I accepted it. Carla believed it, I know. And I doubt that even Maria, the most sophisticated of the three of us, ever suspected anything else. She would have told us; we shared everything we knew. We talked about Frau Schafer and Herr Glauer, we whispered, we speculated. Maria even reported that once, when they thought they were alone, they had called each other by their first name. But we never doubted the accounts.

Many years later I would hear and read of the cynicism and decadence of the thirties. It totally evaded us. We, my contemporaries and I, were of an innocence that the post World War II generation cannot even fathom. Even now, more than half a century later, I can only marvel at it.

Shortly after nine o'clock we would stiffly and sleepily get off the chair and carry the lamp into the kitchen, where the glass cylinder would have to be polished the next day. The kitchen girl banked the fire in the tile stove and each one of us, holding a candle in one hand and protecting the small flame with the other, would drag off to our sleeping quarters.

And then some nights—perhaps not more than once a fortnight—I seemed to have barely drowsed off when the door opened and a flickering candle appeared. Enter, Lady MacBeth. Wrapped in a long, white nightgown, dark hair, streaked with gray, streaming down her back, her eyes in the candlelight two black pools, she walked the three steps from the door to the crib and bent over the sleeping child. Her hair fell forward and covered the red, feverish spots on her cheeks.

"Darling, my darling little boy." She spoke in a low, urgent voice. "My prince! My son! You are my own little love. Do you know that, sweet child? Do you love your mother?"

The child stirred, sat up, startled: "Mammi?"

"Love of my life," she stroked his hair with short, passionate strokes, "You are all I have. Don't ever leave me . . ."

"Mammi . . ." the child's voice grew tearful.

"*Ach, Liebchen, mein Liebchen*, sleep well, sleep well . . ." and the white-clad figure was gliding out of the room, closing the door firmly behind her.

"Mammi!" This time it was a plaintive cry. The child was awake and thoroughly frightened by now.

"Mammi!"

"Shsht, it's all right," I whispered furiously, "lie down and go back to sleep. I am right here . . ."

"Mammi!"

Oh, darn it! Darn that woman! This might mean that I would have to get out of bed and stand there in the icy room with my toes freezing fast onto the floor to calm down the frightened boy.

One more try from the distance: "Be quiet, *Schaetzchen*, your Mammi is asleep right next door. If you stop crying and go back to sleep right now, I'll let you lick the pudding spoon next Sunday!"

Sudden silence. The whimpering stopped. The offer is being considered.

"When is Sunday?"

"In two days."

"Are you going to cook the pudding?"

"Yes, it's my turn."

"Can I lick the pot, too?"

Oh shoot! "Yes."

A little sigh. I heard him rustle around a bit as he settled back under the featherbed. And within two minutes we were both fast asleep.

Saturdays the chicken coop had to be cleaned; another job none of us looked forward to. Chicken coops reek. The chickens slept clinging to horizontal poles fastened throughout the coop. With long, rake-like tools we scraped the boards underneath those poles clean of the drippings. When we came out we smelled like the bird house in the zoo, and we had lice. Chicken lice, sprightly little yellow dots with legs, leave humans on their own accord after a while and one becomes used to this brief encounter; but the first time I saw them crawling up my arms, I almost threw up.

"You must take your turn with the geese," Frau Schafer said to me during my second week. Immediately, my stomach twisted into a knot. I was terrified of geese. I don't know about geese internationally, but German geese bite. They pinch people on their calves. The ganders are always on the attack. They can run fast and they cheat; they do a sort of half-flying act between steps and catch their victims in the legs.

I asked the girls what we had to do with the geese.

"You have to feel them for eggs," said Maria, laughing.

"Feel them for eggs? What does that mean?"

Maria just kept laughing. "You tell her, Carla," she said.

"Well," said Carla with a grin on her broad face, "you have to catch them and hold them under your arm and stick your finger into their behind to see if they are going to lay an egg that morning."

This had to be a joke. They were teasing me and I wasn't going to fall for it any more than I had swallowed the story about the youngest one always carrying the water from the barn.

Maria watched my face. "It's true," she said.

And with a horrible sinking feeling in my stomach, I knew it was true.

After breakfast the next morning, Frau Schafer walked ahead of me to the goose shed.

"It will be your job this week to let the geese out in the morning," she said, "but before any goose gets out you will have to make sure she is not about to lay an egg. Geese don't lay eggs into nests; they lay them any place at all and they are hard to find. Goose eggs are valuable; if we have enough undamaged ones, we have them hatched. So, any goose about to lay an egg cannot leave the shed until the egg is laid."

The wooden shed was vibrating with ominous sounds of hissing, rustling and bumping. Frau Schafer opened the door and coolly kicked the onstorming geese back into the darkness. She singled out the gander and let him escape, then closed the door. In the thin light coming through the cracks between the boards, she began working. While I stood in near panic as far away from the geese as possible, she picked up one goose after another and proceeded to do exactly what Carla had said would be done.

Two of the geese she threw back into a corner, the others she let out of the door.

"Tomorrow you do it," she said, and walked back to the house.

The next morning I walked toward the shed, alone. For a long time I stood before the closed door, trembling, listening to all that mad commotion inside. Then I opened the door about two inches. Instantly a whole white hissing cloud hurled itself against the opening. I slammed the door shut again, leaned against it for support, and contemplated my future. Maybe I could lie down in a dead faint. They would surely come looking for me within an hour. Or maybe I should just run away? I thought longingly of the man with the ear muffs. He never would have sent me into a goose shed. All he had wanted was to marry me and have me cook his meat and potatoes at noon and go for a walk in the park in the evening, with a chaste kiss once in a while on the upper corner of my left cheek. Now he could not come to my rescue because he had no idea where I was. I hadn't even answered his last, rather urgent letters—picked up during solitary "health walks" of which my mother approved—from a post office box and eventually torn into tiny pieces and flushed down the toilet because I trusted neither the waste paper basket nor my mother. Act in haste, repent in leisure. This was getting me nowhere. I began to look around for a suitable weapon. The long rake we used to clean the chicken coop seemed perfect. I went back to the shed, threw the door open and flailed the rake around like a windmill. The geese stormed by me toward the farm pond. No more hissing inside. I peeked in. Empty. I put the rake back and went into the house and reported that not a single goose wished to lay an egg that day.

The next morning was a complete repetition, except that it took less time. I picked up the rake on my way to the shed. The third day Frau Schafer frowned. No eggs, again? I knew I could not keep this up forever. I had decided that the most ferocious one of the bunch had to be the gander, so the next morning I opened the door just a crack and half hid behind it, and sure enough, the gander was the first one out; a few others escaped before I could slam the door shut, but at least some were left inside. Then, grabbing my rake, I went in to join them. I wildly waved my rake at them and discovered with relief that without their obnoxious leader, those geese seemed remarkably meek and ready for some sort of truce. That morning I must have actually examined one or two and left the rest out, and after that, it just got easier each morning. The gander, however, was no friend of mine; he would hiss threateningly each time I crossed his path in the farmyard. "Teach him a lesson," said the hired hand, and he told me how. And so the day came when, instead of hurrying out of his way, I turned around and stood my ground. He came at me, hissing fiercely, large white wings flapping. I grabbed him by the outstretched neck and, turning on my heels, whirled him around two or three times like a mad carousel. Then, dizzy with the motion and my own courage, I let him go suddenly. He fell flat on his stomach, tried to get on his feet, wobbled drunkenly a few steps, and, barely regaining his balance, staggered away as fast as he could manage. After that, all I had to do was walk up to him and say: "Want to dance?" and he would waddle back to his lady geese as quickly as his dignity would permit.

Geese are notoriously bad mothers. Whenever there were enough suitable eggs, Frau Schafer would look for a hatching turkey. Turkeys are marvelous mothers. They are also incredibly stupid. Suddenly, for no apparent reason, eggs or no eggs, a turkey might get this tremendous urge to hatch. They are easy to spot; they just sit there on some sandy place, all round and puffed up, looking determined and defiant and not getting up and out of the way for anything or anybody. They are protecting their non-existent eggs. So Frau Schafer would make a nest in some safe corner of the barn, grab one of those squatting turkeys and set it down on top of five or six goose eggs. Fresh goose eggs are not always available. Neither are squatting turkeys. When they did coincide, we were in business.

While I was the goose girl, some seven little goslings got hatched, and shortly afterward the turkey mother got run over and died and had to be eaten. Seven goslings are a small fortune for a poor farm. Frau Schafer came to me and, for once pleading rather than ordering, said: "You must raise them."

Seven tiny, yellow balls, downy and quivering; huddled together, I could take all of them into my two hands. She had them in a basket under a towel and when she pulled the towel off I looked bleakly into seven wide-open, tiny beaks from which emerged a concert of such high, shrill cries that Frau Schafer quickly covered them again.

"They will have to be fed at least six times a day," Frau Schafer said. "Boil potatoes, mash them, mix them with bone meal, but mostly they should get greens. Fresh greens; I'll show you what to pick."

What she showed me turned out to be mainly burning nettles, a plant that grows abundantly along the ditches and country roads of Germany. The burning nettle is a milder version of poison ivy, which does not grow in Germany. What it lacks in viciousness, it makes up in quantity. Wherever skin comes in contact with it, small painful blisters appear. They do not spread, however, and are not contagious. This, as it turned out, along with other tender green sprouts, was the goslings' favorite snack. It was spring and there was no shortage of it. Armed with woolen gloves and a big basket, I would set off at any free moment, crouch down in the ditches and start picking.

Potatoes were boiling on the stove, a sack of bone meal stood in the kitchen corner, and I was forever chopping nettles. The goslings' appetite was voracious and never appeased. During the first week, I lifted the whole peeping cluster of goslings out at once and put it down on a large tray where I had spread the food. For the first few days I hand-fed them, but they learned fast and very soon gobbled the stuff up with lightning speed; I only had to watch that they didn't push each other over the edge of the tray and that each one got its fair share — rather like the Sunday pudding. If I was to be a Mother Goose, there would be no "runt of the litter" drama.

Soon there had to be a bigger basket; more greens and nettles had to be picked and chopped; I chopped off the thumb of the wool glove and discarded them in the end, since they slowed down the process. There were always some burns on my fingers or palms or wrists. The moment they saw me the goslings went wild; their cries were still shrill, but I fancied that there was affection in them now. They didn't greet anybody else with this piercing racket. They got larger, rounder, more golden; they ate ravenously. One day Frau Schafer appeared in the kitchen carrying five chicken eggs.

"They were partially hatched," she said, "but the hen ran off; she must have been frightened by something. The eggs are dead now, feed them to the goslings."

"Feed them how?" I asked, perplexed.

"Hard boil them and chop them," Frau Schafer said and departed. She was not the only one who departed. The kitchen was all mine once I started chopping up those dead eggs. I don't know what was worse, the odor or the debris inside. But by that time I was really beyond caring; all that mattered were my goslings. Maria and Carla stuck their heads through the kitchen door. Maria yelled: "She is at it again!" and they ran. The goslings loved the stuff.

They became too large for any basket; they fought. They still slept in one big golden ball, but during the day they showed signs of individualism and varying dispositions. The hired hand built a larger cage for them. Then came the glorious day of their first excursion through the farm yard. In famous goose step, they marched, one behind the other, right after me. They went everywhere I went. If I stopped, they stopped; if I ran, they fluttered and waddled in such mad rush that they would fall over their own beaks at every third step. They would have followed me to the end of the earth. In the meantime, I was happy just to lead them to the next ditch and let them pick their own nettles. They were fair sized now, strong, still golden, proud, cantankerous, and beautiful.

One morning while I was scraping out the bread trough, Carla came running into the kitchen.

"Herr Glauer let the sow out and she killed your goslings," she cried. My heart stood still.

"How many?" I whispered.

"All of them," said Carla with some satisfaction. "She ate them."

My knees gave way under me. I sat down on the nearest kitchen stool.

"You look real white," said Carla wonderingly. "Why, aren't you glad? No more nettles, no more stinking eggs. You'll have your lunch hour back!"

I started to cry. Maria came into the kitchen looking at me in surprise. "The sow ate Eva's goslings," announced Carla.

"Who let the sow out?" Maria demanded. "She is not supposed to run free." The sow was a killer; she had killed some of her own piglets.

"Herr Glauer. He left the barn door open and she escaped." Carla glanced at me quite uncertain now. "I told her she ought to be glad. No more messing around the kitchen at all hours . . ."

"Ach, shut up, Carla," said Maria disgustedly. She went to the bread trough and picked up my scraping knife, swearing softly under her breath. Maria had a lot of pet names for Her Glauer. And while she went on cleaning the trough for me, I sat on the kitchen stool, bereft, desolate, and wept for my little goslings.

* * * * * * * * * * * * * *

Spring was upon us. Lilies of the valley and violets glowed in white and purple patches all through the young birch woods. The robins were nesting; the cuckoo called ceaselessly from the depth of the forest. Mutiny was in the air. The three of us, showing as always a united front, declared that we would no longer drag the large, devilish heavy milk canisters up the cellar steps and out the front door to be picked up every morning by the dairy truck driver. There were at least two men in the house, each one as strong as the three of us together. Maria and Carla announced that they would note in their work diary that we had no washboard for the laundry and that we had to scrub the dirty sheets and towels over the knuckles of our hands, which broke the skin and gave us painful sores that never healed before the next laundry day came along. They said they would mention that the same dust pan that was used to remove dog and cat dirt from the stone entrance was also used to sweep the last flour out of the dough tray. And when one evening, as Maria walked into the barn to feed some kitchen garbage to the pigs, Herr Glauer jumped out of a dark corner to frighten her; she threw the kitchen towel with all the potato peelings right into his face.

It produced some results. A washboard appeared and a second dust pan. Frau Schafer grew more remote, and Herr Glauer was at all times as unpleasant as he knew how. Yet our work drew us together daily. Potatoes had to be sorted, seed potatoes bagged, and all of us, master, mistress, and hands, went into the field to plant. The girl on kitchen duty would leave after a few hours to prepare a noon meal which she and the boy would carry to the field, and we all sat, side by side, tired, dirty, with aching backs, peacefully eating our bread and sausage and listening to the cuckoo call and watching the robins feed their young.

Once the potatoes were in, we girls were dispatched to the garden. Vegetables had to be raised to feed us in spring and summer. Onions, carrots and cabbage were grown to last all through the winter.

There came spring days when the sky was an immense velvet blue dome and the air around us was full of sweet, intoxicating smells. The lark was rising out of the field straight into the air, trembling with the power of its voice. The three of us would straighten up, lean on the spades, and look up to the tiny silver plane moving over our heads.

"Pilot, say hello to the sun . . ." sang Maria softly.

"Give my love to the moon and the stars . . ." Carla had joined her.

Flieger, grüss mir die Sonne; grüss mir den Mond und die Sterne . . . Our eyes followed the silvery speck in its vast arc through the blue air, flying slowly into the hazy distance, away, away from us, into a mysterious, wonderful, unknown world that lay behind the horizon and my heart would grow heavy with such vague, painful, sweet longing that it seemed to fill my entire body. I was sixteen and I hadn't a clue to life, but I knew that one day, one day a silver plane would swoop down from the sky and I would not be left behind.

The hired hand quit and Maria took over the milking of the two cows. And one morning the shepherd boy was gone. I suppose Frau Schafer paid them next to nothing. I got five marks each month, less than a dollar a week. Not enough to get new soles for my broken shoes. I did not realize the extent of the calamity of the boy's disappearance until breakfast time, when it became clear to me that this seemed to be a major upset.

"What's the matter?" I asked Maria. "Why all the fuss?"

"This is spring; there is no feed left," said Maria. "The animals have got to be taken out."

I had not thought of that. Why did everybody suddenly look at me? I didn't chase the boy away. I had always been very nice to him. Once I even wrote a letter for him to his grandmother.

"Well, Eva," said Frau Schafer with a notable lack of conviction, "you will have to herd. You are the youngest."

I stared at her, speechless. "The dog will help you," she said encouragingly.

Great! The dog didn't even come when I called him for his food.

Herr Glauer walked ahead of me through the farm yard. He opened the doors to the stables and the cows moved slowly and majestically out into the yard; the goats galloped towards the lane; the geese were already off in full cry. The sheep tried to squeeze through the door all at the same time, got stuck and had to be sorted out. Last came the two calves, already big but having as yet no sense whatsoever. When I went to feed them in the evenings, I never knew what to do with the bucket filled with sheep milk. If I put it on the ground, they hurled themselves on it and pushed it over, spilling every drop of it. If I held the bucket up, they nearly threw me to the floor. I would stand with my back against the wall for support, holding the bucket high, yelling and pushing back, getting that lousy stuff splashed over my arms and face, worrying about my rib cage.

"The calves take watching," warned Herr Glauer. Thanks a lot. He was grinning like a fiend. He had no illusions about my shepherding talents.

"Well, get going," he said. "Keep between the lane and the creek and stay clear of the stone quarry."

The only ones still around were the two cows. The geese, sheep, and calves had disappeared with the goats in the lead. I picked up a switch and ran after them.

When I think of those herding days, they all run together into one vast nightmare. The geese were the least of my worries; they stuck together and could always be found at the nearest nettle patch. The dog started off chasing the two calves down the road until all three disappeared from my view. The goats headed straight into the neighbor's barley field. And the sheep made a bee-line to the stone quarry.

I don't know about sheep. I love King David's 23rd Psalm; it's very sweet and soothing, but, personally, I don't think the man had ever been near a sheep.

"He leadeth me beside still waters . . ." Had he ever tried to lead a sheep beside waters, still or otherwise? The first thing they would do is push him into it. Failing this, they would undoubtedly knock each other in.

At noon Maria came to get the goats for the mid-day milking. She had some trouble finding me. I was down by the creek trying to get some idiot sheep out of the water. Its leg had got caught under a stone. My own left leg was in the muddy water up to my knee.

"How is it going?" she asked.

I looked up for just a second.

"That bad!" she said. She climbed down the low embankment and helped push with her powerful hip.

"Don't let them go so near the creek," she said. "Use your switch."

"They don't even feel it with their thick wool!"

"Don't hit the wool," said Maria. "Do like the dog—get them around their legs. Where is the dog?"

"It started chasing the calves down the road first thing in the morning," I said. "They are probably at the Danish border by now."

"Where are the goats?"

"In Pritzow's barley field," I said in despair.

"Well," said Maria, giving one last well-aimed kick at the rear of the sheep which made it run up the embankment bleating indignantly, "don't take it so hard. They never expected you to last that long. Old Glauer has been cracking jokes and looking up the road all morning. I know he thought you would be back within the hour, bawling."

When Maria brought the goats back she brought my noon meal along. She plunked herself down besides me in the field. The midday sun had warmed the air and caressed our backs; the pussy willow bush beside us was covered with gold dust; dragon flies were dancing in the air, here now and gone again; the geese quacked in the distance; the cows were quietly ruminating at the far end of the field. The goats, heads low, eyes on us, were searching diligently and virtuously for grass tips between the roots and stones.

"This is not so bad," said Maria, stretching and yawning like a big, contented cat in the sun. I just looked at her, ancient wisdom of shepherding misery written all over my face.

"You don't know," I said.

"It beats carrot weeding," she sighed.

When she got up, the goats lifted their heads to watch her. Their dark, cunning looks followed her down the lane and when Maria's sturdy figure finally disappeared around the bend, the goats took off in a body towards Pritzow's lupine field.

Even the longest day comes to an end. Sometime in the late afternoon I was sitting on a stone, inspecting with great concentration the damage to my left shoe where the sole had separated from the top and a gaping hole surrounded by caked mud had appeared. Something nudged my elbow; I looked up and saw with utter amazement my wretched herd gathered around me. The cows, at a dignified distance, were looking at me with their great brown, mournful eyes. The geese in a bunch had squatted nearby; even the sheep for once were not involved in any suicidal activity but stood a stone's throw away, broadside to broadside, bleating softly. All the goats were gathered closely around me and the young ones were beginning to nibble with friendly curiosity at my blouse and hair. The older ones were facing me in a half circle; their dark, sparkling, intelligent eyes seemed to send me an affectionate signal of encouragement. It was as if they were saying: "It's time to go home now. Didn't we just have a lovely day?"

* * * * * * * * * * * * * *

Many years later — about forty, to be exact — I was reminded one day of this scene that happened so long ago and so far away. I was substituting in Hell's Hole, my name for our junior high school then, standing in for an absent library science teacher. The class I was supposed to teach was well known for their uncanny ability to speed substitute teachers towards nervous breakdowns.

I never taught them anything that day; all through that harrowing hour I had my hands full keeping them from climbing out of that open window or crowning each other with the full wastepaper basket. Little paper wads catapulted through the air from nowhere, chairs squeaked rhythmically but could not be located on approach; some girls in the back of the room seemed to practice subdued cheerleading yells. When the bell finally sounded, I was half dizzy with relief but I faced the departing kids with severity, determined to have the last word.

"It's a shame that you were so bad," I proclaimed sternly. "We could have had such a good time together."

One of the worst culprits, a boy with a round face and merry eyes, looked at me with genuine surprise.

"But, don't you know?" he exclaimed, "We *did* have a good time!"

* * * * * * * * * * * * * *

Getting home was easy. The animals out-ran, out-jumped, and out-jogged me by half a mile, and when I appeared, Maria and Carla had them safely tucked away in their pens and stalls. Frau Schafer ignored my mud-covered legs and gaping shoe. There was nothing to be gained by asking how the day had gone. Herr Glauer was not around. Somebody had come by with a bike to tell him that our calves were in the village eating the flower boxes in front of the houses and Herr Glauer had gone to borrow a neighbor's pick-up truck and haul them home.

I herded all that week, but the calves stayed in the barn and by the end of the week Herr Glauer had fenced in a piece of land for them and a young man came from a few villages away and brought his own dog and switch and I went happily back to weeding beets and cleaning chicken coops.

* * * * * * * * * * * * * *

Spring yielded to summer. The air began to quiver in the noon heat; our arms and necks got dark from working outside; more and more vegetables appeared on the dinner table. In the evenings, the three of us hiked over the hill to the pond and splashed noisily around in the dark water. None of us wore a stitch of clothing. Herr Glauer and Frau Schafer were safely locked away with their accounts, and the village boys never ventured that far. Besides, Maria's arm was known to have a mighty swing. Afterward we rubbed each other's backs dry and warm, got into our clothes, and sat in the tall grass that swayed a little in the warm night air. Above us were the June stars and all around us the mighty crescendo of a thousand crickets. We never wanted to go back to the house to bed.

The news came on the wing of the village swallows, who told it to our barn swallow, who sang it to us: the maneuvers had started! The soldiers are here!

The very next day an open military vehicle pulled into our farm yard. It carried two officers. Frau Schafer received them in the parlor and sent for us.

Off flew the smocks and aprons; up we flew to our rooms and the small cracked mirrors over the washbasins. The faces were scrubbed, the unruly hair coaxed into some order, and down the steps we came, neat and demure, to meet our guests.

During my entire time at the farm I entered the parlor only three times — not counting the house cleaning in spring — once on Easter Sunday, a second time when Frau Schafer gave a party for some neighboring farmers and local dignitaries, and once on that day when the two lieutenants came calling.

They were both handsome fellows. They were young, twenty-one or two. I was sixteen and awe struck. One of them was tall and dark. Even though he did most of the talking, I have long since forgotten his name. The other one was short and blond. His name was Paulus. First Lieutenant of the German Air Force, H. D. Paulus. The tall, dark one who did the talking looked amiably at each of us in turn. Paulus looked only at me.

The tall lieutenant, whose name I have forgotten, talked about the maneuvers, the quarters the men had taken with the village farmers, and the ball at the end of the week. They were here to invite us to the ball.

"Will you come?" Paulus asked, looking straight at me.

"We will all come," answered Frau Schafer with a thin smile.

For once Frau Schafer was on our side. While Herr Glauer retreated into a vast sulk that lasted all week, we women were busy every spare minute. We baked large flat cakes with fruit on top and high cakes with poppy seed filling. We polished shoes and dug deep into drawers for stockings without runs; we washed and ironed our "best" dresses and borrowed or lent each other little pieces of jewelry. When the great evening arrived, we worked with lightning speed, Frau Schafer lending us a hand right along. The animals were milked, the milk strained, centrifuged, and dragged to the basement. The milk buckets were scrubbed, the centrifuge was shining, the dishes washed, the kitchen swept, the chicken and geese locked into their coops, and up we went to do the best, the very best, with ourselves. It didn't take long; none of us used cosmetics; it didn't occur to us and we would not have had the money to buy them anyway. I rubbed my cheeks red with a rough towel and used the burnt end of a match stick to give my wayward eyebrows a more enticing arc. Then, very carefully, the ironed white muslin dress was slipped over my head, with the flaring skirt and tight bodice, over which I wore a short, flowered bolero jacket. On either side of my head, over my ears, I rolled a strand of hair before I pinned it up into the bun, which, I thought, looked more feminine and festive; and Cinderella was ready for the ball.

They had sent a car for us with a driver, an open little military vehicle, forerunner of the American jeep. Frau Schafer sat in front beside the driver and the three of us squeezed into the back seat, each one balancing on our knees a platter with a cake. We were too excited to talk; every time the car hit a bump we just giggled and hung on to our cakes.

The dance was a big success. It was colorful, noisy, and hot. I really had eyes only for Paulus who sat beside me, serious and attentive. Once a boisterous young corporal came to ask me for a dance. I shook my head. He looked baffled and uncertain, then bowing slightly again, he left.

"You must not turn my men down, Eva," said Paulus mildly.

"But he is tipsy," I protested.

Firmly: "No, he is not."

"Didn't you see how crazily he danced with the girl in the red dress?"

"He would not have danced so with you," said Paulus quietly.

I sat out the dance, chastised, with flaming cheeks. I could not tell him that I had only wanted to keep myself free for him. He did not dance that dance with me; I knew it was because he did not want to offend his man. I felt awful—angry, humiliated; yet I found myself liking him all the more for it.

It must have been around four o'clock in the morning when we drove home. Frau Schafer sat up front again, holding all the empty platters on her lap. This very conveniently immobilized her. The two lieutenants sat in the back, filling the seat with their larger frames, and we three girls sat on their laps. Two laps for three girls, arms and legs all over the place. We talked, we teased, we laughed hysterically and we sang a little. When we drove up to the farmhouse and the three of us jumped out of the car, we heard one of the lieutenants exclaim in surprise.

"Oh, damn! Have I been holding *YOUR* hand all that time?" yelled the dark one.

"And squeezing it." Paulus grunted, disgusted.

"You squeezed it right back," his buddy accused him.

We were laughing and singing and dancing into the house, ignoring Frau Schafer's shushing and warning that it would not enhance Herr Glauer's mood if we were to wake him at this hour. We made some coffee, went upstairs and changed into our working clothes; Maria and I grabbed the milk buckets, Carla began poking around in the stove ashes and the day had begun. The princesses had turned into pumpkins.

One more time Paulus came, to say good-bye to me. We walked up the lane a little, away from the curious stares of friend and foe, and sat down on the mossy stones at the edge of the birch woods.

"Will you write to me?" Paulus asked with some urgency.

Would I write to him? Volumes. Deluges.

"Yes," I said.

He scribbled his address on the back of an old envelope. Then he held my hand for a while. When he left, before driving around the bend, he turned for one more wave and smile. Then he was gone, leaving his girl by the wayside. A vast, numb sadness engulfed me, but at the same time I was happy. My heart seemed quite broken and yet it seemed to join the lark on its way into the blue sky. I was a bundle of the most wonderfully confusing emotions. I was alive. I was in love.

Unlike his great biblical namesake, my Paulus was no writer of letters. I wrote him the first long letter three days later, and another one two days later, in case the first one should get lost. I lived only for the one minute of the day when the mailman leaned his bicycle against the bench in front of the house and started sorting our mail. About a week later I got a card. It showed a picture, a cartoon drawing, of a little plane with a jolly pilot waving to a crowing rooster below.

"Greetings from Augsburg," read the card. "Flight weather has been great lately. Hope you are well."

Of course, the man had no time to write long letters! He did select the card ever so carefully to suit the two of us. That could not have been easy. I answered him with a long letter two days later. There was no response. This meant I could not write to him again. There had to be something, the tiniest bit of encouragement, before I could turn another one of my long epistles loose on him. One day, when we were at the county seat, I bought a picture post card with the city hall on it. On the back I drew a lone question mark. A week later, a second card arrived with a picture of a windmill, any old windmill.

"Greetings from Hamburg," it said. "Duty and work are very demanding. Hope you are fine and things are going well for you."

Well, my little lieutenant, what did you think? You had just broken my heart. I was not fine. I was anything but fine. I was wretched, bewildered and unhappy.

Maybe he had met a girl a day, a week, a month later, whose fingernails were not broken and grimy, whose hair did not smell of hay and whose clothes did not emit, if ever so faintly, odors of goats and kerosene. It did not really matter. My happiness and my suffering were all my own. My heart grew in those days, expanding with dreams, hopes, love and grief, never to revert again to its childish, innocent and unthinking limits. That was good, for life has given me much to love and all the room was needed.

Unlike so many of his contemporaries, Paulus survived the war. I know because of one of those odd twists that life sometimes produces to tie up loose ends. I met a man, years later, who had been in a prisoner-of-war camp in Canada with a young blond German pilot named Paulus. They were repatriated to Germany together six months after the war.

Well, then, "Greetings from across the sea! Hope things have gone well for you, too, Paulus, my first young love."

* * * * * * * * * * * * * *

Once a year Frau Schafer opened her parlor and gave a party for neighbors and selected farmers from the village. The most prosperous farmer came, who had, as befitted him, the plumpest wife, and the farmer who helped us out, once in a while, with his pick-up truck. The burgomaster came, the pastor, and the tailor who had married the village teacher, who was also the village shrew.

The parlor was opened some days before, aired, swept, dusted, and polished, till everything gleamed. The odor remained, however, the peculiar odor of the unused Good Room. It was the smell of floor wax and candles mingled with the moist cellar odor of a room unheated through many winter days, an autumn air of dead flowers, and from the curtains emanating a whiff of strong cigars and stronger coffee. It cannot be exactly analyzed, this odor, but anybody who ever lived in a country house with a parlor knows it and will recognize it at any time in life — in fact, will be awash in a powerful flood of memories which it invariably evokes before consciousness even takes actual notice.

At the party that evening I met Herr Anaberg. He was a neighbor and his acreage qualified his farm to be called an estate, at least in his own mind. There was always an air of slight melancholy around Herr Anaberg. The truth was that there were a number of things for him to be melancholic about. His estate might be bigger than anybody else's around, but that meant it was just so much more sand, stones, and scrubby pines. If he had more potatoes, more rye, and more cows, he also had more to worry about. He was as poor as the rest of them, but he was not like the rest of them, and herein lay the source of his melancholy. Herr Anaberg was an officer and a gentleman. He was well educated, he was young, and he was very handsome. But handsome alone will not do for a young man if he is also, alas, very poor. There's got to be a certain dash to him, a devil-may-care attitude which totally eluded him. Indeed, he cared about a great many things: his appearance, his image, his dismal prospects. He was, also, completely humorless. In consequence, he was the butt of dozens of jokes and a never ceasing topic of breakfast conversations. He had a little car that he never drove without gloves, summer or winter. That was always good for a wisecrack or two. He had one well-groomed horse which he rode for pleasure. Not that he ever looked very pleased when he rode it, but it belonged to his idea of a gentleman farmer. "Who did he think he was?" the farmers asked mockingly, "Count Ribbeck of Ribbeck in Havelland?" The stories and jokes about him were well worn and redundant, but the villagers never tired of them. How he planted potatoes according to his college books and not the farmer's almanac, and how they all rotted in the fall rains before he could harvest them. How he was treed by his own bull and had to be rescued by his farm hand. How he got stuck with his car in the spring rains and had to wade through two kilometers of mud in his country squire outfit to get help and be pulled out by a team of oxen. The more they joked, the more he hung on, tenaciously, to his style of living, his image, his hopes. He was a reserve officer in a cavalry corps; I saw a picture of him in uniform on his horse and he looked truly splendid.

From the very beginning of the party Herr Anaberg singled me out. I don't remember what we found to talk about. We had many meetings after that but I have forgotten all but our very last conversation. I liked him; I felt flattered by his attention and I was a little sorry for him. And he sensed, perhaps, that I did not think of him as peculiar or ridiculous. The truth is that he was neither. He was a nice, timid young man, not exactly a tower of intellect, who was just as trapped—and for the same reason—as was Frau Schafer, in the dreariness of a dirt farm, with no money and no prospects. But, unlike Mme. Schafer, he refused to drown in sheer hopelessness. He clung, against all odds, to his horse, his gloves, his "estate," and his image as a country squire.

After the evening of the party, he would stop by once in a while and take me for a drive. I do remember those famous gloves because he used to put them on, quite leisurely, while the car was plowing ahead driverless. At the farm those outings only served to step up the jokes and derisive remarks about him, prejudiced and merciless, from Herr Glauer, Frau Schafer, and Carla, and, more good natured, from Maria, who carried a secret torch for a first mate of the Merchant Marines and felt a certain empathy for us. The ridicule did not stop me from seeing him but I was too young and defenseless to rise above it. It certainly prevented me from falling in love with him.

Nor was he in love with me. Twice after I left the farm he called me when he was in Berlin and we met in a little restaurant. Each time he looked the part of the young country squire, right down to the green hunting jacket, boots, and pipe. With nobody around to poke fun at him, I found him not at all unattractive. Besides, I was bored out of my wits with my life, and things at home looked pretty bleak. When he called a third time, some months later, I decided to advance our case a bit. By that time we called each other by our Christian names, but he had never even kissed me. This did not worry me unduly, since every time we met I had a truly phenomenal head cold. My closed sinuses came through on the telephone, muffled and unmistakably. Herr Anaberg was not given to treat calamities like this with a light touch.

"Eva! Not again!" he said, appalled, but we met just the same. I asked him about the estate.

"Not much change," he said with a melancholic smile. I took the bull by the horns.

"You should get married, Gunther," I said, hoping he would not notice my blushing.

"Who would marry me?" he asked. He looked more downhearted than I had ever seen him.

A good start! "You must marry a girl with money," I said lightly. "That would end most of your problems."

No answer; the gray eyes rested thoughtfully on my face.

"You must try to meet a rich girl." No answer. The man was missing all his cues.

"You cannot afford to marry a poor girl like me." Now, if that would not do it, nothing would. Life came into his sad face; he looked positively animated. For the first time there was warmth in his eyes as he took both my hands into his. My heart jumped. As always on such occasions, I became a bit frightened.

"Ach, Eva," he murmured, "you are wonderful. You are wonderfully understanding. You can see it, too, can't you? That's just what I must do, and I will do it, so help me!" He looked quite decisive and manly for once.

I don't know what we talked about for the rest of the evening. Probably about ways and means of meeting wealthy maidens. He was tender and solicitous; I was gracious. We fondly said goodbye; I took the subway home, told my mother I had had a very nice time, hopped into bed, and, before I fell asleep, took Herr Anaberg mentally off my list of possible candidates.

He never managed to meet and marry his heiress. Two years later my melancholic friend was dead, killed during the first months of the war.

* * * * * * * * * * * * * *

It was on a Friday morning when Carla came charging into the kitchen waving a letter in front of me. I recognized the elegant, slanted handwriting and instantly felt the familiar small knot in the pit of my stomach, a phenomenon that never totally disappeared through the sixty-odd years of my relationship with my mother. Her handwriting remained elegant, flowing, and steady into her nineties, and in all those years I never knew if, once I opened the letter, it would leave me happy, angry, or wildly frustrated.

That morning she wrote that she was on her way to a visit up north and that she would break her trip in Lychen, our county-seat. She had made reservations at the Inn. Would I ask Frau Schafer to give me a day and night off to join her there? She did not intend to visit the farm; I am sure an instinct cautioned her away from it.

Saturday morning I went to say goodbye to my fellow inmates. Maria was churning butter in the darkest, coolest corner of the stone hall. It was tedious work because on hot summer days the cream obstinately refused to clump. Carla was looking leisurely for the filthiest smock she could find; she was getting ready to clean the chicken coop. She was in no hurry.

"Well, good-bye, children," I chanted gleefully. "Be good now, look lively. You know the old saying: for idle hands, the devil and Madame find work quick enough. I expect everything to sparkle when I come back tomorrow night."

"Shall I leave the calves out?" asked Carla maliciously. "They will be happy to accompany you to town!" I chose to ignore this indelicate reminder of my shepherding days.

"I'll bring you something from town," I promised.

"Lemon drops," said Carla, her face lighting up.

"Two pounds of butter, preferably not goats'," said Maria, giving the churn an unfriendly kick with her wooden clogs.

"Right." I pushed my bike over the rough cobblestones of the farm yard, skillfully avoiding the slippery poultry droppings. Little Herman was crouched beside a squatting turkey and poking it with Maria's treasured *genuine pig-bristle* brush. I patted his head fondly in passing and I was off. And as I was riding down the lane and around the bend, my overnight bag bouncing merrily on the handlebar, I had not the faintest idea that I would not see any of them ever again.

Six miles of country road lay ahead of me. We were deep into summer and it was a glorious day. The sky was blue and cloudless, the fields of rye were like a gently rippling golden sea around me. There was a smell of fresh hay and ripening grain in the air, the whole earth shared my contentment. Occasionally a small rabbit hopped out of nowhere right into my path, joyfully twitching nose and ears; most often it was followed by its mother or nanny who smacked it soundly right back into the high grass.

I was no more than a mile or two out of Lychen when my bike hit an unexpected bump. The little bag swung wildly against my knee and the handlebar swayed out of control. The front wheel jackknifed and I flew over it, landing with my solid weight on my left knee.

When I had gathered my wits sufficiently about me again, I sat down on the side of the ditch and inspected the damage. The whole countryside seemed to be represented inside my knee; between the blood and dirt, small stones were embedded, along with grass, wild flowers, rabbit dirt, and a smashed blackberry or two. The stinging pain brought tears to my eyes. I attempted to clean the mess with a highly inadequate handkerchief, gave up, wiped my hands, sniffled, and, with some difficulty, picked up my bike. There was not a soul around and there might not be for a considerable time. If I wanted to reach my destination before the knee swelled and stiffened, I had better push on.

My mother's pleasure in seeing me again was somewhat dampened when I limped into the hotel lobby covered with streaks of dirt, blood, and dried tears. She hauled me up to her room where she cleaned the wound and the rest of me as well as she could under the circumstances. A visit to a doctor, she said, had to be postponed for a few hours as she had other plans.

As it turned out, her main purpose in stopping off at Lychen was to take me to the famous orthopedic hospital nearby where she had actually wangled an appointment with the hospital's formidable Chief of Staff, Prof. G. A scar on my right leg--the result of a series of operations during early childhood--which exposed the bone from the ankle to just below the knee, was a source of much more grief to my mother than to me—I could not even remember when I had two sound legs—and she was going to consult the famous orthopedist about the possibility of a skin graft.

This was all a very long time ago. My mother did all the talking for the two of us and most of the listening. I was much more occupied with the pain in my left knee and, anyway, only mildly interested in the whole interview. I have later searched my memory for more details of this meeting. I remember that the Professor was a man between forty and fifty, very lively, with florid coloring, a sportsman more than a scientist in appearance. He gave us his undivided attention. He looked at the x-rays my mother had brought along; he was kind, and, I remember gratefully, he did not squeeze and poke the scar as so many other doctors had done. His conclusion was firm: no skin graft for at least another two years. He suspected that I was still growing, in spite of being in my seventeenth year. Time, incidentally, proved him right. I did actually grow more than an inch between my 16th and 18th birthday.

The consultation over, my mother rushed me to a doctor's office. There we were faced with a full waiting room, a long wait, and, in the end, with a tired, exasperated, and sour country doctor. He soundly scolded me for taking such poor care of the injury, cleaned it till I thought I would faint, gave me a tetanus shot with something that looked and felt like a cake decorating tube, and told my mother that I was to lie flat and not walk or dangle the leg under any circumstances.

"You want to lose your knee, go right ahead," was his last encouraging remark to me.

My mother was in a quandary, but never for long; she was a woman of solutions. She had a taxi drive us to the town's youth hostel. There I was deposited on a bench with my leg propped up, while she disappeared to negotiate with the hostel parents. (Hostels in those days were run by married, middle-aged couples.) I don't know what she said and how she overrode their protests; she could be exceedingly persuasive when she wished to be, appealing either to her opponents Christian spirit or to their social conscience, whichever she deemed to be more effective at the moment. In any case, they agreed to let me stay and rest and to serve me meals in bed. (The bed turned out to be the lower bunk in an empty dormitory.) Next, she called the constable in the village and persuaded him to send a boy on a bike to Frau Schafer to let her know that I was injured and unable to return at least for a few days. She then bought me some toothpaste, a towel, and a magazine, impressed upon me not to dangle my leg, and departed for her visit up north.

The next days are rather blurred. Nobody and nothing sticks out in my memory. My mother came back within three days, speeded, I think, by an unsatisfactory phone call to the hostel mother, to find me swollen, spotted, with an all but immobilized leg and a high fever. I had developed a serum reaction. She wanted to know what had happened and why I was in such a bad way. Feverish and at times delirious, I entertained her instead with anecdotes of life at the farm. She gradually began to ask a few questions about our working hours, our free time. Wasn't Frau Schafer trained to handle young girls? Were there no recreational activities in the evenings? "No, no," I said, and while my mother listened in stony silence, I tried to explain about the farm accounts. That, however, was boring; I wanted to tell her how we had gotten hold of one of Herr Glauer's suits and stuffed it with straw and made a strawman and had our picture taken with the strawman's arms around us and fooled everybody, most of all Frau Schafer. My mother's face was set; no more questions; the strawman went by the wayside. I slept. My mother called the constable one more time to tell him her daughter was very ill. Yes, very unfortunate; but in any case, she had decided against my going back; there were other plans. Would somebody be good enough to pack all my things and send them on to the hostel. The box came with the milk wagon the next morning. Maria had packed it. "Lucky you!" the little note said that she had smuggled into the box.

Maria, the stout-hearted, the strong, the undismayed. Eventually she married her sailor. I like to think that they made it through the war and raised a handful of sturdy, jolly, no-nonsense youngsters; the world can use them. Carla: I don't know what happened to Carla. She was no letter writer.

The next thing I dimly remember is lying in my own bed in our Berlin apartment. I remember somebody giving me a mirror, and that I looked at my swollen, patchy face, the moon of the misbegotten. I remember the doctor bending over me and giving me an injection. I slept a great deal. My mother washed me, bandaged me, fed me chicken soup, and, after the fever left, brought me glasses of red wine into which a raw egg and sugar had been beaten. (This is a remedy still held in high esteem in Germany.) She nursed me with energy and dedication as she had nursed the sick in our house as long as I can remember, from her husband and children, maids and cook to the big shepherd dogs, who were so finely bred and highly strung that they fell ill if anyone looked cross at them.

My bed was turned toward the window and from my pillow I could see the leaves of the linden tree turn slowly golden and begin to drift downward, and as they danced gently and gracefully past the window, I wondered idly what the girls were doing right now.

The great farm experiment was over.

Chapter 4

My mother could now concentrate on me. That was not as easy as it sounds. I had neither the age nor the school level to enter a university. The farm experience had put a temporary damper on overly hasty decisions. But my mother was far from throwing in the towel. Everybody knew that a woman's career began with a knowledge of shorthand and typing; that was the bottom line. So shorthand and typing it would be: I was enrolled in Baumeister's Commercial School, a twenty-minute walk from our apartment.

The school occupied four rooms on the third floor of an old apartment building. The ceilings were high and decorated with stucco garlands. The long, narrow windows vibrated with the roar of the traffic below. Herr Baumeister himself cut an awesome figure. He was well over six feet tall, had a sinister limp, and he frequently exposed very large teeth in a wide wolfish grin. It didn't take me long, though, to discover that behind that fearful exterior dwelt the soul and disposition of a six-week-old kitten.

About a dozen of us sat on both sides of a long table, at the head of which Herr Baumeister, leisurely slouching in an oversized chair, introduced us to the mysteries of stenography. At regular intervals he heaved himself to his feet to inspect our efforts. My papers, he said judiciously, looked like a bunch of fishing worms. He never ceased to be amazed that I could decipher them. I couldn't really, of course; I simply remembered most of the stuff, because he dictated it in small installments. And if I was completely stuck I asked my neighbor. It did not matter much because he never gave us a graded test. Neither those fishing worms nor my mother's phoning him and bawling him out for letting me play hooky (only twice, I might mention) could change Herr Baumeister's good opinion of me. His heart was without vengeance. It was, also, without any common sense. Herr Baumeister was the only person I knew during the twelve Hitler years who would tell political jokes in a circle of strangers. What did he know about us? We were a motley crowd, all ages, from all walks of life. He thought nothing of "brightening up" our day with a nice juicy joke about Goebbels (known for his whopping lies and his numerous extramarital affairs, but not known for his sense of humor) while we sat like pillars of salt, not knowing how to respond. It needed only one indignant student to denounce the rest of us and we would all have been in the devil's kitchen. Nobody did, though — at least not during my time. I hope the dear man got away with it or else somebody enlightened him before it was too late.

At the end of three months we got our diplomas. He handed them to each of us with a large wolfish grin, shook our hands, and wished us good luck. He never flunked anybody. It wasn't in him.

* * * * * * * * * * * * * *

"*Oh weh!*" said the handsome, blond woman bending over the ghastly piece of cloth on the table in front of me; then she bit her lip because she was sorry it had slipped out. I had pushed the cloth toward the far corner of the table, disassociating myself from it as much as possible. This was my first day in the sewing class of the Lettehaus and we were off to a bad start.

Let me tell you about the *Lettehaus* of Berlin. It had a sterling reputation; its name stood for quality, integrity, and tradition. The Berliner Lettehaus taught everything that was safe for a girl to know in those days. It was the West Point of female achievement. My mother had enrolled me there for a sewing course. On the first day we were to bring thread, tape measure, scissors, a piece of material, and a pattern we would like to try. I had no pattern and my piece of material was a bit of stiff, oak-colored imitation velvet that gave me goose pimples when I touched it; already its edges were frayed just from stuffing it into a bag that morning.

So I knew why my teacher had exclaimed when she saw it. Translated into normal speech her comment meant "What on earth is *THIS*? If this is the best you can come up with, why bother at all?" My face went hot with embarrassment and I remained silent. There was no way I could have explained things to her: You see, Madame, I am here only because my mother has temporarily run out of ideas on what to do with me. She does not believe for one minute that anybody could really teach me how to sew. She kept forgetting to buy me material and the day before, at the end of a shopping trip, she rushed back into the department store and grabbed the first likely piece from a remnant table.

My sewing teacher with the merry eyes never again let on what she thought of me, my material, or my sewing talents. She brought me the pattern of a short jacket and she spent as much time, interest, and patience on me as she did on the girl next to me, who was sewing her wedding nightgown out of yards of lovely Swiss cotton batiste. In return, I adored her and tried very hard and turned out, after some weeks, an honest-to-goodness little jacket (oak colored, stiff, unpleasant to touch) with a pentagon-shaped neckline (by design, not accident) and long sleeves gathered at the shoulder. The five hand-sewn buttonholes, which, given the cheap, stiff material, would have tried the skills of an experienced seamstress, were a true labor of love, dedicated to my teacher.

My mother was shocked. I think she was sorry about the material but for her to say so would have momentarily put us on equal footing, and that was something she considered at all times inconsistent and imprudent. Some time during that month, though, she bought me a new blouse and she never asked me what happened to the jacket. I wore it a few times. It matched none of my clothes, it made me look sallow, it gave me goose pimples, and it eventually disappeared in the back of a drawer.

In the meantime, my mother had come upon yet another opportunity to broaden my education. A baby hotel was looking for a nurse's aide. I don't remember the interview; my mother must have answered all the questions to the satisfaction of the two ladies who ran the hotel, and a new experiment was under way.

The baby hotel was situated in a large, old mansion in one of Berlin's lovely, tree-shaded suburbs. It was owned and operated by two middle-aged unmarried women. Miss Bissell, a small, blond, energetic person oversaw the different departments and all personnel and seemed to be every place at the same time. Miss Trump, a fat, pale woman with pepper-and-salt colored hair which she wore in a pageboy cut, ran the business part and was only seen at meal times. There were three nurses, each heading a department, and five aides, not counting the kitchen staff. The nurses had their own rooms; the five aides slept in one large basement room-turned-dormitory. The undisputed ruler of this dormitory was Lotte, a tall, thin girl with the most rampant case of acne I have ever seen. She was irrepressible, though, and full of *Lebensfreude*. I used to watch her get ready on her day off. My own cosmetic endeavors at that time still consisted of trying to darken my unremarkable eyebrows with a burned match stick and rubbing my cheeks vigorously with a dry washcloth. Lotte paid the most meticulous attention to every detail of her appearance. At the end, sitting very close to her mirror, she spread a tinted cream all over her face and neck, which she then covered with numerous layers of pink powder, followed by applications of rouge and lipstick. The effect was staggering; it was beautiful and, at the same time, horrendous. I always admired her courage when she ran up the basement steps and into the brightness of the world outside.

"She is my best girl," I heard Fräulein Bissel once say to a visitor. "The quickest, most efficient help I ever had. And I have to put her in the laundry! What else can I do? Look at her! What would the parents say if I would let her work with their babies?"

Lotte certainly was quick and efficient. She established all the rules in the dormitory and settled all disputes. One day when one of the girls got hold of a copy of "Casanova's Memoirs," she took it away from her and read it first, ruling that it should be passed down by age, which meant that I, being the youngest, would get it last. When my turn finally came, I had heard the other girls whisper and giggle about it for so many weeks that I thought something was wrong with me when I began to be royally bored around the middle of the third chapter. I never dared to let on.

We had an infant department for babies between two weeks and six months. The room adjacent to it had eight cribs holding babies from six to twelve months. Downstairs were two larger rooms, the crawler department. I didn't know much about the crawler department except that there was a rather steady turnover of children. Most of the "crawler parents" were stage actors and left their children in the care of the home when their show went on the road. Unlike our babies upstairs, almost all children in the crawler department had a set of married parents.

I worked in the six-to-twelve months department and I still remember every one of my babies and its background; all of them were heart rending. Sundays were visiting days, and most babies were visited by a parent or a grandparent. Our babies seldom cried. We were permitted to pick them up only for meals, bath, or a change of diapers. Nobody played with them during the week. I was told that this would make them cry afterward. Besides, I did not have the time. The nurse in charge was a friendly, easy-going girl who never scolded and never taught me anything. I just watched her and copied what she did and after a while she even let me bathe the babies. I helped with the feeding, bathing, changing; I washed and steril-ized the bottles, scrubbed the burned porridge pots, and cleaned the room. When I cleaned the room I was alone with the babies, and I talked to them a great deal, but I didn't dare to pick them up; I had been told not to do so and if they started screaming I would most certainly have been ques-tioned about it.

Our two eleven-month-old babies were the most sociable. In spite of their brief existence, they had developed personalities of their own. One was a beautiful child with black, curly hair, pink cheeks, and eyes like dark cherries. Her parents would appear every Sunday, hand in hand, very young, very much in love and very unhappy. The father was a civil servant and was not able to obtain permission to marry his beautiful fiancée whose deceased father had been Jewish. They had written and sent half a dozen applications begging for an exception (that was made at times) but had only been shoved about from one government department to another.

The other little girl was not exactly beautiful but had such a compell-ing personality that even the nurse could not resist keeping her on her lap a little longer at feeding time. Hers was a hopelessly entangled background. Her mother, a smartly dressed, handsome young woman with a haunted look about her would most often come during the morning hours, never on weekends. She was always breathless when she arrived. She would pick up the child, hug and kiss her fiercely, and carry her around singing and talking to her. When she left the child, she was always in tears. She had another child, a girl, eight or nine years old. She had been an unmarried mother but somehow had managed to keep her job and support herself and her child. When the little girl was about six years old, the young woman fell in love again, only to be abandoned once more even before her second child, another girl, was born. She brought the baby to the home and went back to work where, after a few months, she met another man who fell in love with her and proposed marriage. He knew about and accepted the little girl who, by now was in school; he thought everybody was entitled to one mistake. She did not tell him about the second child. She was terrified at the thought of losing him; every time she tried to tell him, fear strangled the words in her throat. They married and led an apparently happy family life together, but as often as she could inconspicuously get away, she came to see her baby.

We had two babies who lay in their cribs, awake or asleep, as inanimate as two little wooden dolls. The mother of the one had, during a severe post-partum depression, jumped out of the hospital window; the widower had not yet found anybody to care for the child. The other baby's mother was an actress who worked as an extra or in small walk-on parts. She came every Sunday, a homely, ill-dressed woman over forty, sitting helplessly and sad for hours beside the crib while the baby was lying quietly on his back, staring at the curtains moving in the summer air, and giving no sign of knowing her.

The fall that year was cold and wet and influenza made the rounds. I caught it from the other girls, who were up and about again by the time I took to my bed. I was too sick to remember much of the following days. Once, when I opened my eyes, I saw Fräulein Trump, the plump one with the pageboy cut, sitting beside my bed. Lotte must have called her when she found her nursing skills over-taxed. When she saw my eyes open she began to ask me questions. I thought it was nice of her to come and visit me (Fräulein Bissel never came near our room) and I tried to be sociable, but I fell asleep again before she left.

My mother appeared that evening to fetch me home. Fräulein Trump had called her. "Your daughter seems to be quite ill," she said. "We have no way of nursing sick employees. I went down to see her and she was delirious. She asked me if I wanted a cup of tea, for heaven's sake! It might be better if you take her home until she is well again. The nurse is pleased with her; we shall keep her job open for her."

But my mother did not send me back. She had not liked our basement bedroom or the belated phone call. Besides, she had other plans for me.

My mother had learned of a language seminar associated with the University of Berlin that did not require a university entrance exam but only an adequate background in a foreign language. My six years of high school French qualified me. "It never hurt a girl to be fluent in two languages," she said.

Monsieur le professeur was a short, jolly Frenchman who looked older than his years; that is, he had a kind of timeless, owlish face, with a great many wrinkles around his small, twinkling eyes. His laughter sounded like the cackling of an old man, but his movements were quick and graceful. He never sat still, but moved back and forth incessantly through the classroom and seemed to come upon a surprised student out of nowhere. He talked German with a thick gallic accent that amused him and which, I suspect, he cultivated. Most of the time he talked to us in French. Half the time I did not understand what he was saying. I often wondered about the other students. They all *looked* as if they understood everything. So I tried to look as attentive as the rest of them and took care to laugh when everybody else laughed.

We must have been three or four weeks into the course when one day he descended upon me from the back of the room startling me not a little. He tapped me lightly on the shoulder and asked me in French:

"Did your father write books, Mademoiselle?"

"*Oui, Monsieur,*" I stammered, hoping that I had understood the question properly.

"*Mais oui, certainement, . . .*" he smiled at me and continued in German:

"I read those books, Mademoiselle. And do you know where I read them, eh? I read them as a young soldier in the big war, lying in the trenches for weeks and weeks. And the German soldiers were lying in the trenches across the line from us! I comforted myself over those bad Germans with the books of a German writer: *Monsieur votre père! Alors*—what do you think of that, Mademoiselle? It is a joke, a good joke, eh?" And cackling and shaking his head he continued his walk through the room.

"*Non Scholae Sed Vitae Discimus.*" Not for the school but for life do we learn. It was written over the entrance of our village school. I wonder how many children who walked under it for the best part of a century knew what it meant? Ah well, it does not matter, I suppose. They would not have believed it, anyway.

Would you have believed it when you were twelve years old?

* * * * * * * * * * * * * *

"How can a daughter of mine . . ." my mother began, and I curled my toes in my shoes. Experience had taught me that any sentence with this particular opening tended, in no time at all, to take a most discouraging plunge. I was not wrong.

"How can a daughter of mine be so ungraceful!" said my mother. I could not help her there; I had wondered about that, too, at times. Besides, my mother did not really expect an answer. This kind of lament came in different variations and was purely academic. Some of those "daughter-of-mine" questions I might have tried to answer; I had a fair guess as to how and why. But I had decided long ago that the best way all around was to simply ignore them.

"How can a daughter of mine be so untidy!?" Well, this, actually, had been nothing but a small error in timing. I did not consider myself any more untidy than the rest of the world, my mother included. Once, when I took my wastepaper basket down to empty it I forgot to pick it up again on the way back to my room. This lapse of memory took somewhat longer than intended and in the meantime—since I dislike a cluttered room, a mitigating factor which my mother failed to appreciate—I stuffed a few odds and ends under my mattress. Unfortunately, the German custom of turning mattresses at regular intervals caught up with me before I caught up with my wastepaper basket. One would have thought I kept a boa constrictor under my mattress the way my mother looked at those few poor squashed items stored temporarily under it. For a week she walked around as if a dagger had been pushed through her heart. She was rather good at that sort of thing. I suppose if all that freely dispersed guilt had not, over the years, set in motion a kind of immunization process, I might conceivably have wasted away during that week.

Admittedly, I was embarrassed. It must be said, though, that my mother's own tidiness was also somewhat sporadic. Her shoes were lined up like marines at a 7 a.m. roll call. Her linen closet was a work of art hewn in marble: pristine white, razor-sharp folded household linen, sorted according to size and use, were bound together by dozens of purple satin ribbons. Nobody was permitted to touch anything in there. Nobody wanted to. Her kitchen, however, was a different matter. After she had prepared a two-course meal for an average sized family it was one vast disaster area. My mother was an inspired cook, but she had never had to clean up after herself. During her married life there had been servants and now there was me.

"A daughter of mine . . . so lacking in vanity!" Thinking back to that time I can only be grateful that this was so. After my father's death there was never enough money to buy new clothes for all of us. (My brothers just then had begun to grow in alarming spurts.) So my mother's dresses were made over for me. I rarely liked the color, pattern, or style of any of them, but there was nothing I could do about it, so I relegated, perhaps subconsciously, the entire matter of clothing to a low priority rank. It was an impasse of sorts: since I seemed indifferent to anything the seamstress had altered for me my mother concluded that I simply was not interested in clothes.

"How can a daughter of mine have so little ambition?!" This, at last, was true. I was not ambitious. Most specifically, not in the sense that my mother had in mind. I did not like to compete; I do not crave to be a winner. I did not want to be a doctor or a lawyer or a second Dagmar Olsen. I wanted to read or daydream, to write letters to my friends or sit in the sun and think about people I had met or fantasize about the future. I was, in those years, very much my father's child. That's one thing Caroline's daughter never fully grasped.

My mother thought, with some justification, that I moved awkwardly. It always grew worse, though, when she was watching me. I seemed to have suddenly acquired an extra arm and leg with no place to put them. Periodically those additional extremities would bump into the tea table or against my mother's glass vitrine. On account of my bad leg, my parents had kept me out of all sports during my childhood. ("How can a daughter of mine be so unathletic?" my mother would wonder aloud ten years later.) She was now looking around for a possible remedy for this lack of grace. She thought she had found it when she discovered, within walking distance of our apartment, a sign announcing private and group gymnastic lessons.

She called the same day. A brisk woman's voice answered. My mother was rather fond of briskness as long as it was not pointed in her direction. Since in this case I would be its beneficiary, she greatly approved of it. I cannot say that I shared her views in this matter. It had occurred to me more than once that brisk people were never fully satisfied unless they stirred up a good deal of commotion in other people's lives.

My mother registered me for a group course and thereafter, twice a week, I trotted off to 117 Breitenbachstrasse to take lessons in grace. I didn't mind going. In fact, I almost enjoyed it, though I was careful not to show it. My mother's inquiries as to how it was going I answered with all the usual teenage effusiveness. But one evening over supper I tripped up.

"How are the gymnastic lessons coming?" (The usual artless opening.)

"Fine."

"How about the teacher?"

"What about her?"

"Is she good?"

"She is all right."

"Does she think you are all right?"

"She thinks I am fine." Nettled, I was raising my voice a little.

"What do you do in those lessons?"

"Oh, just different things. Exercises . . . you know . . ."

"No. I don't know. That's why I am asking."

"Well, stretching and bending and stuff like that. Sometimes we skip rope — not everybody but whoever wants to," (honesty compelled me to mention that) " . . . and floor exercises."

My mother's eyes narrowed a bit.

"And she thinks you are doing fine?

I fell right into the trap.

"Of course she thinks I am doing fine." I said, exasperated by so much incredulity. "I can do more somersaults than anybody else. And last time I did a shoulder stand for almost half a minute and everybody clapped," I added with modest pride. When this report met with silence I looked up to see my mother, fork frozen in mid-air, staring at me with an expression that could only be called unfathomable.

On the following Tuesday my mother was waiting for me outside the building. She had not told me that she was coming, she just stood there on the street when I came down the steps with Frau Treyse and Frau Bierbaum, the two people in the group I liked best. Frau Treyse was a cheerful woman who was trying, so far with unspectacular success, to shed some thirty pounds she had put on since her last baby. Frau Bierbaum was a sweet lady with silvery hair and a youthful spirit.

"Such joy to have your daughter in a group like ours," Frau Bierbaum beamed at my mother. "It's so seldom that young people join their elders at recreational activities." Her hand dug into the large woven handbag she always carried with her. She is going to pull her grandchildren's pictures out, I thought, appalled. But she was only fishing for a mint.

"Come on! Let's go, Mutti!" I was trying to navigate her into a ninety degree turn. My mother stood as if she was rooted to the pavement. I could hear Frau Stuevesandt's cane tapping on the stone floor, and shortly afterward her stately figure slowly emerged through the door. My ship was sinking. Unerringly, like a celestial body, Frau Stuevesandt moved toward us.

"Is this your mother, dear child?"

There was no getting around an introduction. Frau Stuevesandt's eyes rested benignly on my mother's gold-and-lapis circle pin. She had a way of stretching out her hand as if she expected it to be kissed.

"Your little one adds so much youth and spirit to our staid little group. We have quite taken her to our hearts . . ."

I didn't dare to look at my mother. We made our way home in ominous silence. Once my mother gave me a sidelong glance as if to say: "The most somersaults, eh?" but not a word escaped her tightly compressed lips. When we arrived at the apartment she dropped her gloves on the hall table and without taking time to remove her hat she went to the telephone and canceled all further lessons.

"The Body Beautiful — Individual Attuned Exercises — Gymnastics — Interpretive Dancing." My mother handed me the paper clipping across the dinner table. I glanced at it.

"I am not going!" I said, highly alarmed.

"You can take the subway to Wittenbergplatz and then change to Bus Line 1," my mother said.

"*I AM NOT GOING!*"

My mother was busy figuring the fare. "Or else you can walk the last stretch. It can't be much more than ten minutes."

It was fifteen minutes. I stood a few more minutes outside the entrance studying the BODY BEAUTIFUL sign with profound misgivings before I began climbing the steps to the "studio" on the top floor. The door was ajar; the lesson had apparently started. A young woman, finger reproachfully on her lips, pointed to the dressing room. There I pulled off my dress and dumped it on the nearest bench. Underneath it I was wearing my old school gym suit. The young woman had disappeared and I tiptoed my way toward the sounds of a piano and a series of short commands enunciated in a clipped, nasal voice that did not encourage argument. In a large loft, decorated here and there with artistic touches, some twenty elfin figures were already hard at work swooping up and down to the rhythmic sounds hammered out on a piano by an old, bald piano player. The maestro himself, Herr Renaldo, was a thin, middle-aged man with a great deal of multicolored hair; he wore a tight outfit and swayed, clapped, and nodded along with the rhythm of the music. When he noticed me he smiled and nodded, waving me into the room, never losing a beat. I made my way along the outer periphery and found a place in the farthest corner of the group, carefully placing one of the large wooden pillars between me and Herr Renaldo's line of vision. Watching the graceful figures in front of me for a while I slowly started swooping along. Since everybody's back was turned to me and the pillar was between me and the maestro, it didn't go too badly. Everybody swayed and leaped to the tune of the piano and I hopped up and down a little, doing my own thing back in the corner.

When the music stopped Herr Renaldo came over to bid me welcome. That's what he said: "I bid you welcome!" He smiled warmly; his gold tooth sparkled, his toupee trembled a little while his eyes went over me from the top of my head to my pigeon-toed gym shoes, appraising me so coolly and knowingly that I knew my mother must have had one of her long soul talks with him.

He knew, he said, that I would do very well as soon as I would *adopt a positive attitude*. He personally had witnessed miracles happening in this group. Apparently he thought I would require one. He then steered me away from the pillar and to the middle of the back row and returned to the front of the class. The music started again; I moved back behind the pillar and we all swooped some more. This time the music was more intricate and the stretches more extended. Now everybody was leaping with arms outstretched longingly toward the ceiling, then they all seemed to be sinking despairingly toward the floor. I skipped all the strenuous parts and was doing just fine when the music stopped once more and we were told to gather into a group in one corner of the studio.

"Today," Herr Renaldo said, his eyes closed pensively, "today I want you to give expression to what I like to think of as 'The Dance of the Autumn Leaf.' Imagine yourself to be a leaf dancing in the autumn wind.

Imagine that, after a long dusty summer of immobility, for one splendid moment of glory, you are free! Let your fantasy reign! Imagine the abandon, the ecstasy, the weightless grace!"

I imagined and started to perspire freely.

For the next ten minutes while each girl floated singly and in various degrees of weightless grace through the studio, I made myself all but invisible. As the girls returned walking along side the wall to form a new line in the corner, I stepped back behind each one, always keeping to the end of the line. I hardly dared to breath for fear I would be noticed. Finally, to my tremendous relief, the music stopped.

"Fräulein Eva!"

It sounded like Gabriel's trumpet on Judgment Day.

"Have we seen you yet?"

He knew darn well we hadn't.

"Fräulein Eva? Ah, there . . . will you step forward, please? You understood the theme? Good. Now: may we have music. 'The Dance of the Autumn Leaf,' *if you please!*"

I now had the undivided attention of everybody in the room including the old piano player who, while pounding the keyboard, twisted his bald head to get a better look at me. Every second I hesitated compounded my misery.

All I had to do, I told myself, was to pretend I was alone in the room. I stepped forward and did a tentative little hop on my right leg, then on my left leg, after which I jogged to approximately the middle of the room; another brave little hop and then I caught a glimpse of a girl on my left, staring at me, her mouth half open, in ultimate disbelief. That was it! No more ecstasy folks, no more hops. Exit: one autumn leaf.

I ran past the startled faces, past Herr Renaldo's ineffectively outstretched arm, to the end of the studio and out the door, into the dressing room where I grabbed my dress and ran down the steps. I only stopped for a second at the bottom of the stairs to pull my dress over my head and I was out on the street.

"I shall never, never, *NEVER* go back there again!" I announced to my mother. It was probably the most determined pronouncement I had ever made.

"Nonsense," said my mother, "of course you are going back."

It was the maestro himself who settled the matter. He called that evening and gently informed my mother that not everybody had a calling for the creative arts.

"Perhaps a track team . . .?" Herr Renaldo was suggesting helpfully just before my mother slammed down the receiver.

* * * * * * * * * * * * * *

Enid never actually met Mr. Tuesday; at least I don't think she did. Heavens, I was not even sure that I ever met the man (though, at times I had a hunch that I had). She was fond of him, although, of course, not nearly as much as I was. He often was the object of some benign speculation between us when we sat around the small, cream-colored table at our favorite sidewalk café; never for long, though—we had a thousand other things to discuss. But since it was by courtesy of Mr. Tuesday that we sat there at all, we always spared him a friendly thought or two.

Mr. Tuesday was not his real name, but I had to call him something and that seemed to be the most appropriate one. It was always on a Tuesday that he took my mother off my hands. Eventually, even my mother referred to him as Mr. Tuesday (if she referred to him at all), and she always blushed when she did so.

Once a week the angels of Duty and Propriety—who so diligently helped my mother rear me and with whom she entertained such splendid relationship—once a week those angels turned their heads and covered their faces, at least to my mother's way of thinking. Personally, I think they were jolly glad for the little breather. Once a week my mother rushed around our apartment looking young and vulnerable and, miraculously, a little guilty. Feeling guilty was supposed to be entirely my domain, considered by my mother essential for the tempering and managing of an intractable teenager. For herself, however, feeling guilty seemed to be, each Tuesday, a new experience all over again and she handled it with all the aplomb of a young girl eloping through the bedroom window and promptly falling off the ladder.

Every Tuesday around three o'clock my mother added the last touches to her rather exacting preparations for her meeting with the elusive Mr. Tuesday: her rich, brown hair was newly waved, a dab of color would be applied to her high cheekbones, a dash of lipstick followed. Out of the protective cover came the silky white coat that made her look slimmer than she was. Her best sensible shoes were given a last brush (my mother owned *only* sensible shoes and I sincerely hoped that Mr. Tuesday was a sturdy hiker) while I hunted for her reading glasses which she then rather unceremoniously stuffed into the lovely petit-point handbag that had been a Christmas gift from Mr. Tuesday. All this was done in congenial silence; we both shared a fervent interest in seeing her departure go off without a hitch. There were none of the usual questions and admonishings which would have poured down on me at any other time: "Where are you going?" "With whom are you going?" "Don't forget to clean the bathroom first and clean *behind* the commode this time." "What are you going to do?" "Get the top shelf in the pantry done before you go any place; you were supposed to do that yesterday." "When will you be home?" "No, not 'about,' *exactly*?" And then the most dreaded stipulation of all, the one that made me perjure away my soul a dozen times even before I was seventeen: "Promise you'll wear a hat!" My mother never bought me a hat since—as she said—I treated them so badly, so she always insisted that I wear one of hers. It was her unshakable belief that only housemaids on their day off went into the city without a hat.

At the door I handed her gloves to her and gave her a quick peck on the cheek. I knew better than to wish her a good time; that innocent wish, coming from her young daughter, might have quite possibly made her turn around and stay home. Bouncing down the stairs she would call up: "The theater tickets are on the dining room table!" and she was gone. The rest of the day, the long, blessed, marvelous Tuesday afternoon, was all mine.

Once a week I chose my own clothes; I wore what I thought looked "cool." "Prima," we said in those days, which meant first class; or "toll" which meant crazy or wild. I often wore one of my brothers' broad brown leather belts, even with a thin summer dress; I doubt that it was first class, but it definitely was my idea of "toll."

Freedom, just like happiness, if counted by the hour, is so much more precious than if it is taken for granted. My own brand of freedom every Tuesday afternoon began by walking through the front door out onto the street without gloves, hat, or umbrella, a happy housemaid on her day off. The subway took me to the Wittenberg Plaza, the heart of Berlin-West, our stamping grounds, where Enid would already be standing, waiting at the flower stand, equally without hat and gloves, though sometimes she carried an umbrella. Since nobody in her family insisted on it, she quite sensibly took one if it looked like rain.

When my mother moved us back to Berlin I had to leave all my friends behind. There was Hanne, my bosom buddy and partner in every mischief. And Jutta, the only one with whom I ever engaged in battles of scratching, pinching, and hair pulling, and the only one who ever got me to play with dolls. And there was Carola, who sat two rows behind me in school and who drew pictures of little dancing girls during geography class or fat little cherubs shooting love arrows through bleeding hearts (to which she helpfully added initials for better identification) and which were then passed along under the desks for our edification. Carola could laugh so hard — soundless though it had to be during class — that it infected everybody around her. It went like ripples of water down the rows — we sat six to a bench on either side of the room — until half the class was rocking with suppressed laughter and nobody knew why. Our teacher, "Eagle-Eye Arns," used to walk on top of the desks rather than around them, which gave him a better view over his charges (we were seldom less than fifty kids in the room). It also gave him an unfair advantage in locating culprits. He rarely lost any time in quelling potential riots at the root. He dispatched Carola into the last free corner (behind the map of Europe) for an undetermined length of sentence, threatened the distant offenders with dark looks, and soundly smacked the one nearest to him — if it was a boy. We were still living in the wondrous age of double standards and if it was a girl he contented himself with verbally conveying to her his extremely low opinion of her and her entire sex. This didn't particularly devastate anyone; we had heard it all so often already that it served only to send Carola in her corner into a new fit of helpless laughter. (Young as I was, though, I remember wondering at times if Frau Arns ever heard her husband's estimate of our sex and, if she had, what her thoughts on the subject might be.)

The whole crowd I had grown up with and had shared every experience in those years from one day to the next, disappeared out of my life. With my brothers gone, too, I felt that everybody close to me had left me.

Girls were copious letter writers in those days, but letters were not the same. Until I met Enid, I felt totally abandoned by my own kin and kind, and that at a time when I was most in need of them.

A teenager's emotional state is a fragile thing, precariously balanced at its best. It has occurred to me more than once that it was Enid's and Mr. Tuesday's combined efforts during those years that kept me from total despair at times.

Enid lived in Berlin. I met her in dancing class at the Bornim Academy for Cadets. We were twenty girls gathered there for the first time; sorted, sifted and selected most carefully for the solemn purpose of assisting and supporting a class of cadets in their pursuit of gentlemanly behavior and ballroom dancing. I did not know a single soul there; twenty scared, whispering teenage girls, pressed closely into a small anteroom.

I see this scene before me as if it were last week. The rustling of the gowns, the clicking of high heels, the nervous giggling, the shoving, the heartbeat in the throat. A scent of soap and cologne and of new taffeta mingled with a faint whiff of vinegar. (No commercial deodorants were on the market then and many of us put a few drops of vinegar into our wash water.) One girl opened the door just a crack and we all pushed forward to have a peek. What we glimpsed in there was worse than a nightmare. The huge ballroom seemed yawningly empty. In the farthest corner (simply *miles* away!) was a lady seated serenely in a stately chair: the wife of the ranking officer. She was flanked on one side by a tall, exceedingly good looking gentleman, our dancing instructor, whom we had met previously and who had instructed us how to proceed; on the other side, in full dress uniform, stood the officer in charge. The cadets were lined up along the wall to the right, doing their manly best to look bored, but their heads kept turning expectantly toward the door. They were bursting with curiosity and ready to mock, heckle, and criticize — all under their breath, of course, and inaudible to the three people in the far corner. But none of us had any illusions about the reception in store for us. The girl closed the door again and squeaked *"NOT ME!"* which just about expressed the sentiment of all of us.

"This is stupid!" said a voice suddenly, and a tall, blond girl moved out of the crowd and toward the door. She hesitated only for a second, threw back her shoulders, lifted her chin, and marched straight into the lion's den. Without giving the grinning young men on the right a single glance, she walked evenly and unfalteringly through the endless ballroom, the rest of us hustling after her, all but clinging to her skirt. When she arrived at the far corner, the seated lady stretched out her hand, the tall girl curtsied lightly, took the hand and bent her head over it, her lips stopping less than an inch above it. (Only men's lips ever touched the skin of a woman's hand in a hand kiss.) We all followed suit.

The girl's name was Enid and she became my friend.

After the self-conscious confusion of the first few classes, certain preferences began to crystallize. We all knew the unwritten rules of the game. The young man would let a particular girl know—without ever putting it into words—that he would like her more exclusive attention. If the young lady responded favorably, a date would be requested and granted. This, then, would be duly reported by the cadet to the charge officer and on the very next Sunday morning the cadet would present himself to the parents of the young lady in full dress uniform, saber, white gloves, polished buttons—the works.

We are not talking marriage proposals here, just a simple first date. The visit was to be no longer than half an hour and not less than fifteen tortuous minutes. It entitled the young man to take the girl out on a date— that is a visit to a café and a movie afterward, or, if his pocket money had dwindled toward the end of the month, a long walk through the Botanical Gardens.

For a while Enid and I double-dated "our" cadets, and when they faded out of our lives into distant assignments and, eventually, into war duty, we just went out by ourselves.

Enid's father was a publisher and a free-thinker; as far as he was concerned, Enid had the run of the city. It was not that he was a weak or uncaring father; on the contrary, he simply could not conceive his proud and level-headed daughter ever making a wrong choice. Her mother was a pleasant, bustling woman who kept a little closer track of her daughters but generally shared her husband's faith in Enid's good sense.

She was a level-headed girl, but she was also full of fun. Enid had spirit; I never knew anybody to whom the term "proud carriage" applied more perfectly. I remember thinking that first evening: if I could walk like that I would not mind being the first one through that ballroom door either. She was not beautiful in the conventional sense; she was striking looking with dark blond, wavy hair, a short nose, and a large, sensuous mouth. Her best features were her eyes. They were large, almond shaped and of a luminous gray.

And now it was Tuesday afternoon and there was Enid, waiting at the flower stand near the subway entrance of the Wittenberg Plaza. We would already have discussed on the phone what we planned to do. We rarely ran out of ideas. We headed straight for the Kurfuerstendamm, then one of Europe's most elegant and expensive avenues. We would do a great deal of window shopping, but once in a while when we were on our mettle we would enter one of these exclusive little shops – thick rugs, gilded mirrors, tiny curlicued chairs – where no merchandise was displayed and one would have to ask for a certain item. We had a hard time deciding what to ask for; it had to be something they could not possibly have, so we finally arrived at a white blouse with orange embroidery or beads. A splendidly coiffured lady in an understated black dress, an impressive string of pearls around her powdered neck, and long, blood-red fingernails would ask our wishes and the fun would start. One slim young girl after another would appear from behind a velvet curtain parading the most exquisite white blouses for our perusal. None of them, of course, had any orange embroidery. After a while we would make regretful little noises and take our leave, only to try again some other Tuesday in another equally refined establishment. The painful end of this lark did not come, as one might expect, by our sailing into the same store twice, but rather by something we had not thought possible: a white blouse with orange embroidery was produced. The price: about the monthly salary of a good secretary. There we sat, Enid and I, on our curlicue chairs, totally unprepared for this possibility, not daring to look at each other, dying a slow death while the lady in black held the disastrous little thing up in the air with her blood-red fingertips and asked which one of us two ladies were to try it on or was she to wrap it immediately? Enid took a breath, stood up – all regal 5'9" of her; a fine, cool inclining of the head, "I would like my husband to see it before making a decision," she said and we swept out of the store having trouble not to run the last three steps.

We went to have our palms read by a gypsy in a side street, a proper cave with curtains of beads and colorful scarves draped all over the place. And once we went to an old woman who drew horoscopes. To see her, we had to climb a great many steps in an old house. The door was ajar and we just walked into a dark, high ceilinged loft with charts hanging on every wall. The old lady was sitting at a large table that was nothing but a wide, unfinished board supported by two kitchen chairs. A bright electric light glared onto the papers and charts spread out in front of her while the rest of the room lay in darkness. The woman was wrapped in blankets, even though we were wearing summer clothes. I remember wild, white hair and sunken eyes. She looked as if she had not seen the light of day for many months. We gave her the dates and hours of our births and paid her in advance, and were told to come back in a week for the finished horoscope. I have forgotten most of the things she told me. She was not very explicit; apparently I was going to do all right and have lots of children. She spent a great deal more time on Enid's horoscope; in fact, she seemed to have trouble parting with it. Enid would have a very interesting life, she told her, " . . . ah, yes, a fascinating life . . ."

Once — on one of the few evenings I had permission to stay at Enid's place overnight — we talked Enid's cousin into taking us to a night club. Neither of us had ever been to one, and that was not something we could have done on our own. No reputable bar or night club permitted unescorted women to enter the premises. Enid's cousin was eminently suited for the job; he was almost forty, unmarried, and undersexed. Very safe. Good natured, too. He took us to two different bars where we perched on high bar stools to the right and left of him and at each place had one brandy. That was two more than we were used to and we felt wonderfully wicked and just a little fuzzy. The cousin took us home in a taxi, brewed some peppermint tea for us (a sure prevention for hangovers, he said) and saw to it that we were safely in bed. We were quite satisfied that this was the way it was done and that we had gotten on in the world very nicely that evening. Not until years later did we admit to each other that the whole thing had been rather a bore and that we had expected it to be a great deal more exciting. I cannot speak for Enid here, but it effectively deferred my next trip to a night club for about fifteen years.

Sometimes we went to a book store, and that would always be the end of the first part of our afternoon program. Neither of us could ever tear herself away from it. Between five and six o'clock we would at long last make our way to an outdoor café. There we would order the largest, most luscious piece of torte filled with rum-and-mocha creme or marzipan and pineapple (pineapple was considered very exotic in Germany) and a pitcher of tea, which we would consume very slowly, talking and watching the people stream by. It was said, then, that anybody who was somebody in Europe would, at one time or another, walk down the Kurfuerstendamm in Berlin.

Enid was much better at spotting famous faces than I was; I was not even particularly looking for them. The whole panorama of the moving masses fascinated me: the clothes they wore and how they wore them, the expression on their faces, the unlikely company they had chosen at times. The people who strolled by looked at us with the same curiosity with which we regarded them. All of us sitting around those small tables along the sidewalk were part of the grandiose scenery of the avenue they had come to see.

We would sit for hours; nobody rushed us, no waiter gave us a hostile glance, nobody wished us to leave. There were enough tables and chairs for everybody under the awnings and trees of the Kurfuerstendamm. Gradually the sky between the branches of the trees above us would turn pink, the air took on a luminous rosy haze, and suddenly the lights of the avenue would come on, blazing at the strollers, competing with the last translucent shimmer of the day.

The scene changed so quickly that one could not have said just when and how it did so. The leisurely afternoon strollers had disappeared and in their places would be men and women dressed for the evening, hurrying faster down the street, having a destination in mind. Taxis would suddenly flood the avenue, honking their horns impatiently at tardy pedestrians. An excitement was in the air that had not been there before. The city prepared for the evening. It was time to start for the theater.

Berlin in those years wore her nights like a bejeweled coronet and her theaters were its sparkling diamonds. There were more theaters in Berlin than I can name now, but towering over all of them were the two giants: the Staatstheater and the Deutsche Theater. Involved in fierce competition, they strove to outdo each other in excellence. The patron of the Deutsche Theater was Goebbels who, after all, was the German Minister of Culture; but the great Staatstheater was under Goering's patronage. "Staat" in this case meant Prussia, not Germany, and Goering was, among a dozen other things, the Prime Minister of Prussia. Gustav Gruendgens and Heinrich Hilpert were the managers and producers of the two theaters. Both were shrewd, highly gifted men, obsessed with perfection, but only Gruendgens was also his own theater's best actor. Like cunning children playing two hostile parents against each other for their own advantage, they gained unheard of concessions from their patrons and they produced and spent pretty much what they liked. The result was dazzling.

I don't remember ever seeing a political play, but I do remember the vast, international fare that the Berlin theaters offered in the thirties and into the early forties: Ibsen and Strindberg, Shakespeare, Wilde and Shaw, Molière, Sophocles, and all the classic and romantic German authors up to the realistic and naturalistic plays past the turn of the century. If they ignored the theater of the absurd or surrealistic, we did not miss it.

The productions were magnificent, and so were the actors. Under a government that lavishly subsidized its theaters and flattered and pampered its actors, directed by men with spirit and genius, playing night after night before full houses in front of an audience that adored them, the actors grew larger than life. How could they not? Surround a rare and fine plant with absolutely perfect conditions and see a wonder unfold in front of your eyes.

Berlin's theater did not die with the arrival of the Nazis. (That is as ignorant a statement as to say the Russians could not possibly produce a good ballet because they are built too stocky.) It did not even die when the great playhouses burned down during the war. The German theater perished after the war under the hail of abuse and accusations aimed at it, not only by ignorant or malicious outsiders, but by its own hostile youth.

It died when it became a tool in the hands of unskilled "visionaries" who wished to produce "shock effects," when Hamlet, in the end, was played by a naked egomaniac and the "symbolic" stage settings were empty orange crates which signaled nothing but the glaring arrogance of otherwise vacuous minds. It died when half-baked *Wunderkinder* presented their dreary experiments on abstract stages in front of empty seats.

My mother was on good terms with most of the publishing houses in the city, and when one of their plays had a successful run she would sooner or later receive two courtesy tickets for an evening. It was a rare Tuesday night that would not find Enid and me seated in the middle section of one of the first ten rows of a beautiful theater while on the stage before us that special wondrous magic unfolded that never failed to enthrall me. Did it spoil me for the years to come? I would say it did.

The last time I saw Enid was a few years ago on her sixtieth birthday. It was at a garden party given in her honor by her husband and daughter in an exclusive suburb of Hamburg. The food and waiters came from the most expensive caterer of the city. With the exception of one single dinner in Japan, I had never seen a more exquisitely served meal: fourteen bite-sized courses (each a blue-ribbon dish) served on transparent china plates, each placed into our hands and relieved of them again almost unnoticed by soundless spirits. The guests strolled around the gardens or sat at the large, round tables under yellow and white striped garden umbrellas that matched the table linen. Enid's husband was leisurely mingling with his prominent guests. I had met him right after the war, during the first year of their marriage, a talented young architect, six foot high, a half-starved string bean of a man, already slouching and with a perpetual mocking smile on his lips. I thought at the time that this smile hid a great deal of uncertainty and self-doubt and I never quite knew how to get around it.

The country's economic recovery and consequent affluence had carried him straight to the top. His body had filled out over the years; his shoulders were stooped and he carried his weight badly. Lines of sardonic misanthropy were irredeemably etched into his features like permafrost under the thin veneer of urbane affability. The daughter helped receive the guests and supervise the service. Towering over her guests, slouching like her father, she had a dark and brooding face that at rare moments broke into a warm, open smile.

I was sitting beside a buxomy, pretty woman, very blond, very expensive looking, a well-known illustrator of children's books. She was in the midst of telling me about her own daughter.

"She called that morning," the woman said with the husky voice of the perpetual smoker. "She wanted them right then and there. 'Mother, I *need* those golf clubs *now*,' she said, 'I have been asked to play in the championship tournament, for Christ's sake, don't you understand?' What could I do? I dragged that bloody golf bag into the car—never mind the 400 kilometers—and drove it all in one stretch. Well, what d'you think?" The woman dropped her half-smoked cigarette onto the lawn and ground it down with her heel. "It turned out to be the wrong bag! It seems she had a new one in the guest room closet. How the hell was I to know?!" She lit another cigarette and took a few short, nervous puffs. "Do you know what she said to me?" A quick, mirthless laugh. "'You are a shit, mother,' she said, 'you can't even do a little thing like that right . . . ,' never mind that I had driven all day . . ."

A small brown hand tugged at my sleeve and I looked into a pair of large, gray, almond-shaped eyes staring solemnly up at me.

"Grandma wants you," said the little girl.

Enid was standing close to the house beside a very old, frail little woman who had been seated in the protective corner of the entrance.

"You looked as if you needed rescuing" Enid murmured, smiling and nodding at a passing guest at the same time.

Her hair was still dark blond—with a little help, I think—her shoulders were still straight, and her waist slender, but her large eyes were hooded and showed underneath them deep, brown circles foretelling the illness that would take her away within two years' time. None of us, not even she, knew of it that day. ("I think I caught whooping cough from my granddaughter," she said smilingly to me, "I get some awful spells sometimes.")

She introduced me to the seated old lady.

"This is the only person who knows me longer than you do," she said, putting her arms around the frail shoulders for a moment. "She was my first-grade teacher."

"But does she know you *better* that I do?" I asked. "Does she know about your wild and wicked past?"

"You of all people asking a question like that!" said Enid. "Who dragged me into a marriage bureau at the tender age of seventeen!?"

"Oh Enid, I did not!" I protested. "I remember no such thing." But I had to laugh in spite of myself. It certainly sounded like me.

"Oh yes, you did." Enid said unperturbed, "At the Kurfuerstendamm. The most refined, the most expensive institute in all of Berlin."

My mind raced back, sorted through memories, arrived at a profusion of colors. "Lots of oriental rugs?" I asked tentatively.

"Lots of oriental rugs," affirmed Enid. "And the woman with the three gold chains around her neck."

"She showed us two albums with photos of all those good-looking men?"

". . . and you said we lived on estates in Pommern."

"You said that! And then we told her that we were bored with living in the country and wanted to marry into the city . . ."

" . . . and then she said . . ."

"She said we were to come back with our birth certificates and some snapshots of those boring estates!"

"And, of course, it was Tuesday!" said Enid.

We looked at each other fully now; the party around us disappeared. We were sitting at a little cream-colored table on the Kurfuerstendamm under the pink evening sky, just before the lights of the avenue came on. There were no deep brown circles under Enid's eyes, and my hair showed no gray. People from all over the world were strolling by, glancing curiously at the two young girls who were laughing—laughing so hard that they were in need of a handkerchief, and the one who finally found one at the bottom of her handbag shared it with the other.

This is the picture I want to see when I remember Enid. And when the hurt of her death is gone it will erase the other one, the picture that comes to my mind now whenever I think of her. It is the end of an old fairy tale when the mistress of the castle stands alone high on the castle's tower gazing over her husband's wide domain. She is not young anymore, her eyes are clouded with age, but her carriage is proud and she is still beautiful. She looks over the fields and forests and the sleepy villages toward the western horizon where the sun has set behind the distant river, and to the dying day she says: "You have brought me much honor and little happiness."

Chapter 5

Periodically, my mother asked me what I wanted to be. The first time she asked I had no trouble answering.

"I want to be a nurse," I said like a shot.

Certainly this was not an overnight idea. It had been resolved in my heart and mind for a long time. Nebulous memories, rooted within the first years of my life, had turned into an increasing awareness as I grew older: a nurse was somebody who could make a distinct difference in the life of a sick child. I had been fond of all my nurses but I had truly loved the ones with the gentle hands. Early in life I discovered that all hands were not alike. A change of bandages, the cleaning of a wound, that might bring stinging tears to the eyes when performed by one nurse, might be almost painless when done by another. I wanted to be a nurse with painless hands.

"A nurse!" my mother exclaimed. It was not an alien idea to her. As a young girl she herself had wanted to be a nurse but had failed to get her parents' permission. The memory of her own disappointment did not permit her to utter an instant and emphatic *NO*. Instead, her eyes unfocused and achieved the distracted look I knew so well and which signaled a temporary dilemma. She stalled, feigning surprise.

"A nurse?" she repeated slowly as if not quite trusting her ears. She could not have sounded more astonished if I had said a ski instructor. Or a meat inspector. A nurse, she said a third time and shook her head.

The subject was not mentioned again for a few weeks. Then, one morning over breakfast my mother announced that she and I, that day, would visit Professor S., a well-known surgeon in a large hospital. (How my mother wangled all these weighty interviews was nothing short of a miracle.)

"Why?" I asked, instantly on alert.

She muttered something about the benefit of an occasional check-up (I never had one before) and showed no inclination to discuss the matter any further. As we set out to the bus station, she positioned her handbag in a way that was meant to hide, or at least minimize, the large manila envelope she was carrying: Exhibits #1 ad infinitum, the collected x-rays of my right shin bone. The lump already present in my stomach doubled in size. All during the trip she chatted away merrily. Her jauntiness served only to confirm my misgivings. Ordinarily she would not have so blissfully ignored my moody silence; my mother was never above administering a sound slap when she thought me sulking.

The professor was equally jaunty. He was prepared to give us seven minutes of his time. (For which, I am sure, he did not charge my mother a cent. None of those stalwart men whom my mother called to her aid from time to time ever did.)

"So, this is the young lady who wants to be a nurse," he said cheerfully. My mother's warning glance came too late; he did not even notice it. He had already opened the envelope and was studying the pictures. An examination of my leg followed—the turning, tapping, pressing of the scar which I had come to expect over the years with considerable apprehension. However, the professor was a knowledgeable man with skillful hands and did not hurt me unnecessarily.

"Well, nursing is out, young lady," he announced at the end of the examination, just as cheerfully as he had greeted us. "That leg would not stand a twelve-hour shift, I can assure you." (There were only two nursing shifts in a 24-hour hospital day when I was young.) He gave me a friendly pat on the shoulder, shook hands with my mother, and departed.

Now that her victory had come so easily, my mother was genuinely sympathetic. She said some kind and reasonable words but I could sense that she was anxious to switch tracks. About half way home she ventured to do just that.

"Wouldn't you like to be a journalist?

"No."

"I always think journalists have such interesting lives."

"I don't want to be a journalist."

"Think of Dagmar Olsen! What an exciting life she has! What interesting people she meets. Wouldn't you like that?"

Everybody who read a good newspaper or looked into a reputable magazine once in a while knew Dagmar Olsen. She was the most prominent woman in the field of German journalism. She was the *only* woman in that field. Over the years I had seen numerous photos of her. Dagmar Olsen, slender, short blond windswept hair, squinting into the sun over the vast Sahara desert while a few Foreign Legion soldiers grinned sheepishly in the background. Dagmar Olsen in Tibet, windswept and without a thought to vertigo, peering down some fathomless abyss. Dagmar squinting into the camera, her arm around an old chieftain. Dagmar, elegantly groomed and not the least bit disconcerted, shaking hands with royalty. I enjoyed her articles, but I had never even for a second envied her life. I might truthfully say that I no more wanted to be Dagmar Olsen than I would have wanted to be Napoleon. He, too, had met a great many interesting people in his time.

"No, I wouldn't. Besides, even if I would want to be like her — which I don't — I would not have the talent."

"Oh, but you do! You write lovely letters," said my mother enthusiastically.

"Mutti, there are thousands of people who write nice letters but there is only one Dagmar Olsen."

"But you could be another one!"

"I could not and I would not want to." I said with finality and went back to mourning my nursing career.

My mother let it rest there. When necessary she could bide her time. However, newspaper articles and clippings, written by or about Dagmar Olsen, were finding their way beside my dinner plate. Magazines appeared on the living-room table, conspicuously opened to photos showing exotic surroundings and daring explorations.

Dagmar Olsen in one or all of them, windswept and squinting into the sun. But no more verbal attacks.

At that time I was attending a cooking school. It was rather fun, even though it seemed a bit disorganized. There were too many girls, three stoves and only one teacher. I was in my second week, past potato soup and into Spanish rice (a dish consisting of cubed beef, canned whole tomatoes, green peppers, and rice) and was just about to be promoted to omelettes when my mother took me out of the course again to accompany her to a spa in Southern Germany. Once a year she went "to take the waters" (a prescribed series of baths in hot mineral springs followed by massages and bed rest), and she disliked going alone.

On the train back to Berlin she reopened the subject.

"What do you want to be?" It was asked, as artless and easy as if we had never talked about it before.

"A teacher."

"A teacher! That takes years of university," said my mother shrewdly, knowing my dislike of studying.

"So does journalism." I said, giving tit for tat. But my mother ignored the remark. Logic, in her opinion, was something only desperate people employed who couldn't think of any better arguments.

"I want to be an elementary school teacher." I said. That took three years of seminar training and my age and my school level qualified me for it.

"Have you thought about being a journalist?"

"Yes. And I don't want to be one. I want to go to a seminar and become an elementary school teacher!" It took courage to say this right into the stark displeasure of my mother's face.

She did not pursue the matter. I sat across from her in the train compartment and watched her as she looked out the window.

As her frown slowly dissolved and her face took on an almost beatific expression I knew she had planned her strategy.

I was not kept in the dark for long. Coming home from my babysitting job one afternoon—I was watching a little brat of a girl, the daughter of a young woman doctor, three times a week—I saw through the frosted glass of our living room that my mother was entertaining. She called out in the high, melodious voice that she often used when visitors were around: "Would you come and join us, Evchen."

I was surprised to see the table laid with one of my mother's prettiest tea services and her tiny embroidered tea napkins. Expensive little cakes were arranged on the Meissen cake platter. My mother sat beaming on the sofa. The seat of honor, an ancient Biedermeyer chair, was occupied by a stiffly prim, forlorn-looking, middle-aged woman in a starched white blouse with a black velvet ribbon tied around her collar. She did not look at all like the kind of person my mother usually entertained.

"This is my daughter, Eva," my mother said, still with the same determinedly cheerful voice, "and this is Fräulein Schnitzler." A place had been laid for me and I sat down.

"Fräulein Schnitzler is a teacher in an elementary school in Mahrndorf" (a rural community just outside the city limits). "She has kindly accepted my invitation to tell us a little about herself and her job."

So that was it! She was the one elected to do the hatchet job. Fräulein Schnitzler looked as if, a long time ago, the last drop of joy and hope had been squeezed out of her extremely thin, sallow-skinned body. As she began talking in a slow, plaintive voice, I glanced at my mother who seemed to be listening spellbound. How does she do it, I wondered. How many pretty, reasonably happy young teachers had she passed up until she found this perfect specimen? For a cup of tea in my mother's graceful living room, for a chocolate eclair served on a Meissen platter, for just that bit of excitement and recognition in her barren life, this woman, this tightly knotted, discontented creature, was ready to sell her soul. Then and there I resolved that nothing she could say would make the slightest difference in my decision.

She spared us no gloomy detail: poor pay, poor lodgings, no intellectual stimulation, ungrateful children and parents, unreasonable supervisors, back-breaking workload. Goaded and guided by my mother who kept filling her tea cup and asking leading questions, she told the whole sorry story of her embittered old maid's existence while I hardened my heart against this onslaught of misery, and, stony-faced, ate a third eclair in spite of my mother stepping on my foot under the table.

My mother sent quick, probing looks in my direction; she gauged my game as well as I did hers. Presently she dropped the air of innocence and prepared to go for the kill.

"Tell my daughter about the instrument," she said lightly.

Outwardly calm and uninterested, I prepared myself for the *coup de grace* I knew was coming.

Fräulein Schnitzler shrugged her shoulders. This was really of no great importance, not nearly as pertinent as the heartlessness of the school supervisors. But my mother apparently wished it to be mentioned.

"There are some added qualifications now," she said listlessly. "The young teachers have to play at least one musical instrument to get certified."

I caught my breath sharply and shot my mother a quick glance. She was rearranging the last two pieces of cakes on the platter and biting her lower lip—not to hide pain, to be sure. Not only was I unable to read music, I could not even hear the difference between the notes of the scale. Learning to play an instrument would, in my case, take nothing short of an act of God.

I know now that I gave up too quickly. With a great deal of encouragement, under the guidance of a patient teacher, I might have managed the musical requirement. If, under those circumstances, I could produce five faultless double-seamed buttonholes in a piece of fraying, unwielding material, I might have conceivably learned to play a few children's songs on something like a recorder. After all, they were not asking for a Paganini.

On this particular afternoon, however, nothing by way of encouragement or guidance was forthcoming. Unnerved and undermined by those two women sitting across from me aligned in common cause, I saw my hopes crumbling again. My future seemed once more the dreaded vacuum that often frightened me in my dreams.

With the opposition so effectively weakened, my mother pursued her advantage. Two more visitors followed, not as easily dismissed as their predecessor. The first one was a professional guidance teacher, a soft-spoken, intelligent woman who was, even though recruited by my mother, no mere tool or mouthpiece for anybody. She was, above everything else, a listener, and she discerned within a very short time the underlying tension in the air. She refused to play my mother's game; she sincerely wanted to find a solution for both of us.

She asked me about my interests — which were reading, writing (letters), children, people, theater, traveling — and she said smilingly that they did seem to point toward journalism. For the first time I was asked my reasons for opposing the idea.

Liking all those things, I said with some urgency, was only a very small part of becoming a good journalist. The most important ingredients, it seemed to me, were self assurance, strong elbows to push one's way up to the top, physical fearlessness, a talent for bluffing, a certain bloodhound quality, and more than a dash of ruthlessness, none of which I felt I possessed.

"What nonsense," said my mother (who was amply endowed with all of those qualities). "That can be learned! There is nothing to it." The guidance counselor was silent. There was a look of such warm understanding in her face that I would have liked to get up and hug her. When she left, her good wishes were given wistfully; she was too intelligent not to know that she had solved nothing.

My mother had the ace of trump still up her sleeve. She told me that she had a letter from Minister B., an old family friend, who, she said, had business in Berlin and would stop by to see us. Herr B. had been Minister of Culture and Education during the Weimar Republic, a physical and mental giant of a man and a good and loyal friend to our family. Now my mother had called on him to cast the decisive vote.

Minister B., it turned out, had read all my letters. He had been unaware that my mother had sent them to him without my knowledge and very much regretted mentioning it when he saw me wince with embarrassment. Nevertheless, having mentioned them, he had to go on. He thought the letters were good. Journalism, he said, was a field that cried out for more participation by women. There were vast areas where women might do an even better, a more empathetic job than men. Take Dagmar Olsen, for instance. He did not bully me; he spoke in an even, friendly voice; he addressed himself to me, not to my mother; he talked objectively and intelligently; I could have no quarrel with anything he said. I just did not want to be a journalist.

After this memorable visit my mother gave me time to mull it over. It did shake me into action. I had heard about a training in social pedagogic. It had to do with teaching, with children. In a way it also had to do with easing pain. There were no twelve-hour shifts and very definitely no musical instruments required. The guidance counselor who had visited us had such training. But what was even more tempting, graduates in social pedagogics were in charge of the country's orphanages. Adoptions in Germany were rare; the laws were stringent and entirely oriented toward the protection of the legitimate child. One-hundred percent proof of infertility had to be brought (or the woman had to be over childbearing age) before a couple was permitted to adopt a child. Abandoned babies and orphaned children were reared in state or church homes, staffed by people trained in social pedagogic programs. They were the ones responsible for the guidance, discipline, love, and care that were needed to bring up those parentless children.

Without telling my mother, I wrote to the Department of Education for information. The answering letter was prompt and, miraculously, slipped by her unnoticed. It would take four years, divided between seminars and on-the-job training. The costs were not prohibitive; a small salary would be paid to the trainee during the last year.

Well, that was it, then! A dozen orphanage matrons invited to tea by my mother would not change my mind! However, there was no getting around the fact that I was underage and had to get her permission.

I agonized over the right moment to tell her. I checked out my "exhibits," and the exchange of letters. I anticipated her questions and objections and prepared my answers. I finally approached her on a Sunday morning (having slept hardly at all the night before) and opened my plea:

"I would like to talk to you about something, Mutti."

"Good," she said, "I would like to talk to you, too. I have a great surprise for you."

I had a surprise for her, too, but it seemed better diplomacy to let her have a go at it first.

"What is it?" I asked, pushing my papers unobtrusively between me and the chair cushion.

"I have arranged for you to go to the French part of Switzerland in an exchange with a Swiss girl. You will stay with a family there for eight weeks and their daughter will stay with us for the same length of time. You will go there first; then both of you will come back to Berlin together. No exchange of money will be necessary."

This last item was all-important, since no German money could be taken out of the country or exchanged for foreign currency. The whole thing was a tremendous coup, there were no two ways about it. Precious few of such exchanges took place any more; the number of foreign parents who wanted to send their children to Germany had been dwindling rapidly during the last years. I was thunderstruck.

"That is fabulous, Mutti!" was all I could say. My own exhibits (on which I was sitting) seemed to pale by comparison. But loyally I stuck to my intentions of presenting my case then and there.

"I want you to look at those," I said, pulling the papers out from under me and, with a pounding heart, handing them to her. "That's what I want to do when I come back!"

One fleeting glance at them and my mother returned to the subject of the Swiss trip.

"I want you to read this," I said firmly. "I really mean to do it."

"Yes, yes," said my mother with another quick glance. "I see, social work. Poorly paid, I understand; very poor social standing. Certainly I shall look into it," she added quickly, seeing my face, "but first things first. About this Swiss family . . ."

The family lived in a small town deep in the Swiss mountains. Monsieur H. was a lawyer, as was his oldest son, Bernard, who still lived at home. It was not clear what Gaston, the second son, did. Michelle, my future exchange sister, had just finished school. She was about my age but had gone on to university level and would, after her stay in Germany, begin her studies in pharmacy. Neither Monsieur nor Madame spoke a word of German, which would certainly speed my French along. My mother showed me a picture of Michelle. I liked her immediately.

I was to leave at the end of July. My mother was jubilant; it seemed that Dagmar Olsen spoke a number of languages fluently.

I was packing my suitcase, walking between the hall and our bedroom, when I heard my mother talking to a friend on the telephone.

"Yes," she said in her ringing voice, "yes, she is very excited. I had to do something, you know. The child has simply no idea what she wants to do with her life."

* * * * * * * * * * * * * *

The day the Germans marched into Poland in the autumn of 1939 my Swiss host family ceased to talk to me. Monsieur H. and Bernard simply left the house earlier than usual for work. They were gone when I walked out of my room. Gaston, whom I met on the steps, turned around with an absent air as if he had just remembered something and headed toward the kitchen. Gaston liked me on general boy-likes-girl principle and because I had never tattled on him when he pinched me in the dark hall. He didn't care a fig about politics, but he cared a good bit about his mother's ill humor. So he walked into the kitchen and sat there all morning, well out of the way, eating grapes and spitting the seeds into the sink and bothering Madeleine. Michelle had locked herself in her room and was crying. So it was only Madame H. who was waiting for me in the dining room.

She invited me to sit down, poured coffee and hot milk simultaneously out of two pitchers into my cup and pushed the warm croissants toward me. Then she said what she had to say.

She was fond of me, she said, but she had never made a secret of it that she detested the Germans. War had been declared, the borders would be sealed within hours. Madame was sorry to seem to be in such a haste, but I would have to leave that very morning. She was not prepared to take upon herself and her family the responsibility and embarrassment of harboring a German citizen.

She realized, she said with a sigh, that I had no money; Germans were not permitted to take any kind of currency out of their country. Monsieur, out of the kindness of his heart, had agreed to incur one more expense on my behalf, which, she was sure, would never be repaid under the circumstances. He would pay for my ticket to Basel where I would have to make my way to the German Consulate. It would be the consulate's responsibility to see that I would arrive safely back in Berlin. Would I, please, begin packing immediately? There would be a taxi to take me to the early train to Basel.

My reaction was one of relief. For days now the radio had been blaring incessantly, excited voices speaking in rapid French which I could not follow, but I could read the message in Madame's compressed lips and in the averted eyes of the rest of the family. I had spent hours alone in my room, trying to stay out of their way, sick with dread and excitement and longing to talk to somebody who would look at the events from my own confused perspectives. So dense was the atmosphere of silent reproach and animosity, that there were times when I had trouble breathing. I certainly agreed with Madame H. that I should go back to my own kin and kind as quickly as possible.

When the taxi came Madeleine was ordered to help me with the luggage. She looked sullen and hurled the innocent suitcase into the trunk with rather alarming force. Madame H. shook my hand in a friendly way and said she was sorry that things had come to such an impasse. Bon voyage. Henceforth she washed her hands of me and the whole regrettable episode. Michelle came running down the stairs. She looked red-eyed and disheveled. She hugged me fiercely for a few seconds and then turned and ran back into the house. Gaston was nowhere in sight. I suppose he was kept well out of the way so he wouldn't make some unsuitable remark in the end. You never could tell with Gaston.

At the Basel railroad station I stored my suitcase at a check-in counter and began walking toward the consulate. I had no money for a bus or cab. Asking for a German agency that day in high German rather than Switzer-Dütch was a painful experience. People glared at me and some would not answer at all. When I finally got there my stomach was in knots and I was close to tears. The lobby was crowded with other travellers caught in various dilemmas. Eventually I was taken to a room where a large man with a florid face was sitting behind a cluttered desk. I remember most clearly his booming voice. He told me that his office had absolutely no money for cases like mine. Could I imagine, if you please, for even one moment, what would happen if word got around that the German Consul was paying for return tickets to Germany? I think he would have liked to expound this hilarious idea but relented when he saw my face. He told me to go to the Salvation Army, which, he said, was routinely helping stranded people like me. After a moment of hesitation, he pulled out his wallet and gave me a few francs for a sandwich and bus fare.

At the Salvation Army I was told that they never heard of such nonsense. The responsibility for a case like mine lay clearly with the consulate. There was nothing for me to do but to return to the gentleman with the booming voice.

He greeted me like a long lost daughter.

"We have been looking for you high and low," he exclaimed, getting up from behind his desk and pulling a chair up for me. "Where did you go? Right after you left we received a wire from Colonel Koenig of our Berlin main office. The money for your return ticket is on the way. Why didn't you tell me you had these connections?" he added reproachfully. I was at a loss for an answer. The entire day was turning into a nightmare.

He handed me the train fare plus a few francs for a taxi, assured me that they were always of service to people like me, and told me to give his compliments to the Colonel. And I was back on the street.

At the station I got a ticket for the night train to Berlin and then went to get my suitcase.

"That will be two francs," said the unfriendly man behind the counter. Two francs! I had tipped the taxi driver who had driven off without a thank-you almost before I had closed the cab door.

"I have only one franc left," I said in my timid high German.

The man looked at me, a sudden glint in his eyes. Like Madeleine this morning, he saw an opportunity for a fine patriotic gesture.

"Then you cannot have your suitcase," he said loudly, looking at the people around us for approval.

By now I was so tired and overwrought that I had no fight left in me. It would be useless to walk back to the consulate, since it would be closed by the time I reached it. Neither could I board the train without my suitcase. It would never be forwarded. I could imagine my mother's face if I arrived without my luggage. I stared numbly at the man who shrugged and turned to the next customer.

"Could I help you, Miss? said a gentle voice in perfect high German behind me. The voice belonged to a short, plump man in a brown suit. He was a lawyer and a bachelor and his name was Herr Plume.

Herr Plume lived on the German side of the border and practiced law for a German and Swiss clientele. He was on his way to Freiburg to evacuate his old mother. Freiburg was close to the French border and could be bombed any minute, he felt. He was quite old, at least thirty, and he looked a great deal like a medicine ball with legs. His head was round. He had no neck to speak of. His chest and stomach were one perfect circle around which the brown suit jacket strained in an effort to reach the long-suffering button on the other side. Herr Plume not only redeemed my suitcase from the disappointed patriot at the counter, he carried it to the station restaurant and there revived my drooping spirits with a hearty meal. I didn't protest much; he already knew I had no money. It made everything much simpler.

From the very beginning his intentions were strictly honorable. I think it was my growing realization of this that, in the end, forced me to such desperate measures. This was no fun flirtation. Herr Plume might have looked like somebody who had stepped out of a Wilhelm Busch cartoon, but beneath that absurdly globular exterior beat the heart of a troubadour, a 13th century knight in search of a damsel in distress at whose feet he would lay it all: his splendid law practice, his little house on the banks of the Rhine River, his old mother in Freiburg, and his undying devotion. When he saw me in front of the baggage counter at the mercy of a smirking villain, he knew his search had ended. As far as Herr Plume was concerned, I was it.

He watched me eat with a disarming delight, urging ever more sweets and fruit on me. While I was eating my dessert he asked for my train ticket which I meekly surrendered. He disappeared with it for a quarter of an hour. Just when I was becoming somewhat restive, he appeared again, beaming with the surprise he had in store for me. He had turned in my ticket, he told me, and purchased instead two reserved window seats for the night train to Berlin.

"*Two* tickets to Berlin?"

"I shall accompany you," said Herr Plume firmly. "I would not dream of permitting you to travel alone under the present conditions."

"What about your mother in Freiburg?" I protested, appalled.

"They would not attack Freiburg on the first day," declared Herr Plume, sweeping aside with one grand gesture the entire French air force.

"I shall attend to my mother after I have seen you home safely."

"Isn't she expecting you?"

"I called her." Herr Plume looked pleased with my concern for the old lady. He patted my hand reassuringly.

After consulting his watch, he announced that we had well over an hour until departure time and that he would show me a bit of the city. He disposed of my suitcase with the greatest of ease and, once again, I found myself walking the streets of Basel, this time under the protection of my self-appointed knight.

One part of my brain was feverishly trying to find a way to prevent this odd little man from accompanying me to Berlin. The very idea was preposterous: two thirds of Germany lay between Freiburg and the capital. The other part was making polite conversation. I didn't want to offend such genuine kindness.

We stopped in front of a display of local arts and crafts.

"What lovely things," I exclaimed quite sincerely. "What a beautiful tea set!"

"Permit me to buy it for you," said Herr Plume, heading toward the entrance.

"No!" I almost screamed. "Please, don't," I repeated, trying to smile. Things were slipping out of my control at an ever faster pace.

"I . . . we could not possibly carry it. It would mean a very large parcel. You saw the crowds."

Reluctantly Herr Plume let go of the door handle. He had to admit that I was right. We wandered on and thereafter I was careful never to praise anything smaller than a China cabinet in an antique store. Past the beautiful Swiss jewelry shops I hurried, talking a mile-a-minute. I had noticed my companion's hesitant step, his longing glance at the displays.

When we returned, the station was a madhouse. All night trains north were under siege, people pressing into the narrow corridors and the already filled compartments. If my heart sank at this sight, Herr Plume's rejoiced. He seemed to grow inches at this first true challenge threatening our progress. He simply rolled through the crowds with such imperious momentum that a path opened before him and I followed in his wake. He located our compartment and politely but firmly dealt with the people who were occupying our seats. He stored his overnight bag and my suitcase on the overhead shelf. He tested the seats for cleanliness and the window for drafts and, having satisfied himself that I had the better of the two, we settled down in our opposite corners. Almost a dozen people crowded into the compartment which was meant for six travelers. Every one of us, with the possible exception of Herr Plume, was suffering from various degrees of shock. Perhaps it was a good thing that, once we had crossed the Swiss border into Germany, all the train lights went off. The darkness was depressing, but the imposed inactivity seemed to relax the tension.

Exhaustion took over. We were too cramped to do more than doze off for a few minutes at a time. The train raced through the dark countryside. My country, that was now at war with its neighbors. My oldest brother would have to go . . . Somebody sitting on the floor was sleeping with his head against my knees. I cautiously peeked through the darkness at the seat across from me. Every time a light from the outside flitted through the compartment I could see Herr Plume's open eyes, like two black dots, resting on me. His gallant vigil seemed to know no fatigue. Whenever his head fell backwards and half buried itself into the window curtain, he lifted it with a start, and the black dots were searching my corner to reassure themselves that I was still there. I leaned my head back and tried to keep my face expressionless lest he would read, even through the darkness, all the frustration and helpless fury that filled me. How had I gotten into this? How was I to extricate myself? I dreaded the approaching morning. What would happen once we arrived in Berlin? Would this tenacious round little man follow me now all the days of my life? Or would he bid me farewell and head for the next train back to Freiburg? He most certainly would not. He would hold on to my suitcase, hail a taxi cab, and accompany me to the very threshold of my home.

The closer we came to Berlin the more desperate I became. The thought of arriving at our front door escorted by Herr Plume, whose presence I felt totally inadequate to explain, drove me frantic. My mother would guess the situation. She would listen to Herr Plume's gentle, persuasive voice; she would see the devotion in the man's eyes. Of course, she would check him out carefully. But what good would that do me? Herr Plume had integrity written all over him. My mother might see in him, quite conceivably, a heaven-sent, happy solution to all her troubles with me. She would side with him, against me, and I had yet to win a major argument with my mother.

When our train pulled into the station in Berlin masses of disheveled, hollow-eyed travelers poured onto the platform. Once again Herr Plume proved invaluable when, with a mixture of firmness, courtesy, and cunning, he steered us through the milling crowd into the main hall. We both showed the effect of the long night. He looked gray, wrinkled, and generally awful. So did I. Not that this would make the slightest difference in his feelings toward me. Herr Plume was a man who, having made a commitment, would see it through for better or worse, come hell or high water. There was no escape for me.

It was he, though, who showed me the crack in the stone wall. He suggested we go to the washrooms and freshen up a bit before leaving the station. My knight was preparing to present himself to the head of my clan. Here was my one and only chance.

"Yes," I said, "and I need my suitcase for this, please."

He gallantly carried it to the door of the ladies' room and with a smile and a wave turned and crossed the hall. Pretending to be busy with my suitcase, I watched him out of the corner of my eye until he disappeared behind the closed door of the men's washroom. Then I grabbed my suitcase and ran.

I didn't really run, of course. The suitcase was much too heavy. I dragged it, pushed it, and thumped it down the stairs, stumbling, hitting my ankle with it, losing a shoe and having to retrieve it, heading all the while toward the exit doors. I was in full flight. Nothing could stop me. Once outside I got into a taxi and sank into the seat, gasping for air.

When we arrived at the Laubenheimer Strasse I told the driver to wait while I ran upstairs and got the fare from my mother. She was glad to see me home safely. If I seemed to have a case of nerves, that was understandable enough, considering the circumstances. I washed my hands and face while she heated some milk for me, and I crawled into bed, pulling the covers over my ears. Then I waited for the inevitable ring of the phone.

It did not come until thirty minutes later. Among all his other virtues, my knight was endowed with extraordinary patience. I heard my mother's voice, her steps approached the bedroom door.

"There is a Herr Plume on the phone," she said, frowning slightly. "He wants to speak to you."

"Tell him I am asleep," I mumbled.

"He said he waited half an hour in front of the ladies' washroom," said my mother. She sounded puzzled. "What is this all about?

"Well, . . . he helped me. I didn't have any money. He paid for a meal for me. We missed each other when we came out of the washrooms. I thought he had gone," I added cowardly.

"He wants to speak to you."

"I don't want to speak to him."

I felt my mother's eyes resting searchingly on my face.

"If he helped you, you will come and thank him," she said severely.

"No, I won't!" By now I was at the end of my rope and half hysterical. "I won't come to the phone. You talk to him. Thank him. Tell him I am asleep. Tell him anything you want. Tell him I am dead."

For once my mother did not argue. Obviously, fatigue had made me irrational. She closed the door behind her and went back to the phone.

And that, except for the occasional rumblings of my conscience, was the end of it.

Dear, kind Herr Plume. If you are still around. You must be pretty old by now. After all, you were pretty old, then, and that was almost half a century ago. Have you ever forgiven me? I haven't. Not quite. You, or rather my abominable treatment of you, are one of the few genuine regrets I have carried around with me all those years. Whenever I think of it (which is not all that often any more), I am heartily sorry. You deserved much better. Truly, you did. But, given the same circumstances again, I would probably do the same all over again. There is no way I could have dealt more wisely with this spontaneous and consuming affection into which I had stumbled so unexpectedly. I was thirty days shy of my eighteenth birthday. I was not ready for the Plumes of this world.

PART III

1940-1942

Not for school, but for life, do we learn*

*Latin proverb

Chapter 6

All four of us were back in school. Three times a year during holidays my younger brothers—like two jolly, irrepressible poltergeists—descended upon the long suffering tenants of our apartment building. For the rest of the time they were firmly tucked away behind the vine-covered walls of the old Templiner boys' school. Wolfgang, having simultaneously acquired his corporal stripes and an impressive appendix scar in France, had returned to Germany to study medicine under the army's educational program.

After my hasty return from Switzerland, my mother had announced her new plans for me in clear and precise terms. I was to go back to school and study toward the "Abitur," the standard European university entrance diploma. The experiments had to end, she said. (*Whose* experiments, I thought truculently.) It had been a mistake, said my mother, to allow me to leave school at sixteen, three years before reaching university level. It had meant diminished options and, in any career opened to me, an early promotion ceiling.

I knew her reasoning was sound. I was tired of being sent down dead-end streets. The war had a sobering effect on all of us. My only condition was that I would not have to return to a regular high school where, I protested, I would be ancient—at least two years older than my classmates.

Accordingly, in the fall of 1939 I registered at the Berliner Goethe Institute, an evening preparatory school located at the Wittenberg Plaza to which I could commute by subway. The Goethe Institute conducted small classes of a sternly academic nature. No frivolous subjects such as art, music, or sports were offered; no discussion groups, assemblies, or field trips were even remotely considered. Every evening from six to ten the nine required major subjects were taught at a concentrated and accelerated pace: German, English, French, history, math, physics, chemistry, biology, and geography. Spring and fall holidays did not exist; summer and Christmas vacations were severely trimmed. The students were young men and women who were already holding jobs during the day. They had entered the program because they had essentially come to the same conclusion: no Abitur, no hope for advancement or significant promotions.

Once I had agreed to go back to school, I kept my end of the bargain. For the next two years I dug in tenaciously. In the mornings I would do the household chores; around ten o'clock I would hit the books. By one p.m. (German dinner time), I had three hours of solid homework behind me. For a while I kept my afternoon babysitting job, but when school became tougher and the pace faster, I gave it up. Enid and I still met on Tuesday afternoons, but often only for a stroll through the parks. At the cafés food stamps had to be turned over for a slice of cake and theater was only possible on weekends. Around five in the afternoon I would eat a bowl of soup or a sandwich and at twenty to six, my book satchel slung over my shoulder, I would be on my way to the subway. I was eighteen and I was back on the school bench.

* * * * * * * * * * * * * *

When we moved to Berlin I had taken with me an interim diploma, entitling me to a variety of trainings, and the best wishes of my old school administration. When my mother seemed indecisive about enrolling me in a new high school, I jumped at the chance of quitting school for good. It must be spelled out here at least once in complete honesty that I had never liked school. To be sure, there were some subjects that I had loved: German, history, advanced French . . . well, I am afraid, that's it. Everything else I tolerated with some boredom, or cordially disliked, or outright detested. But my quarrels were always with the subject, not with the teacher. For somebody who so greatly objected to school, I had a singularly sanguine approach to my teachers. I didn't even dislike the unpopular ones; deep down—and not very strongly voiced in the face of so much opposition—I always had the feeling that they, too, had a point, that there also was *their* side of the story. This positive attitude must have come through somehow; most of my teachers liked me despite my less than spectacular achievements in their subjects. The rest were either indifferent or so worn down that they did not like anybody. Thus, I was caught entirely unaware and defenseless when at the age of fourteen during my Potsdamer high school years, I was suddenly faced with a teacher who singled me out in a most deplorable way. (Or, as Jane Austen would have put it, who ill used me.) In other words, I was unprepared for my encounter with Karlchen Ratz.

His full name and title were Karl Franz Ratz, doctor of philologie. To his face we called him Herr Doktor Ratz, but out of earshot the entire school called him Karlchen ("little Karl"). It escapes me why that was so; there was nothing cute or cuddly about him. He was one of our younger teachers; handsome and soft-spoken, he moved with the elegance of a cat. He had a perpetual tan, a charming smile, and a fine, treacherous streak. Half of the all-female student body cautiously adored him; the other half regarded him with some misgiving. He was never known to have any discipline problems. He had favorites in every class with whom he would at times converse or even joke during lessons, but not even they would have dared to presume on the strength of these moments of grace.

He was my Latin teacher and, unfortunately, for two years was also my homeroom teacher. We had Latin three times a week and I dreaded those hours more than any trip to the dentist. There were twenty-seven girls in my class, which meant that normally a student might be called upon for translation or conjugation once every other week. I had the dubious honor to have Karlchen's undivided and concentrated attention for several minutes at almost every lesson. Sometimes he would call on me just a few minutes before the bell rang. Our eyes would meet — and I would read in the malice of those blue eyes that he knew I had hoped he would forget about me just this once.

I scrambled out of my seat — we had to stand when we answered a teacher — and already I felt my hands tremble and knew my voice was unsteady. If I knew the answer, he would ask the next question, and then the next. Soon I would reach the end of my rope and remember nothing at all. I just stood there and stared down at my desk. He calmly persisted, asking questions in his low, smooth voice, even though (or because) he knew there would be no response forthcoming. Only the top students in the class might conceivably have known the answers to those questions, but none of them was ever subjected to this kind of exposure. I would dig my nails into my palms and repeat to myself: I will not cry! I will *not* cry! But already I felt my eyes filling with tears, and, once again, I knew that he knew. An almost imperceptible mocking smile would lift the corners of his mouth. "Sit down," he would say softly and then go on with the lesson, entirely ignoring me for the rest of the hour.

I had weathered my share of scoldings in the village school and had stared at grades on my high school report cards that were rather lower than expected, but never had I felt cause to cry: Foul! This blatant unfairness, however, was beginning to unhinge me. For the first and only time in all my school years I appealed to my mother to intervene.

In my mother's school days a teacher often punished children by hitting them over the knuckles with the sharp edge of a ruler. Having to answer questions more difficult and frequently than those addressed to the rest of the class did not seem to her much cause for lament. (How could I tell her about the malice, the smile . . .?) However, after a number of urgent appeals, she did make an appointment with the teacher.

I awaited my mother's report with nervous apprehension. Added to this, oddly enough, was a touch of genuine curiosity. (*Why* did the man do this to me?) I met her in the hall when she returned. Every fiber in me, my whole still rather small frame was one large burning question mark. She began to tell me about her shopping in town.

"Tell me about your talk with Dr. Ratz!"

"Ah, yes. Dr. Ratz. Well—he seems to be quite interested in you."

"I *know*! But why? Why? What did he say? What did you say? Tell me from the beginning."

"Well," said my mother, frowning in an effort to remember. I saw with despair that the whole incident had already been pushed into the back of her mind by her shopping trip afterward, by the friends she had met in the bus, and by the mail she had found when she came home.

Faced with my obvious anxiety, though, she relented and tried to recall the interview.

"Well, I said to him: 'Dear Dr. Ratz, my daughter has the impression that you expect more from her, that you are a little more severe with her than with the rest of the students.' "

Ah, that was clever. That was a good opening.

"What did he say to that?!"

"He admitted that this might be true. The problem is, he explained, that he likes you particularly well and that he is afraid of showing favoritism.

So, he said, it may well be that he is overcompensating by being a little stricter with you than with the others."

"He didn't say that!" It came out more like a cry than a question.

"Yes, he did," said my mother, surprised by my violent reaction.

"And you know," she added judiciously, "I can understand that. A teacher should never show favoritism. The other students might begin to resent this and . . ."

But I was listening no more. I thought rage and frustration would choke me. And yet, out of this rage came something good and helpful. The brazen lie (spoken very probably with a charming smile and a look straight at my mother) broke an evil spell. It put an end to my caring and longing for this man's good opinion. It freed me of all moral obligation I felt toward him. No longer did I feel fear and trepidation when I saw him enter the classroom. When he was in a good mood and whimsically conversed with the rest of the class, I did not sit glued to my seat any more, hanging on every one of his words, hoping against disconsolate hope that I might be included in the general benevolence of the moment, that a single friendly glance might be sent in my direction. Instead, filled with the courage of pure contempt, I would open my library book under the desk and read. He still grilled me from time to time, but since he never again saw me in tears, he seemed to lose interest and contented himself with ignoring me while I, enthralled and breathless, finished the marvelous *Hunchback of Notre Dame* right under his very nose.

When, eight weeks before the end of the school year one of the infamous "blue letters" arrived at our house (the standard warning to parents that a student might fail a major subject—Latin in my case—which would prohibit promotion to the next grade), I bought a German translation of Caesar's Gallic Campaigns. It was against every rule in the book for a student to own such a translation but I felt not the slightest twinge of conscience. My home assignments improved and I managed to squeeze through the two last tests of the year. At the beginning of the new school term I dropped Latin in favor of English and acquired a new homeroom teacher.

Karlchen Ratz lived to be a very old man. Many years later Hanne, my childhood friend and confidant, would still run into him when she visited friends in his Potsdamer neighborhood. They would talk about the weather, their health, and old times.

"He always inquires about you," Hanne wrote. "And he never fails to add in the end: 'Tell her I said hello.' "

"Tell him I said to go to the devil," I wrote back. There are a few sentiments that don't seem to mellow with age.

This must be one of them.

There were four good and true men during those interminable years of school whom I may have tried beyond endurance. They had much cause to erase me from their list of students worth their time and efforts and to cast me into oblivion. They never did; they were without exception kindhearted men of a patient and generous nature. They liked me and never completely gave up on me, although they must have been sorely tempted at times. They were my math instructors.

I am not including Eagle-eye Arns. He had been an old-time schoolmaster, a teacher *par excellence*, who had taught three generations of village youngsters to read and to write. And if he could teach Kurt and Kunz and Little Stoffel some simple addition, subtraction, and the tables, he certainly did not regard me as a particular challenge.

No, *"The Great Math-Disaster Era"* did not begin until I left the village school and started the daily bicycle ride to the Potsdamer high school for girls. And it did not end until the day I took my university entrance exams.

Believe me, I have tried to get to the bottom of it, but all I have come up with is an assumption that there has to be a missing enzyme or a frayed synapse. Nothing else can explain the bleak vacuum in my brain which occupies the exact spot that normal human beings are able to fill with numbers and figures and their relationship to each other.

Papa Leer was my first math teacher. I don't know his full name and neither did anybody else. It was of no consequence, since everybody called him Papa Leer. But unlike "Little Karl," whose nickname had been coined tongue-in-cheek, Papa Leer's name was born out of genuine affection. He was an old man when I knew him, at least he seemed ancient to us with his snow-white hair and his mighty, drooping moustache. He was tall and a little stooped and half of what he said was lost in the white underbrush around his mouth. He must have been a good teacher, because everybody learned at least some math; that is, everybody but me. Papa Leer carried me on his stooped old shoulders through four high school years. He never sent my mother a blue letter and he never failed me. He always gave me the lowest possible grade that would allow me to be promoted. Sometimes he hung a little minus on the end—to soothe his conscience, I suppose.

He had a system by which he could drag me through the year without breaking every rule in the book. During the course of a math lesson when some material happened to be repeated for the third time or a problem came up that was as good as solved already, he called on me. I would then somehow muddle through to the end of it and he would scribble a passing mark in the little black book in which he kept score on every student. That way he would manage to have, eventually, half a dozen passing grades behind my name. We wrote three major tests during each semester. I promptly failed the first two. When the third test approached, he would announce it well in advance. If I flunked that one, too, no passing marks or kind hearts could save me from failing the subject. Now Papa Leer had no wish to flunk a dense but otherwise pleasant and, at this point, very frightened fifteen-year-old out of class and, eventually and inevitably, out of school. He was obviously dealing with a particular type of retardation. But there was no way he could rescue me without some help from me.

So, a recess or two before the fatal test, I would knock at the faculty door and ask for Dr. Ratz. (Unfortunately, the permission to leave school had to be given by the homeroom teacher.) When he appeared in the doorway, slightly peevish at the interruption, I would tell him that I felt ill and would like to go home. Since it was a matter of life and death for me anyway—and since it was Karlchen, of all people, whom I had to face with this fabrication—I looked distraught enough to be believed and was excused.

There was one horrendous exception, though. It must have been the third or fourth time of this charade and I had spent a sleepless night wondering if Karlchen might not be catching on to it. Anyway, I had taken the precaution of bringing an onion along to school that morning. At the beginning of recess, armed with a paper napkin, the onion, and a kitchen knife, I disappeared into the girls' bathroom. Usually one hefty cut into the bulb was enough to start tears rolling down my cheeks, but not this morning. Another cut, a deep sniff—nothing happened. I mean absolutely, positively *nothing*, not even pink-rimmed eyes. Fear, excitement, an outpour of adrenalin, whatever the cause, I seemed completely immune to the odor. I was still locked in the toilet and by now was frantically stuffing onion pieces up my nose when I heard the death-knell sound of the school bell announcing the end of the recess and the beginning of the math test.

I threw the entire useless paraphernalia into the wastebasket and rushed into the hall. Reeking of onion, disheveled and clearly on the brink of shock, I hurled myself into Karlchen's path as he was about to leave the faculty room. For once his complacency wavered. He was so taken aback by my wild-eyed appearance that he offered to call a taxi cab. I bravely whispered that I thought I could manage on my own. Looking doubtful and annoyed, he hurried away to his classes.

If it was summer I headed for a park bench in the gardens of Sanssouci, where nobody but a few forlorn tourists would be wandering about at this hour of a week day. On cold or rainy days I would sit at the post office where it was warm and nobody ever came who knew me. A few minutes before school left out I would start for home, slowly bicycling along the country road until Hanne caught up with me. The next day, miraculously recovered, I would return to school. If I met Papa Leer in the hall he would answer my greeting with a non-committal nod, and at the first possible opportunity he would send me to the blackboard to repeat a problem that he had all but spelled out for us a few minutes before. There was no such thing as a make-up test in our school system. Papa Leer would open his little black book and, poker-faced, pencil another passing grade behind my name.

Surely, there must be a special place in heaven for people like him.

* * * * * * * * * * * * * *

Now I was back in school facing a new math teacher with a flicker of hope and a good deal of apprehension. The scene was different now and could not, by any stretch of imagination, be called uplifting. I was no longer sitting in a large bright classroom where three windows opened toward the row of majestic chestnut trees that lined the old Potsdamer canal. Neither was I surrounded by two dozen girls, all my own age, with heads full of laughter and nonsense. Here were about fifteen young men and women huddled around a large table; the windows were closed and rigorously draped to comply with the general black-out rules. One single, powerful ceiling lamp threw its cold light directly onto the table and on the books and papers in front of us; our faces were already shaded and the rest of the room lay in morose, uncertain darkness.

What happened during those math lessons, however, was nothing but a repetition of by-gone years. It is true, there were no tests now. No little black books, and no playing hookie for that matter. There was only concentrated, hard work and each man for himself. But this math teacher, also, was a good-hearted, astute old man, who came of peasant stock from the northeastern border of Germany, and for many months he, too, refused to accept the fact that I was a lost cause. There came an evening when he turned to me with a math problem that to him seemed so clear and obvious that it could hardly be called a question, and, once again, I sat there looking at him with big, unhappy eyes in total silence.

"Little Miss, Little Miss," said the old man shaking his head sorrowfully and falling back into the ancient dialect of his native village, "I like thee well, I truly do. If thou wouldst only answer me a single time!" If I had been permitted just one moment of mathematical enlightenment in my lifetime, I would have liked it to be then and there.

Enter: Bertram the Giant, mechanical engineer during the day, co-student at night, and mathematician extraordinaire at all times. He was a shy, unassuming young man, but to miss his entrance into any room would have been next to impossible. He was the tallest human being I had ever met until then. He was also slow, deliberate, and homely. The incongruity of his towering appearance and his great shyness was irresistible to me. Besides, I was starved for some fun in this gloomy, unimaginative atmosphere. Cautiously I began to tease him; becoming bolder in time prompted by his slow, good-natured and surprised response. When, during recess, the students left the classroom to stretch, smoke, or have a sandwich in the dreary corridor, I would grab Bertram's notebook or scarf or pen and hide it away, the higher the better. When he returned to his seat he would miss that item almost immediately, shoot a glance at me and then look around the room. When he located it he would walk up to it, lift an arm (barely) and pull it down. This went on for a few weeks and then two things happened: I ran out of hiding places and Bertram, reading the signals all wrong, fell in love. With me. Being used to a couple of quick-witted brothers, I had expected some kind of clever retaliation. Instead, one evening Bertram, stretching just a little, removed his gloves from inside the dusty globe of the ceiling lamp and asked me for a date.

After that I went out with him once in a while, to a movie and a few times to the theater. The thrill of having people nudge each other or even stop to take a better look at him soon wore off. I found Bertram to be a decent, diffident fellow, wearily resigned to being stared at. Conveniently forgetting that it had been his overdimensional size that had drawn my attention to him in the first place, I soon indignantly decided that all those people were indelicate clods.

As the second year at the Goethe Institute drew to an end and the exams moved from a distant abstract threat into stark proximity, I began to panic. I knew my own shortcomings too well to indulge in any kind of hazy optimism regarding my chances. My mother had taken up whispering rather than talking in her normal voice to anybody who happened to be in the hall with her, and she ostentatiously tiptoed past the room where I was studying. It was her contribution toward my efforts and it tended to send me straight up the wall. When she tiptoed into my room one morning and ever so unobtrusively put a plate with bread and marmalade beside me, I turned on her rather frantically:

"Did it ever occur to you that I might fail this exam?"

It took her only three seconds to regain her usual form.

"No child of mine fails," she said coldly and walked out of the room. Desperation made me reckless.

"Am I to jump into the river, then?" I yelled at the closed door.

The kitchen door slammed shut; I never knew if she heard me.

When Bertram offered to tutor me in math, I eagerly accepted. From then on until exams started we met twice a week one hour before class began. He must have given up his supper time and come straight from work. We sat beside each other in the cheerless, empty classroom, united in an effort to salvage a few dismal remnants of twelve years of mathematical endeavor. While Bertram dived into the fundamental analysis of trigonometry, I had a hard time concentrating (for sixty unrelieved minutes) on those appalling figures and curves that popped out of nowhere onto the paper. My mind began to wander; I was thinking that this soft-hearted giant beside me had the patience of Job, and why did he always smell like a basket full of fresh apples? And while he tenaciously plodded ahead, I found myself wishing I could bury my nose, fleetingly, in his hair and neck and discover where all that nice apple smell came from.

However, since this might have been misunderstood, I sadly returned my attention to the paper in front of us on which Bertram was attempting for the seventh time to show me how to construct a tangent from a given point at a required angle onto a parabola. For some reason he had settled on this one problem and given up everything else. He seemed to believe if I could grasp just this one thing I might at least have an inkling of how some of the other problems should be tackled.

The severity of the Institute's program permitted us to cram three years of high school material into two years. During the summer of 1941 we began to apply to the city's school administration for admittance to the end exam, the Abitur. Four written exams and one full day of oral exams awaited us on fixed dates at a designated city school. Written exams in German and one foreign language were obligatory; the two other subjects could be chosen by the candidates. I was the only one in my class who chose history and French for the two elective tests. When the first day of exams arrived and I went to the assigned school at the other end of the city, I found myself not only faced with examiners and supervisors who I had never seen before, but also without the comfort of a single one of my classmates. Altogether we were some twenty students, all coming from different preparatory schools.

We sat through four days of written exams: German, French, English, and History, a three-hour essay in each subject. A ten-day waiting period followed in which the essays were graded. Only if all four grades were satisfactory were we given the date and hour of the oral exams.

When the morning of this formidable day dawned, I awoke with a fever. I had been fighting a cold and it had turned into a sore throat and regular flu. (The time was B.A. — before antibiotics.) My mother struggled heroically with her conscience. Normally the most cautious of nurses, she slowly rationalized herself into permitting me to go. Staying home would have meant a six month's postponement of the exams. And neither she nor I could envisage another six months of this nightmare. So it was hot milk and honey and a couple of aspirin and a taxi instead of bus and subway. My mother took up her station in a little café across the street and I disappeared through a pair of ominous double doors.

We met in a large room. The twenty desks were as far apart from each other as the space permitted. In a half circle along the wall were seven small tables lined up, one for each subject: German, history, biology, chemistry, physics, math, and geography. Two people sat on one side of each table, the examiner and the recorder; facing them was the unnerving spectacle of seven as yet empty chairs. Seated at the other end of the room at an elevated desk was the Area Schools' Supervisor, a squat, homely woman with a manish haircut (very stylish now but then almost unheard of). In front of her rested a large book containing our names and the grades of our written exams. She would keep score of our various marks during the day.

Each student would come forward, pick up a small piece of paper with an assignment written on it, return to his or her desk, and wait to be called. This gave us sometimes as little as four minutes, at other times as much as twenty, to think about our assignment.

There were no smiles, no talk between us. Everyone looked strained and apprehensive. When I picked up my first assignment, it turned out to be German, the theme: poetry. I sat down and stared at the paper. I could hardly believe my good fortune. Fervently I hoped it might be a good omen for the rest of the day.

Within a few minutes I was facing my first examiner, answering his questions, quoting, falling all over myself with joyful enthusiasm. His face lost its slightly pained look; his expression became at first incredulous, then kindled into pure delight. He, too, began quoting poems. We helped each other out with a missing line, a forgotten title; we could not cover enough ground, time seemed of no importance . . . Finally the recorder, who had listened to us in somewhat of a daze, pointedly tapped her finger against her watch and we regretfully parted.

My next assignment was history. This was my second best subject and I hardly dared look at the paper. What if my theme was somebody like Charlemagne? Not that I could not have talked for hours about him if needed. For some things I had a memory like an elephant. I could have talked about his many daughters whom he loved so much (he said) that he did not permit any of them to marry. (One of them ran off and married anyway which, reportedly, made him quite sour.) And how he never really learned the German language, although it was spoken in more than one third of his empire. He humbly accepted his homework assignment from his German tutor and if it had been one of those days and he simply did not get around to it, he hopefully put it under his pillow at night (a custom that many of us still followed before an important test). Or how his great, gray stone chair in the cathedral of Aachen was placed behind a large pillar so the people would look at their sweet Jesus during mass and not at him. But what if the examiner was not interested in the aspects of human nature and would cut a swath right through this enchanting thicket of trivia and find Sleeping Beauty behind it not just napping but passed out cold? I knew none of the names or dates of those terribly important and terribly bloody battles he was always riding to. I wasn't even sure of the borders of his empire, and I had only the dimmest notion when the great man lived, give or take five-hundred years.

My luck, however, ran true. The paper said: "Events at the turn of the 20th century," and I started breathing again. The date was right there on the paper. And as to the events that took place during that handful of years, they had practically been spoon-fed to us.

My third assignment was Mendel's Laws. Biology was a wobbly subject with me, but Mendel's Laws and the ongoing research of chromosomes and their importance in the making of a human being had been the one part of biology that had truly interested me.

And then my luck ran out. It had to, of course, eventually, but by now I was so dazzled by my three windfalls that I was beginning to believe that somehow, magically, I had acquired the Midas touch overnight. The fourth assignment, however, was math.

You are about to meet the last of my four math instructors. I never knew his name; I faced him no more than twenty unspeakably awful minutes of my life, at the end of which he flunked me unconditionally. And yet, he belongs right up there with the rest of my saints.

My assignment was . . . ah, well might you ask. There is a nebulous memory in the back of my mind that it went something like this: If a 1, 10 m long rod is planted onto the ground at a 90-degree angle and the sun culminates that day at 12:15 p.m., how long would the shadow be? Or maybe the shadow was 1, 10 m, and how long was the rod? It really did not matter; it could have been written in Chinese for all I got out of it.

I returned to my seat, contemplated the text once more and slowly stuffed the ghastly piece of paper into the empty inkwell. Then I just waited in bleak numbness. The girl whose desk was closest to mine came by on her way back from getting her German assignment. She looked sick.

"What's the matter?" I mumbled without looking at her. For a second she rested the paper with her theme on the top of my desk. "Name the highlight of Schiller's drama *Maria Stuart*" it said. I tore a corner off my squashed math paper and scribbled on it: "The confrontation of the two queens." That would have been my answer, anyway. When I was called to the math table I dropped the paper in passing on the floor beside her desk. If this did not stir her memory, it couldn't be helped. It was all I could do for her.

It is strange that I cannot remember more clearly what the examiner looked like. He was bald, I know, and he wore glasses, because I remember him taking them off and cleaning them more than once during our mutual ordeal.

He greeted me cordially: "Well, young lady, how did you do with your problem?"

"Not very well, I am afraid." It didn't even sound like my own voice.

"Are you on the right track?"

"I don't think so."

"Ah, well," he said good naturedly, "let me see how far you got and we'll figure out together where you went wrong."

"I don't have the paper any more," I said very low.

"Why? What happened to it?"

"My start was so wrong that I was embarrassed and I tore it up." The recorder's head shot around, looking first at the examiner and then at me in silent consternation.

"You should not have done that!" the examiner exclaimed, looking very perturbed.

"I am so sorry," I said, and I must have looked it. I had trouble not to burst into tears.

"Well," said the dear man with a little sigh, "I'll just have to give you another problem." And he did. And another one. He drew them on a lined geometric paper and pushed them around to me and each time I just shook my head. Small drops of perspiration began to show on his bald spot. "How about this one?" he'd say, encouragingly, wiping his forehead and cleaning his glasses. If he failed me it might mean the end of my schooling, perhaps the total upheaval of a young life. He was aware of this and clearly getting distraught. Not for the first time in my life I wanted to put my arm around a math teacher and comfort him: Don't mind so much, please! You see, I am quite resigned . . . But I wasn't resigned, not really; there was too much at stake here. Suddenly, my harassed friend bent forward over the table and, avoiding the recorder's eyes, he asked gently:"

"Is there *anything* you know?"

A sudden spark of hope gleamed in the ashes.

"I know how to construct a tangent from a given point at a required angle onto a parabola."

His face lit up with desperate relief. He carefully drew the parabola, positioned the point and turned the paper over to me. Immediately my face fell: the point was on the left side of the parabola. For some reason Bertram had set his dots always on the right side.

"Would you, please, put the point on the other side," I said in a very small voice. "I cannot do it this way."

The recorder's pencil froze in mid-air. My examiner gave a heavy sigh and leaned back in his chair. Once more, he took off his glasses and slowly began wiping them again. He seemed to have aged in the last twenty minutes.

"No," he said simply. "No. I cannot do that." And then he marked a failing grade on a piece of paper. It just about killed him.

I got up and gave him a tremulous smile. I wanted him to know that I was not mad at him. But he would not meet my eyes. Then I walked over to the podium to face the supervisor.

The woman looked at my grades, looked up at me and then back at my grades.

"You are presenting me with a dilemma," she said soberly. "How can I ignore a failing grade in a subject like math? On the other hand, I cannot ignore the fact that you have brought me more A's and B's so far than any other student during these exams." Again she scanned the pages in front of her.

"The only A's so far," she corrected herself, shaking her head.

There was a long silence. She was obviously wrestling for a solution.

"What do you intend to study?" she finally asked.

"Literature and social pedagogic," I answered.

Again a long pause. "Go on with the exams," she said. "Mind you, I make no promises! But go on."

I don't remember very much about the rest. I got through chemistry and physics by virtue of manageable assignments. When I walked to the geography table the room had emptied. The failed students had long since left; I had been too much involved in my own struggle to notice their leaving. The rest of the students had finished. The girl who had sat closest to me was just leaving. In the door she turned her head and gave me a radiant smile. And then, at long last, I, too, was done. The weary examiners gathered their stuff together. We had been in that room for almost six hours. My head was burning; the aspirin had long since worn off.

My mother stood directly at the entrance door. She told me that she had just about resolved to charge into the building and carry me off, finished or not, when a girl had come whirling through the door. Seeing my mother she stopped and said: "She will be out in a minute!" and then all but danced into the sunset.

I forgot how we got home. Not dancing, I know. I remember lying in bed, swallowing medicine, drinking more hot milk and honey; my mother had closed the curtains, the pillow seemed pleasantly cool and I was floating on air. There was only one rosy, shining, beautiful thought in my head: I passed, I passed, I passed! I had my Abitur! Miracles still happened.

Chapter 7

The Abitur entitled us to enter any university we chose. However, simply waving our brand new diploma in front of the ancient gates of Heidelberg or Marburg did not open those venerable doors any more. Since the beginning of the Third Reich, every student who aspired to an academic career had to live, for a designated time, by the sweat of his or her brow. This was to be a life-long lesson to us that digging ditches and cleaning stables was not the easiest way to make a living. Nobody had thought it was, but we were to experience it first hand. It would instill in us a lasting respect for the work of the farmer and laborer. It was not a bad idea. There was a resigned compliance in all quarters. (I remember meeting a cheerful young girl at a party, a Princess Salm, whose hands were red and chapped from scrubbing the stone steps of a country schoolhouse, a daily task assigned to her for that month by the work unit of her camp.)

There were separate camps for boys and girls, almost all of them situated in the country. The young people slept in large dormitories and during the day were assigned to farmers and tradesmen. The requirements for those girls headed for advanced education were either six months of work camp or twelve months at a place where manual labor was needed. The latter could be chosen by the student but had to be approved of by the state. Any farm or large family without domestic help qualified.

Of course, I chose work camp. All my friends had gone there and were forever swapping stories and photos of that unique experience. This dream ended abruptly when I flunked my physical.

"Ooooh—now she is crying!" said the examining woman doctor, not unkindly. She had told me that work camp was out of the question. And I was; big tears of disappointment were running down my cheeks.

"Well, child," she said, handing me a tissue, "I would be very amiss if I let you pass with that leg and your irregular heartbeat."

The irregular heartbeat had never bothered me much, except for not being able to run or climb as well as my contemporaries. And the leg . . . well, darn it, anyway!

So, it was the "Pflichtjahr" for me, the twelve months "tour-of-duty." My mother was less shaken. Her views of state institutions had been rather jaundiced for some time now. Within a week I found myself in the office of a fashionable heart specialist. He knew of a rest home for children in the Bavarian mountains that needed domestic help. He had sent young patients of his there at various times. At my mother's request, he wrote a letter of introduction and recommendation to the owner-director of the home. This heart specialist had seen me for less than half an hour during which time my mother had done all the talking, but he must have written a grand letter, for I was accepted sight unseen. The Home was approved for the tour-of-duty year; it was overflowing with children and chronically understaffed.

Together with the letter of acceptance came a snapshot of a woman with a small child standing in front of a spacious two-story mansion. The woman was young and blond; she wore the native costume of the region. Standing very straight, she was looking over the child's head toward the mountain range above. This was Frau Thomas, head of the Home, my future "boss." When I think of her now, half a century later, I think of her as she looked in the picture that day when I was sitting on one of the stiff, dark chairs in our dining room, the mail spread out on the table before me, studying for a long time the little photo in my hand.

A bare fortnight later I was facing her in the entrance of the Home, my suitcase beside me, my heart thumping in my throat. By now I was something of a veteran of first-day-on-the-job encounters, but they did not seem to become any easier with time.

"Let me show you where you will be staying," Frau Thomas said, "and then I will give you a tour through the Home."

When I picked up my suitcase, she took hold of the other half of the grip and together we walked down the steep path to a farmhouse in the village where I was to room for a year. During the walk, she talked about the Home and the children and the people with whom I would be working. There was nothing pedantic or patronizing in the way she talked; she spoke to me as she would to a friend or a welcome visitor.

The main house and an adjacent, smaller school building had been built to accommodate twenty children with respiratory or heart problems. Their bedrooms, as well as the social rooms and a small apartment for Herr and Frau Thomas, were on the upper floor. The rooms on the ground floor had originally been occupied by the personnel. However, when I arrived the house was bulging at the seams with forty healthy, noisy kids between the ages of four and fifteen. They came from cities in the north and west of Germany that were subjected to heavy air raids. The children had taken over both floors and the personnel had been moved to rooms in the village.

The Home, smartly designed, bright and cheerful, with large windows and terraces, stood on a grassy slope well above the little Alpine village. Hemmed in on three sides by the Allgäuer mountain range, we could, on clear days, see the tips of the glaciers beyond the valley beneath us. In spring the small mountain creeks turned into rushing waterfalls. Cowbells would ring us awake in the mornings. The house was surrounded by pastures where wild flowers, ancient rocks, and fresh cow manure were strewn about in abundance. Shimmering, and lording it over all, stood the rare silver thistle, respected by beast and protected by man. As the summer wore on, the smell of hay drying in the sun was all around us; it clung to our clothes and hair and followed us into our rooms in the village. Even the outhouse in the barn smelled sweet. Gradually, the pastures began to show a purple sheen; the small, blue, stemless flower of the meadow saffron (called the Autumn-Timeless in German) covered the fields. The leaf trees, lost during summer between the evergreens, showed up suddenly in golden spots.

In winter the snow ruled our lives; not snow that comes, grows gray and wet, and disappears again, but deep, cold, lasting snow, descending slowly from the mountaintops into the village and to the valley beneath it and remaining there, white, hard and glittering, for many months.

My room was on the second floor of an old farmhouse. It had a low ceiling, a round little iron stove, and a million-dollar view. In winter my landlady would start a fire in the stove an hour before I came home in the evening. On my free afternoons (of which she conscientiously kept track) she began heating the room at noon. I always came home to a warm place, though the featherbed was still icy when I crawled under it at night. Most evenings I went into the kitchen first and sat with the family for a while. My landlady was a placid, motherly woman, dressed in perpetual mourning, as most of the village women were; but there were freckles on her nose and smile crinkles all around her eyes. Her husband was away, in a war she did not understand, and her nightly prayers were neither for victory or defeat, but solely for his safe return. She was a seamstress and when I came into the kitchen at night I always found her sitting at the table, her measuring tape around her neck, bent over her sewing. The two older children would be sitting beside her, doing their homework. A younger child would be busy dressing up a much-handled, balding doll in pieces of cloth that had fallen off the kitchen table. The baby was sleeping in an ancient cradle in the dimmest corner of the kitchen. The whole scene was like a nerve tonic after a long and hectic working day among forty clamoring children and a dozen tasks that had to be done all at once.

The position of a girl during her tour-of-duty year was any place at all between a "daily," as the English would say, and a daughter of the house. We were paid less than half the minimum wage. Job descriptions did not exist. During my year at the Home I scrubbed tiles and toilets, waxed stairs and floors, made innumerable beds, changed linens, polished windows, packed and unpacked an unending stream of suitcases, hunted from the ground floor to the storage places on the rooftops for lost sweaters and swimsuits, supervised lunch hours, set tables, cleared tables, washed necks and ears, treated athlete's feet, and inspected (late at night) small bottoms for pin worms. As the months wore on, my scanty typing talents were discovered and Frau Thomas began dictating to me the quarterly reports that were sent to the parents. There came a day when, being summoned away for the fourth or fifth time, she called over her shoulder as she left the room: "You finish it, Eva!" After the initial shock and a good deal of meditation, I did as told. When she returned she read the letter and signed it without any corrections or changes. From that day on this would happen more and more frequently; sometimes I would write whole letters by myself. Frau Thomas just glanced at them and put her name at the bottom. This took a burden off her and I liked writing those letters. The truth was that I saw more of the children than she did, and it was easier for me than for her to report on their daily activities.

The demands made on Frau Thomas' time and endurance were horrendous. The Home ran its own private elementary and high school, but a number of children living in a nearby resort place also attended the classes. Herr Thomas saw to the administration of the school and the overall finances. Everything else rested on his wife's shoulders. The meals were her greatest worry; finding ways and means to supplement the scanty food coupons to feed this multitude of youngsters three adequate meals was a relentless daily challenge to her strength and resourcefulness.

She was a handsome woman, grandly designed in every respect. Blond, blue eyed, of regal posture, she was endowed with an artistic sense of beauty, a love for color, music and poetry, and she possessed a shrewd knowledge of people. I was a little afraid of her—of her changing moods, her cool stare and sharp words, caused by the unmitigating stress of circumstances. I was afraid of her, but I also loved her, and in time she and her husband came to love me, and I was not afraid any more. Even before I left, a growing mutual trust had changed our relationship into the beginning of a lifelong friendship.

I have gone back many times over the years and have always been given a warm and happy welcome. She is very old now, my lady of the mountain, over ninety, and quite blind. Herr Thomas is dead. But she still writes to me in large, slanted letters, six lines to a sheet of paper. When I visited her the last time, a few years back, I brought her a silver thistle in memory of the one she and I had picked during a mountain hike some twenty years ago. It grew on a steep rock and we nearly broke our necks trying to reach it, holding on to each other for dear life, laughing and panting and slipping precariously on the crumbling stones. She was quite old then—too old, really, for such climbing adventures—and I never was good at any kind of athletic endeavor even when I was young.

But I have jumped ahead of my story and left myself standing with bucket and brush at the door of the boys' bathroom, looking with some satisfaction at the gleaming facilities and threatening each approaching boy with a dire fate if he did not aim straight into the toilet bowl. I got along well with those urchins; not for nothing did I have three brothers. I had no quarrel with the girls, either, although I always took my own sex with a good bit of prudence. Perhaps the fact that I had no sisters or female cousins to banter, fight, or share with had something to do with this cautious approach.

There had been some dark moments, particularly during the first months, when the year seemed to stretch interminably before me. We worked long hours for little pay; the work was often tedious, and there were times when tempers were short and we were scolded like children. More than once, after a discouraging day, I was tempted to pick up a pen and write a moving and repentant letter to Bertram, with whom I had had a rather breezy farewell date before leaving Berlin. Breezy, that is, on my part; Bertram was about the least breezy person imaginable.

"Good bye. Good luck to you. Thanks a million for absolutely everything. You were a brick!" Not exactly the kind of speech an enamored young man wants to hear from the departing object of his adoration.

Actually, moving and repentant letters were not exactly my way of doing things. It would have been more like a jolly report of my daily efforts and pratfalls and then, in a closing paragraph: How were things in the old hometown? Were the air raids getting worse? Did he see any of the old chums? Any good movies? Was he pleased with his studies, and what would he think of getting married sometime in the future, like next month or so?

I was twenty years old and I had never made a single decision concerning my life. I never even had a voice in it. It seemed to me that since the day I stood up and walked somebody always told me where to go, when to go, and what to do once I got there. The worst part of this was that I could see no end to it. On and on it would go, like a squirrel in a wheel. The only way out would be that mild-mannered, earnest giant back home in my beleaguered Berlin. Granted, I did not love him, but I liked him and I most certainly got along with him a great deal better than I did with my mother. Love, just then, was not my first concern. Much more worrisome was the fact that our combined training and finances did not as yet amount to a hill of beans. Every time I actually sat down to write to him, this sobering thought kept cropping up and interfering with the "after us the deluge" attitude that I was about to advocate.

There were two young women working in the Home, a few years older than I: Lilo, who was the elementary teacher of the Home school, and Pauline, who was a native girl, born and raised in the village. She had been working in the Home longer than anybody else and had become something of a second-in-command. She was loved by the children and grown-ups alike; she was the salt of the earth, and she, Lilo, and I became good and true friends. With such comrades-in-arms and an inborn inclination toward the practical, my sporadic bouts with unhappiness never got to the point where I actually went ahead and did anything foolish, including writing catastrophic letters to unsuspecting young men.

So I just plodded on, one day at a time. One of the things I learned in life is: Never run *away* from anything. If you have to run, run *toward* something. Don't run away from despair, walk toward hope! It's as simple as that. Otherwise, your troubles will run right alongside you, and they are every bit as speedy as you.

Once during that year my mother came south and I saw her for a few days. She did not travel into my distant Allgäuer Valley, but wrote that she would stop over in Munich and I was to ask for a three-day leave to join her. She was staying at a clean, no-frills bed-and-breakfast place and I slept on the couch in her room.

Those were some clear, cool autumn days and together we toured the city, which neither of us knew very well. On the second day we went to a picture gallery. After an hour or so peculiar things began to happen: the pictures would not hang still on the wall and the floor began to undulate, either meeting my foot too soon or disappearing just when I was ready to step on it. This was somewhat disconcerting, though not entirely disagreeable, and I wondered if I should tell my mother about it. When my stomach signaled approaching seasickness, my mother decided that I was hungry and took me to a restaurant for a bowl of hot soup. Unfortunately, the restaurant walls showed the same inclination as the picture gallery; they slowly turned around me and I could not swallow the soup. My mother's experienced hand reached for my forehead, which was burning. The next thing seems to have been a taxi, followed by a place with painfully bright lights and a man in a white coat saying " . . . bed!" My mother must have explained to him that there was no bed; in any case, soon afterward I found myself between wonderfully cool sheets in a large room amidst a veritable sea of beds. A plump little woman in a long black gown, a white cap with large wings pressed deep down over her eyebrows, was busy arranging an ice bag alongside each of my ears. "Why?" I tried in vain to shake them off.

"You have bilateral inflammation of the middle ear," said the little white-winged woman, rearranging the bags.

"My mother uses warm oil and a heating pad," I mumbled.

"I know," the little nun said, reassuring me with a smile. "It's ice bags now. You'll see, it will feel good."

It felt wonderful. I slept through the rest of the day and the night. The first thing I remember clearly was my mother coming in the next morning to say goodbye. Having scrutinized the floor, the nurses' station, and the little winged woman who was to be in charge of me, she declared herself satisfied and continued her travel. I felt better, the room did not turn around me any more, and I inspected my surroundings. There were ten beds in all, five on each side, headboards along the wall, feet pointing toward the middle aisle. A fever chart was fastened above each headboard, the curve drawn with a red pencil. My own curve was very short; it started at an interesting height but had dipped toward a more unexciting middle line in the morning. My bed was closest to the door and to the screen behind which the washbasin, mirror, and our numbered towels were hidden. The beds were occupied by women of all ages and backgrounds; the one thing we seemed to have in common was that there was something wrong inside our heads or throats. Toward evening the red line above my head shot up again and I slept during most of the visiting hour. I wasn't expecting anybody anyway. The next day the fever began to abate and, having nothing else to do, I took more of an interest in the visitors who trickled in and out of the room. Pretty soon the girl in the third bed across the aisle drew all my attention. She had lank, sand-colored hair, an upturned little nose, and a bad complexion. She looked about fourteen but had to be older to be on the women's floor. Her visitor was a young man in workman's clothes whose ears stuck out a good deal and tended to turn beet red when he was embarrassed. Obviously intimidated by this assembly of night-shirted women, he tried not to look at any of us. He would sit on the edge of the bed of his "fiancée" (as she told us) and hold her hand in a fervent grip while she wiggled and whispered and tugged on his sleeve. Every once in a while all that wiggly pink flesh under the disarranged nightie would simply get too much for him and he would bend over and begin tickling her. This would set off some thrashing around and an almost hysterical giggling fit. He took this for an encouraging response and the tickling efforts would double.

"Franzi," gasped the girl between little screeches and giggles, "Don't! Stop it!"

The young man straightened up and caught some of the outraged looks from the neighboring beds. His ears turned red and for the next quarter hour he would sit again in awkward silence just holding the girl's hand until he could restrain himself no longer and would make furtive attempts to tickle at least the sole of her bare foot, with which she kept giving him little pokes in the ribs.

I was one of the lucky ones for whom apparently nothing had been ordered but bed rest and ice bags. (No antibiotics as yet on the medical scene, remember.) Other patients were not so fortunate. On my third day there the little girl with the turned-up nose and the ardent fiancé had been scheduled for an "invasive procedure." She was very quiet that morning. Her face was white and blotchy and scared. Some time within the next half hour she would be taken down to the operating room, seated on a hard, tilted chair, and held tight while something inside her head would be snipped off or cauterized or totally removed. She would be given nothing to alleviate the pain. German doctors at that time were not great on anesthetics.

* * * * * * * * * * * * * *

My eyes kept wandering over to the third bed across the aisle. I had had more than a passing acquaintance with pain. When I was five years old, the doctors had taken a swollen red ankle for a sprain or a hairline fracture and had put my leg in a cast. While my parents and a nurse helplessly stood by and I sobbed through the nights, a bone marrow infection, insidious and unchecked, made its way up the leg. When it had reached an inch below the knee and I was delirious, the cast was opened. That night three doctors operated, having given my parents scant hope for my survival. I survived (obviously) but five months passed before I took my first step out of bed. During the weeks that followed the operation, the bandages were changed every second day. Ether, which was then the sole anesthetic, was used only during the operation and for the very first dressing. After that it was do or die for the five-year-old. My hands were tied to the sides of the stretcher, the dressing was removed from the bone cavity, the wound was cleaned, and the cavity was packed again with sterile gauze. I don't remember the pain as much as my own screams. I have sometimes wondered that they were not afraid I might die of shock right there under their restraining hands.

When I was nine and ten, stray bone splinters had to be removed. They were located by x-rays; a surgical tong was inserted through a tiny hole in the flesh above the location, and, after some probing, the splinter, larger than a thumbnail and with jagged edges, was forced out through the opening. There was no general or local anesthetic whatsoever. I remember one time after such a procedure when I was being helped up, trembling, bathed in perspiration, tear-stained and hoarse, my mother, herself rather drained, turned toward the nurse and said: "She may have a glass of water now." When the nurse looked bewildered by the phrasing of this request, my mother explained that we were usually not permitted to drink water, since it filled up a child's stomach without having any nutritious value.

* * * * * * * * * * * * * *

The cart came for the girl in the third bed across the aisle; she was wheeled past me, rigid, her eyes black with fear.

After the door closed behind her, a heavy silence hung over the room.

"They oughtn't to let that man in here," said a harsh voice from across the room. "Somebody ought to tell Sister."

The floodgate had opened.

"Her fiancé! I wonder where she picked him up."

"Did you see how he went after her? Disgusting, if you ask me."

"She egged him on, that's what I say. He wouldn't have dared to go after her the way he did without her egging him on."

"She spilled her coffee this morning. Sister had to . . ."

". . . and when she dropped that piece of candy, giggling like a loon, he picked it off the floor and stuck it right back in her mouth." (This from the woman in the bed next to her.)

"D'you see his filthy hands? He don't even wash up before he comes here and has his paws all over her . . ."

"Well, speaking of *that!*" said the woman across from me; from her bed she could glimpse into the screened-off corner. "She never washes! I watched her for three mornings now and she never *really* washes. A few dabs . . . it's ludicrous. She just pretends to, you know, she turns the spigot on so we'll hear the water run . . ."

For a moment the voices died down as the women let that bit of news sink in. Hospital days were monotonous. At some other time I might have considered this unrehearsed scene greatly entertaining. But not then. Not at this moment.

"I think, right now she is in a lot of pain," I ventured into the silence.

Instant freeze. Nobody answered. Hostile quick stares and then a blank dismissal. The woman next to me ostentatiously turned her back on me and started a whispered conversation with her other neighbor. The woman across the aisle picked up a magazine and began to leaf through it. The woman next to her patted her pillows and seemed in need of a nap. Nobody looked at me. Nobody spoke to me. I had broken ranks. It would not easily be forgiven.

When they brought the girl back after an hour, her hair sticking to her head, her face puffy beyond recognition, she crawled under her sheet like a hurt little animal and quietly sobbed herself to sleep.

My ice bags did their duty. The red curve above me fell and was straightening out. Our little winged nurse assured me I would be permitted to get out of bed the next day. I was idly watching the door that evening when a woman entered, carrying a bouquet of flowers. She was middle-aged, thin; dressed primly and inexpensively. She looked like every tired middle-aged woman who has a job during the day and a household at night and tries to keep herself neat and clean for both. I had seen her before; she visited the young woman beside the window in the last bed of my row. This time, though, she headed straight toward my bed.

"Wrong bed," I was about to say with a smile when she spoke to me.

"My daughter told me what you said the other day." Her voice was friendly, almost matter of fact.

"What I said? What did I . . .?"

But the woman had already walked on. The flowers lay on my blanket.

Sister helped me to get dressed the next day. I finally had a visitor; Wolfgang had taken a few days off and was there to take me on my first outing. The hospitals in Germany do not discharge anybody unless they are able to walk three times around the block. All right—I made that one up, but it's close to the truth. Most hospitals have parks and the patients are encouraged to walk and move about, fully dressed, for as long as an hour at a time. My hospital was in the center of town and did not have a park. Hanging on to Wolfgang's arm, my legs wobbly, we walked around the streets and to the plaza until I was ready to fall into bed again. The autumn days continued to be cool and clear. Wolfgang came the next day for another walk. After the third day I was declared fit to be discharged; Wolfgang went back north to his studies and I went south. And after two trains and a bumpy bus ride, the mountains had swallowed me up again.

Good things began to happen. I remember a beautiful luminous winter night. Pauline had promised Lilo and me a nightly outing into the mountains and we had been waiting with some impatience for it to happen. So many conditions had to be just right. The air had to be cold and still and the snow high and hard on the ground. The sky had to be clear and there had to be a moon, since there would be no other source of light anywhere at all. None of the children in the Home should be ill, so that Consuela, the pediatric nurse, could come with us. And, of course, we had to get permission from Frau Thomas for all four of us to leave at the same time.

Just such a night did come and around nine o'clock that evening we began walking up the road that cars and wagons used to reach the hot spring spa, which lay half way up toward the mountain pass. This pass was one of the few accessible roads leading into Austria. The climb was not steep but it was steady, and we were pulling two wooden sleds behind us. Perhaps the three other girls could have made it in less time, but they amicably adjusted to a more sedate pace. Up the mountain we stomped for hours, never spotting a car or another human being or even a curious deer peering at us out of the dark. Just the silent, towering evergreens on both sides of us, the moon above us, and the glittering snow protesting softly under our feet. It might have been close to midnight when we finally saw the spa hotel silhouetted against the sky. Only then did we turn around and begin our descent. Pauline and I took the first sled; Pauline was sitting behind me, guiding and braking with her strong mountaineer heels. Consuela, to accommodate her long stork-legs, did the honors on the second sled; exuberant and optimistic as always, she plunged down on the back seat, although she had no more experience in steering a sled down an Alpine road than playing a bagpipe in a Scottish Highland parade.

Gliding down, evenly, soundlessly, endlessly through the enchanted winter forest, guided only by the light of the moon, a thousand stars in the black dome above us, their shimmer mirrored and answered by the sparkle of the snow in the treetops, it was so moving, so magnificent an experience that I wonder if it is possible to truly convey it.

Ever since I had arrived at the Home I had heard casual references to a party that had taken place a few years ago, or, more specifically, to a play that had been performed at that party. It seemed that this play had been written by one of the young women who had worked in the Home at that time. There were still a number of children and grown-ups around who had seen the play and they used to reminisce about it with a kind of wistful admiration.

Now every time this happened something like a tiny prick of an electric needle went through my system. I felt challenged, a sensation entirely new to me. I felt challenged to compete with a girl I had never met, in a craft I had never tried, and I wanted no part of it. In the future I simply would, I decided, ignore all references to this memorable achievement.

One evening—clearing the tables after dinner, addressing nobody in particular—I heard myself say quite loudly: "I guess I'll write a play for you kids for the holidays."

And so I did. It was incomprehensible to me that I had uttered those fateful words, but—having made the grand announcement—I was committed. Within hours the news had spread through the Home. Everything I had expected and dreaded rushed at me and engulfed me: the questions, the requests, the pressures, the feeling of inadequacy, the sleepless nights, and the overwhelming wish for flight, not to mention the stomach ache. But there was also a sense of elation, a resolution of action and a consummate desire to win that people like me with few competitive needs rarely ever experience.

I chose Andersen's fairy tale, "The Snowqueen," because I had loved it as a child. It was very dramatic and I could write into it any number of parts for children and adults. I had decided that the whole thing was to be in rhyme—hang for the saddle, hang for the horse. Frau Thomas, swept along by the general current of happy anticipation, gave me time off during the day to work on the play. And so I sat in lone splendor in the smaller of the two dining rooms, and after rearranging a few pieces of furniture, closing the curtains to keep the winter sun out, opening the curtains because it seemed too dark for creativity, cleaning a number of clogged keys in the typewriter with a bobby pin, cleaning the bobby pin, inspecting a noise in the hall, getting a cushion for the chair, getting rid of the cushion on the chair, counting the carbon papers, and blowing my nose, there was nothing left to do but to start typing.

By the end of November it was finished. It was a good play, written in good, solid rhyme, dramatic, exciting, and with a happy ending. The next step was casting the parts. That turned out to be almost as difficult as the writing had been. Everybody wanted to be in it but nobody wanted to memorize pages of script. In the end, I had to take the role of the hero's sister (the one who wanders off toward the North Pole to rescue little Kai); not because I wanted to shine on the stage, but because nobody was willing to learn such a long part. Consuela was a natural for the snowqueen. The important part of the gypsy girl posed another problem. She had to sing and dance and be quite airy and naughty and lovable. All the twelve and thirteen-year-old girls in the Home were in the process of growing like weeds. They were self conscious of their height and had no idea what to do with their arms and legs. During try-outs I was reminded at times of a certain performance of a dying autumn leaf. Finally, in a moment of enlightenment, I tabbed an eleven-year-old little rascal of a boy, thin, jolly, and forever into mischief; and after some minimal bribing (like getting him excused from homework for play practice), he agreed to be my gypsy girl. He was marvelous. He brought down the house. But so did Consuela. This tall, sinewy young woman with her mop of unruly brown hair and her fine, pale face, looked every inch the snowqueen.

I don't know what had possessed Consuela to think she should become a pediatric nurse. She was as suited to this profession as I would have been to be a demolition engineer. She was a free spirit, needing unrestricted wide open spaces. Since she was to play the title role in the play and the whole performance stood and fell with her, most rehearsals were scheduled for her evening off. On those occasions she invariably appeared late; her thick dark curls, which she usually (unsuccessfully) attempted to stuff under her cap, framed her face like a halo, her cheeks were glowing, and she was just the tiniest bit tipsy, having loyally broken off a lovely evening in the village pub to rush to the rehearsals. At such moments she was magnificent, irresistible, ad libbing with astonishing fire and talent and throwing everybody else off their lines. Guiding her back onto the straight and narrow path of the script without dampening her spirit, or having her announce that she would rather go to bed and couldn't she just read the whole thing from behind a curtain, required a great deal of persuasion and patience and left me limp at the end of each rehearsal.

By necessity writer, director, stagehand, and producer of the play, I learned a number of things first-hand and quickly. One of them was that the more talented the actors, the more fragile their egos and the more vacillating their moods. I learned to appease, coax, cajole, and flatter; I learned all about the iron fist in the velvet glove. And besides that, I had to learn my own lines. Do not think because I wrote them that I knew them by heart. Only people who never write poetry themselves can be caught in that error.

All is well that ends well. The play was a great success; even people from the village came to see it, and the rosy glow it shed over everything around me lasted for at least a week.

Consuela, incidentally, departed not long afterward by mutual agreement with Frau Thomas. It just did not work. She could not function in such a structured environment.

She had been the only member of the staff who had lived in the Home on the children's floor. And even she had to take a crib with one of the youngest children into her room. After she had left, Frau Thomas asked me if I would move into the Home and into Consuela's room. She was not going to engage another nurse. I was flattered and a little overcome. It meant a great vote of confidence. It also meant giving up the treasured privacy of my room in the village and my much-cherished nightly kitchen visits. It also meant less sleep, as I found out very quickly, since every night at eleven o'clock I had to make rounds with a flashlight and put all the chronic bedwetters on the potty. It is one of the lesser-known facts of life that chronic bedwetters frequently don't consider themselves as such and are not inclined to be cooperative. There were always those, of course, who meekly climbed out of bed — never even opening their eyes — and plunged themselves on anything I pushed under them. It was then just a matter of pulling up their nightgowns with lightning speed before they sat right down on it. Changing those little somnambulators from a warmly dripping nightgown into a dry one was greatly hampered by their desire to roll back into bed, dripping or not. The rest of them did not fancy being awakened in the middle of the night for a purpose they deemed entirely unnecessary; until I had developed a workable method, I had a few bumps and bruises to show for my promotion. It was strictly on-the-job training as, it seems in retrospect, were most of the things I learned in life.

I was carefully raised to be physically timid. The words I heard most often during my childhood years were: "Be careful! Try not to get hurt."

I don't blame my parents. Even a scratch on the scar took months to heal; any honest-to-goodness bump might have caused additional trauma to the bone. Being constantly admonished not to take chances, however, was bound to lead to extreme results. Either I would — in defiance of their protectiveness — turn into a veritable dare devil, or for the rest of my life I would automatically respond negatively to all physical challenges. Need I tell you which way I went? I was the successful product of an overly cautious upbringing: anything more venturesome than a three-rung step ladder I approached with the greatest of misgiving.

This does not mean that I did not have my share of daring experiences. I most assuredly did. It simply means that I never looked for them.

I probably suffered more fears in embarrassed silence than I admitted to my peers. I can recall three incidents, though, when I wanted to scream at the people in charge: "Stop it! Right now!! This is *not* what I had in mind!" only to realize with profound shock that they were in charge no longer. They could no more have stopped the course of events than they could have turned off the Niagara Falls for a minute because some tourist had dropped his watch into it.

There was the time at the Montreal World's Fair when my family lured me into a hollowed log that was gently weaving about on a little pond. Too late did I discover that the waterfall thundering down a hillside nearby was to be part of the fun! Another time when I was all for quitting and beating it home was during the rather prolonged delivery of one of my babies. And the third time was a bobsled ride down the steep and twisted mountain road between the Home and the village below.

It is difficult to explain what possessed me to get onto that bobsled, given all the above facts. I was neither blackmailed nor drugged and entirely immune to being challenged to any kind of physical feats. There was only this thirteen-year-old kid who simply talked me into it during my lunch hour.

"Come on, Eva," he coaxed, "it's lots of fun. It really is."

I was skeptical, to say the least. "Do you know how?" I asked rather unenthusiastically. If he had answered something like "Bah, there is nothing to it!" wild horses would not have gotten me on that thing. Instead he looked at me almost as if surprised at the foolishness of such question.

"Of course, I do," he said with simple dignity.

The Wretch! I should have remembered that, like me, he came from Northern Germany where an anthill is considered an elevation.

I regarded the sled, compact, solid, with a sort of guiding device, and then the boy who was one of our "toughies" at the Home. He certainly looked competent, the way he inspected the runners, tested the steering.

"Aw, come on, Eva," he said, "sit down!"

And so I pulled my knitted cap deeper over my ears, spread my coat to both sides and sat down, right behind him, my arms around his waist. He adjusted his position and then the steering in a most knowledgeable manner and we pushed off. The sled started slowly; the driveway near the Home was almost level, but we seemed to gather speed rather rapidly and in no time at all things were flying by on both sides of us in a very disquieting manner. I don't recall exactly at what point it became horribly clear to me that we were out of control. Probably when the postman ahead of us looked over his shoulder and jumped into the nearest snow bank. By the time we approached the village with its narrow alleys, twisted corners, and plaster saints in wooden niches, without slowing down the least bit, I knew we were in big trouble. When I saw us heading straight at the stone wall around the village pump, I was certain we would die. Less than a second before impact the boy, with a tremendous onrush of fear and adrenalin, forced that devil-thing to the right and we shot under the lowest slat of a wooden fence onto a snow heap in front of an apple tree, where we came to a lopsided stop.

I was stretched flat on my back on the sled seat, my driver just as flat on top of me. Neither of us stirred. I thought it likely that he was dead. Definitely, his face would be gone, scraped away by the wooden slat. After all, we had shot through that fence at approximately the speed of sound.

They say that a drowning man sees his entire past rush by him within a few seconds. It wasn't my past but my future that flashed through my head. It seemed to have taken on new aspects in view of the fact that a thirteen-year-old boy was lying motionless on my stomach with no face left, no nose, no chin to speak of, probably no eyebrows . . .

I don't know which one of us moved first. Eventually we both rolled off the sled into the snow. As soon as I was vertical, I was sick. While my eminent driver held a handful of snow against a scratch on his cheek, I threw up behind the apple tree. Later on, when we were trudging up the mountain hauling that cursed sled behind us, we aired our mutual feelings. After the boy, rather squeaky voiced, confessed that he had lain so still on top of me for so long because he was sure I was done for, squashed to death by him and the fence, I decided to forgo killing him at the first opportune moment.

When every four years during the Olympic Games I searched the TV program for the bobsled races, my family was astonished. They could never understand why I sat in front of the tube staring like a hypnotized rabbit at those well-padded, helmetted men flying through the engineer-designed curves of a carefully prepared track. And they just rolled their eyes and tolerantly grinned at each other when I modestly remarked "Well, you know, I did that once. Only my ride was a great deal more daring."

A few overtures of job offers had been made to me toward the end of the year, not only by Frau Thomas, but also by some of the visiting parents whose children had become attached to me. I had no trouble turning them down. There was a strong restlessness in me in those years. Whenever I arrived at a new place, I would say to myself almost fiercely, "I do not have to like it here for I shall not be staying long." There was great comfort in those words and I felt less vulnerable.

So I left my friends at the Home regretfully, but the confinement of the valley I left gladly.

* * * * * * * * * * * * * *

Lilo departed a few months after me. A year later she married a young soldier and became bride and widow in the same month. After the war she returned to the valley and her work at the Home. Pauline never married, and after many working years the two friends moved into a small, cheery apartment on the second floor of one of the village houses to spend their retirement years together.

The last time I visited them, the three of us sat on the corner bench in their kitchen as we had many times before; brightly covered cushions stuffed behind our backs, elbows on the round, white scrubbed kitchen table, the window open toward the mountain range. We were, once again, reminiscing about those bygone days; three graying heads huddled together, giggling over half forgotten sins and mishaps.

"Imagine," I said in wonder, "three neat girls like us being together for a whole year and not a single date among us!"

"But we did have a date, you and I," Pauline said unexpectedly.

"No we didn't." I was indignant. "I would never have forgotten a thing like that. Not in a lifetime!"

"We did," said Pauline, quite matter of factly. "We had a date with two soldiers in the Rathskeller in S. We had a heck of a time getting the evening off together and almost didn't make the bus."

"Well—what happened?" I challenged her, still convinced that she had me mixed up with somebody else.

"Don't you really remember?" Pauline looked at me curiously. "We got to the Rathskeller, in our Sunday best, and they were waiting for us. And you sent them away because they hadn't shaved that morning."

Silence fell around the table. All my ready denial withered in the bud. I still did not remember the road I was to have taken but I recognized the footprint.

For a disquieting second I found myself wondering if I had ruined something possibly permanent for Pauline, but I dismissed the thought immediately. For every unattached male floating around in those days—most likely a soldier on furlough—came at least a dozen date-starved girls. Any fellow so smugly aware of this sorry fact that he would show up for a first date with two-day-old stubbles all over his face surely was not worth grieving over.

Chapter 8

On my return to Berlin I found our apartment invaded by two gentlemen. Living quarters were already at a high premium and a rent control had been imposed to prevent abuses. But the control was enforced only on empty spaces. In the case of furnished rooms it was to a large degree left to the landlord to fix a price on the value of the furnishings. My mother, as I have mentioned before, held quite a high opinion of her furniture. As the one and only concession to her renting purposes she had squeezed a studio couch into a corner of the dining room so that the unfortunate tenant dressed and undressed in the approximately two square feet of space in front of the couch. The rest of the barely medium-sized room was taken up by the large dining table with its circle of chairs, an oversized chest, and two imposing sideboards displaying ornate silver spoons, delicate Meissen plates, brass candlesticks, and ancient pewter pitchers. There was also a beautiful but highly unreliable coffee table of inlaid old Delft tiles; a rounded, antique Luther chair, its carved legs sticking out in all four directions; and an awe-inspiring corner cabinet (dated 1728) filled with crystal and genuine Roemer goblets. The last shapes my mother's roomer would be aware of every night when he hunted for the light switch under the drooping golden silk shade of the floor lamp, would be the life-sized contours of my ancestors looking severely down at him from three of the four walls. For the privilege of living amidst such splendor my mother felt completely justified in charging the government a hefty rent. The second tenant stayed—less elegant and less expensive but a good deal more comfortable—in our former bedroom. My mother had moved into the small room and I was to sleep on the couch in our living room. The living room and the dining room were connected by a double door of frosted glass panels which had been kept open all those years but was now haphazardly "leaned-to," since it had neither bolt nor lock and the latch did not click. This was a direct oversight in my mother's shrewd financial arrangement of things. It was one of those astonishing blank spots that happen once in a while to the most watchful parent or the most careful planner, and it cost me a great deal of anxiety.

Our two tenants were army buddies, career officers working out of headquarters and assigned to the same job. They were the army's liaison men to the *Reichsjugendführer*, the head of the Hitler youth, Baldur von Schirach. I know that in the eyes of anybody who is non-German or not of my generation this would brand the two officers automatically as Nazi-friendly. The truth would very probably be the opposite. The army would have carefully selected such officers for their tempered and realistic view of the political scene, since it was their job to keep the enthusiastic and rather foolish Baldur effectively out of the army's way. In other words, those two men were sort of glorified but low-key babysitters, assigned to keep the head of the youth organizations from interfering with army rules and recruiting, without antagonizing him. I don't know if they liked or despised their job. They joked about it sometimes but only cautiously; a sense of humor was neither required nor valued in official places.

These two men, while best of friends, were quite unlike each other in build and temperament. Both were in their mid thirties; Joseph was large, somewhat phlegmatic and inclined to be pouchy; Walli, quick, jolly, and good humored, was of average height, broad shouldered and of athletic build, all sinew and muscle.

Managing Baldur was one thing, getting around my mother was a different matter. Both men seemed to be well aware of this when I arrived. One evening, a few days after my return, I encountered the two officers in the dark corridor tiptoeing toward the front door.

"What are you doing?" I asked blankly.

Almost simultaneously their fingers flew to their lips, quickly shushing me.

"We are going to the cinema," Walli whispered.

"Why are we whispering?"

"Well . . ." Walli looked slightly discomfited, "You see, we already went there twice this week. And you know your dear mother. She does not approve of going to the movies more than once a week."

He looked at Joseph for reinforcement of this explanation and Joseph nodded in agreement.

"Yep," he said philosophically, "that's a fact, you know."

Keeping Baldur occupied involved a good bit of partying and more than once the two men would return after a "happy hour," cheeks flushed and a gleam in their eyes, with an aura of wine and song about them. Joseph, who occupied our bedroom, was unmarried and had a steady girl friend somewhere in the city. After changing into a clean shirt with unusual speed, he would depart for greener pastures and a night away from home. No such luck for Walli, although the glint in his eyes quite equaled that of his buddy. He was a married man and had a wife and four children living at the other end of the country. Lying wide awake on the corner couch, looking through the darkness toward the unlatched glass door, Walli became very restless, indeed. And one night a very determined Walli decided to pay me a visit. The first of several, in fact.

It wasn't my heart that was in trouble during those midnight appearances. But this knowledgeable, virile, square-built man handed me some of the most horrendously difficult feelings I ever had to deal with. My body, very unfortunately, seemed to become a thing apart from me, ready and willing to fall into some unknown and awesome precipice. It was my head, struggling to stay clear, telling me over and over again: If there was something to that great and mysterious event in a girl's life about which our elders had kept us at arm's length all those years and of which we had only rather nebulous information from our peers, it was not to be shared with this sturdy father of four on a silly living room couch with my mother sleeping two doors down the hall.

And so Walli, falling first over the Luther arm chair and then over the floor lamp, returned to his carved Frisian furniture and corner bed, mission unaccomplished — rejected but never permanently discouraged. During the days he strutted about looking frighteningly optimistic while I grew more apprehensive each day and very resentful toward my mother, whose breezy oversight in her financial arrangements had placed me in this impossible situation. Complaining to her was out of the question; a confrontation between my mother, Walli, and me was simply unthinkable. I would rather have died.

As with so many unsolvable problems, this one resolved itself. Within a few weeks my suitcase was packed again and I was on my way to Muenchen to study journalism.

* * * * * * * * * * * * * *

My year in Munich, my so-called "Lustige Studentenzeit" (merry student days) was a remarkable accumulation of fiascos. One at a time, they might have been manageable; as it was, they compounded each other. I lived in a city whose dialect I could not speak, studying a subject that I did not wish to master, and attending classes I did not understand. I was employed in an office that did not need me and I roomed at a place where I was not welcome.

Initiation to this comedy of errors was swift. Standing rather forlorn in the huge, drafty hall of the Munich railroad station, I asked several people for directions and was answered with blank stares or an unfriendly muttering. The reason for this poor welcome was the way I spoke. Hitler was by birth an Austrian and his rise to power had been largely accomplished in this very city, but the people of the Bavarian capital, with inimitable native logic, blamed the bad times on the people up north; in other words, they made anybody who spoke high German directly responsible for the inconvenience of the war. I finally took a taxi, silently showing the driver the slip with the address.

Ahornstrasse was in one of the oldest parts of the city. Shaded by weary old trees, Nr. 56 was a five-story house, all dignity and decay. The elevator, encased in graceful, handwrought iron grill, had not run for years. The leaded stain glassed windows of the staircase were dingy and unwashed, and the wooden steps showed the bare brass rings of a carpet that had long since been removed.

After my prolonged ringing, Frau Platte herself opened the door. Enid had warned me that her grandmother was eccentric but I was not completely prepared for this bird-like *Gestalt* facing me. A tiny arrow-straight figure in a black wrap, with cropped white hair over deeply hooded eyes and a short, beaked nose, she was so white and thin and bloodless that one wondered how she kept herself vertical.

In blazing anger the hooded owl eyes fastened first on me and then on my suitcase; the old woman's voice, high pitched and imperious, ordered me to leave. I told her my name; I said that Enid had written to her about my arrival. No recognition registered in the sunken eyes, but she did not quite slam the door in my face. When I ventured a few steps inside she did not stop me.

Frau Platte occupied the large, high-ceilinged apartment all by herself except for a small room off the kitchen that was let to a red-haired burly woman, a waitress in a sidewalk café who lived rent-free in return for keeping an eye on the old lady. Mysteriously, the housing shortage had not yet caught up with this situation. Frau Platte either ignored the questionnaires sent out by the city's housing department or else filled them out in such a lunatic fashion that the agency kept postponing all decisions until further investigation.

The two of us were standing in the dark entrance hall, eyeing each other with mutual distrust.

"Get out of here," my prospective landlady rasped in majestic scorn, "I don't take people off the street."

"I am not off the street, Frau Platte. I am a friend of Enid. She wrote to you about me."

"Nobody ever tells me anything," said the old woman querulously. A long, angry tirade against her family, the world at large, and the Prussians most specifically followed this statement, interrupted only by repeated invitations for me to leave.

I had a long journey behind me; the experience at the station had been disheartening, and now this. The only reason I did not grab my suitcase and walk out the door was that I had no idea where else to go. So I just stood there and listened until Frau Platte ran out of steam. Her fury simply evaporated.

Looking once again at me and my suitcase she sighed, all dignity and suffering now.

"Well, I am quite resigned that I shall be murdered in my bed one night by strangers sent here by my family. What time is it? It must be past seven! I must revitalize or I shall be ill. Which will be your fault," she added but without much rancor. She walked off into the living room, leaving me to find my way around the apartment. Enid had told me which room I might use and where I would find bedding and linen. And so I had found myself a place to stay only because I had refused to be thrown out.

From then on Frau Platte accepted my presence as merely another one of those unjust and undeserved incidents that befall helpless old women. This was a subject that was near and dear to her heart and about which she could lecture me for hours. Although she began to depend on me a great deal for errands and company, she never stopped boycotting my stay, pretending to forget my name, periodically hiding the toilet paper, and charging me an outrageous rent. At the same time, she sent a bill for my rent to Enid. Since Enid and I were too tactful to talk money in this delicate set-up, we didn't find out about this double billing until years later. On the other hand, I had to thank my erratic landlady for not being evicted by the housing department when they finally got around to investigate, since I was staying there without official rent permission.

A single person occupying so large a place was practically unthinkable. Her family, worried about the old lady and the circumstances, had at one time succeeded in moving her on a trial basis into a home for the aged. It was a large, sprawling manor outside the city, surrounded by a park and a vegetable garden. Frau Platte used to wander about there, a rhubarb leaf on her head against possible sunstroke, poking her cane into the vegetable beds to see how the radishes were coming. Inside the house she had taken to wearing a genteel veil over her face; that is, she tied a strip of black gauze around her head, covering her eyes and forehead. Since she could barely see through the gauze, she kept bumping into the furniture which she then rearranged for her greater convenience. When, during a temporary stay in the infirmary, she got out of bed one night and stuck a clothespin on the nose of her sleeping roommate to cure her snoring, the administrator gently hinted to her family that she might be better off in a place of her own and so she returned triumphantly to her apartment on Ahornstrasse.

The day came when a city official appeared to inspect the apartment and inquire about those odd questionnaires. Frau Platte gave the agent a similar reception to the one she had given me, and when the man, at long last, lost patience and demanded to see the entire apartment, she announced that it was past the time for her revitalization and that all further postponement would result in her fainting dead away.

"Go ahead," said the exasperated official, who had a mental picture of bottles of pink and green pep pills, "I can wait."

And while I in joyful anticipation faded into the farthest corner of the room and pretended to study my notes, Frau Platte seated herself in the middle of the sofa and prepared for the daily task of rejuvenating her system.

Carefully rolling up the black tube-like woolen garment she always wore, she exposed a kind of Isabella-colored cotton slip. (This color derives its name from Queen Isabella, Columbus' patroness, who, at Columbus' departure, is said to have vowed not to change her shirt until his safe return.)

"What is she doing? Make her stop!" the nervous official demanded.

Tears of suppressed laughter were running down my cheeks. Not trusting my voice, I shrugged my shoulders to indicate that I was powerless. I couldn't have stopped her even if it would have meant our imminent eviction.

The slip, too, was now daintily rolled up and the tips of two withered little nipples appeared. The official's eyes flew to the door, evidently considering flight. Resolved, however, not to be tricked by the antics of a crazy old woman, he was standing his ground.

Holding the two rolls of clothes with her elbows, Frau Platte turned her attention now to her petticoat and a pair of bloomers slowly peeling them down toward her hips and presenting the aghast official with the unobstructed view of about five inches of wrinkly skin around a dark brown belly button. Next she opened a black box beside her and took out a long electric cord with two handles on one end. Freeing one arm for a moment, she expertly plugged the other end of the cord into the electrical outlet behind her.

At that point her visitor gave up. Announcing over his shoulder that we could be sure he would be back, he fled through the nearest exit, and shortly afterward we heard the front door slam.

The old lady, unmoved by either victory or threat, had already forgotten about him. Pushing the vibrating handles into either side of her belly button, she was fully and pleasantly occupied revitalizing herself.

There is nothing cheerful to tell about my so-called employment. The deciding factor in choosing the university of Munich had been a financial consideration. My mother had a publisher friend in Hanover who had assured her that I would have a part-time job in his branch office there. All details would be explained to me when I reported for work. In consequence, my first trip, after I had found living quarters, was to the indicated address where I hoped to schedule my working hours around lectures and seminars. I found a flight of rooms filled with intimidating activity, and after having been given the usual run-around, I finally faced a woman of undetermined age who seemed to be the office supervisor. She had been informed of my coming. Her instructions were short, her voice non-committal, her face, under make-up applied to perfection, was pure marble. I was to be a stenographer-on-call, she said. My working hours would be irregular. She then handed me a paycheck for one month and turned back to her desk.

"Don't you need my address and telephone?" I asked, not a little taken aback by this total lack of congeniality.

"Yes. Of course," she said, sounding bored by the fact that I was still standing there. "You may leave it at the front desk."

Slightly squashed by this encounter, I wondered if I would like working in such an unfriendly atmosphere. But the check in my pocket felt good; it would be sufficient for rent and food that month.

Weeks went by and I was never called. When I went back on the first day of the next month, the same woman, barely looking up from her desk, held up another check. I did not reach for it.

"I have not worked at all so far."

"Well, you are on call; you were probably not needed." She shrugged her elegant shoulders.

"Why am I paid then?" I asked, embarrassed.

"You are paid because you are on call," she said, waving the check impatiently in the air.

I took the check because I needed it, feeling depressed and mortified. Every time the telephone rang during the next month my heart started pounding; I hoped and feared at the same time I would finally be summoned to do some work. I fretted over the possibility that they had called and gotten Frau Platte on the phone. That might conceivably have terminated the most solid employment.

When I returned to the office for the third time I was determined to have it out with the supervisor.

"I have not been called!" I said, braver than I felt.

"Here is your check." Again that impatient waving without looking up from her desk.

"I am not on call at all, am I?" I said with sudden enlightenment.

"I have been instructed to give you a monthly paycheck. Please, take it. I am very busy," said the woman.

"Why am I getting paid?" I said angrily.

For the first time the woman looked me full in the face, a long, silent stare that drove the blood to the roots of my hair. Quickly losing interest again, the woman's attention returned to her desk.

"Take your check, please."

I took it and left and never went back again. My mother's friend had meant well, but he had gone about it the wrong way. It left me angry and bitterly humiliated. I began feeling better only after I had firmly resolved to pay them back their money, every blooming penny of it, as soon as I could afford it. The mental picture of my walking into that office one day and dumping the money (in coin!) silently and contemptuously on that woman's desk, right under her arrogant nose, went a long way toward lifting my spirits. But when I finally could have afforded this impressive gesture, the publisher was dead, his company had been swept out of existence, and I could not have remembered the woman's face or name if my life had depended on it.

No tuition was charged at German universities. A few dues had to be paid for membership at the mensa and athletic organizations. There were no prescribed curriculum and no advisers. The registrar told me to study the announcements of lectures and seminars posted in the large entrance hall. Completely at sea, I asked the advice of anybody near me who seemed to be taking in this maze of messages with a certain amount of comprehension. In the end I registered for two classes in journalism, one class in philosophy, and two seminars: one in advanced French and one in drama critique, all of which I faithfully attended in the beginning. My initial excitement soon turned into dismay when I discovered that I understood less than half of what was being said. Neither the books nor the professors seemed inclined to explain the missing other half. Nobody ever mentioned to me that there was such a thing as prerequisite courses and introductory seminars that would open the way to an understanding of the subject. Dismay turned into frantic frustration, which in turn became a general listless disenchantment. It effectively extinguished any spark of scholarly curiosity that might have been present at one time. The worst of the classes was philosophy, where I had chosen a lecture series on Emanual Kant for the simple reason that I had heard him often quoted as the last instance of intellectual wisdom and insight. It never occurred to me that for this very reason he also should be the last of the philosophers to be studied. I was somewhat in the position of piano student who has just mastered the scales to his teacher's satisfaction and is attempting to play one of Bach's Brandenburg Concertos that night.

It was not the professor's fault. He was a slender, prematurely gray man, somewhat above medium height, with high color, lively blue eyes, and a youthful, sportsman's way of dressing. He was neither remote nor condescending; he addressed his students directly and his voice was invigorating. He spoke high German and he did not mumble or slur his words. So why did I not understand what he was saying?

I remember many desolate hours spent in one of the gloomy study rooms of the university with its row of high, narrow windows and its book-lined walls; an open chapter on Kant or an essay on 18th century classic French poems in front of me, staring at the sky outside and wishing myself a thousands miles away. Not during the worst of math tests or the most boring physics class had I ever experienced such an overwhelming feeling of intellectual inadequacy. This was the only time in my life that I ever wondered if I might not be stupid after all. Missing entirely were a sense of self-challenge, any trace of tenacity, the slightest wish to "hang in there," come hell or high water. I wanted to deal with people, with flesh-and-blood situations; I wanted to learn how to find viable solutions to real problems. Instead I was being propelled into the realm of the abstract where I could feel no ground under my feet and the air was too rarefied for me to function. Miscast and confused, I wanted to be gone and out of there.

* * * * * * * * * * * * * *

One more dark and awful fact has to be added so that this account might be complete and can be laid to rest.

I have known many young men who met a violent death, all of them of my generation. There is nothing selective about a grenade or a machine gun. But I have also known four men, much older than I, who were executed singly and deliberately by people who thought it was right and fitting to do so. One of them was hanged by the Nazis; two were hanged by the Allies, and one died under the hands of Tito's guerillas.

The one executed by the Nazis was my professor, the teacher of Kant. He had been working with the underground, printing and distributing leaflets, calling for civil and military disobedience. I did not learn this until much later, and it seemed sadly ironic to me that a man who taught generations of students Kant's categorical imperative: "Act so that every one of your actions could be the law of the land tomorrow!" died because he had set his own conscience above the law of his land which he had judged unworthy of obeying.

The second man was the prominent orthopedic surgeon to whom my mother had taken me when I was sixteen and who had been kind to me and given my mother good advice. He had been hanged by the Allies for experimenting with bone transplants on prisoners.

The third was the general who had been in charge of the German military forces on the Greek Islands when Italy switched sides. He had followed orders from Berlin to treat captured Italian officers who had actively entered into combat against German troops not as prisoners of war but as traitors.

The fourth man was a member of the Admiral's staff of Athens who had elected to walk home with his sailors, retreating north across the Balkan Mountains, rather than board the last plane out of Greece. He was skinned alive by some of Tito's bandits, his crime apparently being that he was the ranking officer in that little group of captured men.

I had known those four men, talked with them, laughed with them, and liked them. Some of their executioners, eventually, were executed themselves. Others were decorated. A few of them might have simply gone home and, for the rest of their lives, tried to forget that there was a time so disoriented and brutal that it had turned human beings into monsters.

My guess is that most of them went back to their ordinary lives with the conviction that they had, at one time, been instrumental in meting out this most pliable and elusive of human concepts, justice.

* * * * * * * * * * * * * * *

The first month of each summer vacation a student had to spend in the Labor-Replacement Force (we had such wonderful names for everything.) For one month the students were assigned to various factories, enabling workers to take some time off. Once again we went through a routine physical examination, after which we received our assignment in the mail.

My letter arrived three days after my physical check-up. "Report June . . . at 6:30 a.m. at the gate of compound XY at Gernersdorf," a small borough outside Munich.

Compound XY at Gernersdorf turned out to be an ammunition factory. At the gate I had to identify myself and was tagged. As far as I could make out, there were no other students around. My shoes were confiscated and I was given a pair of felt slippers, two sizes too big, and a smock.

"Why the slippers?" I asked, and was told that nailed shoe soles might set off sparks.

In a large hallway two rows of women were seated along the walls, each one with a scale in front of her and a long, wooden tray at her left elbow, filled with something that looked like concentrated coal dust.

The foreman deposited a stack of flat, round, silky looking bags beside me, about the size of a tennis ball, and told me to fill each one with so many grams of gun powder. The black stuff, it turned out, was not coal dust. The scale, though rather large in appearance, was finer tuned than a postage scale; grams and milligrams were clearly marked.

"Be precise," said the foreman. "A fraction of a gram too much means missing the target, too little means hitting our own people."

End of instructions. There was no speech on safety measures, no warnings, precautions or moral support. There was no hello or goodbye. I didn't even know if there were any emergency exits in the building and I never thought of asking. From then on it would be five and a half days a week sitting in front of the scale, eyes glued to the black, quivering arrow in front of me, fingers digging into the gun powder with a small spoon, feeding and unfeeding the silky bag . . . a little too much means hitting our own people . . . hitting our own people. At night in bed, the black arrow would dance in front of my closed eyes. A deep furrow began to appear between my eyebrows, directly over my nose.

The other women never talked to me, and after some half-hearted attempts I gave up trying. A whistle blew at noon announcing a forty-five-minute break. We sat outside on the few wooden benches or in the grass and emptied our brown paper bags, which were then carefully folded and put away for re-use. (Paper bags had become irreplaceable.) The whistle blew again and we silently got up, trooped through the door, and sat down behind our scales. As I write this down now it seems to come straight out of a horror movie, but I didn't think so at the time. It was just one of those things, then.

The wooden trays were carried by prisoners of war. They carried the full ones into the hall on their shoulders and came back for the empty ones. These POWs were young and poker-faced. I would have loved to start a conversation with them, trying out my French; even in English I could have managed a friendly exchange, but I quickly abandoned the idea. Talking to prisoners-of-war in a foreign language while weighing gun powder for German grenades would have been sheer lunacy. However, I often stole a glance at their faces—they were like shuttered windows—and I wondered what they were thinking while carrying that deadly stuff to us. "Be precise," the foreman had said. Too much would overshoot the target . . ." The target had to be their buddies, their comrades . . . Lord forbid we should overshoot the target.

Once at a movie, the newsreel showed enemy planes unloading para-troopers. The young soldiers drifted down slowly, strapped to their parachutes, while the German ground forces picked them off, one by one, like ducks at a carnival booth. After a while I started to cry hysterically. The young man with me panicked. "Stop it, stop it!!" he kept whispering, shaking my shoulders, "Those are *enemies*!" But I could not stop.

There was a single army corporal in charge of the POWs. He was called the fireworker—not exactly a confidence-inspiring name for some-body working with gun powder. Since he was positively the only non-robot-like figure in the whole ghastly assembly, and more out of boredom than anything else, I struck up a mildly flirtatious acquaintance with him. He responded like a drowning man.

When the whistle shrilled at the end of the day, our hands froze. There was no question of finishing what we had started or tidying up our work-place; the whistle blew and all work ceased; the spoon was dropped in mid-air, the chair pushed back and the hall emptied in seconds. The night shift would take over where we had left off.

Toward the end of the second week the foreman stopped at my chair.

"You the student? Well, don't come back after tomorrow."

"What?"

"You are out. Dismissed. You didn't pass the physical."

Not again! Hot anger stiffened my whole body.

"There must be some mistake," I said, trying to sound indifferent.

"Notice came this morning. You quit after tomorrow. Take it up with them." He shrugged and moved on.

"There is nothing wrong with me!" I shouted furiously at his back.

The woman in front of me turned around and stared.

"You crazy or something?!" she hissed.

It brought me to my senses. The full meaning of the message sank in. I was discharged, free to walk out of this nightmare. Heaven should be thanked on my knees. My whistle had just blown.

I dropped the half-filled spoon back into the tray, pushed the chair back, stood up and stalked out. Tomorrow be damned. The war would just have to do without me tomorrow.

Chapter 9

The gangly youngster, a book under his arm, crossed the street and went into the park. The apartment often seemed too small for his growing bones, and his mother's list of things to be done was unending. He walked through the narrow path where the untrimmed bushes on both sides were beginning to form an archway and came to an open space that spread, green and airy, along the width and length of a city block. Grass was reclaiming the once carefully tended flower beds. The pebbled walks were dotted with wooden benches. Sturdy and comfortable in spite of their peeling paint, they were half hidden in little groves of trees and bushes. He flopped himself on the first bench, occupied only by an elderly man, opened his book and began to read.

"Go away, boy," said the man at the other end of the bench.

The youngster looked up in amazement. He doubted what he had heard.

"Go away," said the man again. He was not looking at the boy; his arms were crossed over his chest and he was staring straight ahead over the meadow that once had been a lawn.

"Find another bench."

The boy scowled at him. Another grown-up who was trying to tell him what he could or could not do.

"I can sit here if I want to," he said.

"You don't want to sit here," said the man. His voice was tired, unargumentative.

"I do so! You can't tell me . . ." the boy began and then stopped. The man had dropped his arms; his hands were resting on his knees now. He still was not looking at the youngster. Sewn onto his dark jacket, over his chest, glared a large yellow star with the word *Jew* written on it.

Almost half a century later — and only because I had asked him: "Where did you see the first of those yellow stars?" — did my brother tell me this story.

"What did you do then?" I asked him, although I knew the answer before he spoke.

"Nothing," he said. "I wanted to stay to show him that I didn't care, but I was scared. I got up and went to another bench."

Like my brother Dolfi, I had spent the last years in parts of the country where there had not been any such stars. Like him, I was not prepared for it when I encountered them for the first time.

It happened on the subway during one of my visits to Berlin. As usual the car was overcrowded; people were standing in the aisle, hanging on to the straps overhead. At one station a small, elderly lady entered; she looked so frail that a seated passenger felt moved to motion her to take his seat. The woman seemed to shrink within herself. With a quick, nervous shaking of the head she declined the offer. Just then the train thudded around a corner and the woman's hand, which had been clutching her handbag against her chest, reached out for a hold, revealing a yellow star: *Jew*. I was standing opposite her, and this unholy thing was glaring directly at me. It seemed to erase the small figure who wore it. It was large, dominant, hideous. It was like a whiplash across the heart.

The man who had offered her his seat glanced around quickly and furtively to see if anybody had noticed his sympathetic gesture. But the passengers near us were looking expressionless into space. The woman was once again pressing her bag against her chest, covering the ancient symbol that isolated her from us and us from each other. The aura of fear around her was almost tangible. I found myself struggling for some kind of emotional plateau from which I could deal with this experience. While doing so I averted my eyes, and my face seemed to be taking on, entirely on its own, the same kind of vacuous expression I saw on all the faces around me.

* * * * * * * * * * * * * *

When I returned to Berlin I told my mother that I was not going back to Munich. From the distracted air with which she listened I concluded that she had considered the possibility herself. Her two officers had been reassigned and had left. They had been cheerful and attentive; they had spoiled her in a way, and she missed them. She was reluctant now to take in a new set of strangers. To live alone in the apartment, on the other hand, to weather the terrifying air raids at night without human companionship, was unthinkable. The Department for Housing would, eventually, have come to the same conclusion, although for different reasons. My refusal to go back to Munich appeared to be the ideal solution and so there was little protest.

Within forty-eight hours I had found a job as a medical secretary in the practice of an elderly professor, a specialist for allergies and thyroid diseases. Once again I commuted by subway, leaving at 8 a.m. and returning at five in the afternoon, early enough to do the household chores. My mother did the cooking, and every evening we faced each other over the supper table as if I had never been away. Once again, on Sunday mornings, we would go on long hikes just outside the city limits, after which my mother treated us to the weekly visit to the cinema. Within our fragile relationship we were back to square one.

A few years ago I read in an article that people tend to think of the "Dark Ages" as having been literally dark, sunless, steeped in perpetual twilight. It struck an instant chord in me: that is precisely the way I think of those months, my last war-time stay in Berlin. It was summer when I came back, yet I don't remember a single bright morning. All those long days seemed to have been dusky and bleak. Our windows were draped for the nightly blackout, and not all the drapes could be removed every morning. Our already dark apartment was now, in truth, steeped in perpetual twilight. At night, the city was like the inside of an inkpot.

The population was divided into three elements. There were those — invisible to us — who set up and enforced the rules. And there were those who watched and denounced the offenders, delivering them into the hands of their judges. They were visible but unknown to us, and, in consequence, they were an element to be feared. And there was the vast majority who worked long hours each day; who prayed to find a letter from Russia or Africa when they came home at the end of the day; who stood patiently in long lines in front of the butcher or grocery store; who tread lightly, spoke cautiously, and in general tried their prudent best not to stand out in the crowd.

We were told by radio and newspapers—all of them controlled by the state—what was happening in the world and on the fronts. My mother, more often than not as soon as the evening news came on, would say to me almost automatically: *"Stell den Quatschkopf ab."* ("Turn that drivel off.")

We were informed by our minister of propaganda, Goebbels, in a regular radio broadcast, of the state of affairs, officially called: "The Hour of the Nation," and promptly dubbed by the sardonic Berliners: "Little Clubfoot's Story Hour."

We were not told of the concentration camps although we knew about them or thought we did. We did not know how many there were, or exactly where they were located, but we thought we had a pretty good idea who were in them: dyed-in-the-wool communists; people who had shown signs of passive resistance to party or state programs; preachers who had delivered ambiguous messages from the pulpit; people who dragged their feet complying with war regulations; and, most of all and closest to home, people who told political jokes.

I knew only one person who actually had been in a concentration camp, our neighbor, who lived in the apartment beside us. He was an author and a poet who had written some sarcastic lines about German politics. He had been sent away for "re-education." Only once did I hear him talk of that time, when he mentioned during a conversation that they had tried to get a theater group started in the camp. He did not look and talk like a man who had seen unspeakable horrors. They apparently kept the political prisoners away from the Jewish inmates, at least in the beginning.

The political jokes were the people's only recourse, their single hidden vent to let off steam and frustration. Nobody knew where those jokes came from; they cropped up like mushrooms after great rains and found their way across the country overnight, which is all the more astonishing, since no one of sound mind would ever have told such a joke to anybody but a very good friend.

In the beginning they were mild. Amused by the weaknesses of our three "incomparable leaders" — a term they sometimes bestowed on each other — these stories zeroed in on target.

There was Goering with his boundless vanity. "Did you know that he has two sets of all his medals and ribbons? One for his uniforms and one for his nightgowns."

Or Goebbels with his lies and flagrant affairs with beautiful actresses. "Have you heard that he signed up for the Olympics? In two categories: Breast crawling and sidestepping."

And Hitler himself with his delusions of grandeur: It seemed that the Lord had invited all the heads of state for an interview. As they entered, St. Peter introduced each one in turn and each time the Lord rose from his throne and inclined his head in greeting. However, when Hitler was introduced the Lord stayed seated, just nodding slightly. "Lord," whispered St. Peter, "he also is a head of state. Will you not stand up for him, too?" "You think I'm crazy?" whispered the Lord. "He'll sit down on my throne!"

Each one of these stories, told to the wrong person, might have gotten the unlucky storyteller into a heap of trouble. There would have been political probing and unpleasant Gestapo interviews and, if these were not considered satisfactory, a few months of re-education in a concentration camp. (It was said, though, that Goering made his aides tell him political jokes and that he roared with laughter at some of them. I suspect those were the ones about Goebbels.)

Some jokes were genuinely funny, some were hard hitting, all were surprisingly perceptive.

As the war wore on, the jokes became harsher, more hostile. So, too, became the punishment to anyone who was caught. There was no question now of re-education. Those bitter "jokes" were high treason and were punished accordingly. I know of a party given by one of the Hohenzollern princes, during which some of these stories were told. It ended in the execution of two of the guests. All it took was one wrong person in the room.

People still groped their way through the darkness to theaters and concerts, often interrupted by air raids. Once in a while my mother entertained a gathering of friends; the refreshments were meager, the conversation lively. I probably heard most of the political stories I know at those times. I remember my mother standing in our little entrance hall one evening greeting the guests as they arrived; while taking their coats, she would announce to each guest in turn that she had invited Herr B., the new assistant director of a publishing house. "I believe he is rather in tune with our government," she would mumble into the coat as she adjusted it onto the hanger. At that party no stories were told. A host owed it to his guests to inform them of an outsider. The trouble was that the hosts were not always informed themselves.

* * * * * * * * * * * * * * *

The star of David was seen less and less on the streets of Berlin. One weekend my mother and I went up north to visit my brother's boarding school. Our train had pulled into a village station; we were sitting, eight to a compartment, looking idly out of the window. At a side track, a stone's throw away from our train, another train had pulled up seemingly to no purpose since it had not stopped alongside any platform. Slowly our minds registered that it was filled to capacity with people sitting or standing very close to each other. Somehow they looked different, and suddenly, as they shifted their positions, we could see the glare of yellow stars. "Jews," said somebody in the compartment, as if that explained things. Silence. One never knew what one's neighbor was thinking. That was part of the horror.

"Where are they going?" asked a woman who was either very brave or very naive.

"Madagascar?" said another woman. This was not meant or taken as a joke, however sad. All of us, at one time or another, had heard of a plan to deport the German Jews to the island of Madagascar. Few had believed it.

"They are being settled in the liberated Polish territory," said an authoritative voice. "Farming, you know."

That was the end of the conversation among us. Did we all jump at that straw? I must have believed it — or wanted to believe it — because I remember saying to my mother after we were alone: "But they don't know *anything* about farming!"

* * * * * * * * * * * * * * *

Food became scarcer with each ration period. Diabetes, heart and gallbladder diseases declined; people began to suffer from long bouts with boils and trench mouth; tuberculosis was on the rise. With the December ration cards, special coupons for sweets were given out, our Christmas treat. On the day the rations were issued my mother asked me to take some letters to the mailbox. I would find them ready and stamped on the dining room table, she said. The table was, as usual, overflowing with papers, bills and lists, my mother's business and private correspondence. I located the bundle of letters and walked to the nearby mailbox. A few hours later my mother was frantically looking for the Christmas coupons. Had they, by any chance, been between the letters? It soon became hopelessly clear that they had. I had stuffed our Christmas coupons into the mailbox.

"Go and get them back!" ordered my enraged mother. I was aghast. "How can I? There is no way I can get them back!"

"Then find one! Look at the mail box; the postal district should be marked on it. Then go there and bring them back."

Slowly I got into my coat and opened the front door. I had not the foggiest notion what I was to do.

"Don't come home without them," my mother called after me, by way of putting more bounce into my departure.

The district office was marked on the box as my mother had predicted. It was three subway stations away. This was not a regular post office but a central place for collecting and sorting mail. Somehow I got inside. Desperation rather than courage made me tenacious. Somehow I made somebody listen to me. In the end I found myself in the part of the immense hall where the mail of our region was being sorted. The men working there were tired, sullen, and greatly inconvenienced by my bizarre request. But they were not entirely unsympathetic. They, too, had gotten that day their first ration of sweets in many a month. They began to sift through the large carts in which the mail was transported from one end of the hall to the other. And somehow they found the coupons.

Near the central building I passed an open candy store. Miraculously there were no lines of people waiting and I went in and exchanged my coupons for two large chocolate bars and a small bag of marzipan.

"You are awfully quiet," said my mother while we were eating our supper. Since I had arrived with our candy rations in my bag she had been very cheerful.

"There was a little boy standing across the street from the candy store. He wore a star. He looked so bad. I don't mean his clothes. I mean his face . . . I wanted to give him one of the candy bars."

My mother stopped eating and looked at me.

"There was nobody else around," I said hastily, interpreting her wary glance correctly.

"But he would not take it. He backed away from me; he was frightened. I could not make him take it."

Now my mother was quiet, too, and we finished our meal in silence. It was the last of such stars I remember seeing.

* * * * * * * * * * * * * *

Two of my brothers came home for a short Christmas furlough. It was during that time that my mother called us into the living room one afternoon. She was sitting on the sofa, looking at once solemn and deeply disturbed.

"Close the door," she ordered and then spoke to us in whispers even though there was nobody else in the apartment.

"I have heard something terrible! I have heard that they actually *beat* people in the concentration camps!"

We looked at her, wordlessly, trying to absorb yet another element of the unknown and fearful.

My brother Peter was the first one to speak.

"Did you talk to someone who got beaten?"

"No," said my mother, a little reluctant, "but . . ."

"Did you talk to somebody who *saw* such a beating?"

"No, . . ." My mother was floundering now, on the defense, "but I heard it from a very reliable source."

"You heard from someone who was neither beaten nor had he seen such a thing," Peter said sharply. "That someone, very probably, heard it from a similar source. That's how rumors get started. Don't do that!"

My other brother and I silently sided with him. It made sense and it gave us a way out. Nobody wants to lie in bed at night wrestling with terrible images. We were barely twenty and we preferred to doubt; it gave us a little space for some laughter and light-heartedness. Not even my mother went about agonizing all the time, although she was much more convinced of the evil around us than we were. It is difficult to worry constantly about your troubled neighbor when your own life is badly in disarray.

The air raids became heavier and ever more frequent. Berliners in their opaquely blacked-out city had rediscovered that there were nights of full moon and starlit skies, but they rejoiced little in this discovery. These were the nights when the sirens shrilled more than once and the hollow bark of the flak resounded through the shimmering darkness and the buildings trembled beneath the ceaseless explosions above. Search lights slid over the sky like long, thin, pale fingers trying to get hold of a deadly insect. Earlier, when the bombings had been limited to the industrial parts of the city, I would sometimes watch those fingers, watch how one of them would catch a small, silvery dot in the purple dome and pin it down to be joined instantly by half a dozen other beams. The plane, thus caught in the cross-point of many search lights and the visible target of every flak fire around the city, would desperately try to escape this web. I would watch this life and death struggle above me breathlessly and feel the inexplicable urge to root for the underdog stirring within me, quickly to be quelled by reason.

This was not the underdog. Not any more. Firebombs would rain now onto the residential districts, coming ever closer to our part of the city.

At the start, when the sirens screamed, we struggled out of bed but we would not go down to the basement. Neither did most of the other tenants. Regulations said that we had to go, but everybody would simply claim that they had slept right through the warning. Our air raid warden, who was responsible for the appearance of all tenants in the basement, did not for one moment believe those excuses and he put an end to them once and for all by patrolling the stairways armed with a frying pan and a hammer. The racket would have raised the dead; nobody could have slept through it. Still, we would not go down but would sit on the floor of the narrow hall, under the frame of an open door with cushions around us and on top of our heads in case of flying debris. But the night came when we heard for the first time the soft, screeching whistle of the falling bombs and we were frightened enough to get up and try to make a dash for the basement. It was too late, though; flak shells seemed to explode directly over our heads; the windows above the stairs shattered, splinters flying everywhere, and we ran back into the apartment and crouched down on the floor, burying our heads in the pillows.

After that night we always went to the basement, as did everybody else, although the first people to die in our neighborhood had all been in the basement shelter of their building. It was our corner drugstore and we had known some of the dead people. It was whispered that they had not been killed by the tumbling walls but were still alive after the air raid was over and had drowned from the bursting pipes in the basement long before any help arrived on the scene.

After that I never felt safe in our so-called air shelter. Pipes were running everywhere along the ceiling. Even down there we could hear the whistling of the descending bombs. Those nights we spent in that basement shelter are all melted into one single image in my memory: sitting on a hard, narrow chair near the wall alongside the other tenants, not talking, listening . . . thinking over and over again: "I will *not* be the first one to panic!" cupping my chin with my hand to keep my teeth from chattering.

When the all-clear sirens sounded we would file out of the basement, climbing over broken glass and ceiling debris, everyone anxious to check the damage to their own apartment. Often it was the fall-out from the flak that broke the windows and pock-marked the walls. Eventually, most windows were boarded. After the first firebombs fell in our neighborhood we all went to help extinguish the fire. I remember how everyone was willing to go out into the raw winter night, risking, as it were, life and limb, but nobody wanted to risk their bucket. Buckets could not be replaced. They would be going, water-filled or empty, through the human chain and simply disappear in the end. There were enough hands but never enough buckets at those first fire rescues.

Eventually, when circles of fire were thrown around whole city blocks, nobody bothered with anything but trying to come out alive. But by that time I had left Berlin, and this is not part of my own experiences, and I shall not talk about it.

After a night of air raids, people in the subway the next morning would look bleary-eyed and gray but anybody whose house was still standing and whose limbs were still sound would go to work as always. The daily routine was dreary and, at the same time, sanity-sustaining.

My work as a medical secretary was interesting and would have been pleasant but for my professor's assistant, Fräulein Zell. A woman in her thirties, dark-haired, slender and rather pretty, a malevolent sprite of considerable magnitude, she was bluntly vocal and at the same time secretive and conniving. The professor himself was an elderly man, large, a bit stooped, with a round, rosy, childlike face. He was slow of speech and motion and invariably kind. I think he would have liked to retire, to be done and gone, but for reasons I did not know, he was still practicing full time. He was a thyroid specialist and had developed a method of treatment about which he had given a series of lectures at the university. He had also done work with allergies and it was Fräulein Zell's job to give the extensive allergy tests and prepare patients for examination. Originally she had been the secretary, and when the professor lost his assistant he had trained her for the job. I was her replacement, and she was as jealous and suspicious of me as any secretary who had bettered herself by marrying the boss. My job was to schedule appointments, receive the patients, help them fill out questionnaires, record the history of their illness, and see to it that the professor's and Fräulein Zell's work ran on smooth, parallel tracks. I marked down all treatments the patients had received and eventually billed them. Every time Fräulein Zell crossed the room she looked disapprovingly over my shoulder. Whenever she had a free minute she sat at her desk next to mine manicuring her nails, and when she was not giving me the benefit of her sexual experiences she was bad-mouthing any living being she had ever met, with the possible exception of the professor and her cat.

PART IV

1943-1944

Athens, Greece

Chapter 10

The war, like a monstrous bulldozer, rolled into its fourth year and came to a grinding halt before Stalingrad, sending shockwaves into the farthest corner of Germany. During the first Russian winter, word had spread like wildfire: our boys are freezing to death! In spite of history's lessons, the army had not been prepared for the awesome Russian winters. Never officially admitted, a gathering of warm clothing was set into motion and every wife, mother, and sister turned her closets and chests inside out. Blankets, sweaters, gloves, socks, and woolen underwear were carried by the armloads to the big trucks that made the rounds through cities and villages. The hope that any of the clothes you gave would reach your own kin was nil, but somebody else's blanket would warm your son or brother, just as your gloves and socks would keep an unknown young boy from freezing his feet or hands off in the icy Russian nights.

Now, in this fourth winter of feeble hope and growing misery, it was metal that was demanded. Any metal at all that was not necessary for survival. Again the trucks rolled through the city, again the knock of every door.

"What are we going to give?" I asked my mother.

"Nothing," she answered grimly.

"We've got to give *something*" I wailed. "We are already in bad grace. How about the umbrella stand?"

"There is not going to be a single bullet made out of anything coming from my house!" said my mother with great finality.

And there wasn't. When the knock came, I was sent to the door to announce that we did not have any spare metal whatsoever.

How very much this incident typified our relationship in those days. First my mother's courageous decision, which, if repercussions should follow, would rest on her as the head of the household. Then my feeble intervention, and her firm insistence; yet, when it came to the embarrassing and disagreeable execution of the decision, it was left to me. And, lastly, the proud phrasing: "My house!" meaning our modest four-room apartment. And did I not live there, too? There is, however, no getting around the unflattering fact that, if I had had a voice in this matter, I would very likely have surrendered the umbrella stand.

It rained a great deal that fall. The drooping linden trees shed their leaves listlessly, foregoing all golden glory. I remember standing at the kitchen window, looking out at the dreariness of the November afternoon and seeing no silver lining at all on any horizon. I stood there often when I came home from work, lost in a morose moodiness, which I found hard to shake. Perhaps I remember this so well because never again in my life did I feel as forlorn and hopeless as on those dark November evenings at our kitchen window in the autumn of 1942.

My mother and I had returned to a kind of status quo in our relationship which she seemed to accept for the time being, but which I felt threatened to wipe me out. Every minute of the day was lived by my mother's rules, every conversation was initiated and ended by her, just as her rising in the mornings and bedtimes at night had to be mine, also. Every ounce of self-respect and independence in me was endangered. I knew I could and should no longer submit to being treated like a child, yet I did not know how to help the adult in me to emerge. I only knew with ever-growing certainty that I had to break away or go under.

Help came without fanfare or drama. Young women, not engaged in war-necessary occupations, were drafted systematically to war service. It was simple mathematics to figure out when my turn would come. If I wanted a choice in the matter, I had to stay a jump ahead of the draft. I had passed my twenty-first birthday and it gradually dawned upon me that, legally, I was a free agent. For the first time I would not need my mother's permission to act.

With this overwhelming realization in mind, I met with Hanna one Saturday afternoon in a little café. While drinking ersatzkaffee and poking our forks absentmindedly into something that looked and tasted like a soggy billfold, she told me about her job. She had graduated from a prestigious language school as an interpreter and translator of English. Her

aptitude and marks were high and she was employed at the Navy Intelligence in Berlin. She told me that she loved her job and that the men she
worked for were courteous and intelligent. Men! Not grandpas or school-
boys. Men, who had all but disappeared from my life.

"Apply to the Navy before they catch you and stick you in another
munitions factory," Hanna urged. I did not need much urging. The following Monday, during lunch hour, I got the application; Tuesday, on my way
to work, I mailed it; and a week later I had the acceptance in my hands.
Only then did I tell my mother. I *told* her, I did not ask her. My heart was
pounding, my scalp prickled, and the first words sounded squeaky and had
to be covered up with a little cough, but I told her.

My mother received the news quite composed. It occurred to me that
she might even have been a bit relieved. During the next weeks she hired
a seamstress for a few days who stitched, patched, mended, and altered
some of my mother's clothes to bolster my meager wardrobe. Anything at
all might do, if given a proper turn. When I was five, I had a swiss-
embroidered little dress that I loved. (I still have it, brittle and transparent
with age, wrapped in tissue paper, at the bottom of an old chest in our
guest room.) The seamstress added material to its sleeves to widen them
and turned it into a blouse to go with a skirt she had made out of a kitchen
curtain.

We fought little during that time. There was an easing of tensions and
a sharing of the beginning of a new adventure. One morning, late in March —
March had many beginnings for me, now that I think of it — she accompanied me to the station. She hugged me and gave me a cautious goodbye
kiss, careful not to show approval by being overly moved by the occasion,
and the train chugged northward, toward the camp in Schleswig Holstein,
which was to be the first step of my navy career.

* * * * * * * * * * * * * *

We were met at the station and taken by truck to the camp. Instructions were sparse. Somebody gave us a room number and told us to as-
semble at 19 o'clock sharp for the evening meal at the mess hall. When I
finally found my room, five other girls had just arrived. There were six

bunk beds, three upper and three lower. For reasons I have never been able to discover, the upper bunks were always more popular.

"I take this one," said one girl, slapping the side of an upper bed. "Me this," said another, doing the same to the neighboring bed. The third girl just pitched her suitcase on the last upper bunk.

Conversation did not exactly flow. "I don't feel well," said the girl who had taken the bed next to mine. She seemed to have a little greenish tinge on her face. We began to open our suitcases, looking doubtfully at the thin, long closet doors, side by side, on the opposite wall. "I take this," said the first girl, slapping the handiest door on the right. "I don't feel well," said the girl next to me again, and then she threw up. Holding on to the bedpost, she emptied what must have been the entire last twenty-four hours' content of her stomach on the floor at the end of the bunks.

For a moment, silence of surprise and consternation followed this unexpected performance. Then, like lightening, the first girl was at her side.

"I am taking her to the infirmary," she announced, grabbing her by the elbow and steering her toward the door.

"I'll help!" The second girl hopped off her bed and got hold of the other elbow.

The sick girl, who was beginning to look a lot better, might conceivably have made it on her own, but the two Samaritans had a firm grip on her and were guiding her out of the door. An unlovely smell began to fill the room.

"Girls," a voice said from the third upper bed, "I am sorry, but if I stay here another second, I'm going to throw up, too." A figure came sliding down and headed for the door. "Me too," said the fifth girl, and covering her mouth and nose with both her hands, she followed on the other girl's heels.

That left me. I slowly unpacked as much of my stuff as I could squeeze into the closet and stored the suitcase out of the way. Then I sat down on my bed and hoped somebody would come in and explain things to me.

After a few minutes the door was pushed open and an older woman came into the room. (Anybody over 35 was an older woman in those days.) She stopped short, sniffed, and stared at the floor.

"What is *that*?" she demanded, entirely unnecessarily, I thought, because it really could not have been anything else.

"Somebody threw up," I explained.

"Well, what are you waiting for?" asked the woman indignantly. "Get a bucket and mop from utility and start cleaning!"

Utility was, eventually, located. When I returned with the cleaning stuff, the room smelled worse than ever. None of the others had returned. As I began mopping up, trying to keep my eyes unfocused and not breathe through my nose, I thought: "Navy lesson No. 1: *DON'T* hang around when there is trouble!"

I spent three weeks in camp together with about a hundred girls, too short a time to form any attachments. There were tests for ability and aptitude, and various medical examinations, and, while the results were evaluated, we went through the most half-assed attempt at boot camp training the human brain can possibly imagine.

I can still see us newcomers in our various garments (no uniforms were issued): long, warm winter jackets, rubber raincoats, time-worn rabbit furs, wool skirts and sweaters. Some girls were wearing high-heeled shoes, some gym shoes, and a few lucky ones wore hiking boots. We staggered through a muddy field, backward, forward, right flank and left flank, as the spirit moved us, to the unintelligible barks of an old mustached petty officer who had been mobilized out of his well-earned rest in an old sailors' home for this patriotic purpose. Since all parties concerned were well aware of the fact that everyone of us girls would wind up either in an office or a kitchen, this was an exercise in futility of some magnitude and the camp commander was not about to waste an able-bodied seaman on this nonsense. So the old gentleman in his flapping blue uniform—his round sailor hat with the two little ribbons pushed low over his forehead—just gripped his pipe with some of his more dependable teeth and hollered his commands while each of us marched to her own drummer. Around and around we stomped in the spring mud until we got quite fed up with it and drifted off, one at a time, until in the end only six or seven of the more earnest ones were still marching about, bumping into each other, and finally giving up.

For the rest of the time we stood around the old seaman, who would smoke his pipe and tell us anecdotes of World War I and help us knock the mud off our shoes with a stick. He was dearly loved by all his "recruits" because, I think, he really was the only one there who paid the slightest attention to us.

As for men: well, I had one afternoon date during those three weeks with a very handsome Navy lieutenant who was in a hurry and lost no time kissing me rather passionately within the hour, which took me quite by surprise. Hanging limply in his arms, I wondered when we would come up for air and if it would be rude to wipe my mouth with my handkerchief afterward. His parting words at the camp gate were: "Well, kid, you have a lot to learn." Of course I had a lot to learn. What did I join the Navy for? Wise guy!

* * * * * * * * * * * * * *

Our fate quite often is shaped by conscious decisions; sometimes by circumstances only. Most frequently, I think, it is a combination of both. However, once or twice in a lifetime, some seemingly insignificant event takes place, so small, so incidental, that it might not have merited a single thought afterward had it not set the course of our destiny at this precise point. Twice this has occurred in my own life, and it happened for the first time during those three otherwise uneventful weeks at the camp.

We were told that young women over twenty-one might apply for service in foreign countries. I promptly got hold of a shoelace and a map of Europe and measured the longest distance between my home and any such possible place. The northern tip of Norway and the southern seacoast of Greece ran just about the same length. Norway made me think of my room at the farm and the frozen water in the wash basin. Norway was out. Greece sounded lovely.

Applicants to foreign countries had to see the medical examiner one more time. We were scheduled at twenty-minute intervals. When I arrived at the doctor's waiting room, only a few minutes went by before the girl who had been ahead of me emerged from the office. She wasn't one of the girls I remembered seeing before. Generally we took little interest in each other during this transient stage, but when she crossed the room on her way out, I saw that she looked very unhappy and that her eyes were red. She had already started opening the door when I got up the courage to speak to her.

"Why are you so sad? What made you cry?"

The girl stopped and turned around to look at me. Her voice was unsteady when she answered.

"The doctor asked me if I get headaches and I said yes. So he ruled out Greece. And I wanted to go to Greece so badly. It's all I thought and dreamed about." Her eyes filled with tears again and she hurried out of the room.

I stared after her, thunderstruck. Since my fifteenth year I had been tormented by migraine headaches at regular intervals By now, they belonged to my life as much as my right-hand thumb did.

The examination was routine, nothing but the filling out of a large questionnaire that would be added to my medical records and sent along to my destination.

Any allergies? Insomnia? Bed wetting? Menstrual cramps? Headaches?

"No," I said, not batting a single eyelash.

"*Tropentauglich*," "Cleared for tropical climate" wrote the doctor on the margin of the questionnaire. Destiny had taken a turn.

* * * * * * * * * * * * * *

On a breezy April morning I found myself with six other girls waiting for the train to Berlin, the first leg of our long trip to Greece. We expected Greece to be sunny and warm and none of us had known how to dress for this trip. There was hardly a sign of spring around us in the north country. We were all shivering, partly from the sharp wind, partly from excitement into which had crept a slight apprehension. We were setting out on an adventure of which every facet was unknown to us.

Two days before our departure we had been issued one seabag, one long-sleeved, dark wool turtleneck sweater, and one pair of black, low-heeled, laced shoes, standard navy equipment, no matter if you were on your way to the Arctic or Africa. The rest of the bag was stuffed with our own belongings, such as they were. None of us had handled a seabag before, nobody showed us how, so we dragged this monstrous roll for the most part behind us in the dust. In addition to it, we had some bags with food provisions and our handbags with money and marching orders as well as our overnight gear. As soon as it got warmer, we carried our coats and jackets over our arms. For the moment, however, we were wrapped tightly into our warm clothing, since the April wind was chilly and brisk, chasing little white clouds over the pale blue sky.

It was just about time for the train to pull in when a young sailor arrived at a trot, looked around, and headed straight for us. He carried a large parcel in his arms—about the size of a bread box, I'd say—and he was red and out of breath from running.

"You are the girls going to Greece?" he asked. "Will you take this parcel to my girl? Her name is written on top, see? It's a sewing box; I made it myself. I am a cabinet maker by trade. Please?"

The train was approaching; he held the box out toward all of us. Impulsively I wanted to stretch out my arms when a sudden picture flashed through my mind—that of a mop and a bucket—and my arms stayed glued to my sides. Another girl, with the same urge and no mental image to warn her, held up her hands. He dropped the box into them, which made her stagger a bit. "Thanks a million! Tell her Karl sends his love." And with a wide, endearing smile he added: "I don't even have a platform pass! Have a good trip." And down the platform he tore and out of sight.

The expression on the girl's face I remember well: I have seen it a few more times in my life. It was the "mop-and-bucket face," innocence slowly grasping that something had gone awfully wrong. For eight long days the girl dragged a heavy, clumsy parcel with her that contained a lovingly carved wooden sewing box big enough for a family with six active children, sent from a young man in the most northern part of Germany to his girl in the south of Greece who would never even pick up a needle and thread to fasten a button during her entire stay there. Once or twice, the hard-pressed carrier "forgot" the parcel on a station bench or a train seat, only to race back at the last moment, guilt-stricken, to retrieve it again. We all took turns with this awful bundle, but the responsibility always rested with her.

Berlin was our first stop, a lay-over of a few hours. Spring had arrived in Berlin; even the chestnut trees were blooming. Now that I was leaving it behind, it looked lovely. I called my mother from the station. Her comments were diplomatic. She wanted to keep her options open. If this adventure should prove disastrous, she reserved all rights to say: "I knew it!" If, on the other hand, I should, in the course of events, become engaged to some full captain with a little villa in Blankeneese, she would like to have been in on the ground floor.

The train we boarded in Berlin took us to Vienna. It was a long, tiring haul. We had three seats for the seven of us. Taking turns with them, the other four made do, sitting on a seabag or standing at a window in the long, narrow train corridor, watching the still, lightless countryside rush by. The train was overcrowded as all trains were. This was the first time I ever saw human beings sleeping while standing. Soldiers hanging on to the overhead grips with almost spastically closed fists were sound asleep, their heads sunk onto their chests, while swaying on their feet. Sometimes during the night, the train would stop in the midst of nowhere to wait out yet another air raid going on in some city ahead of us. There were no lights in the train, no lights in the villages; a few ghostly blue bulbs marked the stations we passed.

We arrived in Vienna during the late afternoon and it took some time until we had carried, pushed, and dragged ourselves and our luggage out of the train, fighting to stay together and not lose sight of each other. Instinctively we formed a little circle on the platform, like the wagon trains of old, letting the waves of people break and stream around us. Eventually we found our way to the station's Navy office and, after an hour of waiting, our bags and we were loaded into a truck and taken to a convent. The nuns had been persuaded to move over a bit into the west wing of the building and the east wing now provided sleeping quarters for travelers such as us. The nuns served us a meal; none of them spoke to us. I thought that they were probably mad at us for taking their chairs in the rectory and their beds to boot. Much later in life I learned that those were the hours of the daily Great Silence in convents the world over during which no nun talked to anyone but God. Well, very likely they were mad, too, but it did not matter too much just then. We had not slept for some forty hours and the large dining hall turned slow circles around me. A silent nun took us to a vast dormitory, where we crept under two thin gray blankets onto a very narrow cot with a wafer-thin mattress. As soon as my head touched the pillow I was gone.

I don't remember too well how we got to and from the stations. I recall only what a terrible time we had staying together, defying the force of the unending masses ever threatening to draw us apart. It was during one of those struggles that we were suddenly a circle of eight; a young soldier had joined us at the Vienna station and, without speaking much or moving unnecessarily, he began to look after our forlorn little group. He located lost hand luggage, carried seabags, secured seats, and, uncomplaining, took a few turns with the sewing box.

It was in the train from Vienna to Belgrade that I really took stock of my travel companions for the first time. Thanks to the soldier, we all had seats in the same compartment, the eight of us filled it, in fact. The first one I had noticed was the young widow, since she wore deep mourning. Her shoes and stockings, her dress, her scarf, all were black; her cap even had a little black veil. She was very young and I thought her quite a pretty woman, but she was very pale. I was not the only one who noticed her first. It soon became clear that our blessed helper was not exactly heaven-sent but had joined us because he felt a quite earthy and uncomplicated attraction for our pretty young widow. Within hours they were inseparable. Far from begrudging her the conquest, we were delighted and grateful.

They sat side by side, as close as if grown together, the same dark coat spread over both of them during the long, cool night, his head on her shoulder, or, shifting, her head on his chest and his arm around her. Toward morning, their hands were under the coat, caressing, and a warm, pink color came into the young woman's face. They never talked much, they just clung to each other, giving comfort to each other in a way that, in those days, was still beyond my experience and comprehension.

The oldest one of our group — older perhaps by eight or nine years — was a small-boned, graceful woman to whom, in my mind, I had given the name "The Hazelnut." I have long since forgotten her real name. Everything about her was brown, her eyes, her hair, her skin; she was like a tidy little gypsy woman, well-groomed to the end, never looking as dishevelled and done-in as the rest of us. We began talking to each other and looking for seats together. Then, of course, there was the girl with the sewing box at whom I looked with sympathy and, sometimes, I must admit, with a suppressed grin. I thought I knew how she felt. Two of the girls I don't remember at all; the seventh one was a long-legged girl who was extraordinarily white. Not the sad paleness of the young widow, but an inherent complexion made this girl so light as to be almost colorless. Her skin was an opaque milky white (and later it would not even tan under the Greek sun), her lashes were pale blond over her light blue eyes, her hair was a finely spun ash blond. Her movements were slow and deliberate and so was the way she talked. She spoke with the soft, a bit singing intonation of the people of East Prussia, then Germany's most northeastern province.

When we arrived in Belgrade, we learned that we would have to stay there a few nights, since the single train track through the Balkans had been, once again, blown up by guerrillas and would have to be repaired before we could continue our trip.

The days in Belgrade were pleasant. Jugoslavia was an "occupied" country, but we were free of air raids. The hotel room I shared with the Hazelnut was clean and comfortable and we were served three meals a day of a quality we had not seen in Germany in a long time. Nobody supervised our coming or going as long as we checked twice a day with the office of transportation. On the fourth morning we were told the trip would continue that afternoon. So, off we were once again, with bag and baggage and the widow's guardian angel lending us a hand and the girl with the sewing box bringing up the rear. The train, awaiting us at the station, was long and empty. The first three cars were open freight cars, filled with sand. This, we were told, was for our protection, in case the newly repaired tracks were dynamited again. I thought of the four men in the engine cab but pushed that thought out of my mind as fast as I could. We all trooped into the same compartment (out of sheer habit, I suppose) which immediately took on the same overcrowded look as in all the previous trains. The eight of us tried to get comfortable for a trip that would take two days and a night, if all went well.

We were the only females on the entire train. All the rest were soldiers and sailors coming back from furlough and leave or, like us, going south for the first time and wondering what lay ahead. The night seemed endless and when morning came we were stiff and sticky and out of sorts. The wait for the washroom was long; the water came in a trickle. The Hazelnut and I decided to go exploring. It did not take us long to discover that the train was far from full. Within a short walk down the train aisle, we found an empty compartment; nobody had staked it out; nobody claimed it. We walked back to our compartment and began moving our stuff. Unlamenting and unlamented, we took our leave of the group. After spreading out, happily, all over our new quarters, I discovered that I had forgotten my coat. I went back to the other compartment, did not see it, and finally discovered it on the floor between the benches, everybody stepping over it and on it with the greatest unconcern.

"Why did you throw my coat on the floor?" I yelled. "Why are you all tramping on it?!"

Some of the girls looked surprised and a bit guilty, but nobody answered except the pale girl.

"We did not *throw* your coat on the floor," she said.

"Well, somebody did!" I said furiously, "and you were not paying the slightest attention to it."

"Neither, obviously, were you," said the girl, not raising her soft sing-song voice a bit. I grabbed my mauled coat and in silent rage, stomped out of the compartment.

"They are a bunch of a stupid geese," I announced to The Hazelnut. "And the one from East Prussia is the worst!"

My companion helped me clean the coat and inspect it for damage. We told each other that we were heartily glad to be rid of the rest.

We had more room to stretch, more air to breathe; we could lie down on the benches; we walked up and down the corridor, peeking quickly into the neighboring compartments. Gradually the landscape outside was changing as the train rolled on—through the day, through the night, through another day. The flat Puszta gave way to hilly country and tiny villages with ancient stones house. Steep mountains appeared with flocks of grazing sheep and once in a while we glimpsed a shepherd leaning on his long staff and gazing wistfully at the passing train. I never failed to wave at him.

On the morning of our last day came a knock at our door, and a very nice-looking young sailor entered. He told us that he came as a messenger. The guys next door had sent him. "There are four of us," he told us. (We knew that.) "We pooled our rations and came up with three bars of chocolate. The guys want me to tell you that we would like to give them to you if you would kiss us once."

The Hazelnut and I sat in thunderstruck silence. This was unexpected, to say the very least. Three bars of chocolate—I didn't know about her, but I had not had any chocolate since Christmas and then just a very small Christmas ration piece. And—I didn't dare look at my companion—those guys in the next compartment were cute.

"You don't have to answer now," said the messenger a bit nervous. "Think about it and I'll be back in half an hour." We nodded assent.

And then we agonized. We really did. I don't know anymore what all we said to each other, but in the end we knew we had to decline. When our messenger appeared again, we told him so. We were flattered, we said, really, but no, thank you, no.

"The guys will be disappointed," he said, shaking his head in disbelief, and back he went with his sorry message.

The Hazelnut and I faked unconcern. After all, we knew we had done the right thing. It seemed, however, that noble decisions are not always rewarded with instant elation. I looked out of the window, she got out her cosmetic bag and began filing her nails. All of a sudden the file was hurled back into the bag.

"Oh, damn! Why did they have to *offer* us something for it?" said The Hazelnut with great feeling. I couldn't have agreed with her more.

Chapter 11

When our train pulled into the deserted station just outside Athens, even the most travel-happy ones of us were ready to become stationary for a while. One more time our luggage was rolled and tumbled down to the station platform. We were tired, stiff, and dirty and were dressed much too warmly. The sky was a deep azure, seldom seen in our country, and the air was windless and soaked with sunshine. We were perspiring freely; great, dark, wet blotches had appeared on the back of our dresses and blouses. In time we got used to this and gave it no thought at all, but during those first days, we were perpetually mortified by it.

A golden apparition floated toward us, taking in our wilted crew without any surprise. A young woman dressed in a cool white outfit, hair a sun-bleached gold, skin a sun-drenched bronze, long, dark lashes over gentle cornflower eyes — one of Greece's young goddesses to welcome us!

"I am Anita Lavade," said the apparition in very good German. "I work in the Personnel Department. Welcome to Athens!" A friendly smile accompanied those words.

As if hit by an electric spark, one of the girls moved forward.

"Anita Lavade?" she said. "Do you know a sailor named Karl?"

The goddess seemed confused. "Yes, that is my . . . that is a very good friend of mine."

"Well, then: *Here*!" said the girl, and, with a mixture of rage, relief, and pride, she thrust the heavy, messy bundle into Anita Lavade's arms. "He sent you this!"

"What is it?" asked Fräulein Anita, appalled. She was definitely earthbound now.

"It's a sewing box." " He brought it to the station." " He made it himself." We all volunteered information now.

"A sewing box? Oh . . ." Our goddess had crash-landed. The dismay on her lovely face was unmistakable. For a moment it looked as if she was going to drop the parcel. Then she had caught herself. Good manners came to her rescue. "Well, thank you so much," she smiled feebly at the girl. "It must have been . . . awkward . . ." Her voice trailed off.

"We'll put it with the rest of the luggage," she added, brightening.

"Only two of you will stay in Athens," she told us, all business now. "The rest will go on to the Islands — after a good rest," she added kindly, looking at the weary faces. She was just a sweet and pretty girl, after all.

"Staying in Athens . . ." she began to read from a list. The first name was mine. "And Kristin Gardner." I looked around curiously and was not a little taken aback when the girl from East Prussia stepped forward. Any girl would have been all right. The Hazelnut would have been great. But not this one. Fräulein Gardner remained poker-faced; she rarely showed any emotion at all. Nobody could have guessed how she felt about our future togetherness. We got into a Navy bus and headed into the sun-bathed capital of Greece.

Kristin and I were the first to be dropped off in front of one of the few darker buildings of this dazzling white city. It might have been a low-priced hotel in pre-war years. I don't think it was frequented by American visitors, since there was only one toilet and one bath to each floor.

We were received by a large, untidy looking older woman whose name was Frau Gnade (Mrs. Mercy) which in itself was a bit of a joke. I don't know how Frau Gnade had wangled the appointment to be housemother of a dormitory full of young women. She always reminded me of a half-baked loaf of rye bread to which accidentally too much yeast had been added: flabby, grayish and overflowing on all sides. It was impossible to tell her exact age, but it could not have been too far from fifty. We did not know when we climbed the steep, dark steps after her that Frau Gnade would play only a very minor part in our lives. In fact, she would be all but invisible, since she spent most of her time in her room with a bottle of Samos wine to keep her company.

At this moment, however, she was the person-in-charge for us. When she opened the door to a sparsely furnished room with one bleak window facing the wall of the next house, darkened even more by an iron fire ladder going right past it, we did not dare voice our disappointment. It was only when I saw the two narrow beds, side by side, and the one cracked, wooden cabinet that would hold the clothes for both of us, that I gathered some desperate courage. Even if I had to sleep in a room worse than this one, I would prefer it to sharing such close quarters with this wretched girl. Frau Gnade had already left the room when I ran after her, leaving the door open in my haste to catch up with her. I asked her if there was another room, any other room, any room but this one, into which I might move. She told me that there was not another free room or bed at the moment but that she would keep me in mind for the very next vacancy. When I slowly returned to our cave, as I already called it in my mind, Kristin was sitting on the edge of one of the beds. She sat there as she always did, very still, very white, not a flicker of emotion on her face. But she looked straight at me and said in her quiet, slightly singing voice:

"Couldn't we at least *try?*"

The fact that she had overheard me did not trouble me much, but she could have hardly asked a more effective question. It showed me up as one so lacking in good will that I was left standing in the doorway, disquieted and without an answer. Kristin herself broke the tension.

"Well, let's unpack," she said quite matter-of-factly. And "Isn't this a ghastly room. I wonder if they are all like this."

Those were the first few minutes of a friendship that has lasted a lifetime. I came to know Kristin better than perhaps even her own family. I learned to read that poker face of hers as a lawyer reads very fine print, having a vested interest in it. Every flick of an eyelash, the tiniest movement of the corners of her mouth I could interpret. Kristin had a good sense of humor but she seldom really laughed at anybody's jokes and never at her own. Coaxing a smile out of her was a major achievement. Yet she was capable of love, anger, fear, furious frustration, and real amusement. I have met during the years few other people with this curious phenomenon and most of those that I did meet came from Kristin's part of the country, the high northeastern Baltic border of Germany. Kristin's hands, however, had a life of their own. They moved when she talked and—what her face never did—they gave emphasis to anything she wanted to stress. She was a different breed, my friend Kristin was.

We slept in "the cave" for two nights. On the third day, a Sunday, we climbed out the window and up the fire ladder and found ourselves on a sizable flat rooftop from which four narrow doors were leading back into the building. We opened all four. The first one led down the regular flight of steps, the next two opened into tiny rooms, each one equipped with a bare iron bedstead, a chair, some open shelves, a few hooks on the wall, and a rusty washbasin. The fourth door opened to a space no bigger than a closet, featuring a lone toilet with ants crawling all over the cracked seat. However, there was water in the spigot and the toilet actually flushed. Obviously, this had been the servant quarters. The view was beautiful, gliding over the rooftops of Athens toward the violet mountain range in the distance. Kristin and I hugged each other—that is, I hugged Kristin, and she lifted the corners of her mouth to a smile. We knew we had found our home away from home. We were on top of the world. We had finally arrived in Athens!

Spiro was the name of the only hotel employee left, Spiro Hachalapopulus. (I don't know if it was spelled that way, I never saw it written, but that's what we called him.) Spiro was young and friendly and willing, but he spoke no German and we spoke no Greek. We went down to the ground floor where he sat in his chair during the day in the open front door, observing the sidewalk with never lagging interest. Half pushing, half pulling, we coaxed him upstairs, and we pointed to the rooms on the roof, smiling and nodding and talking with our hands, until Spiro's face lit up with comprehension. By afternoon the two rooms had undergone a somewhat dubious cleaning, the ants had temporarily disappeared, and we had carried our bedding and clothes up the steps and settled down in our lovely penthouse apartment, each with a room of our own. We quickly learned to keep the doors wide open during the early morning hours and late in the evening hours and tightly closed against the heat of the day. Spiro found us some old garden chairs for our rooftop, and Kristin started some flower pots in a shaded corner. We were the Kings of the Mountain and we were blissfully happy. It took the bedbugs a whole week to find us up there.

Our working day was from seven until noon, and from four until seven. We soon discovered the reason for those peculiar hours. The entire city closed down at noon for one vast, leaden, sweat-soaked nap and it did not stir again until the sun threw slanted shadows from the west. It sprang to life in full cry only after the sun had disappeared in a sudden, mad drop behind the distant mountains of the Peloponnesus.

On this, our first morning, Kristin and I walked the fifteen minutes to our future working place with great trepidation, yet taking in everything around us with a feeling of enchantment and wonder that did not leave us for many a day.

The Administration of the Admirality of the Aegaeis was housed in a large government building facing a park. We went through the long corridors in search of the paymaster's quarters, to which we had been assigned. I think we would have liked to hold hands and take comfort in each other's presence and ignorance, but we were immediately separated and placed into different rooms. I found myself sitting at a large desk across from a young petty officer with mild brown eyes and a nice smile. In his role as instructor he seemed more timid than I. The entire desk, his side as well as mine, was covered with sheets of paper full of numbers. He mumbled explanations and instructions in an almost apologetic tone, as through he wished to imply that he knew that I knew all that stuff already, but that he was forced to run it by me just the same. It did not just run by me, it ran off me with lightning speed and evaporated without a drop of it sticking to my brain. The entire morning I sat there, staring at the papers in front of me, staring out the window, staring at the people walking in and out of the room, staring at my petty officer, staring at the clock. It didn't escape him, of course. "You'll catch on," he said encouragingly every half hour or so. When we left for the noon meal to our separate mess halls, I looked frantically for Kristin. As soon as I saw her, I hurled myself at her.

"For heaven's sake, Kristin, what are we supposed to do?" I pleaded. Kristin explained. Apparently we paid people, both German and Greek. I would be given vouchers, receipts, and accounts, for work done, hours spent, goods delivered, for travel, lay-overs, room-and-board expenses. I was to estimate future costs and check on past ones. I was to discover honest errors and not-so-honest slip-ups. I was to figure, calculate, add, multiply and subtract. I would be dealing with numbers morning, noon, and night until they came out of my nose, ears, and throat, and I would fall dead off my chair! Kristin did not seem to mind a bit. I wondered what they did with people who counted on their fingers and could not multiply eight times seven without filling a number of scratch papers with various approaches and possibilities.

For the next three days I sat at the "Desk of Dwindling Hopes" and drew daisies and little birch trees (my doodling specialties; also back views of bunnies) around itemized bills, while the nice petty officer sped through his papers so he could do mine before the noon break and before quitting time in the evening. For his efforts I gratefully went out with him at night to have a glass of Samos in one of the dozens of little restaurants that had placed their wooden chairs and tables invitingly outside on the sidewalks. Kristin, who was catching on fast, joined us with her instructor and desk mate. It was our introduction to the nights in paradise, the nights of the brilliant stars and velvet air, of the thousand crickets, and the sound of singing and bouzoukis bursting out of open doors and hidden courtyards and carried to us on a wind more gentle and caressing than we had ever known; the nights of the tangy, burning retzina wine and the sweet dizzy Samos. The nights of Athens, the nights of Greece.

Late in the afternoon of the third day I was called to the paymaster's office, where I was faced by a disagreeable older man in a warrant officer's uniform. He was one of those people who never look at you when they talk but seem to address themselves to the ghosts of Christmases past behind your shoulder. He informed me, rather sourly, that he had been requested to send me upstairs to the Department of Operations. He obviously had not had time to check on my performance in his department or he would not have grieved so excessively. But what was the Department of Operations? Who operated up there on whom? Small matter, everything considered. It could not be worse than what I was escaping from.

My angel of rescue came in the shape of a red-haired, freckled, near-sighted lieutenant; merry blue eyes twinkling behind thick glasses, he came to escort me to my new job. In the elevator on the way up he proudly took credit for my transfer.

"Fräulein Lieske is leaving," he explained, taking it for granted that I knew the lady, "and the workload is simply too much for just Eleanor and Horsie. I looked through the records of the new arrivals and you seemed just the person we needed." Oh Lord!

We walked down the hall and he opened the door to a large office room that seemed hardly filled by three desks, chairs and typewriters. Two young women were sitting behind their typewriters; the third desk was vacant.

A quick introduction, a formal nodding of heads in all directions, and my jolly escort disappeared, handing the doorknob to an older heavy-set man in a lieutenant commander's uniform.

"I need a typist, please," said the newcomer politely. He had a long, worried face.

"She . . ." a nod toward me by one of the girls, "is free."

"You won't need a pad and pencil," said the officer. "And no pocketbook, please."

He led the way, followed closely by me, my heart pounding, my scalp itching with nervousness and perspiration, down long, winding corridors, around corners and through connecting doors. A few times he opened a door and shut it again, finally finding what he was looking for, a large, high-ceilinged room, void of any furniture, except a small table with a typewriter and one chair. There was not even a calendar on the wall nor a waste paper basket near the desk. One long, narrow window looking out at a courtyard gave scanty light. It was a most discouraging room and gave me instant creeps. The sad-faced man told me to sit down and carefully counted out five sheets of plain paper and four sheets of carbon paper. He watched me insert them into the typewriter, my fingers trembling slightly. He then produced one more sheet, this one covered tightly with small pencilled figures — all numbers.

"Please type this," he said politely, "We will proofread it afterward, but try not to make any mistakes."

"What is it?" I asked, against all good judgment, staring at this monstrous thing.

"A mine field," he said, not cheering up one bit. "That's why accuracy is so vital."

He walked to the door, turned around and gave me a little apologetic smile.

"I will have to lock you in. Regulations, you understand." He said it and went out of the door. I heard the key turn twice in the lock and his steps echoing away down the long, empty hall.

For a moment I felt like jumping up and hammering at the door with all my might. The whole thing seemed like a very bad dream, the hideous room, the locked door, the narrow window looking toward a blank house wall and that awful piece of paper with those hieroglyphic numbers with dots and dashes and commas all around them. No room for daisies and little birch trees here. Slowly I began hitting the keys, double-checking before each touch that I had the right number, the right dash, the proper distance, the right line. I figured at that speed I would have about one third of it done by the time he came back. Click. . .click. . .click went my fingers. Drops of perspiration ran through my hair and down my back. C111 . . . better check again, all right, click. . .click. . .. Room, heat, and time were suspended. I became disembodied, only my fingers and the pencilled numbers were real. Hours must have gone by. I was down to the last number. Click. . .dash. I noticed for the first time that I was still breathing. Then, slowly, meticulously, I checked over the two papers, number for number, dot for dot. Another hour—or was it a day by now?

The sun had gone down; it was getting quite dark. How long had it been since I entered this room, since I had been locked in? I went to the door and listened. Not a sound outside. The dirty window showed nothing but the brick wall across. I began walking back and forth with mounting dread. What was meant by "Department of Operations"? Why had they taken a new, unknown girl to type a mine field? Why did nobody come to let me out? What happened to people around here after they had finished typing a mine field? My throat began to constrict a little; I found it difficult to breathe. Why had that man looked so sad? Everybody must have left the building by now. It was dark.

I was sitting on the chair, my throat parched, my blouse wet, my body stiff with apprehension when steps approached. The key was turned and my jailer entered. This time he looked twice as worried as before; at the same time there was relief in his face.

"Oh, thank goodness!" he exclaimed. "Mein liebes Fräulein, I am so very sorry. You must be very hungry by now. You see, I have only recently arrived and do not know this building and I had forgotten in which room you were sitting. I kept going in circles and opening the same doors twice. Frankly," he said, a little reproachfully, "you had me worried." I had *him* worried!

He counted the papers and the carbon sheets, thanked me, courteously escorted me to the elevator, and disappeared. With trembling knees I made my way home. It was too late for the mess hall.

Kristin appeared in the open door of my room.

"Did you like your new job?" she asked.

"Don't talk about it," I said, hollow-voiced, "I am trying to forget." I crawled into bed and pulled the sheet over my face.

"Anyway, I don't see how I can survive another day!"

But survive I did, not only one day, but many, and this was not the last mine field I had to type. But not until the day of my departure from Athens was I again as frightened—and then with a great deal more reason.

* * * * * * * * * * * * * * *

"The new girls have to report for vaccination," a girl said dropping the memo on my desk, "Next Monday, in the infirmary." She was gone before I could ask her any questions. Kristin came home in the evening with the same order.

"What is this all about?" we asked our escorts when we sat together at night with a glass of Samos. They told us that all personnel had to be inoculated against typhus, cholera, and yellow fever.

"It's no fun, but you'll survive," they said.

"I won't go," said Kristin, her mouth set firmly. "I hate shots. I get sick just thinking about them."

"Well, everybody has to," she was told.

"And if I just don't appear?"

"Then your records will show that you did not get vaccinated and they will either make you or ship you back home."

Kristin's face was a study in marble.

"Oh, please, Kristin," I said, "nobody likes to get shots. But it's just a second or so and you don't want to be sent home!"

The petty officers joined me in reassuring her. A tiny relaxation of the corners of Kristin's mouth showed that she was wavering. I breathed a sigh of relief. The young men nodded approval.

"Sure," the younger one assured her, "nobody likes it! But we all live through it. Oh my," he said, shaking his head and grinning a bit. "I remember us guys standing there, stripped down to the waist, the needles sticking out of our chests—they do it in the chest, you know—and waiting for the medic with the shot to come around. They just screw the shot into the needle, that way they shoot you three times with the same needle. Yep," he said, shaking his head again wistfully, "there we stood, looking dumb and scared, and the old needle whipping up and down in our chest with every heartbeat . . ."

A withering glance from one side and a kick from the other under the table against his shin brought this happy reminiscing to an abrupt end. But a quick glance at Kristin's face showed me that it was too late. The damage was done. Kirstin's face had simply closed down; she had retired behind closed blinds and would be unapproachable.

"Kristin," I pleaded, when we were alone, "they are going to send you home! If you refuse the shots, they'll just pack you off back to Germany."

"Not if I don't get the shots," she corrected me, "If the records don't *show* that I got the shots."

"Well, it's the same thing," I said unhappily.

"Wrong, little Eva," said Kristin calmly and retired to her room for the night.

In my mind I already saw Kristin fading into the distance. Nothing and nobody would induce her to take the required shots, of that I was certain. There was no way out, I could lose a friend I had begun to need and cherish, and I would have to watch helplessly and furiously when she was packed off on a homeward-bound train. I had not counted on Kristin Gardner's two most remarkable qualities: her single-minded determination and the mysterious appeal she held for men. Kristin, as I was to find out over the years, with her still, white face, her rare smile, and her slow talk, could get any man she set her cap for.

She was not wanton, not even frivolous. She was slow and deliberate, which does not always mean wise and full of insights. She did not take life lightly. She was not in love with love, as I had been since I was sixteen. Romance, to her, meant only one of two things: a tentative investment in the future, or a matter of life and death. Standing in front of a young medic, stripped to the waist, a long, quivering needle sticking out of her breast, fell definitely into the second category.

For the next several days I saw very little of Kristin. She did not join us in the evenings for our glass of wine. She was going out with somebody she had met at the office, she vaguely explained to me.

"She is going out with the fellow who runs the infirmary," said her ex-date, whose nose was considerably out of joint.

I could hardly believe that I heard right. What did she think she could accomplish in the four days left until we had to report for our vaccination? Oh, poor Kristin, I thought, what a pathetic attempt. The medic was sure to have a girlfriend some place—and here comes Kristin, slow, inscrutable, Kristin—and only four days to go!

We were only a few girls on Monday morning. We stood there, sick with dread, smiling casually at each other, and we got our shots in the breast, and we lived through it. Kristin was not one of us. We got dressed and went to work. I got a fever and felt wretched for three days, and Kristin brought me water and fruit juice and my rations and looked after me. She still went out at night, but less and less, and after a week or so, when I was well again, she seemed to be a free agent once more and joined in anything that came our way. Nobody sent for her; nobody came and made her pack her suitcases. We never talked about it. If she had made promises she didn't keep, she was not exactly torn apart by remorse. She slept well enough. Life was so good just then, so sweet. There were wine and friendship and nights like velvet under desert stars, the blue clear sea and the soft white beaches, the white marble city and the teeming Bazaar, and music, music everywhere—the bouzouky sound of Greece.

There were, also, ants, mice, mosquitoes, cockroaches, and bedbugs. The first item we had been issued in Athens was a large mosquito net. None of us had ever seen one before. Spiro proved valueless when it came to putting them up. We tried our hand at it and got hopelessly entangled. Eventually we just slept without one. Mosquito nets had many other wonderful uses. The mice and ants we took philosophically. I remember on Saturdays and Sundays unwrapping my rations, which we took home with us from mess hall, and automatically blowing and scraping the tiny ants off the cheese before biting into it. It was just one of those things.

Now cockroaches are a different matter. You never really get used to cockroaches. I have heard a lot about New York's famous cockroaches, but when I finally saw one running across a washbasin in an old hotel off Central Park, my first thought was: Is that all? Compared to Greek cockroaches, the New York ones are pets. The cockroaches in our hotel in Athens were about three times as big and much darker. Maybe the New York ones are feistier, but if they ever met their Greek cousins, it would be like a gazelle meeting up with a rhino. We were assured that they were harmless, useful even, keeping smaller bugs at bay. Ha! When you open a water spigot in the dark and find yourself with one of those pre-historic miniature monsters crackling in you fingers, this comforting biological fact is not the first thing that comes to your mind, you can be sure.

Never an evening went by that one of us—usually the one who came home later—did not slip into the other's room to sit on the edge of the bed and share the experiences, laughs, and worries of the day. For, more and more, Kristin's days and mine were spent differently, nor did we spend each evening or weekend together any more.

Our work places now were separated by two floors. Kristin kept working for the paymaster's department. As long as she did not have anything to do with the head of the department himself, she was quite happy. It did not take her long to catch on to the mechanics of the work, and she became an expert with those numbers and figures, additions, deductions, and percentages that had been so frightening to me. She could smell a padded travel account or some fictitious hours on a worksheet through a closed envelope. She was simply good at her work. Within a few weeks she began dating an exceedingly thin and long young seaman with deep set eyes and a wicked grin. His name was Harry. Dating a girl like Kristin must have been quite a new experience for him and something of a surprise to boot. He was a bit of a rascal and she was not the type he usually chased. But, once Kristin had set her cap for somebody . . . Harry drove large Navy trucks. Back home he had a father who had a furniture factory in the south of Germany. Kristin, who was two years older than I, had begun to invest in the future.

Chapter 12

Four days after our arrival in Athens I had been pushed up the ladder, so to speak, by a freckled, near-sighted, jolly junior lieutenant who had been ordered to produce a typist-secretary within the hour. My new place of work was a large room with three bright windows from which the view was almost but not quite as spectacular as that from our penthouse. My co-workers were two girls, one definitely named Eleanor. The other's name, when introduced, had sounded so much like "horse" that I did not dare address her for the better part of a week.

As it turned out, "Horsie" it was. Her real last name was "Gaul," and Gaul being an old-fashioned word for horse, it was only a skip and a hop to Horsie. This name was born out of a mixture of affection, amusement, and exasperation, I think, and it fit her eminently well. Horsie herself quite approved of it. There were times when I tried to imagine what she might have looked like if she had been permitted to stretch properly at the right time. As it was, some unknown force must have given her a solid swat with a two-by-four just when she started stretching. The result was astonishing. Horsie's face was absolutely square; her forehead was low and wide, the eyes beneath it were slanted and slightly bulging. Her nose was flat and her lips wide and thin. Her neck was short and thick and sat on powerful shoulders. Her whole figure had been squashed and squared by that one mighty swat. Her hair was not only colorless but textureless and she only just managed it with two thin pigtails behind each large ear.

I know it would gratify some deep romantic need in us if I were to add now that beneath this rough exterior beat a heart of gold. But, alas, it would not be the truth. Beneath Horsie's flat bosom beat the heart of a horse trader. Horsie had made herself invaluable, not by beauty and grace, but by being able to purchase, requisition, persuade, steal, coax, and produce almost anything anyone might wish for, but thought was impossible to obtain—until he or she met up with Horsie. Everybody but the highest echelon availed themselves of Horsie's talents and services. A spare mosquito net? Horsie requisitioned it. A hot plate needed to throw a little party? Horsie clattered down the hall with it to the party-in-need. A four-hour pass to see a girlfriend in Piraeus? Horsie twisted somebody's arm. Everybody's gratitude was sincere but cautious. Horsie, as it was well known, did nothing for nothing. Her brain computed and stored away every service rendered and, like a benign Godfather, she called in her favors when the time came. The lieutenant commander whose party's success had depended on the presence of a hot plate would be the one who signed short-term passes. The girl who needed the extra mosquito net would cover a few hours for a girl whose boyfriend happened to be in charge of kitchen supplies.

It must be said that once every blue moon Horsie did cancel a debt. If admiration and gratitude came through so loud and clear that Horsie was the heroine of the hour, she would bend a little, glow a little, and bask a little in all the fuss, and temporarily stop the computer. She was human, after all.

Horsie had one very disconcerting habit. On the wall beside the door hung a little mirror, just the right height to catch a fleeting glance before flying off, pencil and pad in hand, to one of the offices. Since throughout most of the year our faces shined with perspiration and our hair stuck to our head with moisture, we all but forgot about the mirror. Unfortunately, Horsie did not. Once in a while she left her place behind her typewriter, walked over to the door, unhurried and deliberate, and took a long, wistful look in the mirror, at the end of which she would shake her head and say, slowly and wonderingly: "Did you ever see anything so homely?" At such moments, Eleanor's long, nimble fingers would fly faster over the typewriter and I would bend my head a little lower over my steno pad to decipher what my teacher had called years ago "a bunch of fishing worms." We secretly dreaded Horsie's mirror encounters and never learned to take them in stride.

Eleanor was as much the opposite of Horsie as a girl at the same age, in the same room, with the same kind of job could possibly be. She had a fine, narrow, aristocratic face; her skin was almost transparent; she had large, green mermaid eyes, and her dark blond hair was parted simply and bound together softly and firmly at the nape of her neck. She was without moods, friendly and helpful at all times. When I first met her, she seemed reticent and shy, but when I knew her better I found that she was entirely at ease within her own silences, which stemmed neither from shyness nor a pouting disposition. Eleanor was a very private person. Unlike Horsie, who was the Queen of Gossip and a walking company newspaper, Eleanor never divulged anybody's secrets nor, for a long time, did she talk about her own life to me. She did not live in our hotel but had quarters in a private house. Anything I did learn about her came, of course, from Horsie.

There were two men in Eleanor's life and I never had more than a few fleeting glimpses of either of them. According to Horsie, Eleanor kept company with a man who was older than she by some fifteen years. He belonged to the rare specie: a male civilian working for the military. He was an engineer, a brilliant man, and, I suppose, this brilliance kept him out of uniform. They took him on any terms they could get him, and those were his terms. He gave his talents and ingenuity to the job they required of him and seemed to do jolly well what he pleased any other way and time. He was a married man, away from his family since the beginning of the war, seemingly an eternity; good looking, a little balding, with a sharp, dry wit, which both attracted the military men who had to deal with him and kept them at arm's length. And he found rest and companionship with this quiet, even-tempered girl with the mermaid eyes.

The other man was a seaman with no rank at all. He was, in civilian life, a teacher of classical languages; he was a scholar and a loner, and nobody and nothing, not even four years of war and many well-meaning and exasperated attempts by his superiors, could make anything more than a seaman out of him. He had a desk job just outside of Athens, and he came to see Eleanor as often as he could manage, which was not often. I remember this man and his serious, gentle face, the face of a scholar and thinker, and the dark blue simple sailor suit that looked on him as if he had donned it as a joke for a costume party—and not a very apt joke at that. He was not married and he must have known of Eleanor's attachment to the engineer, but he courted her with a serious, unwavering loyal devotion and affection that was not lost on her, although she never talked at the time about this conflict in her life. It was not until much later, when Kristin was gone and Horsie had ceased to live vicariously and was occupied with her own affairs for a change, that Eleanor and I became closer.

When she began to teach me how to knit baby clothes, she began talking about her own little girl who lived a thousand miles away in an orphanage run by the Sisters of Mercy.

Eleanor came from a proud, protestantic North-German family. When she told her parents about her pregnancy, there had been stares of disbelief, followed by an offended silence and, finally by a coldly civilized request to leave. "Come back when you have a ring on your finger," her father had said. Eleanor's smile when she told me covered the little break in her voice. She did not wait around for any hearts to soften. She packed her suitcases and left for the far south of the country. It was typical of Eleanor that this was no blind and tearful flight into the night; she chose the most sensible way open to her. Many state agencies would have assisted her, but she went to a Catholic order of sisters who would extend the most help with the fewest questions. She accepted their uncurious kindness and shelter, worked for them until her time came, and when fully recovered, left the child in their care in a small town in the Austrian Alps that was not threatened by air raids or other horrors of war. She was particular about the employment she chose. She wished to be out of the reach of her family and yet not to isolate herself. She wanted to live and work within a community, earn good money, and be able to save toward a life that would reunite her with her little daughter. The Navy obliged her on every point.

Those, then, were the two girls with whom I shared that large bright room, all of us very different from each other, but working well together without friction. Rarely, though, did our paths cross during our free hours.

We worked in what would be called today a secretarial pool. We had more "bosses" than fingers on both hands, all of them involved on some level in the naval operations of the Aegaen-Mediterranean theater, which derived their immense importance from the convoys of oil tankers coming from the Near East and attempting to reach German-occupied harbors in Italy and France. Escorting those tankers safely through the maze of islands was the Admiral Aegaes' foremost task. To secure this route, most of the islands held some contingent of German military personnel; Crete was a major stronghold. Shipping supplies necessary for survival to those islands was the other important mission. At one time I could rattle off the names of the Aegean islands in my sleep; they cropped upon my steno pad a hundred times. All orders were taken down by one of us girls, typed out, signed by the officer in charge, and turned over to the teletypist. Our steno pads filled fast with those commands, many of them so crammed with abbreviations that only the initiated could have made any sense of them, and sometimes not even those. There was "G" for secret, and GKDOS for triple secret and KR KR for immediately (empty all wires!) Another code meant that this message could be handled only by officers, including the teletyping of it (which did not automatically make us three girls officers even though we typed them all). Every branch of the Navy, every project, procedure and action had its own code initials. So, when one day a vital message from us to our superior command in Sofia began: "R O M E reports that . . ." Admiral Aegaeis received an urgent message back: "R O M E unknown here; identify!" Our high echelon huddled together in a short, desolate meeting; there was nothing to be done but send back to the commanding Admiral of the Balkans the enlightening message: "R O M E: capital of Italy." It led to one of the last joyful belly-laughs along the grapevines of the German Navy.

The long corridor had flights of offices on both sides; the largest one was occupied by the chief of operations. All officers in the rank of commander or captain occupied their own offices. The aides, ensigns and lieutenants doubled up; they hardly ever sat still long enough to warrant desks of their own. Our working atmosphere was easy-going, even though the stuff we typed was not. Whenever a steno pad was filled, it was rather ceremoniously burned with a witness or two present; the same happened to the contents of any wastepaper basket.

An officer in need of a typist would appear at the door and politely ask for one of us at our first free moment. If it was a KR affair, one of us three would have to drop everything and follow the man to his office. If the commander's rank was of the higher order, he would send an aide to fetch us. The younger officers appeared in person, which we liked because they were full of fun and great teasers. One of them I particularly remember – a journalist in civilian life – who would always show up singing at our door. "Lass, I'm longing for you coming" was his favorite tune. His job was to guide neutral ships through the minefields that protected the Aegaean ports, a job that would have cost me many sleepless nights, but through which he seemed to zoom with mathematical precision and breathtaking speed, dictating the life-and-death course to us, interrupting himself with little songs while re-checking the accuracy of some figures, his legs up on the desk (highly unusual for a German officer) and asking us in between about our latest dates and adventures. Once in a while, when I came to his office, strangers in civilian clothes would be there, speaking in accented German. They were polite, reserved, but the irrepressible lieutenant captain would always have them laughing within minutes. These were Swedes off the Red Cross ships that brought food to the Greek population at regular intervals. As far as I know, our singing captain never lost a ship.

What those Swedish ships brought mostly were canned baked beans. I did not know that, and when I first walked through the streets and markets of Athens I was astonished to see here or there a man squatting in a shady doorway and spooning beans from a tin; or a woman behind a bazaar table feeding a child those orange beans out of a can. I finally decided that this must be some kind of national dish like potatoes in Ireland and North Germany and rice in the Far East. Canned beans as a national staple food seemed very strange to me. I had never eaten or even seen them in Germany.

The long corridor of our floor ended abruptly at a little hall going off to the right and left, so that it took on a T shape. The crossbar of the T led into a few rather large and splendid offices. This was The Inner Sanctum, the Olympus. To the left, the largest of the offices was occupied by the Admiral, with his top aide holding the fort in the outer office. The large office to the right belonged to the chief of staff, who had his own secretary in his outer office. We never really ventured into this sacred tip of the T. Fräulein Henneberg, the chief's secretary, descended once in a while to the lower regions, and a few times she stuck her head into our pool room. She talked to no one in the mess hall or, perhaps, no one talked to her. When I first met her, I thought her old, at least six or seven years older than I was, cool, polite, and distant. She was very blond, with a little help; never a hair was out of place. She was immaculately groomed and she never seemed to perspire. She was the key to the chief of staff's ear, and she doubled as the Admiral's secretary when he was in need of one, which made her even more awe-inspiring.

When I told the girls that I had finally met the famous Fräulein Henneberg, Horsie immediately asked: "Did she tell you about her headaches?" And when I nodded, Horsie yelled: "I knew it! She bores everybody with it."

"She did not always do that," said Eleanor mildly.

"Yeah, but she does now," said Horsie, "and everybody is pretty tired of it."

Our Admiral was hardly known in the building. He was neither arrogant nor shy, he was simply isolated. It came with the territory. He was a rather short man, on the plump side, not young anymore by any means. He had a great deal of responsibility but his desk (when I finally got to see it) was practically bare. He was excellent at delegating. On the desk was a picture of his young wife, Laura-Marie, and I think he spent a good deal of time longing for her. Sometimes he would pick up the phone and ask for a special operator at our telephone center. He would identify himself and ask her to try to reach his home number. She, of course, would move heaven and earth to get a connection, and the Admiral would be able to talk to Laura-Marie for a while. Invariable, after the conversation ended, the Admiral called the operator again and thanked her for her trouble.

Admirals, I decided, have it tough. Despite all the honor and awe they are afforded, they are remote and friendless. The air is very thin around them — thin and sterile. They are so shielded from small and medium-sized annoyances that their world becomes rather unreal. Once they were young ensigns and got hollered at a good deal; they shrugged it off and laughed and mocked their superiors behind their backs. Now they are Admirals and the joke is on them but there is no one to share it with.

Years later I heard an American Navy song that made me think of the elderly, mild-mannered man sitting behind the polished mahogany desk in the isolated splendor of his office.

> *"They tell us that the Admiral*
> *Is as nice as he can be,*
> *But we never see the Admiral,*
> *Because the Admiral has never been to sea!"*

That is certainly how it must have seemed to the young officers who passed through the double doors of the great gray administration building of the Admiralty of the Aegaeis.

Things were quite different with our chief of staff. This tall, handsome aristocrat was tremendously popular. Anecdotes about him made the rounds, from his lieutenants down to the youngest kitchen maid, who very likely had a crush on him anyway. His sense of fairness and inherent, even temper, the low-key voice, his light touch and firm decisions were effective in all matters. Unlike an admiral, a chief of staff deals with an unending stream of annoyances; he is the court of last appeal, the King Solomon of the military. Our chief was equal to the job. The sailors respected and liked him, the young officers idealized him, the girls adored him.

I remember one beautiful Saturday afternoon. I was merrily sailing off into the freedom of the weekend when I met him in the elevator on my way down. We had been told some days before that the political situation was precarious and that our presence and readiness in the office over the weekend would be appreciated; but there was not an enemy lurking any place, not a cloud in the sky, and I had lovely plans.

"Are you leaving?" asked the chief pleasantly. I blushed a little. "Yes, I am," I said, and then, half teasing and half anxious, I added: "You are not going to stop me, are you?"

"My dear young lady," said the chief, smiling faintly. "I shall leave that entirely to your own conscience." My face fell in utter dismay. Anything else I could have defied. We found ways and means around plenty of orders. Anything but this! I took the next elevator up again, wailing and kicking the door all the way.

* * * * * * * * * * * * * * *

The first of May in Germany had been, traditionally, the "Workers' Day." It had been marked by marches, riots, demands, rowdy clashes — workers versus management — and a lot of schnapps and beer. After January, 1933, it had been declared the "Workers' Celebration"; henceforth there were large company picnics, river cruises, folk dances, athletic events, marches, songs — and a lot of schnapps and beer. No more demands, since the workers' paradise had already been achieved! Not so in the military; they cheerfully prepared their demands and celebrated in their own style.

Way out on the bleak and deadly North Sea, the skipper of a *Torpedoflotille* sat gloomily in his cabin awaiting the fate of his beard. And a beautiful black beard it was, well-trimmed and lovingly groomed, the only beard on the face of a German Navy officer. It had taken, so it was whispered, a special permission from the "Führer" for the young skipper to grow and keep that beard. It was known all along the coast and had brought him the nickname "Dandy Andy," recognized by one and all who wore the German Navy blue.

This particular night, the first of May, 1943, his crew was busily raising money which, they had announced, would be turned over to the Red Cross, if the Skipper would shave his beard. After the first shock wave, the officers rallied to the cause. "Save the Skipper's beard!" was the battle cry. They began collecting among themselves and topped the crew by fifty marks. The beard was saved! But not for long. The crew jumped into action again and raised the pot; the officers responded to the challenge, and so it see-sawed all during the day until, late at night, the officers ran out of money and during the early morning hours, Dandy Andy, in the dim light of his cabin, grimly shaved off the Navy's most famous beard.

Word quickly spread along the coasts. A few days later the officers in our building stopped each other in the hall to share the news from the North Sea; it brightened everybody's day. Dandy Andy found few sympathizers. He really needed none.

When Dandy Andy's flotilla sailed into Piraeus some three months later and he came striding into the office to report to the chief, a new magnificent beard surrounded his cheeks and hid the mouth so that only the dark, fiery eyes gave away the reckless, arrogant man inside. He spent a good deal of time straddling a chair beside my desk and murmuring sweet promises in my direction. This was heady stuff, straight out of the Arabian Nights; it made my skin tingle, it kept me from work, it made me laugh, and it made me wonder. How could a man so brave, so competent, so self-assured, be also so stupid? When he whispered the names of past conquests to me to make his pursuit more enticing, more irresistible — would not even the densest girl say to herself: "The next time he sits like this, talks like this, at the next port, to the next girl, my name would be added to his list." Apparently not; the list was long and impressive. He did not know what to make of my teasing; his visit to my office ceased and he turned to greener pastures, to maidens who would recognize a jewel when they were offered one and would not let some perverse sense of humor interfere with so serious a matter. In any case, when he came to the office on his last day to check out with the chief, Dandy Andy did not look like a man who had missed out on what he fancied. He punished me by walking by me without so much as a glance and he decidedly looked quite pleased with himself.

The ensigns and young lieutenants at Admiral Aegaeis celebrated the first of May in their own style. Ten "Demands" were nailed on the officers' mess hall door. We didn't see them, of course—the mess hall was off limits for female personnel—but we heard all about them. Demand No. 3 was: "Down with Frau Gnade" (our housemother). "Surrender the women to us!"

Whatever it was that Frau Gnade celebrated or whatever grief she was drowning within the privacy of her four walls, she was not always without the comfort of a fellow creature.

There were afternoons when she emerged from her dark, unaired room, fully corsetted and coiffured, a silk gray and violet dress rustling about her impressive hips, a small veil fastened to her curls which were piled on top of her head. Like a brig under full sail, she would majestically float toward the city and not return till hours later, as often as not in the company of some grizzly old seaman who would be carrying a number of bottles under his arms, looking slightly dazed about him as he stumbled up the stairs behind her. In other words, Frau Gnade was not the great, unknown recluse we had assumed her to be.

So we were not too surprised when her name appeared in the course of the ten May-Day Demands, which the young officers had nailed to their mess hall door. Sometime during that night, when their May celebration had advanced toward lesser inhibitions and bolder perspectives, somebody must have suggested a little action concerning Demand No. 3. So off they went, marching along the dark streets in high good spirits. Spiro, our able guard and doorman, sat as usual on his chair in the open doorway and was anxious to be helpful. A 100 drachma note refreshed his memory. Frau Gnade's room? 204, just to the left and Spiro's arm waved to the left for additional visual assistance.

"Frau Gnade, Frau Gnade, mercy onto us! We are coming!" they shouted as they thundered up the stairs. All through the hotel the doors opened cautiously; the girls in nightgowns and robes tiptoed out of their rooms. Speculating in whispers, they peered down the hall or leaned over the bannister trying to catch a glimpse of this wonderful spectacle.

A half a dozen fists knocked at the lady's door.

"Open up! Open the door!" the young men shouted. Silence. Frau Gnade could not even have been breathing.

"Open the door, Mme. Mercy, or we'll break it down!" Ghostly silence.

"Frau Gnade" said the leader solemnly, steadying himself on the doorknob, "I repeat: Open the door and surrender the women you keep in this dungeon."

A suppressed, ecstatic giggle went up and down the steps. Frau Gnade decided to negotiate.

"Get out, you ruffians!" she screamed. "I shall report all of you tomorrow to your superiors!"

"Frau Gnade" said the leader with dignity, "let us say we did not hear that! Here is our generous offer: you shall be granted a free retreat and a full pardon if you turn over the women which you keep in this hole."

"I am telephoning the city patrol," screamed Frau Gnade from inside her room.

"You don't even have a telephone!"

"Yes, I do!," shouted the beleaguered lady, "and I am telephoning right now!"

"Let me see," said one of the young men. He bent down and peeked through the keyhole.

"Oh, Frau Gnade," he cried delightedly, "I can see you! I can see your rosy little tootsies! And you don't have a telephone," he added reproachfully.

"Let me see . . ." the leader pushed the other one away and bent down to the keyhole.

"Oh, oh, Frau Gnade, no telephone! You were fibbing. Was that nice?" he scolded. Suddenly a surprised and happy squeal: "Ach, you have a button missing from your nightie! Two buttons . . . what do I see? Oh, Frau Gnade, what splendor! What have you been keeping from us all this time!"

With a piercing screech the lady jumped into her bed and pulled the blanket up to her chin. We could hear the bed creak under the sudden weight. The young men were laughing and jostling each other in front of the keyhole. When they began to look around and up the staircase, the girls ran into their rooms like scared rabbits. Up and down the halls, the doors slammed shut. We heard the men singing and shouting: "See you next year, Lady Merciful!" as they descended the steps and streamed onto the street.

They didn't, of course. For those who were still alive, Greece by that time was just a memory. But, as my mischievous goats would have implied: Didn't they just have a lovely day?

* * * * * * * * * * * * * *

The term "sexual harassment," which covers such a multitude of sins nowadays, had not then been coined. The simple word "NO" seemed to do fine in those days to stop any really unwanted nonsense at the office. Another word which none of us knew was "promiscuous." My old-fashioned dictionary defines it as "lack of discernment" and "failure to make distinctions." Sex is not even mentioned. How did this fine word, then, get such a bawdy reputation? In any case, very little of this was going on in Athens in 1943. I would say rather the opposite; a great deal of distinction was being practiced. Ours was a peculiar situation: a handful of girls surrounded by hundreds of men; something like promiscuity could have spread like a spark in a dry forest. The women's instinctive answer to this potentially explosive situation was stubborn conservatism. Any new girl appearing on the scene was wined and dined by at least half a dozen hopeful young men, was taken to the movies, to the beach, treated to Samos and roast lamb, showered with attention and flattery, and in every way properly courted until she made up her mind and chose one of them as sweetheart and escort. The loyalty then became almost complete. I was in the position to know because it eventually fell on me to recruit girls to show up at some parties and persuading those girls to attend was worse than pulling teeth.

Torpedo boats and S-boats—the ones that Churchill had called "the mosquitoes of the sea"—docked regularly in Piraeus and often the young skippers would make the pilgrimage into Athens to the Administration Building simply to get a party going for their crew. Inevitably they wound up in the office that I occupied and charged me with the task of finding and escorting a group of girls to the boat for a party. I told them that the girls all had steady boyfriends who would sulk and give them a hard time if they went. The young captains, incredulous, refused to accept this.

"Our boys have scrubbed the whole boat down," they would say. "They have saved their rations to have refreshments ready. They have cleared space to dance, and practiced their accordions and harmonicas . . . I can't go back now and say that the girls refuse to come!"

Or, worse, they tried emotional blackmail. "We are leaving again in two days—how do you know we'll be back?"

So, off I'd go, trotting from office to office, floor to floor, making the rounds at the Quartermaster's department where most of the girls worked, to plead, coax, to persuade. Most girls would have come like a shot but dreaded the arguments with their boyfriends. I had to catch the ones between commitments, or those who thought their friend would not find out, or else the few truly emancipated ones who refused to surrender every ounce of personal freedom.

Our little group would take the subway to the harbor to be met by a delegation of beaming young seamen in dazzling clean uniforms. They would escort us to the boat which was decorated with inspired resourcefulness and where we were greeted like so many princesses on a holiday.

Many times, fidgeting on my chair at one of my mother's tea parties, I listened to older people wistfully reminisce about their youth. Inevitably, one or another would look my way and sigh: "Oh, my dear, you don't *know* how beautiful life was before the Great War!" This used to frustrate me considerably. It seemed to belittle all my own experiences and to disparage in advance all future happenings. It is true that opportunities are not always equal, but the capacity to experience magic hours rests within all of us.

So I shall never say to the next generation: "Oh, you poor dears, you will never know what it is like to dance on the piers of Piraeus on a silken night under a starry sky!" Of course, they will never know. They will experience other magic hours, uniquely theirs. Let them make the most of it!

Kristin never went along. Her Harry was demanding of her time and furiously jealous. They went out together at night or he visited at the hotel, and on the nights when he was on duty she was supposed to wash his socks and think of him. Kristin didn't object to thinking of him; she talked of him all the time anyway. But she detested washing socks. Very soon she and I had a deal worked out. My dresses and skirts had never found Kristin's approval; she was a great deal more fashion-conscious than I. For one thing, she declared them all the wrong length. So, on the evenings when we stayed home, Kristin would sit on her bed, shortening or lengthening my skirts, fastening buttons and turning collars on blouses while I stood at her sink scrubbing Harry's socks. Afterward we would go outside and sit on our rooftop, the heat of the sunbaked bricks against our backs, looking over the flickering lights of the city to the horizon, where the purple mountains melted into the dark blue sky and the distant beat of the bouzoukis joined the cry of the crickets.

We never ran out of talk.

Harry, of course, was the main topic. Kristin and Harry's relationship could best be described as tumultuous. Since I was seldom around the two of them, I could never understand how this low-key, seemingly passive girl got into so many passionate squabbles with him. For that matter, I never quite understood how she could be in love with this man. It wasn't just Harry's smile that was wicked. Harry had been walking the wild side more than once in his life. It must have been this to her so mysterious quality in him that intrigued her, while he was attracted to her like a wildly fluttering moth to a quietly burning candle. Yet those two totally different human beings were so convinced that they were right for each other that they announced their engagement to their families at home. From that point on, their arguments centered mostly on their future married life. I remember coming home one night and finding, as I frequently did, the big navy truck parked outside our hotel and Harry, once again, slouched behind the wheel, arms crossed over his chest, staring ferociously into the dark.

"Now what?" I asked.

"She is impossible!" he hissed between clenched teeth.

"What did you fight about this time?"

"Ask her!" was the furious answer.

"I don't have to, I'll hear it anyway," I muttered, beginning to climb the steps.

I found Kristin cowering on her bed, arms around her legs, head on her knees, staring at the wall. The corners of her mouth were drawn downward about a hundredth of an inch, signaling frustration and disgust.

"What did you fight about, Kristin?"

"He is impossible!"

"Want to tell me?" Silence. Then:

"You'll think it's silly, but it isn't." Silence. With the faintest blush of passion in her face, she turned to me: "He said I was to polish his shoes when we are married! My father always polished my mother's shoes. Harry thinks it's up to the woman to polish everybody's shoes!"

"Kristin," I said dumbfounded, "You can't be serious?"

"I knew you would not understand," she said. There were tears of frustration in her eyes, which, however, she did not permit to roll down her cheeks.

At such moments, when her stubbornness was at its peak, I could not tease her out of it. All I could do was make some comforting little noises about men's general unreasonableness and calm her down until she finally would get under the covers and go to sleep.

The early mornings and the last hour at night Kristin and I used to share regularly, and often we met in the mess hall to eat together. Our paths seldom crossed at any other of our day's activities. We did not even share the experience of a visit to the Acropolis together. Twice during my year in Greece I walked up to the beautiful temple and shrine to the Goddess Pallas Athene; once during the sunset hours when the sky turned a transparent green and rose glow, and once in the night when a full moon pointed a white path up the mountain to the Parthenon. Each time I walked with a man I liked, in silence, in awe. It was not the sort of thing one might want to do chattering with a girlfriend, nor even with the very best of girlfriends.

Our working day began at six when I ran barefoot across the night-cool tarred roof to waken Kristin. I don't remember having an alarm clock; I simply awakened at the right time. At six thirty we would walk through the still-shaded streets to the mess hall for our cup of ersatzkaffee and our rations of bread and marmalade. At seven we were behind our desks. At noon all offices closed; we went for our dinner, received our evening rations, and headed home. The city slowed down for a long siesta. In the cooling shades of doorways and the cave-like courtyard entrances, hustlers, street merchants, and workmen would be lying down, their faces lightly covered, sound asleep. All women and children disappeared inside the darkened rooms of their houses which, with their tightly shuttered windows, faced the merciless glare of the streets with blind, lifeless hostility. The heat was phenomenal. It seemed to me as if we were not walking under the sun but in it. Great, dark stains of perspiration appeared on the backs of our blouses; our moist hair was pasted to our scalps. Small, itchy streams of sweat were running down our bodies. I often wondered if I cracked a raw egg onto the asphalt, would it not fry as speedily as on a sizzling skillet?

Kristin always lay down on top of her bed, like the rest of the girls, to fall into a leaden sleep. There were days when I was unable to do anything but follow her example. (I remember getting up after one of those naps. I felt perspiration drops tickling my neck. Walking over to the sink, I lifted my hair to dry my neck and three bedbugs dropped into the sink.) More often, though, I would grab my towel and bathing suit and walk back onto the street to wait for our streetcar. I say "our streetcar" because, in order to reduce friction, different streetcars were assigned to the population and to the members of the occupation. The native streetcars ran much more frequently and once in a while, on my way into town in the evenings, I just stood in line with the natives and made an attempt to board one of theirs. It always remained an attempt. The streetcar conductor, looking so bored and uninterested, would suddenly come to life. Waving his arms wildly at me, he would signal: "*NO!*" Absolutely no. And dejectedly I would climb out again. How did he know? My hair was very dark, I wore civilian clothes, I sweated like the rest of them. I sometimes think my light eyes gave me away, or my tan. Greek women might have very white skin, and if they did, they protected it at all times with scarfs and umbrellas. Never would they voluntarily have exposed themselves to the sun and a darkening of their highly valued milky white skin.

But during those noon hours the natives' cars had all but ceased to run. There I would stand on the treeless, unshaded, empty plaza, slowly perishing in the heat. When our streetcar finally came, I was the only passenger on it. "Mad dogs and Englishmen." The conductor was always the same and acknowledged me with a mere flicker of his eye. Down the tracks we would fly, not stopping at all; there were no passengers waiting anywhere and he knew my destination. We would reach the coast in record time and a five-minute walk would take me to a stretch of white, deserted beach, where I would fairly throw myself into the warm sea. And the sea received me as if it had been waiting for me. Floating on my back in the soft, clear, green water, I would stare at the endlessly deep, blue sky above me, not hurting anywhere, not wishing for anything. If, as someone once said, happiness is the absence of pain, I spent there and then a few of the happiest, most deeply contented moments of my life.

After two hours, I would start the long haul back to the city and arrive at my desk with salt-crusted skin and dried, salty strands of hair hanging down my back. Needless to say, there were no showers. So, one evening, I told Kristin to cut off my hair. I sat on a chair on our roof and gave her the scissors and she said: Do you *really* want this? And I said, yes. She quickly cut off the hair on one side in a straight line under the ear and then lost her nerve. She stopped and asked feebly:

"Do you really want this?"

This struck me as so funny that the coiffuring had to be postponed until I stopped laughing. "If I said no, now, what on earth would you do?" I asked, and then started laughing again. Maybe Dandy Andy was right and I have a perverted sense of humor. Anyway, Kristin shuddered, closed her eyes and cut off the rest. After that, it was much easier to rinse and dry my hair, and in the moist heat it began to curl on its own.

The mess hall was not the place where we spent our most memorable hours. The meals ranged from tolerable to bad to awesomely awful. The potatoes were almost always bluish and glassy, which meant that some time between harvest and consumption they had been exposed to frost. Just where and when this should have happened on their way to Greece remained a mystery. Our evening rations consisted of bread, jam, butter, cheese and eggs. The bread was dark, wet and heavy. At the time I suspected that they lengthened the dough with moist sawdust; quite a few times it gave me considerable pain under the ribs. More likely, though, they added some of those glassy potatoes. The butter was greenish and word had gotten around that it was synthetic and probably made of coal fats. It was a small and unappetizing piece but it was practically tasteless and calmed the stomach. We learned to accept the inevitable. The eggs, however, were a different matter. There was nothing wrong with those eggs when they were delivered to the kitchen. It was the cook who ruined them. He simply dumped them into a great kettle of water and put the kettle on low heat before he retired to his four-hour midday break. When he returned, well-rested, he fished them out and added them to our evening meal. Eggs are not meant to boil for four hours, not even on low heat. When we peeled them, they looked like Chinese eggs aged through a century, and that was how they lay in our stomach: aged, purple, and stony.

We supplemented this dreary fare with as much dried and fresh fruit as we could afford. Grapes and raisins were sold in abundance at roadside stands. We ate fresh dates and lovely fresh figs, the red, sweet juice spurting out of the green shell and running down our fingers. We traded our bread for olive oil and fresh eggs and lemons and made mayonnaise to enhance those purple eggs and watery potatoes. We drank gallons of fruit juice. With this sort of diet and the water we drank straight from the spigot, it was not surprising that all of us suffered at times from various degrees of diarrhea or dysentery. The worst cases were referred to the large military hospital outside the city; the rest of us just bore it rather stoically as we did the sweat, the salt pills, and the bugs. We delighted in the blue sky, the warm nights, the unending summer, and we were resigned to the penalties that the children of the north invariably pay when they trespass into sunnier latitudes.

The sole exception, perhaps, was the illness we called *Papadacci*. The Italians had given it that name and we adopted it, but by any other name it would not have smelled like roses, either. Victims related to it not unlike women relate to childbirth. The ones who had experienced it and were safely on the other side loved reminiscing about it—with much rolling of the eyes and pleasant little shivers—in front of future victims who would listen with long faces and a good deal of apprehension. It was carried by a small mosquito; natives were immune to it but among foreigners it raged like a hailstorm in a wheatfield. Its onset was fast: within a few hours it mowed down its victims and rendered them all but paralyzed. A steadily rising fever, reaching 105 degrees, was the most obvious symptom. Violent headaches made moving and lifting of the head a torture. The skin was so sensitized that the flimsiest nightgown, the lightest sheet, meant painful pressure. But what anybody who underwent this hellish illness probably remembered most vividly were the aching bones, perhaps because this discomfort outlasted the headaches and the fever. Every inch of every bone seemed to hurt, which made it almost impossible to lie quietly in bed hoping to sleep and let this nightmare pass. But pass it did, rarely lasting longer than five or six days, leaving the patient relieved, delivered, and weak as a kitten.

We all had been issued a large mosquito net on our first day there to prevent just that sort of catastrophe. It didn't work for two simple reasons: One could just as well be stung during the day, and almost nobody used them for their intended purpose. Those mosquito nets were exceedingly popular, but I knew few people who actually slept under them. The officers put them away as nuisances after which they were speedily and permanently removed by Greek servants. The sailors stacked them away for souvenirs. The women dyed them and sewed blouses and skirts of the fine, porous material, which was ideally suited for tropical clothing.

Intermittently, memos were received by the supply officers that information of misappropriation of navy supplies, notably mosquito netting, had reached headquarters in Sofia. Those memos were duly studied by the supply warrant officers, who would tell their petty officers to keep closer track of the nets in the future. The petty officers would tell their girlfriends that they might have to wait a few weeks before they could get another net, since the heat was on at the moment. Nobody got very excited about it; it was just another one of those things. So it came like a thunderclap one day when headquarters in Sofia directly addressed our quartermaster and ordered him to take the strongest actions against the stealing of mosquito nets. He was to set a stern disciplinary example that would stop all future mischief in that matter. Headquarters ordered a detailed report of measures taken.

It was a bad situation. The quartermaster ordered the disciplinary board to meet and take such action as was expected by Headquarters. The members of the disciplinary board, having never before been called on for anything like it, were not even sure they were members. A few young captains, a few middle-aged commanders who had been in the reserve and had, in fact, never as much as hollered at anybody who worked for them, were now to sit in judgment on something they knew to be common practice and to find culprits who had done nothing more than most everybody else.

The girls did not hear too much of what went on during those meetings. The members of the board cursed their fate that had placed them in such a miserable position. But immediate action was required. They had no choice but to find a culprit. A young woman was summoned before the board and charged with misappropriation of navy property. At a short hearing she received a mild sentence of five days in the brig. The report was sent to Headquarters and Headquarters seemed to be satisfied. They were the only ones satisfied; they sat a thousand miles away. Everybody felt bad about the whole thing. The whispering in the mess hall was about nothing else. We all knew the involved girl by sight, but none of us knew much about her. She was a loner, she was not friendly and she was, obviously, friendless. For everyone of the most flagrant violators, when named as possible culprit, somebody had spoken up; nobody spoke for her. At the hearing she wore a wide black skirt made out of the offensive material. She had not had any idea what she had been called for. Her offense was read to her; the board asked her for a statement; she remained mute with surprise. The black skirt hung limply around the dumfounded girl as they read her sentence to her.

She spent her five days in the brig. The door was never locked, the cook sent her some decent meals, the embarrassed guards tried to cheer her up. She was not having any of it; she was not letting anybody off the hook; she forgave nothing. If she was lonely before, now she was isolated. If strangers had descended upon her, sentenced her to confinement and departed again, it would have been a different situation. But those were no strangers; those were members of her working community; they had singled her out for punishment and she would see us in hell before she would lift our guilt from us.

* * * * * * * * * * * * * *

Certainly we met up with situations for which nobody had prepared us and we had to deal with them without the advice or input of family or teachers. Neither could we solve the problem by hiding our heads in the sand. There are moments in our lives when there is nothing to be done but — as my old math tutor would say — to address ourselves to the task at hand.

Kristin and Harry had a falling out that lasted longer than usual and I was getting used to finding her, when I came home at night, alone and serenely sitting on her bed stitching on a piece of clothing or putting up her hair. Life was more peaceful around her during Harry's long-term sulk.

One evening she did not answer when I called out coming up the steps. At first glance her room seemed empty, but something was moving under her sheet and there were sounds of stifled sobs. I ran to the bed and tried to pull the sheet off her face, but she would not let me. My questions were answered by increased sobbing and thrashing under the bed clothes.

"Are you sick, Kristin?" I asked over and over again, "What is the matter? Speak to me!"

Finally a muffled, but audible answer. "*I* am not sick! This place is sick! It stinks! It's rotten! I hate it! I want to go home. I never ever want to come back here again!"

Pretty strong stuff from my poker-faced friend. There was more sobbing and mumbling and after a great deal of coaxing from my side, one word emerged: "Lice." Lice? Kristin? Who was always washing and fussing with her hair?

"Not those lice," she enlightened me from beneath the sheet, "the other kind."

"Chicken lice?" I asked, surprised.

"Don't be daft," said Kristin, momentarily exasperated into almost normalcy. "I haven't been near a chicken for almost two years. The other kind, body lice."

No sooner had she uttered that fateful word when the full horror of it descended upon her once again. She pulled her pillow down over her head and temporarily ceased to be of this world.

I had never heard of body lice. Obviously they were nastier than chicken lice and less inclined to leave on their own accord, or Kristin would not carry on like this.

"Listen, Kristin," I addressed myself to the pillow with some firmness, "surely they have some stuff, ointments or salves, for just that. We'll go to the infirmary tomorrow and get some medication."

A muffled, but piercing, scream stopped me.

"Kristin, what is it?"

"I'd rather die than go there!" Kristin had lifted the pillow a little to make herself perfectly clear.

"But why? They are the ones who can help . . ."

Suddenly Kristin's face, pale, tear-blotched, tragic, emerged from under the sheet.

"Have you forgotten who runs the infirmary?"

For a moment I was at a loss and then it dawned on me: the medic! He, of the falsified immunization records and the broken heart! Never would I get Kristin within a mile of that place. We were back to square one. From under the sheet and pillow came Kristin's irrevocable decision:

"I am going to kill myself."

"How?"

"I am going to cut my wrists."

"That hurts!"

Shocked silence. Kristin was against pain. She, also, was against my being frivolous.

"I'll find a way!"

"Can I have your white raincoat?"

"That is not funny," said Kristin indignantly from beneath the pillow. My mind was rummaging through every corner of past experiences.

"Listen, Kristin," I said. "When I was a child we had a favorite book about a little stray dog . . ." Kristin started sobbing again rather energetically; she was not interested in little stray dogs.

"Well, listen! He had fleas and the mother would not let the children keep him till he got rid of the fleas, so their nanny made a sort of broth from tobacco and she bathed the dog in it."

The sobbing ceased. "Did it help?" asked Kristin in a small voice. "Like a charm," I assured her. "Fleas and lice, that's all the same. And now, go to sleep. Tomorrow we'll get rid of the pest."

Kristin did not go to work the next morning but spent her time sitting on her bed, crying and beheading lice with her thumb nail. She looked worn and pathetic when I came back at noon.

"What do we have?" It was time to be practical about it. Kristin had a whole loaf of bread saved up. I produced a bag of cough drops. We pooled our money. It looked good; I was fairly sure that this would be sufficient enticement to get hold of a carton of cigarettes on the black market.

Athen's black market stretched over a number of street blocks. I could never figure out why it was called "black market," implying something secret or illegal. There was nothing secret about the place. It was open, large, and extraordinarily noisy. One could get a great many things there, but olive oil and cigarettes were not among the items exhibited at every stand. Some subtlety was required. Neither Kristin nor I were smokers so we had no experience with purchasing cigarettes, but, just as I had hoped, some urchins approached me already at the edge of the market.

"Stockings, lady? Scarves? Beautiful pearl necklace, almost real? . . ."

"Cigarettes," I said. Immediately they were all business.

"What you have?" And we were off, bargaining. I know they got the better of me, but I was in a hurry and they knew it. The main thing was I had my carton of cigarettes.

I went into our dark, windowless kitchen, lit only by a single bulb dangling haphazardly from the ceiling. With flying fingers I began to slit open the cigarettes with my nails, one after another, pack after pack, and emptying the tobacco into the largest cookpot I could find. The kitchen was rarely used by any of the girls, but it was not off limits and anyone might enter at any moment. What was I to say, standing there ripping precious cigarettes open and dumping them into a greasy old pot? I finished undisturbed, though, put the pot on the stove, and cleaned up any mess I had made. It wasn't until the evil-looking broth started to boil and I was standing over it, stirring it, that two girls came in looking for some dishes to make mayonnaise.

"What stinks?" one of them asked immediately.

"I don't smell anything," I said.

"What are you cooking?"

"Herbs," I said, pushing the last of the tobacco leaves under water.

"It smells like tobacco!"

"That, too," I said.

The girls were about to leave when one of them, driven by curiosity, came over to peer into the pot.

"Yak!" she said. "What do you want that for? Dye?"

What a marvelous idea. "Yes, some guys asked me to dye their socks for them."

"With *that*?" asked the girl incredulously.

"It prevents athlete's foot," I explained. "You should try it."

"Yak!" said the girl again and left. I don't think I had sold her on the idea.

I boiled the stuff for about ten minutes and carried it up to the rooftop. We stripped Kristin's bed, we stripped her shelves and hooks, and we stripped Kristin. And then we sponged. This was total war.

When we had finished, there was not a six-legged creature alive within a four-and-a-half-foot radius. It was a stunning victory.

Chapter 13

The chief of operations was a thin, fidgety man with the unhealthy color of an ulcer candidate. As his military task grew from complex to difficult to pretty nearly impossible, so grew his ulcer and his irritability. His office was the farthest down the hall from the secretaries' room. Whenever he needed a secretary, he would ring for one of his aides who would hurry down the corridor and storm into our room to coax us away from our typewriter. We were not keen on taking dictation from this nervous gentleman but one of us would always immediately rise and leave. One did not keep the chief of operations waiting. However, wait he did, his chair pushed back, his fingers drumming a hectic march on his desk, his mouth lined with pain. Hiding his discomfort as unbecoming an officer, he showed his impatience with the wait he had to endure all the more clearly. He was not an unkind man. During the first months of my stay, when the soggy bread at times gave me violent stomach cramps, he was the most sympathetic soul around. I might even say, the only sympathetic soul. Eventually the ulcer got the better of him and he had to ask for an indefinite medical leave. He stayed on, however, until the Admiral found a suitable replacement.

That was a formidable task. The job was nerve-racking and became daily more difficult. Africa was lost. The safety of the oil tankers rested on convoy escorts that had shrunk to a pitiful number, and the German contingents on the various islands had to be supplied with at least the barest necessities. The Admiral wanted a man with a good solid sea-faring background but even more with the ability to make quick, daring decisions and with nerves like steel cables.

He found such a man in the captain of a destroyer that had sunk near the coast of Africa. The ship, under the command of this skipper, had an impressive record of safe convoy duty. It had done battle with a large enemy submarine, disabling it and taking its entire crew on board. It had survived two air attacks by outmaneuvering the falling bombs. A third attack, some weeks later, hit the destroyer's main screw, paralyzing it. When enemy vessels approached and a take-over was inevitable, the captain ordered his crew to the lifeboats and with all souls at a safe distance, blew up his ship. This was the kind of nerve and decision-making ability the Admiral thought was needed in his chief of operation. No ulcers here, apparently.

Rumors, as always, blossomed over night, nourished by "eye-witness" reports. A few of the young officers had known the man and had served under him. Their reports were so controversial that they only heightened everybody's curiosity. Some of them said it had been their most memorable stretch of duty and that the crew would have gone through hell and high water for him. Others reported that he was disliked and that his temper fits were monumental.

When he finally arrived, he was locked in closed conferences with our suffering old chief and we did not catch a glimpse of him until a few days later. I won't say that we weren't worried a bit. Even Horsie, who liked to swim on top of the soup at all times, owned up to a few misgivings.

On the third day our old boss, looking more yellow and pinched than ever, came in to shake hands with everybody and thereafter vanished from the scene. A new broom was sweeping through the old corridor. All aides went about in dazzling clean shirts, looking duty-bound and busy. It was heartwarming to watch them so earnest and dedicated, trying to move faster and sweat less.

When we came in for dictation, our new boss looked at us with piercing blue eyes, but asked few personal questions beyond our names and how long we had been working there. Within three days he declared that the setup of securing a secretary was a colossal stupidity and a waste of everybody's time. With one casual motion of his hand, he swept his various aides a few offices down the hall and ordered a permanent secretary to be installed in the room adjoining his office.

And so it came about that for the second time within three months, my nearsighted, jolly friend was standing beside my desk saying:

"Eva, you'll have to move. Orders!"

Even though it was only a few rooms up the hall, the move was something of an upheaval. If I was worried about Eleanor's or Horsie's reaction—both of them with more seniority than I—my mind was soon put at ease. Eleanor, serene and uncompetitive, was the fastest and best typist on the floor, and since I was not to be replaced in the pool, she was certainly needed. And Horsie? Well, Horsie just might have made life very difficult for me if it had not been for the fact that this was no job she aspired to. Horsie needed to get around, to keep her contacts, to touch all her bases. Acting as a receptionist and watchdog, having to be available at all times with nobody to cover for her, would have sorely cramped her style. And even though Horsie never said a nice word to me about the move up, she knew deep down in her heart that she would have hated to be selected herself.

My own feelings varied from amazement to pleasure to a slight dread. So far, I had no real clue to the man. I remembered the stories of his temper outbursts and didn't cherish the thought of being placed in the line of fire on possible future occasions. On the other hand, the working atmosphere on the floor was so considerate and congenial that I hoped it would persevere, even over so erratic a temperament. The first morning at my new job strengthened this hope. The new chief's orders were short and to the point: "Do what you want with the office. Get some furniture— people will be waiting there—make it as attractive as you wish. Leave the door ajar. When I need you, I will call." Period. Not, "How many words do you type a minute?" nor "Are you sure you can read your own shorthand?" Two questions I hoped would not be put to me at any time, and especially not on the first morning of a new job.

It was a busy first week. With help from Horsie who was inwardly tickled pink, outwardly sighing and muttering, and with the help of a number of eager aides, I got a small table, three chairs, not counting my desk chair, and a rug. The room did boast a bookcase that contained what seemed at a first look to be an all-Greek library, but an optimistic search through the shelves rendered—oh marvelous surprise!—a German Iliad. Some scholar, in anticipation of a tour of duty in the land of Homer, had probably brought the book along from Germany and later deposited it in the only bookcase on the floor. Horsie, watching my search for books, donated a German Bible that somebody must have pawned with her and she foresaw being stuck with it. Lacking sports and gossip magazines, the Bible and the Iliad went on the table in the waiting area. Horsie, also, got me a coffee machine and some mugs. Coffee and sugar were available; milk or cream, of course, were out of the question. I polished the dirty window, put some flowers on my desk and opened for business.

And business was thriving. Almost anybody of consequence who wanted something from Admiral Aegaeis eventually wound up at the chief of operations' office. With my office now guarding the chief's door, all of the receiving and screening which the aides had done fell on me. The consensus of the new system was that waiting was much more fun than it used to be. Everybody who had to cool his heels was served "sailor's coffee" (black, with sugar) and sympathy. They drank their coffee, leafed through the Bible (looking for the Songs of Solomon) and told me their grievances. The young officers who came from the islands, if and when they could get a ride, came to plead for more supplies and to impress the big brass with their troops' precarious position. They practiced their speech on me first, the undiluted version. I remember one of their biting jokes which they cheerfully told me over their cup of coffee: "Admiral Aegaeis went out to Piraeus to review a parade of his ships. Unfortunately, after an hour, the parade had to be called off because the two men who were rowing got blisters on their hands!"

The skippers of the torpedo boats, the S-boats and the convoy escort ships who had to report to the Admiralty waited their turn in my office. Many of them, notably the S-boat captains, were pathetically young. I asked once why this was so—what happened to the famous years of experience? The answer was mind-boggling. "If they are older," I was told, "they begin to figure out the odds of survival and they can no longer be used successfully in that position."

They came from Piraeus harbor to their headquarters in Athens, their caps at a jaunty angle, captain stripes gleaming, white shirts soaked with perspiration, submitting their log books, receiving their impossible orders, looking for girls so their crew could have a party and some happy memories to take back out to sea. They were barely older than I. They were my brothers, they were the boys next door with whom I had grown up. The war had caught them between school and university, and they were waiting for the war to be done and over with so they could get on with their education and their lives. I remember a young man, captain of one of those cursed S-boats, sitting on the low chair beside the table, opening the Iliad and losing himself so completely in it that when the chief signaled to see him, he was oblivious to the world around him and I had to get up and gently take the book out of his hands.

I will tell you something: even now, more than forty years later, I cannot think of this incident without tears in my heart. Maybe it is so because within a year's time my younger brother was to say to me: "To get out of this uniform, to get back on the school bench, is all I can think about!" Less than a month later my brother was dead. This incident in my office in Athens signifies something so sad, so hopeless, so damnable — and if you cannot understand what I mean, you are very fortunate and I shall not attempt to explain.

I barely had time to miss the girls. Eleanor came to see me when she had some time to spare. Kristin came up once in a while for a quick chat. And now that I had moved so much closer to the Inner Sanctum, Fräulein Henneberg paid me an occasional visit. She did not sit on the chair beside my desk as Kristin and Eleanor did and as Dandy Andy of the black beard fame had done, but sat on the official visitor chair at the little table, daintily holding her coffee cup and telling me about her headaches. They were getting worse, more frequent . . . her sentence trailed off at times, unfinished. Horsie never came; this, decidedly, was not her turf.

Lightening struck again at our poor Admiral's balding head. His second in command, our chief of staff, was leaving us. This popular officer, whose serenity and Solomonic good judgment had benignly influenced the entire administration, was a truly afflicted man. A creeping, crippling arthritis had pervaded his body with ever-increasing pain and immobility until there were days when this proud, elegant man had to be dressed and undressed by his orderly like a small child. Our beloved "C" was going home into early retirement.

Following her superior on a medical discharge was his devoted girl Friday, Fräulein Henneberg. She disappeared in the wake of his departure, almost unnoticed. It was some weeks before confusing rumors reached us at Admiral Aegaeis and, shortly afterwards, the cool, hard facts. Fräulein Henneberg of the impeccable manners and the vague headaches had gotten no further than Sofia. There, twenty-four hours after removal of a tumor on the brain, she had quietly turned her head toward the wall and died.

No replacements were in sight. The duties of the chief of staff fell automatically to the next highest ranking officer, the chief of operations, my boss. This formidable job was simply added to his other tasks. He refused to move away from his staff. He remained in his office, and so did I. There now was no Fräulein Henneberg to shield me from Mt. Olympus. If and when the Admiral wanted to dictate a memo or a letter, he would send his aide to collar me. I won't deny that this thought made me very nervous. It soon became apparent, however, that Admirals don't dictate letters and memos as often as I had assumed. Several days went by before I was summoned for the first time. His head aide, a good-looking captain who in civilian life had a ranch in Brazil and on it, I am sure, a large and handsome family, got up from his chair when I entered and gave me an encouraging little hug. If it seemed to have a bit more warmth to it than necessary, I figured it to be a Brazilian custom. It soon became evident, however, that he had no intention of letting me go, and as the embrace gained momentum and I felt I had all the encouragement I needed, I ducked out of his arms and got away from him. This maneuver was followed by a lively but noiseless chase around his desk. Neither of us had the least interest in having the Admiral stick his head through the door to investigate any commotion in his outer office. I finally got hold of the doorknob to the Admiral's room, which forced the captain to jump hastily back into his chair and frown industriously at a piece of paper.

No, I was not outraged. Far from it. This incident had definitely its beneficial aspects. I had arrived at the scene filled with fear and trembling at my debut in the Admiral's office. By now I was effectually distracted. Particularly the sight of the captain's unceremonious dive back into his chair — which was in visual line with the Admiral's desk — had gone a long way toward restoring my spirits and good humor.

The Admiral sat in a large chair behind a great, wide, beautiful desk that was graced by a picture of Laura-Marie and a few neatly stacked papers. Like Atlas, he carried the ultimate responsibility for the troublesome seas around him on his plump, elderly shoulders. The actual work, though, was done by everybody else. I decided that this was the secret of his restful, vast, empty desk, while my boss's desk, a few rooms down the hall, looked more and more like a disaster area. I sat down on the chair across from him, looking my most composed and competent, hoping and praying all the while that he would talk as slowly as he moved.

The merry Gods of Greece were with me. He dictated two short letters, speaking thoughtfully and deliberately, and I went back to my office and typed them without a single mistake, filling in by memory all the parts which I could not decipher on my steno pad. Early in my "career" I had discovered that I often had total recall of the spoken word, and this useful talent had gotten me mercifully over many a rough spot before.

I loved my job. Since my boss filled in as chief of staff pro tem, the traffic had grown. My office saw a steady stream of visitors, the important and the insignificant, the formidable and the timid, navy brass and army colonels, all waiting patiently or irritably for their turn, all wanting transportation, all needing ships which we did not have and our Admiral could not stomp out of the ground or grow on the flat of his hand. Many came into the office short-tempered and overwrought, and if I was able to turn a frown into a smile with a cup of sailor's coffee, some patient listening, or a bit of teasing, I felt I had done my part to ease the tension and have things run more smoothly.

During that time an incident occurred that probably qualifies for the term "sexual harassment." Early one morning I had a caller, a girl my age whom I should have known but at first did not recognize. It was the young goddess who more than six months before had received us at the station. There was now no radiance about her. Her hair was still blond and the long, curved eyelashes were still remarkably black, but there were ominous dark circles under her eyes, her face was colorless, and there were anxious lines around her mouth. She took the chair beside my desk and tried hard to appear casual.

"I have asked for a transfer home," she began. Her voice faltered. She stopped, looked past me out of the window and seemed to fight to regain her casual demeanor.

"Yes?" I said, puzzled. We had nothing at all to do with transfers.

"My fiancé wants me to come home. We want to get married. We . . ." she stopped again.

"That's great," I said heartily. I remembered the jolly young sailor and his ten-pound sewing box.

"I've *got* to go home," she suddenly said almost wildly. I looked at her haunted eyes, still mystified.

"He won't let me," she whispered, and then her misery swept over her; she stood up and almost fell against me. I put my arms around her and patted her back, completely at a loss for a minute. She would not say anything more but just sobbed into my shoulder. Slowly enlightenment descended upon me. She was the secretary of the head of the department of civilian personnel. It was in this capacity that she had met us at the train.

The head of personnel was a Captain Berner, a man of somewhat sinister handsomeness, built like a whip, with a formidable reputation for wine and women. I had heard rumors that he had been her lover. No civilian within the administration could get a marching order or transfer without his approval.

"Have you applied for home transfer?" The head on my shoulder nodded. I ventured a guess: "He won't process your application?" No answer, but the sobbing grew more violent. Why, the louse! The miserable, fink-faced cad!

"Let's talk to the chief about it," I said. More patting on the back. "Everything is going to be all right. I promise!"

The sobbing slowly subsided. A handkerchief was produced, then a comb. A cup of coffee, a look into the mirror, a grateful, sniffled thank-you, an attempt at a smile, and my blond, unhappy goddess disappeared out of my door and out of my life.

Timing is everything. Well, a lot, anyway. I had to catch my boss in a good mood, but with my righteous wrath still fresh.

"Lord Almighty!" he groaned, "Do I have to look after stuff like that, too?"

"Yes, Sir," I said firmly.

He picked up the phone and dialed. "Berner!" His voice was like thunder. Nobody could have accused my boss of being low key.

"You have a Fräulein Lavade working for you. I want her marching orders to Germany, fully processed, on my desk first thing tomorrow morning. Is that understood? Good!" The receiver slammed down.

"All right?" he said, turning to me. I looked approvingly at the great man.

"Now may I go back to running my ships?" he asked in mock meekness. I nodded graciously and floated out of the office.

Actually, there were a few other things on my mind, little items in need of correction. Ever since my boss had been promoted to chief of staff pro tem the girls in the mess hall had been after me to do something about the purple eggs. But I decided I had done enough meddling for one day. Never overload the circuit.

"What on earth are the black stains on your blouse?" Kristin asked that night. "Up there, on your left shoulder? It looks like mascara." We inspected it together. I told her what had happened. After all, she was my best friend. And then she helped me to wash it out.

When the next time I went to bat, it was on another emergency and again the eggs had to be postponed.

The head of the payroll department was a middle-aged, sallow man of a remarkably nasty disposition. Cringing before superiors, he was a bully within his own department. He set impossible timetables, reneged on promises, contradicted his own orders, and often withheld information, only to throw the necessary papers on the desks of his staff late in the afternoon with orders to finish the job before they left. He was fond of cutting down his subalterns in front of other people and, in general, had a whole bag of chicaneries that he used at various times on different employees. Kristin, who liked her job and her co-workers, deplored a situation that poisoned the atmosphere of the department. I was used to hearing her complain about this man and often heartily joined in her diatribe, partly out of genuine concern but mostly out of loyalty to her. It tended to calm her down when I became properly indignant.

The last straw, however, was about to be deposited on Kristin's own back. The paymaster developed bladder trouble and had to be temporarily under doctor's care. This meant a daily testing of an early urine specimen. Kristin was ordered to his office. With a lopsided grin and a few heavily jocular words he handed her a small, peculiarly warm bottle wrapped moistly and sloppily in a scrap of paper. There are few things as embarrassing as the humor of the humorless. Kristin did not laugh. Numbly she carried her messy parcel five blocks down to the medical labs. On the second morning she was fuming. On the third morning she turned hostile. She planted the bottle on a window sill outside the office and came up to visit me instead.

I did not fiddle around with that one. If there was not an opportune moment, one had to be created. Once on the subject, my report did not stop with the carrier service. There were any number of nasty little incidents to choose from. My boss was not amused. He looked like a veritable thunder cloud. There was something singularly offensive to him about the whole thing. The paymaster was ordered upstairs on the double. He appeared, looking sallow and scared. For the first time I witnessed one of the chief's famed temper outbursts. The noises from inside his office sounded like judgment day. Suddenly an ominous silence and then the chief's voice bellowed:

"What smells in here?" A mumbled reply followed about an unusual tendency to sweat and the use of some perfume.

"Christ Almighty, man," the chief's voice roared through the door, "get rid of that stuff! You smell like a whorehouse!"

At that point I picked up my pencil and pad and fled out of the office. Let the old buzzard, when he came stumbling out, cling to the forlorn hope that the room had been empty the entire time.

I wasn't always the one who stirred up trouble. On at least one memorable occasion I was on the receiving end of the storm, and what a storm it was!

The administration, like a ship on high seas, had to keep a log book ("war diary") into which all important events and decisions of the day were recorded. All charge officers of the department contributed to it. The young ensigns and aides gathered the information for us and we three girls took turns typing it out. It had to be typed on stencil which did not bother Eleanor — nothing much seemed to bother Eleanor — but Horsie and I greatly disliked typing stencils. One morning it was discovered that two stencil pages with the previous day's activities were missing. It started with the fluttering back and forth between offices by various young officers. It soon took on momentum and turned into a hectic search which involved the whole department. Who had seen the missing sheets? Who had typed them? Who had carried them last from where to where? By late afternoon the department was in an uproar, the charge officers were jittery, the ensigns and aides were nervous wrecks, the wastepaper baskets were confiscated, and our desks had been all but turned upside down. There was not a trace of those two pages. Thirty hours after the disappearance it was reported to security. Another search followed, this time by experts. Even the Admiral had to leave his office while they searched the Inner Sanctum.

In the late afternoon of the second day, coming back from a visit with Eleanor and Horsie to discuss in whispers the Evil Deed with all its implications, I sat down behind my desk and almost immediately noticed a corner of yellowish paper in the paper pile beside my typewriter. It stuck out so flagrantly that it was impossible not to see it. My heart stood still — I knew what it was! With trembling fingers I pulled out the two stencilled pages from the pile of paper on my desk.

I dragged myself into the chief's office. He looked up and I wordlessly held out the sheets to him. He only said one word: "Where?"

"On my desk," I murmured. The situation was entirely unreal to me.

"God Almighty!" he said.

I went back to my office and sat on my chair, waiting. A few minutes later an aide appeared to take me to the Admiral.

The Admiral, sitting behind his empty desk, stared at me in silence. He did not ask me to sit down. I stared back, stricken. Finally he picked up his gold knobbed pen and began tapping the top of his desk.

"What am I going to do with you?" he said, not at all unkindly.

"I am so very sorry, Herr Admiral," I said, trying not to burst out in tears.

"This could have gone very badly," he said and sighed.

"Yes, Sir," I mumbled. How could I say to the Admiral that there was no way those papers could have been on my desk during the search that morning or even only an hour before? I suspect the Admiral knew it, too. He sighed again and looked out of the window. Finally he turned back to me.

"This must never happen again." he told me.

"I know, Sir." And I was dismissed.

In my own mind, I long ago solved the mystery. I think that one of the young officers found the stencils where he had misplaced and forgotten them. He could not suddenly, triumphantly, produce them without the truth being discerned by everybody involved. In the shock of it — after all, the Admiral himself had been forced to submit to a search — the young officer panicked. Hastily going over his dismal options he decided to plant the cursed papers where he hoped the least harm would be done. The two pages contained nothing of the slightest importance to the enemy. It had been a simple pragmatic solution to a potential disciplinary disaster. I think the Admiral came to the same conclusion. The subject was never brought up again in my presence. I have long since forgiven the guilty party and I hope he has forgiven himself. There were even times when I thought I might be rather flattered by his choice of desks.

Ah, I was flying high in those days: short, salty, sun-streaked hair touching the cloudless sky. Brown, tar-stained feet in gold slippers barely skimming the solid earth. When I was rushing into the building in the morning, always about ninety seconds late, the guard at the door would smile and shake his head.

"I don't need to ask *you* how you are," he would say.

And I, hurrying past him, would whirl around, laughing, stretching my fingertips out to him: "Want to touch me? It's got to be contagious!"

I lived in a land where it never rained. I had an exciting job. I was in love and was loved in return.

I had found the man with whom, I thought, I could spend the rest of my life. When I first became aware of how his face lit up when I entered the room, my heart skipped a few beats. He saw the girl he wanted; I wanted to be the girl he saw. He thought me surprisingly innocent of the ways of the world (which I was), and funny and clever, which I became, because he thought me so. He coaxed me out of my cautious shell into the rougher winds of reality even as he stood between me and their harshness.

I thought him confident and marvelously unfettered, fearless to the point of recklessness, though never uncaring. And he could listen. How many people do we know who can truly listen? He asked my opinions sometimes, not to humor me, but because he trusted my judgment. He rekindled confidence and self-esteem in me, dormant for years, without either of us ever talking about it.

I could make him laugh as I had been able to make my father smile, even on bad days. I made him wonder — just by being there — if there might not be a future after all. And I stood between him and his impetuous temper.

I built castles in the air for both of us in which neither of us quite believed. Tomorrow, to me, was nebulous and vaguely threatening, but today was real and bursting with the joy of being alive.

Many years later, in a small, dusty book of German poetry, printed on poor postwar paper, I found a poem written by a woman whose name and age I did not know and whose face I never saw, yet she had worn my shoes and walked my road and her poem summed up all there was to say about those few months of my life so long ago:

(I have translated it and, though it could not be her exact beautiful wording, I hope and think that I have taken nothing away from it.)

I was a child when fate led me to you,
Too filled with fears to see, with doubts, to talk.
A child that walked away from all it knew,
Yet knew not whom to ask nor where to walk.

You saw the anguish in my eyes; you saw
The restless longing which, through day and night
Drove me unmercifully. My delight
And my complaints were fierce and I laughed
Too quickly, though I knew not why,
And all the seeds lay, perishing, on barren soil.
You came and lit the stars upon the sky.
The first sweet harvest at the end of night
Came from your earth, came from your loving toil.

* * * * * * * * * * * * * * *

Life took a few steps ahead for many of us just then, not all of them happy. Kristin was withdrawing from her engagement. Harry was becoming ever more demanding; she turned ever more stubborn. It was no match made in heaven. There was no final, devastating blow. They drifted apart, none too gently, and when the separation came, Kristin took it serenely. Now no big black truck — with a sulking driver slouched behind the wheel — was parked in front of our hotel in the late evening hours. Kristin, tearless, was upstairs, washing, mending, sorting, getting ready to leave. We had talked long about our plans. She thought that the handwriting on the wall was clear. No homebound civilian personnel had been replaced lately. Fewer girls gathered in the mess hall each week. Kristin did not want to be sent back to Germany. She had applied for duty in Sofia while there was still a chance. The Navy High Command in Bulgaria was still running on all turbines.

Eleanor, too, was at the time drawn into a turbulence of emotions, although, just as in Kristin's case, one would not have noticed a change in her calm, pleasant demeanor. The moment of decision could hardly be avoided much longer. She must have asked herself many times where her attachment to the engineer would lead her. She had been spellbound by him all those months, but never to the point where all reasoning in this cool, blond, northern head of hers ceased to function. Something happened that fall that reinforced this reasoning and drove her toward a decisive step. Her faithful suitor, the teacher-of-classical-languages-turned ordinary seaman for the duration of the war, had gone home on furlough. Of his ten days in Germany, not counting the long, weary trip, he had spent five days with his parents and sisters. Then, leaving his disappointed and puzzled family behind, he traveled south. He fought his way into dark, overcrowded trains and creaking old buses that took him into the valley deep in the Austrian mountains to the convent of the Sisters of Mercy. In the nursery there he was shown a blond little girl who looked at him questioningly out of Eleanor's mermaid eyes. He spent three days with the child, taking her for walks, picking flowers for the good sisters in the alpine meadows, going into the village for a watery ice cream, taking her on donkey rides.

"He did all that!" said Eleanor to me in wonder.

Not very long afterward Eleanor told us that she was meeting the engineer for the last time. She did not come to the office the next day and Horsie and I, somewhat in the dark ourselves, loyally fibbed for her. We asked no questions when she came back, and she volunteered no answers. But gradually, some color returned to her cheeks and when her eyes had lost the distant look and focused on us again, she told us that she was getting engaged to her sailor. We celebrated a little after office hours with Samos wine and shish kebab, Horsie's offering to the occasion. Some weeks later, after Kristin had left for Sofia, I went with Eleanor to the black market to buy some material for a wedding dress. Late that fall Eleanor and her seaman went to his unit to get married, and, in due time, according to regulations, which keep the human affairs running, come hell or high water, the Navy separated them and he was transferred to a desk job in Saloniki in northeast Greece.

* * * * * * * * * * * * * *

"I hear wedding bells ringing," whispered the cook sticking his damp head out of the kitchen through the mess hall door. He gave me a mighty wink. I smiled vaguely back; first, we had not yet resolved the case of the purple eggs, and secondly, any acknowledgement of the wink would have been precarious.

This first firm commitment of my life was a very private matter. If publicly acknowledged, my transfer or return to Germany would have been inevitable. We desperately wished to postpone such a separation.

In this we had much help. There was a friendly conspiracy of silence around us, born out of comradeship and affection. Curiosity in more distant quarters was rampant, of course, but any question on the subject used to bring forth the most marvelous vacuous expressions on the faces of the young ensigns and aides. (Nobody dared question the higher echelon.)

Early in autumn the officers of our department gave a party. I doubt that anybody who was there ever forgot that evening. The large marble mansion might have presented itself cold and hostile had it not been for the warmth of the human bodies, the laughter and camaraderie. The separation of rank and age, so all-important during the day, had vanished. As the night wore on and jostling and laughter subsided, we sat down on the wide, sweeping staircase that led to the upper halls. The warm, sweet night air, forever foreign, forever enchanting to the people of the north, streamed through the open doors. The moon was rising over the trees of the Royal gardens, distant, pale, waning, promising nothing. Gradually the room fell silent. There was a sense of destiny and loss above and around us all.

Somebody began a song and one by one the others fell in. The voices of the men were strong and harmonized without effort. There was not a soul in the room that night who did not know that our days in Greece were numbered, that the Balkans were lost, that an invasion of the continent was inevitable, that the war could not be turned around any more. Folk songs and *wanderlieder* gave way to the love songs of those days, hour and circumstances lifting the words out of banality and make-believe and rendering them sad and haunting.

"Heimat, deine Sterne:" "My country, thy stars — sent here by my lover to greet me . . ." they sang. And :
"In the late night's misty rain,
when you stand and wait in vain,
who will come, Lilli Marlen?
Who will come . . .?"
As the moon slowly disappeared out of our sight and only its light remained cool and white on the marble balconies, the songs turned toward their one great mutual love, the sea. All of them had heard the call of the sea when they were young or they would not have been here at this place

and this hour. Songs that were sung by the sailors of all seafaring nations since time unknown, of the sailor's longing for home and family during the long, black nights at sea, and of his restless love for the sea when he was safely in port. This they had in common. This they had sung as young cadets when the world was theirs for the daring, this they sang now, wondering in the darkness and stillness of the night if they would ever sit together like this again, they and their songs.

* * * * * * * * * * * * * *

The Italians had overthrown their government. Il Duce was caught in flight. The new government in Rome ordered a complete turnabout: henceforth their armed forces were to regard their former allies as mortal enemies.

It is one thing to make politics in offices in Rome, Berlin, London, and Washington, but another entirely for one man to turn against another who had sailed alongside him so often through so many precarious waters. The German Admiralty in Athens was housed under the same roof as the Italian navy command. Many a cup of coffee and cigarette along with many worrisome decisions had been shared by the officers of both countries.

It was a dismal situation. The Italian captains were dismayed. There were short, unhappy conferences behind closed doors, a quiet withdrawal from the headquarters building, and the sparkling white uniforms with the broad black and gold epaulets, the tanned faces and the wide smiles to which we were so used, disappeared from our workday scene.

The city was at high alert. It had been administered by the Italians. No organized takeover could take place under the circumstances. The Italian administrators, forewarned no doubt, were simply and suddenly gone.

One of the first actions the new German administration undertook was to free some of the Greek political prisoners sentenced by the Italians. It came as a surprise to me that Greeks had been imprisoned for political reasons. I had never heard or witnessed a hostile incident of any kind. The Greek population and the German occupation forces lived alongside each other—a parallel existence with little personal contact.

We were not aware of what went on in the villages and mountain areas. Athens, the capital, functioned orderly and peacefully. There were no air raids, no harsh curfews. No armed police were stopping pedestrians or cars on the streets. Kristin and I were not afraid to walk home in the dark. When I went to the beach at my noon excursions, I was alone at the plaza, alone in the street car, alone at the beach. There seemed to be no reason to be afraid. On the streets, at the market, where we brushed shoulders with the natives, there were no smiles but neither were there fists or covert hostile looks.

Perhaps there are numbers and statistics somewhere refuting this statement. But it has been my intention throughout my story to tell it simply the way I saw it, heard it, or experienced it first hand.

During our last briefing at the navy camp, before we left for Greece, we had been told to conduct ourselves responsibly and to avoid offending the Greek population. We were shown a gesture—the open palm of our hand, fingers spread wide apart, pushed toward the face of another person—that we were told constituted a grave insult which we were to avoid under all circumstances. Not to worry, we would have been just as likely to hop down main street on one leg as to push our spread-out fingers into anybody's face.

I don't remember any kind of non-fraternization orders. When one of the ensigns was placed on report for being caught kissing a Greek kitchen maid, our chief of staff let it be known that he would prefer that his young officers would not compete with their orderlies in the kitchen area. This sounded more like a reminder of cadet school rules than a non-fraternization order.

In the entire year I lived in Greece I learned the names of only two Greeks—Spiro, our indefatiguable doorman, and Despoa, a jolly, plump young woman who was the chief of staff's housekeeper. If this seems preposterous, it was, nevertheless, the truth.

There was the language barrier, of course. People like Spiro and Despoa, the street vendors, the merchants, and restaurant owners had acquired a limited German vocabulary necessary for their business. The rest of the Greeks spoke no German and none of us knew more than three or four words of Greek.

There was a patent indifference on our part, not caused by animosity or dislike but by a singular lack of curiosity. Every one of us was fully occupied with his or her own affairs. I had no idea how the multitude of faces and races that streamed through the avenues during the day made a living or where the people had gone whose houses we occupied. All I really knew about them was that they loved music and resin wine, had a notable preference for canned beans, and shunned the sun whenever possible.

A few years later, when the shoe was on the other foot and Germany was the occupied country, I remembered my year in Greece and all my "*Unterlassungsünden*" as the Germans say—sins of omission, sins of neglect—with gradual enlightenment and a great deal of regret.

* * * * * * * * * * * * * *

In the wake of the general confusion after the Italians' departure, motorbikes appeared at the hotel to haul Eleanor, Horsie, and me to the navy building. A flood of messages would come and go. Nervous, excited, and thrilled, the three of us huddled together through the night. During those first twenty-four hours nobody quite knew what to make of the situation. The city remained quiet. The people gave no indication of violence. I suppose they were simply glad to be rid of half of the lot and decided they could wait until the other half left. The Italian administration had been very unpopular, there had been some personal, political axes to grind between them and the Greeks. Other places were not so lucky. The islands, which had been occupied by both German and Italian troops, were seething. Crete was in uproar. When orders came from Berlin to treat any Italian officer who actively took up arms against German troops not as an enemy but as a traitor, things began to look gloomy, indeed.

In our department, night watches were installed. We were asked to take turns; one of us three would stay awake and alert at the office during the night to be available if orders had to go out. Preparations were made to move high-ranking officers into quarters on the unoccupied top floor of the administration building. The largest room was turned into a well-furnished bed-sitting room for the Admiral, who would spend his nights there during the following weeks. The rooms adjacent to his quarters were small and empty, save a set of bunk beds and a few rickety chairs, not counting, of course, the various bugs and mice who had settled in there during three years of undisturbed bliss. Those rooms were ours, the secretaries' emergency quarters. We avoided them like the plague.

Reality descended at that time upon my own private little world dealing quickly and deftly with rosy clouds and castles in the air. The inevitable separation came, as we had known it would. In the North Sea and the Baltic Sea men with cunning and wide experience were needed more than they were needed behind desks. Thereafter I joined Eleanor in her daily mail vigil, but letters were easier written in Saloniki than on a winter night on the Baltic Sea.

We celebrated Christmas Eve in the officers' mess hall. The men who had toasted us so cheerfully scarcely two months earlier rallied around Eleanor and me now like so many big brothers, chaffing and cheering, not suffering us to become tearful, not wanting us to sit out a single dance. But I did sit out a few just the same, because my head started to spin and at times the most peculiar feeling of sea sickness would overcome me.

The winter of 1943-1944 was an unusually cold one in Athens. Very few buildings were equipped with central heating or any other heating devices. I never saw a stove anywhere. The administration building was barely warm; the hotel was icy. A large parcel arrived one day for the Admiral: Laura-Marie had sent her husband a large down-filled quilt for his bed in the emergency quarters. The rest of us struggled with old navy blankets, of which there was only a very limited supply. Greece was not exactly high on the list for woolens at the military supply centers.

One morning snow was falling. We looked out of the window with incredulous eyes. Wasn't this a sub-tropical climate? An elated Spiro was standing in the open door of the hotel, his face transformed with excitement.

"Never!" he cried, "Never it snows in Athens! First time this century!"

Oh, great! We looked down at our sandals, pulled our sweaters tighter around us and set out to work. We appreciated this historical moment, but not a whole lot. The streets offered a singular spectacle. The city's entire population seemed to be out of doors. Those people who had moved so sluggishly through the quivering summer heat were alive with joy and something close to ecstasy. They were shouting at each other, laughing, and pointing at the white fluff around us. They picked it up and tasted it; they threw it at each other. Young people were holding hands and dancing. The stores and bazaars stayed closed. A people's holiday was taking place spontaneously.

The snow was gone again by late afternoon but the cold hung on tenaciously. The weather suited the general mood. We functioned at all times at a threatening "sudden-crisis level." The admiral had tentatively moved back to the warmer comforts of his villa. But the secretaries of the Department of Operations were requested to be available for night shifts. So Eleanor, Horsie, and I packed our toothbrushes, a few pieces of our warmest clothing, and an extra blanket and moved into our bleak emergency quarters on the top floor. It saved us, if nothing else, the morning and evening walk through the slush. At night we would wrap ourselves in just about everything we had and climb into those awful beds. The springs were poking through the thin mattresses, the blankets smelled musty and were woefully inadequate, and if the cold did not keep us awake, the mice did. They always had something going; they certainly liked to socialize. There was no end to the rustling and flitting about, the pitter-patter of little feet and the squeaky greetings. One evening, when I was getting ready for bed, a mouse jumped over my naked foot. It startled the mouse a great deal more than me, I remember. There came a night when we were lying in our bunks, curled up like embryos for warmth, still wide awake, listening to the mice who seemed to be carrying on worse than usual when suddenly some rather decisive noises came from the direction of Horsie's bunk. She was sitting straight up in her bed.

"That's it!" she yelled. "I have had it!"

She began climbing down from her upper bunk.

"He didn't take his quilt along, you know," she said by way of explanation. "He" presumably was our Admiral. Before Horsie was through the door, Eleanor was already up and behind her. I knew where they were heading. That left me to the mice and the mice to me. I wondered if I could *possibly* overcome upbringing and convention to the point of such outrage as they were about to commit and discovered, as I was running barefoot across the cold floor boards, that it was not nearly so difficult as I had assumed. Eleanor and Horsie were already snugly in the Admiral's French bed when I arrived, but moved willingly to make room for me. For the first time in weeks a glorious warmth pervaded our chilled bones. And so we slept from then on, night after night, and Athens did not burn and the Admiral never showed up in the middle of the night to find his three secretaries sleeping peacefully, like triplets in a nursery, in his bed under

Laura-Marie's heavenly down-filled quilt. Too bad, really, that he didn't show up just once.

* * * * * * * * * * * * * *

In the last week of January, 1944, I learned that my mail vigil was over. There would be no more letters for me from the Baltic Sea.

Chapter 14

My return to Germany was being processed. Helping hands stretched out from all sides. Precious cargo gathered in the sea bag under my bed at the hotel: boxes of cigarettes, a large canister of olive oil, two brand new mosquito nets. Eleanor went with me to the black market to help me buy yarn. She cut out patterns and showed me how to knit little sweaters and pants, the very same patterns I used to knit for my grandchildren many years later. I never learned any new ones.

Horsie, though, Horsie was preoccupied. She still slept with us, but during the day she disappeared more often than usual and seldom showed up in the early evenings. Horsie had discovered another large empty room at the top floor and she was busy furnishing it. She took bunk beds apart and placed them side by side; she washed windows and swept floors and went after the mice with a vengeance. A table appeared and some chairs; the same mosquito net furnished some curtains and something very much like a table cloth. The crowning glory, though, was a hot plate that materialized one day out of nowhere. Nobody knew how she got those things. Horsie had turned into a woman with a purpose. Time was running out and she knew it. Her appearance changed. The sack-like dresses took on shape; a thin belt actually located a waistline. For the first time in her life, and without telling anybody, Horsie went to a hair dresser. The thin pigtails had vanished one morning and a gentle waved hairline covered the big ears. Everybody pretended not to notice anything—Horsie would glare at us, daring us to make a remark—but everybody was watching curiously as the story unfolded quietly and speedily day by day. One evening Horsie brought a guest to her "apartment," a young blond corporal with a round face and permanently surprised round blue eyes. She cooked supper for him. Lovely smells of sauteed onions and browned lamb still lingered in the air when we went to bed. Horsie did not appear; there was a lot more room under the quilt that night. Thereafter she was busy washing and mending shirts, darning socks, tightening buttons, and cooking, always cooking. When Eleanor and I once in a while at night stuck our heads through the door to pay a friendly call before the corporal (who worked in an army repair shop) came "home," Horsie was demure and domestic. Something was always simmering on the hot plate. She never offered us anything, she had not changed *that* much, but she was pleasant and talkative and kept all insults to a minimum. There were moments while I watched her bustling about, peeking into the steaming pot, stirring, setting plates out, when she seemed to have some secret, rosy glow from within and I found myself wondering why I had ever thought her so very homely.

Horsie's domestic bliss did not make me feel jealous, but it brought home the loneliness I was facing. I did not feel singled out by fate. How could I? We were in the fifth year of the war and millions of women had to face a life without a husband and be prepared to be a single parent, although this word had not been coined yet either. To Kristin in Sofia I wrote:

"They are pressing me to name a destination to be filled in the marching orders. I am at a loss of what to do. All my life I have thought that once I was financially independent everything would be changed. I am that now — and it seems I shall be more dependent on my mother than ever before. Where should I go? . . . My mother has left Berlin and the air raids, taking our furniture with her. She has moved to a place in the country, I do not yet know precisely where. Shall I write to her and ask her if she has room for me — for us? . . . Ach, Kristin, this is not the way I planned to go home!"

The population of the city was cold and we shivered right along with them. It rained at intervals, a cold, sterile rain that left nothing greener and sweeter in its wake. None of us had sufficient warm clothing; nobody had been prepared for a winter like this. Most of us caught colds and the coughing spells at night were hard and hurting.

Around the middle of February came Kristin's answer:

"You must go to my parents' house in East Prussia. They are expecting you; they will welcome you. I want you to do this. Please, please, go!"

It was the last week of February when departure time arrived. Horsie got herself out of a sticky goodbye scene by playing the injured party.

"Running off when the going gets tough. Some people!"

"Oh Horsie," I said, "I wish you oodles and oodles of luck . . ." For a moment I felt like hugging her, but Horsie, anticipating the worst, made a face and ran. Eleanor rode along to the airport in the department limousine. My sea bag was stuffed so tightly that I never even attempted to lift it. In the smaller bag I carried two cartons of cigarettes; I would need them all before I would arrive at the other end of the continent.

"Good heavens!" whispered Eleanor. "Look who is going to be your travel companion!" A slim, lonely figure, sea sack and travel bag beside her, was waiting at the deserted airport gate. I took in the dark hair framing the narrow, pale face, the thin, unsmiling mouth, the quick glance at us before the dark eyes turned away again without a flicker of acknowledgement. The girl who had done time in the brig. I remembered her entering the mess hall, lips pressed together in bitter contempt and resentment, not looking at any of us, sitting down at the far end of the table, taking her first meal again with us — or alongside us — after five days of confinement.

"Nobody else?" I looked around in dismay. But the gate remained deserted.

The plane looked dark and lumpish in the gray, damp winter air. It was a transport plane, flying back to Sofia without cargo and giving us a lift. Our driver was loading my sea bag and talking to two large men in air force uniform. They were looking at us, grinning a welcome. I turned to Eleanor; we hugged each other silently, dry-eyed — uncertainty seldom has tears — and she walked back to the car. There was work to be done at the office. The pilots cried cheerfully: "Get in, girls; we don't have all day!" and we climbed in.

We — what shall I call her? She has no name for me any more; maybe a subconscious process of selecting memories pushed it overboard quietly and quickly. As I sit here, staring at the paper in my typewriter, I find it difficult even to make up a name for her. I shall just have to call her "the girl," which makes me wince a little, which might be good for my soul.

We hardly talked, the girl and I, during that nightmarish trip. "The mosquito net incident" stood between us more effectively than a seven-foot barbed-wire fence. I was her natural enemy, she was my guilty conscience. I dared not think of my duffel bag at the bottom of which rested two neatly rolled brand-new mosquito nets that, eventually, would be cut and sewn into two dozen strong, serviceable diapers.

The plane was a yawning, dark cave with narrow benches along each wall. The two pilots came in to enlighten us about the upcoming adventure.

"All right, girls," rumbled the bigger one, "this is a transport plane, not a fighter. We are *slow*!"

"You know, of course," added the other one, "that the airspace over the Balkans is not ours anymore. Furthermore, this plane has only one small machine gun. We thought you should know those little facts."

They were having a grand time of it as they peered into our white faces. They are just like their plane, I thought unkindly, big, damp, and lumpish. Get lost, you dummies! I smiled politely at them. The girl didn't even bother to look up.

"Well, keep your fingers crossed, ladies!" They locked the doors and disappeared into the cockpit.

There was no heat in the plane. I don't know which made me shiver more, the cold or the fear. The girl sat stony-faced across from me, between us the dark vastness of the plane's belly. Neither of us suggested moving beside each other for warmth and comfort. There are times in life that happen to everybody, I suppose, when circumstances divest you completely of the power of decisions, solutions, and responsibility. You are simply delivered into the hands of fate. I know I was determined to keep my teeth from chattering and my knees from trembling. I have no idea what the girl felt; she did not talk to me.

Each time the plane dipped tipsily I saw in my mind a mountain top racing toward us. Every time we banked roughly I imagined an enemy plane in hot pursuit. Most of the time I sat with my eyes closed and tried to convince myself that I had had a wonderful life and that I was resigned and ready now for a quick end. Just then the plane would dip sharply and my eyes opened like saucers and my hand flew to my mouth and I knew that I was not ready for anything of the sort.

When the plane landed in Salonika and I felt firm ground under my feet again, gratitude mingled with weariness to the point of total exhaustion. Salonika is an ancient port city, not offering a serene street scene in the best of time. Now, stirred by past and coming events down to the dregs, it seemed like a city whirled around by a giant egg beater. We walked through many streets to our assigned quarters, and to my bleary eyes we seemed to be walking in an exotic and colorful fish bowl, all images fleeting and blurred.

The room, to which an old and very dirty woman showed us, shocked me momentarily back into reality. It was small and narrow with an iron bedstead on either side along the wall. The only window was on the wall between the beds; cardboard was nailed over the shattered window panes. The single light bulb dangled unshaded from the middle of the dirt-streaked ceiling. There was only one other piece of furniture, a large, cracked cabinet, which was locked. It was the sight of the beds that shook me out of my lethargy. There was no pillow and no top sheet. The bottom sheet was gray and creased and showed stains that gave evidence of a variety of bugs having been squashed there by previous unhappy occupants. Two dirty blankets lay folded at the footend. A large, dark grease spot marked the place where heads had rested. It was that particular sight that made my stomach, already in a precarious state, virtually turn over. I felt the meal we had just eaten rising to my throat. I looked at the girl; she was staring at the same stain.

In spite of our exhaustion, neither of us made a move to get ready for bed. Finally the girl opened the blankets with her fingertips and began inspecting and shaking them. I did the same. Out of my handbag I took the leather folder that held my money and marching orders, opened it up and placed it exactly over the grease stain. Next I took my handkerchief and bound it around my chin, covering my lips and knotting it on top of my head. Then I took my shoes off and climbed onto this sty. Slowly and carefully I placed my head onto the leather case and then pulled the blankets over my shoulders and up to my chin, making sure they touched only the handkerchief. I would have liked to put on gloves but I had none. The girl was already on her bed; she had not even bothered to take off her shoes.

The cold in the room was numbing. It would be no use, I thought, to report this pig pen to the navy office. They would just stare at us and say:

"Be glad you had a bed! D'you know how many men had to sleep on the floor here with their heads propped up on their duffel bags?"

We had not been in bed more than a quarter of an hour when the door opened and into the room rolled — like two deranged train engines — our very own pilots, full of hot air and local wine.

"What is this?" they cried. "You girls are already in bed? What's the matter with you? Where's the old navy spirit? Get up, we want to celebrate!"

We pulled the filthy blankets a bit higher and mumbled something about being tired and needing sleep.

"Aw, come on," the bigger fellow lowered his weight cautiously on the edge of my bed. "Come on, girlie, you live only once. We'll have a little wine, we'll dance a little . . . what's the harm in that?"

From under my smelly cover I glanced across the room. The other fellow had nestled down on my companion's bed, making similar enticing proposals. His large, lumpish frame was bent low, his wine breath steaming all over the girl. I imagined her eyes blazing through the darkness. If he did not stop giving her stomach those benign little pats she might conceivably scratch out his eyes within the next two minutes.

Just then my own two-hundred-fifty-pound, wine-soaked swain had an inspiration.

"If you two ladies won't get up and go out with us," he announced, "we'll get a few bottles and have a party right here!"

"That's a wonderful idea," I said enthusiastically. "Why don't you do that!"

"Yes. Get the bottles," said the girl from the other bed.

With much creaking and sighing of the released bedsprings, the two men heaved themselves up and promised to be back in a jiffy. The moment they were out of the door we jumped out of the beds. For the first time we fully looked at each other. No more invisible barbed wire fence; the bond of sisterhood had taken over.

The door had no lock or bolt. "The cabinet?" whispered the girl.

"Can we manage it?" I whispered back.

Pushing and pulling, inch by inch, we maneuvered the large piece of furniture squarely in front of the door, which, fortunately, opened into the room. Thrusting our shoulders against it, we gave one last strong push till we heard it hit the door frame. Looking at each other with a half smile, we returned to our beds. That smile still lingered, if a bit anxiously, when our thwarted dates began knocking, hollering, and rattling the doorknob. They got the message after a while. They tried no force. We heard them mutter to each other as they stumbled away, the glasses and bottles clinking under their arms.

We got up early the next morning. It was a speedy and silent procedure. The moment of closeness had vanished into the cold, gray air of the new day. Wordlessly we moved the cabinet back. When we walked out of the room, though, one more thing happened that stands out in my mind as clearly as if it happened yesterday. The girl suddenly turned, walked back into the room and gave her bed such an awe-inspiring, powerful kick that one of its legs buckled under it. I have envied her that kick many times. It made her the survivor she was. It set her free.

Our fearless leaders didn't look too well. They seemed to be blaming their ailing condition on us. Neither of them as much as glanced at us; we were invisible to them. The flight was very much like the one on the day before. Neither the fear or the cold subsided. Shortly before Sofia, one of the pilots emerged from the cockpit. He told us that the airport in Sofia had been bombed recently and that another air raid was reported to be on the way. They didn't know, he said, if they could manage a landing between attacks on the heavily damaged landing strip.

"All right, you worm," I thought, "you made your point. We are terrified! Now go back and fly your plane. It's your skin, too, you know." Aloud I said nothing, nor did the girl. The pilot disappeared again. I desperately sought the girl's eyes for some human contact, but she kept staring, unfocused, right past me. A few minutes later we went down for a bumpy landing.

A shuttle bus with a nervous driver awaited us. We climbed in and waited. The pilots were sitting on some debris, chewing the fat with some buddies. Once in a while we heard them laugh uproariously. The driver tapped his horn, they seemed totally unconcerned.

"Anybody else coming?" asked the jittery driver.

"No!" we both said in one voice. And the bus tore off.

Kristin had been bombed out twice during her stay in Sofia. The navy had moved its female personnel to a hotel in a part of the city that so far had escaped the air raids. Our bus driver delivered me to the doorstep.

Kristin received me with open arms, both corners of her mouth lifted to a real smile. A few times she even laughed joyfully. The room was neat, her bed had clean sheets; a glass of milk was standing on her night table.

"Boy, you really must be friends!" her roommate said when she was alone with me for a minute. "She had to go to the other end of the city for that milk. She said you liked milk a lot."

It was the first milk I had seen in a year. Kristin had planned to show me Sofia, but parts of the city were still smoking from the last air raid and one look at me convinced her that I would be a great deal better off in bed. At night time she bedded herself down in a sleeping bag. We whispered a long time before sleep overcame us. There, in the dark, with Kristin on the floor beside me, I could cry a little at long last.

Kristin took me to the station the next day. From then on, until a train, three days later, stopped and discarded me at the small East Prussian town north of the Masuria Lakes, I don't remember any more than a somnambulator would recall of a night's wanderings. As the unheated, dark trains rattled through Bulgaria, Yugoslavia, Hungary, and Austria into Germany, into Poland, and back into Germany they left few glimpses in the dimmest corners of my memory. Glimpses, mostly of outstretched, grimy hands that I filled with long, thin, fragrant Greek cigarettes, after which those hands dragged me and my bags over platforms and tracks to yet another overcrowded train and, ignoring protests and returning push for shove, elbowed me safely into it. I don't remember anybody ever going back on a deal and leaving me stranded.

Kristin's parents met me at the train. Kristin's father loaded the bags on a small wagon. Kristin's mother, a thin, prematurely old woman with Kristin's pale blue eyes, and deep worry lines all over her face, took my arm and steered me toward their house near the station.

I remember a large, warm kitchen with a low ceiling and hand-knotted rugs on the floor, and something hot and tasty in a cup between my cold fingers.

"That cough!" exclaimed Kristin's mother. "Mercy, child, how long have you had that cough?"

Together they got me up the stairs.

"Kristin wrote you are to have her room," said the old lady, "and her clothes, and anything of hers that you want. Mercy! That cough!"

"We have storm warnings," said Kristin's father, heaving the long-suffering sea bag into the room. "Glad you got here in time."

The room was warm and white and shiny-clean, the furniture painted white, the curtains white clouds around the windows. On the bed lay a huge round featherbed in a sparkling white cover. A white and brown tile stove in the corner, reaching from the floor almost to the ceiling, radiated an even, cozy warmth. Kristin's father disappeared; her mother, small and bird-like, hovered near me, ready to catch me should I suddenly decide to drop. After I had undressed she slipped a long, flowered, flannel nightgown over my head. Before I surrendered myself completely to this paradise, I crouched down and opened my sea bag. On top of it was a can filled with untoasted green coffee beans. I had planned to use them—one handful at a time—when the cigarettes ran out, but spontaneously I pulled out the whole can and pressed it in the old lady's hands. She opened it and a gleam of such great, surprised pleasure came into her eyes that I knew I would not regret it.

Kristin's mother had turned off the light and tiptoed out of the room. I sank into the bed and felt another featherbed beneath me. The one on top of me unrolled and yielded, molding itself to my bone-tired body. My cold toes felt a hot water bottle at the foot end. Through the thin cracks in the iron shutter of the tile stove a flickering orange light escaped and danced along the ceiling. From under the door, a whiff of fresh coffee reached me: Kristin's mother was toasting the coffee beans over the open fire in the kitchen downstairs. I was engulfed in a wave of warmth and well-being. Drowsily I watched the dancing fire on the ceiling above me and felt a tiny fluttering inside my body as if a small butterfly had gotten caught down there under my skin. It was such a small, soundless fluttering, yet suddenly I was wide awake, listening to it breathlessly. It came again, and then once more. Outside the wind was rising and the shutters began to rattle. I thought suddenly how close we were to the Russian front. I thought of the soldiers out there in the winter night forming a thin, desperate wall against the ceaseless onslaught of the enemy. Unconsciously, both my hands covered my body there where I had felt the fluttering. "Dear God," I prayed silently, "make them hold! Keep them strong. Oh God, keep them strong!"

And as the black storm coming from the Barents Sea over the Russian plains tore into the tiny border town, hurling snow masses against the windows, stirring the white curtains a little and causing the fire in the tile stove to crackle a bit more spiritedly, I sank into dreamless, deep oblivion.

PART V

The Rock Cellar

1944

Thuringia, Germany

Chapter 15

Before I begin this—possibly most crucial—part of my story, I should pause to explain how I came to live, at that particular time, in an ancient house called "The Rock Cellar" in the midst of Germany's Thuringia Forest.

Let me take you back for a few moments to that day, eight years earlier, when for me and my family life seemed to have come to an abrupt halt, and for an uncertain future a new course had to be charted.

* * * * * * * * * * * * * *

My father died on the last day of September, 1935, which was also my fourteenth birthday. The memorial service for him was held in the old chapel at the Potsdam cemetery. It was the largest turnout of mourners the church had ever seen and the doors had to be kept open during the service to accommodate the people who were standing in the dark stone entrance. One of the persons present in the church was a short, dapper man with a crew cut and a small blond mustache who had arrived in a chauffeur-driven limousine. There was no seating order or reserved seats and during the service he sat in the fourth or fifth row beside my father's barber. The barber was a middle-aged man who stammered and who had shaved my father every morning for the last seven years and had told him the town's news and all the jokes he could remember. He shaved him for the last time on the morning after his death and he cried a little while doing it and looked as if he would have liked to tell him one more joke, if my father would only wink at him one more time.

The man with the little blond mustache, whose name was Benneman, sat beside the barber and his alert, blue eyes wandered here and there and missed nothing. The day after the memorial service, and just before his chauffeur drove him back to his mansion near Hannover, he came to call on my mother. By trade and profession Herr Benneman was a publisher of books and literary reviews. He had published a number of my father's books, and he admired my father's writings, though he admired his character more, his own being quite different. Two years before my father's death, he had published a "prestige book" of my father's poems. This was something publishing houses sometimes did; the books were beautifully printed and handsomely bound collectors' items. The publishers rarely made money on them, but they lent prestige to their company. My father had been a little perplexed and advised against it but, nevertheless, was pleased and touched when he held the first, beautiful issue in his hands. My parents considered him a friend as much as a business partner.

So my mother received him very cordially and served him some of my father's best wine while he told her how much he had always admired her husband. My mother said she knew and was grateful.

"But what you do not know, dear, gracious lady," said the publisher, "is how much I have admired you, how great an affection for you I have carried in my heart all those years. Indeed," said the publisher, warming up to his subject, "I have envied my good friend nothing as much as his lovely wife."

At this point my mother, who had lowered her eyes and shaken her head a little in modest surprise, abandoned all social niceties and began to look quite alarmed. She was, in fact, considerably thrown off balance by this unexpected declaration at this particular time. Undaunted, her visitor continued.

"I have thought of a day when it might be possible for me, after a suitable time of mourning for my good friend, to offer you my heart and fortune in marriage."

"However," Herr Benneman continued, his blue eyes fixing my mother sadly and a bit reproachfully, "this is not to be. A few weeks ago I asked my secretary to become my wife. A very pleasant young woman. She is twenty years younger than I. And no children, of course," he added by way of explaining things. "I think," said my mother when she told me about the conversation afterwards, "this was the only time in my life when I ever sat with my mouth open."

Her visitor then assured my speechless mother that he would always, always, carry a torch for her in his heart and that he had no intention of forsaking her. As of that date, his publishing house would pay a small monthly pension to her in recognition of the fact that my father had been one of their honored authors.

He was as good as his word. He married his secretary; he paid my mother a small pension; he returned her calls and answered her letters promptly, and he took her, a few times, to some splendid restaurant when business brought him to Berlin.

Herr Benneman was a self-made man. This does not mean that he was uneducated. On the contrary, education was the first area to which he applied his driving motivation and iron discipline, and if he graduated without any particular glory, he did so fairly and squarely and with respectable grades. This first goal achieved, he turned (with a mental sigh of relief) toward the real purpose of life: acquiring money and acclaim. While pursuing this with all the necessary vision, skill, and ruthlessness, he never lost his secret admiration for grace and learning (hence his devotion to my father). He gave his former alma mater such generous and concrete signs of his gratitude that the puzzled institution finally bestowed upon him the coveted title of doktor honoris causa. He cherished this token honor more than his bank accounts and was called "Herr Doktor" from that time on by anybody who wished to address him successfully.

With the rise of the Third Reich he saw his little empire, built on free publishing and free competition, shaken to the roots. He ventured into the political upheaval, tested the winds, and saw no foreseeable change. He considered his options and joined an obscure motorized branch of the Party whose purpose it was, as stated in the by-laws, to make their (glamorous) automobiles available to "cause and country" in case of emergency. He then had his picture taken with a number of determined looking men in uniform standing around a large, shiny car. Having thus bought a certain amount of freedom from pressure and chicanery by the government, he retired from the political scene to devote his time again to his publishing house.

A few weeks before I left for Greece, I got a note from the publisher's wife inviting me for a weekend. This was in 1943, in the fourth year of the war, and pleasure traveling was frowned upon and indeed was no pleasure. However, my mother decided that turning down the invitation was out of the question and I very much wanted to go. So, on a Friday evening I took a train to Hannover.

I was met by the chauffeur and limousine and taken to a handsome house outside the city. My hostess, a young woman with the face and figure of an exhausted high-fashion model, received me cordially and I was shown to a splendid guest room. On Saturday morning the three of us, Herr Benneman, his wife and I, had breakfast, during which my host ate the yolks of two soft-boiled eggs and his wife ate the rubbery whites of the two eggs.

After breakfast he told his wife to leave us for half an hour, which she did without any visible signs of annoyance.

Left without her, I fidgeted a bit in my chair. I was not sure what to expect. I had not seen the publisher since my father's funeral seven years before. My host was completely at ease. He lit a large cigar, gave it a few tentative puffs, and began to look me over with the friendly interest of someone contemplating a puppy dog that one might take home to one's family. Inspection over, he gave his cigar one more long puff, settled himself more comfortably in his armchair and told me that he was a great lover. For a few minutes he elaborated on this God-given talent without the slightest embarrassment while I curled my toes in my shoes and tried desperately to look sophisticated and on top of it all.

He then informed me that he considered me eminently marriageable and just the right age.

A little silence followed this observation, during which he studied the tip of his cigar rather wistfully. His wife, he then confided to me, was a good sort who tried hard and by and large did little to displease him. It would not be right to turn around and divorce her, he said with a little sigh, and added that he hoped I would understand.

I cleared my throat and, at the second try, managed to reply that I completely understood, whereupon he patted my arm and called his wife back into the room. He told her to have the chauffeur bring the car around and take me to one of his black market connections (he did not call it that exactly) to get me an Italian-made suit. I got the suit. It was all wool, dark blue and white, beautiful, and for years after, the mainstay of my wardrobe.

Of course, he was as crazy as a cuckoo on the 35th of May. A mad hatter, if there ever was one. But for a while he made our world more colorful. He had loved and admired my father and to the end of his days he was kind and generous to our family. He kept the faith. There are not too many of those.

In 1943 the publisher was still a very rich man, but money bought little and, as he knew, would buy less in the future. An agent was sent out to scout the country for property that could be bought as investment. The agent had been out on the road for almost two weeks and had left no stone unturned, but nobody wanted to sell. He called his employer one evening with the news that he had found a house in a very small town on the edge of the Thuringia Forest which in German geography books is called "The Green Heart of Germany."

"Well," said the agent into the telephone, "it's really not bad. It used to be a pub. The landlord died; the widow is an elderly woman; she cannot run it alone. She wants to move into town."

"Buy it," said his employer.

"It has a bowling alley of some sort," said the agent. "Just one lane. All the men in town used to bowl here. It's pretty run down. The whole place is . . . well, not in too good a shape anymore. No central heating, tile stoves, but they seem to be in working condition."

"Well?" said his employer.

"It's called 'The Rock Cellar' because there seems to be a tunnel leading directly from inside the house into the rocky hill behind it. I understand water collects there frequently."

"Three floors, nine rooms," the agent continued. "She wants too much for it, but it's the first feasible property I have seen. It should not stand empty though. It might fall apart without a caretaker. It has no toilet," said the agent hurriedly, "just, you know, an outhouse some distance away."

"Buy it!" said Herr Benneman and hung up.

The publisher's call to my mother came after three bad nights of air raids in a row. His offer sounded like an invitation to paradise. A house with a large yard in a small quiet town in the country. One could sleep through the nights, one could grow one's own vegetables, there might even be fresh milk. No frantic crowds of people, no endless lines in front of the stores. Most of all: no fear! Tile stoves didn't worry her; she had grown up with tile stoves. Surely, in a place called the Thuringia Forest there was wood to be had.

"You will love it," said Herr Benneman.

"Well, yes — maybe . . .," my mother said cautiously.

"There seems to be no indoor plumbing," said Herr Benneman.

"What?" said my mother, but the publisher had hung up.

* * * * * * * * * * * * * *

My mother had no intention of leaving her furniture behind. Her first errand took her to the manager of a large transportation firm. The man behind the desk looked at her as if she had asked him to spend a weekend with her in Monaco.

"We don't move people," he said, simply appalled.

"You are not to move people," explained my mother patiently. "You are to move my furniture."

"Lady," said the man, recovering from the first shock, "anybody can come in here and say, please, move me and my stuff to Buxtehude, for all I know. What do you think we are doing here? Half the city wants to leave; that's just too bad. Sixty percent of my trucks are confiscated, the others are engaged in war-important work, and you want us to move your sofa and armchairs to Thuringia?"

"Those sofas and armchairs you are sneering at," said my mother with dignity, "happen to be genuine 18th and 19th century pieces. I am talking about priceless antiques which will be even more precious after the war, considering the losses we are suffering daily."

The man behind the desk felt he was losing ground and began to bluster.

"The answer is: *NO*! You cannot tell us what to do," he said loudly.

My mother fixed him with an icy stare. Then slowly she began to gather her gloves and purse.

"Perhaps I cannot," she said regally, "but I am sure the Department for the Preservation of German Culture and Heritage, which is under the direct patronage of Herr Reichsminister Goebbels, will be interested in your callous attitude toward the treasures of our country."

My mother could utter sentences like this as if she lunched twice a week with the gentleman in question.

The man stared at her. He didn't even know there was such a department (neither, for that matter, did my mother) but he knew when he was licked.

"We would have to verify your claims of antiques," he said sullenly. His visitor nodded graciously.

"Of course, any time this week you wish. Except between two and four," said my mother who took a nap every day after lunch. "I might be in conference then."

* * * * * * * * * * * * *

It was March again when I packed my bundle, said goodbye to Kristin's parents and headed west. My youngest brother, Dolfi, was then in his last year of high school. In March was his spring break. He would come as far as Berlin, wrote my mother, and would meet me there and see me safely to the place *where I belonged*.

Getting to Berlin meant once again sitting on my duffel bag for a night in the aisle of an unheated train, but that was nothing compared to the "meeting part" of the plan. Thousands of people, refugees and soldiers, were swarming through the vast station building in Berlin, whose once mighty glass dome was now shattered and open to the elements. Roaming the halls and platforms in search of my brother was out of the question, so I remained stationary, sitting quietly on my duffel bag, pressed against a wall and as much out of the way of the human flood as possible. That was very likely the reason that my brother, against all odds, did find me in the end by systematically covering every square yard of the grounds.

Dolfi was seventeen then, tall, lanky, vastly energetic and at all times hungry. I don't remember the rest of the trip—he took care of everything— but I do remember the apple! A large, firm red apple he had carried in his pocket the entire trip to give to me. It was warm from his body, shiny from rubbing against the rough material of his coat, and absolutely heavenly: a fresh apple in March in the fifth year of the war! I could not persuade him to share it with me; I was to have it all. He later confessed that he had to resist the urge to touch it many times during the long trip to Berlin, and forcefully pushed the thought of it out of his mind or he would have succumbed to the wild desire to eat it himself.

It was dusk when we arrived at the dreary little stop in Thuringia that was to be my new home. There were no taxis; Dolfi grabbed my long-suffering duffel bag with one arm and me with the other and propelled us toward the town. There were no welcoming lights shining through the blacked-out windows of the narrow old row houses to either side of us. Dolfi—

spirits forever undampened—half coaxed, half carried his weary load through the deserted main street and up the winding mountain road toward the Rock Cellar.

My mother received me quite matter-of-factly, which attitude emphatically changed after she had listened to my first coughing spell. Immediately she had a bed put up in the smallest, best-heated room on the second floor and ordered me into it. She then submerged me into a flood of home remedies—beginning with hot skim milk and honey and linden blossom tea to steaming compresses and warm camphor oil chest rubs—with such relentless stamina that whatever had held my chest in such a painful grip for the past two months declared itself defeated and at long last let go of me. I began to recuperate.

While I sat in bed, propped up with pillows to make breathing easier—cutting old newspaper into small rectangular pieces which would be strung on a thread and hung on a rusty nail in the outhouse or hemming large square pieces of mosquito nets for diapers—I began to acquaint myself with my new surroundings.

There was, first of all, Frau Einfalt. "Einfalt" is a benign, old-fashioned word meaning "simple-minded." It suited her wonderfully well. She possessed all the artless innocence and exasperating denseness that the word indicates.

Shortly after my mother's arrival in town she had advertised for a tenant-caretaker. She carefully interviewed the applicants, all women, and she chose this small, freckle-faced, red-haired woman for her gentle voice and timid manners, judging her rightly to be more pliable and less troublesome than some of the more self-assured candidates.

"I have two boys," said the young woman diffidently. "They are good boys, they wouldn't be no trouble."

"That's all right. Just keep them quiet between two and four," said my mother kindly.

Frau Einfalt and her two boys, aged eleven and three, moved into the top floor within the next two days. They paid half the going rate of rent, and my mother kept the hours of services to be rendered open to suit her needs. The freckled-faced, little woman meekly accepted this arrangement. Since her husband had been killed six months before, she had lived with some sour-faced in-laws. She was glad for a place of her own.

One morning, a week or so after I had arrived and while my mother was on one of her food scurrying field trips, I slipped out of bed and headed toward the large unheated living room where I found Frau Einfalt dusting the floor.

"Why are you out of bed? What are you doing in here?" she cried, her little white rabbit face puckered anxiously.

"It's all right, Frau Einfalt," I said soothingly, "I am just looking for a book."

Frau Einfalt straightened up and stared at me.

"Get back to bed," she said darkly, "or your mother will have both our hides!"

I retreated and as I hopped back into bed I thought that in spite of her name it had not taken Frau Einfalt very long to get a pretty good grasp of things.

The town's population was about four thousand souls. Its livelihood was hemp. There were four factories in the northern part of town, rivals in peacetime for the best reputation and the widest market. Now they were working full shifts, twelve hours a day, indifferent toward each other's success or failure, conditioning the hemp and twisting the ropes that would hold overcrowded elevators and tie ships to their docks. The women still took piecework home, as they had done before the war, to knot the fishing nets and bags which now the government distributed.

Some empty barracks at the other end of town had been turned into a camp and most of the factories' work forces were drawn from there. It's never been clear to me just what kind of a camp it was and I doubt that anybody else knew. It was a "catch-all" for the homeless: refugees, forced labor, displaced persons, and a sprinkle of asocial elements, with the latter two categories at the end of the war hurriedly joining the "forced labor" ranks after it was discovered that this merited bigger ration cards and preferred treatment.

But during the last year of the war, at least in our town's camp, the fine demarcation lines were eroding; either the government or the war or circumstances had forced them all to live in the shelter of the camp. They all worked long hours in the factories, got the same wages, slept in large dormitories, and ate the same poorly cooked food. Nobody had volunteered for any of it. It was from those quarters that Katja, our White Russian friend, one day majestically sailed into our lives. But that was not until a few months after my arrival.

* * * * * * * * * * * * *

There was in later years a photograph of the Rock Cellar standing on my mother's chest of drawers in her living room in Berlin, framed and prominently displayed, between the pictures of her children and grandchildren. It was a black and white photo and the old oak tree which towered over the pointed gable seemed to envelope the house in its protective shade. This picture stood there in its place of honor for some forty years, proof once again that it is not the hardest times in our lives which we would like to erase from our mind. My mother wore the memory of those seven years spent in this house in the small town in the Thuringia Forest like an invisible medal, a shiny badge of courage, until the end of her days.

The house stood on a hillside on the eastern end of town with no sidewalk or front yard separating it from the road, the first and the last house of the town. To the American tanks on their cautiously solemn march through town it was the last house and the one they stopped at until the next village was reconnoitered. For the Russians, who some weeks later came rolling down the hill in their various vehicles, it was the first house of yet another hapless little enemy town handed over to them by the departing Americans.

The house had been a pub as long as anybody could remember. It proudly bore its name "Rock Cellar" chiseled into a gray stone plate across the front and no scrubbing, chipping, and hacking away at it—and my mother tried it all—could erase it completely. Since everything that bears the name "Cellar" means pub in Germany, my mother's battle with thirsty visitors of various nations never completely ceased in all the seven years she was to spend there. She simply learned to deal with them more efficiently as time went by.

Directly behind the house some steep, uneven stone steps led up the hill onto a grass-planted plateau that held our garden. Currant and blackberry bushes defined the borders. A washline was strung between the branches of two gnarled old apple trees, and getting the baskets with wet sheets and towels up those bannisterless steps was no mean feat. On a nice summer or fall day hanging up the wash was a pleasant task. With an apron full of clothespins tied around my waist, holding a pin or two between my teeth and fastening a sheet to the rope just above my head, I had the whole lovely panorama of the countryside at my feet. The green and yellow hills rose and abated so gently that it seemed as if the land itself was breathing peacefully in the sun. On the next hilltop, across a dale too small to be called a valley, stood the town's windmill. The large wheel turned serenely in the wind, and each time one of its long arms dipped slowly toward me it seemed to give me a courteous and regal greeting. Sometimes I could see the long, thin miller (who always walked in a gray cloud of flour dust) move the big bags from inside the mill to the waiting wagon. My mother knew the miller, as she knew the baker, and the wife of the butcher, and the old carpenter in town, and she never came back empty-handed from her visits to the mill or without a little speck of flour on her dress, her shoes, or the tip of her nose.

There was only one large double door leading into the house and it could be secured with an iron crossbar. We were delighted with this extra protection, but after the war was over it became a threat and encumbrance. It tended to annoy our conquerors, who were an impatient lot anyway and inclined to take barred doors as a personal affront. They used to work our front door over with the butt end of their rifles until we had come flying down the steps and loosened the bar. I doubt that those doors ever got replaced. If I were ever to go back there, I would know those marks on that door and it would all come rushing back to me: the blows, and the fear and the excitement and uncertainty. What a tightrope walk it all was! And none of us knew if the rope would hold and what precipices lay beneath us.

The entrance hall was large and dark. A rusty iron door on the left led into the famed Rock Cellar. This was simply a long, black tunnel blasted straight into the rock behind the house and during rainy times the water covering the stone floor was ankle deep. Maybe it had been meant as cold storage for the pub; it certainly was always very cold and clammy in there. It was empty when my mother moved into the house, but as the months went by and the squadrons of enemy bombers became ever more frequent and dense so that the air around us vibrated with the steady hum of their motors, we put chairs in the cellar, and anybody who wanted to make it up the hill could join us in this gloomy shelter.

Straight ahead through the hall was the pub's kitchen, which was dank and dark and windowless, and for all its appearance might have also been carved out of the rock. We used it sometimes in summer, but most of the time we used a small room, immediately off the second floor staircase, where my mother had a woodburning stove installed.

To the right of the lower hall were the pub rooms. The first one was a large room with a long bar counter running alongside the wall opposite the windows, a sight which, at first, offended my mother not a little. She soon arranged our dining room furniture around the bar in a way that looked as if it had been part of the plan. The "backroom," not quite as large, was brighter and more pleasant and became for the time being our family room.

The rooms on the second floor were entered through the tiny chamber-turned kitchen, which held a stove, a sink, a table, and one or two chairs. From there, a door led into a small bright room with a large, brown tile stove, and this, eventually, became the very heart of our house and our lives. As heating material became more and more scarce it was the only room in winter that was really warm. The furnishings changed as the seasons and the needs of the family changed. It held, at different times, a daybed, a dining room table and chairs, a cabinet, bookshelves, the large stove and later a baby's crib. It had everything except walking space. A second door led to a large and wide room that accommodated most of our antique furniture and books. My mother used this room as her sitting room all summer and into late fall until the cold drove her out.

On the third floor, under the gable, Frau Einfalt resided with her boys in two rooms and a small kitchen.

My mother, taking stock of her new domicile, found no room suitable for a bedroom of her own. The room downstairs, though pleasant, had two large windows at street level that had neither bars nor shutters and those were precarious times and the house stood lonely. The small room on the second floor was the center of all activities and would afford her very little privacy. The large living room was out of the question. There was, however, the bowling lane, leading, with two steps up, straight off the living room. It had sturdy walls and a good roof. My mother had the carpenter partition off the first few yards of it, creating thus a new little room. The velvet curtain which had not been left behind to perish in the Berlin apartment was strung across the opening toward the living room, and my mother's bed and night table were placed behind it, so that she now slept on a true little stage, not unlike royalty in the great palaces of Europe, a comparison in which she saw nothing noteworthy or strange.

The rest of the bowling alley was used for storage. Here my mother kept much of the apple harvest, each apple resting on the lane without touching its neighbor and being checked and turned at regular intervals, which, as I learned, was the secret of their survival into spring. All faulty apples had been collected in autumn, no matter how misshapen or worm-eaten they appeared, and hauled off in a little wagon to the fruit press. There everything—apples, seeds, peelings, stems, and worms—would disappear into one big tank. Eventually we would climb back up the hill pulling our wagon filled with bottles of golden apple juice. According to my calculations this apple juice contained not only a great many wonderful vitamins but a goodly amount of protein as well. (*If* worms consist of protein. I always meant to ask somebody about it.)

The outhouse, placed somewhat at a distance from the house, really was not too bad a place. It was built of solid, weather-beaten wood and certainly was very airy. It had no more than the usual amount of flies in summer and it never lacked reading material. Nobody had any complaints in summer. Winter, however, was a different matter. It got very, very cold! (When years later I met up for the first time with the expression of "freezing one's whatyamacallit off" I took no exception to it at all but, with memories rekindled, heartily approved. It describes this particular sensation exceedingly well.) A year or so after my mother's arrival, the roof of the outhouse began to leak and not even my mother could get anybody to fix it. Since it rained directly onto the seat, emergency measures were in order. A large, black umbrella was stationed, permanently, right inside the entrance door of the house. It was a matter of honor to restore the umbrella to precisely the same spot where one found it. This newly added feature to our lifestyle was not without its silver lining. It saved us more than once from eviction after the war, when better equipped houses were frequently requisitioned by occupation troops.

Chapter 16

In the spring of 1944 my mother was 48 years old and looked ten years younger. She was short in stature and always well-rounded, but thin was not all the cry then. She was considered a very pretty woman with thick auburn hair and beautiful even teeth. The bridge of her nose showed a slight bump where she had run into a mailbox as a child. (She never quite forgave the mailbox for its malice.) Her eyes were light blue, often with a twinkle but at other times they were like blue ice. She refused to wear glasses all the time, even though she did not see well, and hunting for her mislaid glasses was a family affair. She was lively, energetic, purposeful and she bounced when she walked. Her laugh was hearty and infectious. She was also opinionated and, when crossed, flew either into a furious temper or, if such tantrum would have gotten her foreseeably nowhere at all, she turned coldly hostile. It was easy for her to strike up acquaintances and, if not crossed or inconvenienced, she was a staunch and loyal friend. Perhaps her most remarkable feature, considering the times we lived in, was what she herself called civil courage. This did not mean bravura in the face of physical violence but rather the moral courage of her convictions. Of this she had a great deal. She was never afraid to confront people. She let it be known when she was displeased. She knew herself to be at all times on the side of the angels. This led to a premature parting of the ways with some of her friends and all of her tenants. I don't think that in all those years we ever had a tenant who did not leave enraged. A number of times both parties wound up in court. It did not daunt my mother that she did not always win. Even the courts of law have been known to be wrong.

Into this sleepy little town in the Thuringia Forest she swept like a fresh breeze. She wooed the merchants and tradesmen. She charmed the thin top layer of the social order; she mentally sorted the refugees (who had so far been ignored by everybody in town) and found talent where nobody suspected it. Within three months of her arrival she gave her first "tea," consisting of ersatzkaffee, dry yeast cookies, and a reading of Goethe's *Letters to Frau von Stein*. Thanks to her, our social life was by no means dormant; not, at least, until those times when the business of surviving took up everybody's entire effort.

* * * * * * * * * * * * *

In the first days of spring my brother Peter came home on leave. Of the four of us, he was the most gifted, the most handsome, and the most difficult. He was a pilot in the Air Force and flew reconnaissance on the Eastern front.

"Is that bad?" I asked him one time when I was alone with him. He shrugged and laughed. "Want to hear about it?" he asked. He recited a poem that a fellow officer had made defining the different branches of the flying forces. The "Jaeger" (hunter), forerunner of the jet fighter, was described as the king of the sky, and so on down, I have forgotten the rest except for the last two lines, which ran something like this: "The reconnoiter, skin and bone, flies all alone, comes seldom home." I looked at him with consternation.

"And that is what you do?"

"Not anymore," he said. He had spent the last two months in an Air Force camp retraining for hunter pilot.

"What do they do?" I asked. I could see no task for them anymore.

"They try to detract the bomber formations and push them off course," he explained, "away from cities and heavily populated areas."

"Ach, Peter," I said, thinking of those silvery clouds of bombers droning above our heads, high up in the sky, seemingly uncontested and unassailable. It was then he said that the war had to be gotten over with, that all he could think of was hanging his uniform on a nail and going back to school.

I remembered what I had been told about the young captains: If they are over twenty-five they might begin to figure out the odds. Peter was not yet twenty-one.

I have heard it said that blue eyes could not have "soul." Wrong! Peter's eyes were very blue and they had fire and passion, dreams, laughter, and, at rare times, gentleness. When he left, we looked out of the upstairs window to see him walk down the hill toward the station. He turned back, smiled and waved. He was everything that was bright, young, and promising. When he came back less than a month later it was in a narrow black box, accompanied by four comrades. He died diving into a fortress of bombers over the German Westerwald, heedless of the odds. And he died alone.

My mother took the news of his death with the uncanny strength she mustered in the face of disaster. She came into the room where I was sitting and told me, tearless and in a low voice. Perhaps she was afraid for me; by then I was in the seventh month of pregnancy. She did not permit me to go to the funeral. That night, when I tiptoed through the living room on my way to bed I heard a muffled sound from her bedroom. The curtain was drawn but through the crack I saw my mother kneeling in front of her bed, her face buried in her hands, weeping bitterly. It was the only time I ever saw her cry. She did not know that I had seen her. Her tears were between her and her God.

* * * * * * * * * * * * * *

Getting ready for the baby was a test of one's ability to improvise. "Baby bathtub or bucket? Can't have both," said the woman at the coupon center.

"Bucket," said my mother before I had even begun to ponder that question. "We can always bathe the baby in the kitchen sink," she said to me afterward, "but where and how would you wash diapers without a bucket?" Maternity dress or baby clothes? No contest there. We knew nobody who could spare some baby clothes; without the mosquito nets there would not have been a single diaper. Somebody got a crib down from their attic and, oddly enough, we got hold of a baby buggy. It was made of cardboard but had four wheels and a little sunroof and if we stayed out of the rain with it, all would be well. It was painted a creamy white and I lined it with some flowered material that came out of my mother's "magic" chest. Out of the same chest she pulled triumphantly some maid's uniforms of days

gone bye. Between the maids who came and went, there had been, fortunately, a few plump ones. The uniforms were made of thin, black cotton, cut straight down. A white starched apron had gathered the dress at
the waist. A starched white collar was fastened around the neckline with
invisible snaps. I wore the black gown and the white collar and dispensed
with the apron.

With the baby coupons I bought some shirts and jumpers and a blanket.
For fall and winter, one of our square feather pillows would do very well.
Under Eleanor's guidance I had knitted little jackets and pants, two of
each, both blue and white. I had steered clear of pink even though I had
enough girls' names ready for quintuplets and not a single boy's name. I
was daring fate, I suppose; deep down, I was scared of having a daughter
and felt inadequate to raise one, never having sorted out my own girlhood
properly.

My ration cards were a bit more plentiful than average. I got a pint
of milk every day and a few ounces more butter every week. I craved pudding. No pickles or onion and jelly sandwiches for me, it was pudding all
the way. My mother used to come home from her visits to the mill with a
pound or two of "Gries," a rough-textured cream of wheat, and I would
use most of my rationed milk to cook a pudding which I served twice a
day. I often cooked a vegetable soup, simmering carrots, celery roots, onions
and potatoes, dill and parsley, in olive oil taken from my inexhaustible
Greek canister. I would add water and salt until there was enough soup
for a day or two. We were not hungry yet. That was to come later.

There was no prenatal care in those days. Doctors were rarely involved
in normal deliveries. I went to see the local midwife once, a pleasant and
business-like woman in her forties. She wrote down the date in her calendar and promised to accompany me to the hospital. I barely remember
her. As it turned out she never saw my baby.

The town had no hospital. A twenty-minute train ride would take us
to the county seat where I was registered, by phone, at the hospital for the
approximate time. I was in a state of great anticipation about the approaching delivery. I planned to be alert, intelligent, and observant during this,
nature's most exciting process, which I was about to experience. It was to
be the end, once and for all, of all the vague and muddled tales I had
heard about childbirth since I ceased to believe in the stork. Surely there
would be a way of pinning the whole thing down properly. I meant to take
precise and comprehensive mental notes of all the steps along the way in

the consecutive order of their occurrence. Young women today take such knowledge for granted. In my time it was a somewhat revolutionary idea which I kept well to myself. As it turned out, I found it nearly impossible to realize this idea. To be main participant and objective observer at the same time would take training and preparation which I was totally lacking. I will, however, say one thing: I challenge any statement that it is largely fear that makes women suffer during delivery. I walked into this, my first childbirth, joyfully, excited, and completely fearless!

On a warm summer night around midnight I wakened and, "listening" to my body, I felt a slight pinch inside me, just above my pelvic bone, not unlike, I thought (being alert, intelligent, and observing), the pinch one might feel after eating unripe fruit. This slight cramp returned some eight or nine minutes later and after the fourth reoccurrence I heaved myself out of bed and ran barefoot to my mother's room to tell her about it.

It was only five days before due day, and my mother thought this might be it. We talked for a while and then I went back to sleep, and so did she. By six o'clock we were both wide awake, up and about and getting ready. My mother notified the midwife, who promised to meet us at the station for the first train at ten o'clock. At 9:30 she called back and told us that a woman in the next village had gone into labor earlier than expected and that she was needed there. I found nothing objectionable about this, but my mother was furious. A promise is a promise, she fumed, and the midwife was acting irresponsibly. When I said that the village woman would not be in a hospital and I would, she was furious with me. Under the circumstances, however, she could not keep up her anger, and we set off on our short train ride without a fight.

The hospital was a half hour's walk from the station. I was heavy and carried the baby low. I rather waddled, I suppose, along the residential street, in my black maid's uniform, but what a beautiful walk it was! The day promised to be very warm, the sky was blue and cloudless. All the gardens were in full glory. Above and between the white painted picket fence posts roses of all colors and shades were nodding at me in the summer air: "Good luck, good luck, little Eva." The air was sweet with fragrance. I would have liked to dance and sing and kiss the air and the roses. In reality, I suppose, our progress was a bit clumsy and at a snail's pace. By now I had been in labor for eleven hours and was struggling for breath.

The first thing with which the hospital concerned itself was finding another midwife. The directress of nurses, a big, middle-aged, wonderful woman, finally talked a retired old lady into taking just one more case. She was a tiny old woman with snow-white hair who was close to eighty years old and had been a midwife for more than forty-five years. Half of the population of the county seat must have been delivered by her.

She stayed with me for the next fourteen hours, and it was she who was alert, intelligent, and observant. I was getting restless and perplexed. The contractions had moved higher and were more intense. They appeared every four minutes. But nothing else much happened.

"The contractions are pretty strong now," I reported. My mother shook her head.

"You are not crying out yet," she said knowingly.

"How are you doing?" asked the floor nurse, sticking her head through the door. "I am having contractions now every three minutes," I said eagerly.

"Ah, you are still smiling! It's not time yet," said the floor nurse, setting me straight. So much for childbirth psychology in those days.

The minutes and hours ran together. It got dark. I was not smiling any longer. Every contraction was harder and longer and made my body rigid with pain. At ten o'clock, the midwife called the doctor. The doctor on duty was a young woman straight out of medical school. She was gentle and timid and often looked at the wise, old, wrinkled face of the midwife. My mother sat on a chair in the corner of the room trying to stay awake. At eleven o'clock the air raid sirens began to scream. Only one small lamp was burning at the bedside. The head nurse came in to check the curtains and shutters. I heard the commotion outside in the hall as the patients were carried down to the basement. Two nurses, four hands, formed a seat, and the patient would hang on to the nurses' necks for support. So they carried them down, one after another.

Nobody in my room stirred. It was as if they had not heard the horrible screeching of the sirens.

At midnight, the dark young head and the white-haired head were bent over me in whispered consultation. I suppose I was a mess by then.

"I shall give you some morphine," said the young doctor. "You need to rest. We will work again after you sleep a little."

She gave me a shot; they covered me, and everybody, including my mother, tiptoed out of the room. The terrible contractions became distant, faded, I became drowsy; a warm, wet wave engulfed my lower body. A great pressure I had not felt before bore down on me. I called out and within seconds everybody was back in the room, the young one, the old one, the head nurse, and my mother in the background. They were bent over, me, they whispered, a hasty decision was made by consensus and I heard the clanking of metal. I don't know if the knife in the childwoman's hand trembled or was steady; I cried out just once and then I heard my child pick up my cry and carry it on its own.

"A miracle! My God, what a miracle!" I heard my mother exclaim. She had given life to four children and had never seen one born.

I was aware of soundless, quick activity, but it was so dark that I could barely distinguish the figures. I was cleaned and covered warmly. Something was pushed beside my bed and when I lifted my head I could see my little son, wrapped in blankets, sleeping in a basket on the floor. He was exhausted from twenty-five hours of struggle.

"Me, too, love," I thought. My head fell back on the pillow. From the rooftops a long, uninterrupted wail of sirens signaled the end of the air raid. I felt that I had done the most wonderful and amazing thing that anybody could ever hope to achieve in life. And then I slept.

The baby and I stayed at the hospital for nine days. During the first five or six days I suffered a great deal of discomfort, but I remember my stay as pleasant. The morning after the delivery, the senior staff doctor, with the assistance of the young woman doctor, stitched me together under full anesthetic. By then the tissue was swollen and inflamed and for the next three days, I could hardly move at all. I was flat on my back and spent a good deal of the time contemplating the possibility that I might never be able to sit on a chair again, that I would, in all probability, have to waddle through the rest of my life like a duck, and that I definitely never again would be able to ride on a bicycle.

During one of those rather bleak contemplative sessions, the head nurse came into the room and, seeing tears rolling down on each side of my face onto the pillow (even turning my head was painful) she wordlessly left again. She reappeared a quarter of an hour later with an armload of books. Since the hospital had no library, she must have taken them from her own living quarters. They had been carefully selected to cheer me up. (The memory computer in our brain has a marvelous way of storing such small, unexpected kindnesses, to have and to hold, and to return in kind when the opportunity arises.)

Neighbors from home sent me a basket of strawberries, a truly royal gift in those days, and other friends sent lovingly mended baby clothing.

One day the senior doctor, taciturn, distant, and overworked, during one of his daily visits turned in the door to say with a smile: ". . . and your baby is the prettiest of them all."

The large window looking out toward a garden filled with shrubs and flowers was open all day, and though I could not turn my head toward it for the first few days I could smell the fragrance that the summer air carried into the room and I could hear the birds sing in the willow tree.

* * * * * * * * * * * * *

Bertel was a beautiful baby, but during the first four months of his life, he cried a great deal. I wonder even now if the child was not constantly hungry. I was sure I had not enough milk for him. This creates a great deal of guilt. My mother said that the only way to find out was to weigh the baby before and after each feeding. This sounds simple enough in theory but it was something of a nightmare in practice. I can still see the two of us hovering over the kitchen scale. The baby was placed on a large dinner tray, one of us steadied the tray and kept the wiggling child from rolling off it while the other one pushed the weights back and forth to establish the minuscule amount the baby had gained during the feeding. This we did ten times a day, before and after each of the five feedings. It was sheer insanity, and the baby tried to let us know that. He howled his protest during most of the procedures. By late fall I stopped nursing and Bertel went on the bottle without a whimper. He thrived, and the crying stopped.

The problem now was the heating of the early morning bottle. There was no fire going in the kitchen stove, and the bottle, which had been placed in cold storage during the night, was icy. It was unthinkable in those days to give the baby a bottle without warming it. I solved the dilemma by getting up sometime between four and five in the morning, fetching the bottle and taking it to bed with me. It was not unlike cuddling an icicle to your breast. For the first few minutes I was goose pimples from head to toe, followed by a period of mutual adjustment and then I would fall asleep again. By the time the first feeding was due, the bottle was as warm as toast.

* * * * * * * * * * * * *

We were by now in the sixth year of the war and the population of the Rock Cellar had gained momentum. Bertel was the first one to join us. The next new face around the house was Frau Einfalt's younger sister who moved in with her. She was no younger version of our little Einfalt, though. She was short and there all resemblance ended. She was plump and blue-eyed, with the rosy complexion of a china doll, and blond, very curly hair. I remember best her small, even, white teeth, because she told me once that those were her baby teeth which she had never lost. No second teeth had ever appeared. Her older sister, whose teeth were large and a bit crooked, beamed verification. (I have always meant to ask an expert if this could have been true.)

This young lady might have looked like a china doll, but she was pure steel wool. It did not take her long to discern my mother's firm grip on her meek older sister. From then on she regarded it as her sacred duty to strengthen her sister's flabby backbone. Small flickers of rebellion appeared now on little Einfalt's face when my mother's demands were too frequent or too abruptly imparted. This unexpected resistance only served to call forth my mother's own steely qualities. The whole relationship became a rope-pulling between Miss Milktooth and my mother, with little Einfalt with her frightened, freckled, bunny face right in the middle. The older boy stopped running errands for my mother. If she wanted something quickly from town he pretended not to hear her, and I would have to go upstairs and repeat the request.

The next one to join our little group was Katja, the White Russian lady. At least she said she was White Russian. She spoke German with a heavy accent; she spoke a good but accented French; she could converse in Polish and Yiddish; and she knew a few English words. I often wondered if she did not have an accent in Russian, too. If so, what, on the good earth, was Katja's mother tongue?

She was a stately and handsome woman in her forties.

"Vas I alvays a 'Brremen,'" she once said proudly to us (referring to one of the large, ocean-going steamers) "never a little sailboat! Nah?"

It would be impossible to conjure up Katja's picture without mentioning her favorite word: "Nah?" She pronounced it as if saying: "not" but dropping the "t" at the end, and she always put an invisible question mark behind it. It was, at once, the softening touch after an opinionated statement and her connecting bridge to the surrounding world.

Her life story was nebulous. She had fled from Russia to Germany while still very young. She had been married and divorced. She had either married again or lived in companionship with a Jewish doctor who had been sent to Poland, where she had followed him. Since she was not permitted to stay with him, rather than await the arrival of the Russians, she had returned to Germany. She was now living in the camp outside the town and was sent to work in one of the rope factories. She was a steady and efficient worker, disdaining all chatter and shortcuts, but she quickly became something of a freak show there. During her lunch hour she would descend into the open courtyard of the factory and embark on a series of muscle relaxing exercises that involved kneebends, sweeping circles of her large arms, and expansive breathing — a heaving and receding of her mighty chest like ocean waves rolling in and out. She did this daily, rain or shine, impervious to her noisy audience of fellow workers who were leaning out of every window, jeering and cheering her on. In time, they came to be quite proud of her. She was the first sight shown to each new arrival. Katja shrugged them all off.

"Zey are such small ants," she said of them.

What she could not bear, though, was the dormitory living, the lack of privacy and the inadequate washing facilities. It was the latter that brought her to our house. I have forgotten how she introduced herself. She simply stood in front of our door one day and asked my mother if she might sponge bathe herself once a week in our house. My mother, who had heard about her (and heartily approved of her exercises) was impressed by so much dignity under such wretched circumstances. She agreed to let her come. And so our "Bremen" sailed into the shelter of the Rock Cellar. Thereafter, on Saturday afternoons, a great splashing and moving about could be heard through the closed door of our tiny kitchen, accompanied by little grunts and exclamations, at the end of which Katja emerged moist, shiny, and in high, good spirits.

She did not live with us. My mother found her a cubbyhole under the stairwell of the baker's house that would hold a bed and a small table. Katja persuaded the factory foreman to let her do piecework "at home."

Since she had no chair, she did her work propped up in her bed. She never failed her quota and never had to return to the factory. Her exercises she now did in the baker's backyard. Her spare time she spent in our house. Eight hours a day, six days a week, she knitted nets for her very survival, and in her free time, she knitted little baby sweaters and pants for Bertel out of friendship and the inability to be unoccupied.

On warm summer days she would struggle up the hill behind the house and sit in a garden chair with the baby sleeping in the cardboard buggy right beside her. There my mother found her one day, part of her clothes piled beside her on the grass, knitting and sunning herself, topless, and supremely content. Back in the house my mother told me about it amused and shocked in equal parts. She wondered what she should do about this unorthodox idyll in our backyard. It would be best, she decided, to nip it in the bud. She climbed the steps once more and faced her outrageous friend who was lying in the chair, her eyes closed and all but purring in the sun.

"You cannot do this, Katja," she said firmly. Katja looked up.

"Is wronk?" she asked calmly. "In Russia, ve do it all ze time. Human body is beautiful, Nah?"

"Russia is very large," my mother said, "It can absorb this sort of thing. We are more crowded here. It's not a native custom. Please, keep your clothes on, Katja."

Katja shrugged philosophically. "Nah?" she said with a resigned little sigh and reached down in the grass for her bra.

In winter she remained stationary in a chair beside the tile stove. The little room could not have accommodated a restless "Bremen" sailing about. She sat there, reading, knitting and talking; she was amusing and intelligent and no complainer. It was clear that much of her adult life had been spent under more fortunate circumstances and that money had never been a problem. In many ways, my mother greatly admired her. She was the only person in our house, not counting the baby, with whom my mother maintained a good relationship through her entire stay.

* * * * * * * * * * * * *

The next stranger who crossed the threshold into the Rock Cellar did not come of her own free will and her stay was short and ill-starred.

She had noticed the woman the first time she came into the pharmacy, Frau Lange, the pharmacist's wife, said — she was so tall and gaunt. But it was the trapped look in her deep-set eyes that she had not been able to forget.

"She might be any age between thirty and forty. It's difficult to tell with them, you know," said the pharmacists's wife. The woman had asked for some small item that the pharmacy did not have and very likely would not be supplied with anymore for the duration of the war. When against all expectation one more shipment arrived, Frau Lange had put a little parcel aside in case the woman should return. She came and was handed the parcel and stood for a while, quietly, while Frau Lange put a few cautious questions to her. It was obvious by now that this forlorn creature was carrying a child within her gaunt body. The circles under her eyes were deep and purple.

Where did she stay? — In the displaced persons' camp.

"I knew the answer before she spoke," said Frau Lange with a sigh. She asked her what her name was.

"Mara."

"Mara . . .?"

No answer. Nothing. Mara Nothing.

When she came a third time, she was heavy around her hips and her breath came shorter. The haunted look had given way to dull despair. Only once had there been a spark of animation.

"I will not have the child in that hell hole," she said; and the blotches on her face turned red and angry. "I will not have it with all those people looking on!"

"How about the father's family?" Frau Lange asked gently, "Can they not help?"

"There is no father," the woman said listlessly.

"There has to be a father!" Frau Lange almost said. "I swallowed the stupid remark just in time," she told us.

The Langes had no spare rooms. Their children were grown and gone and the rooms had been taken over by a refugee family.

Frau Lange contacted the hospital in the nearest town. Their staff had been reduced again, she was told. The rooms were overcrowded.

"Surely you can take care of your own deliveries," said a tired, exasperated voice on the other end of the line. "You have a qualified midwife and a doctor in your town. Not all communities are that lucky." It was after this last futile phone call that Frau Lange walked up to the Rock Cellar one evening in late summer and told my mother about the woman.

"Will you let her have her baby here?" she asked my mother.

"By all means!" said my mother without a moment's hesitation. "Tell her that she can have her baby here."

Frau Einfalt and I were set to scrubbing the family room downstairs.

"A room where a baby is born has to be as clean as a whistle," said my mother when she came down to inspect it. Frau Einfalt avoided my mother's eyes. She looked as sullen as her good-natured face could manage.

When I first told our little Einfalt about the woman she had shown a good bit of interest, but when she finally came downstairs to help me I could tell by the way she clanked the bucket around and slammed the furniture back against the wall that she must have had one of her backbone strengthening talks with her sister.

"You are to do *what*?" yelled Miss Milktooth, faking vast incredulity. "Scrub a room for one of them gypsies? She probably slept with anybody who crooked a finger at her!"

"Who scrubbed down the room for you when you had Herbie?" she demanded. "D'you think that gypsy would have done it? She would have spit in your face if you'd ask her, that's what she'd have done!"

My reluctant helper was gone within the hour, "to look after my own family" she said haughtily, properly primed by her little sister. I finished the room and began hunting some baby clothes that Bertel had outgrown. Remembering the joy at discovering the basket with the baby beside my bed less than three months earlier, I asked my mother to let me use our laundry basket. Once again she pulled out of her chest an old flowered curtain with which I lined the basket, with more enthusiasm than talent, it must be said, but the end effect, I thought, was quite pretty. My mother, who could not sew at all, wholeheartedly agreed. Frau Lange had brought a few old bed sheets and Katja and I, in the later afternoons, would sit in the backyard, Bertel between us, and hem large, square pieces for diapers.

Nobody seemed to know exactly when the baby was due, but we were ready for it.

On a mild Indian summer evening, just before dark, the phone rang. It was the local doctor, a short, brusque man whom we barely knew.

"Did I understand that you were willing to take the maternity case out of the camp?" he asked without any introduction.

"Yes, oh yes, doctor," my mother exclaimed. "Is she in labor?"

"Well, yes . . . no . . ." for a second the doctor seemed at a loss for words. He had not been prepared for that joyful note in my mother's voice.

"The baby came prematurely. It was self-induced labor . . . everything went wrong. Anyway, the baby was stillborn. The woman is ill. I'd like to get her out of the camp. Are you still willing to take her?"

"Yes, of course," said my mother. The joy had gone out of her voice.

The pharmacist and his wife came walking up the hill, carrying a bundle of sheets and cotton. Frau Lange looked stricken. She knew before the little pickup truck stopped and the four men had carried the mattress with the prone, covered figure into our house, what they were bringing. And she prepared us for it.

The woman—in a moment of wild and final despair—had taken a lead pencil and with one sharp, hard blow, pushed it toward that unwanted, kicking, living thing inside her. She had screamed just once, and, in the ceaseless tower of Babel noises around her, nobody had paid any attention. She had lain down on her bed and doubled her covers to hide the blood and the writhing of her mutilated body as long as she could bear it. She had not called for help. When her plight was finally discovered, hours passed before the doctor arrived. The child had been born dead or died in the process. The woman was only semiconscious by then. Peritonitis had set in. When she was carried into our house, she was comatose. There were no antibiotics. There was not even a piece of ice I could have crushed and put between her cracked lips. I slept in her room that night, but all I could do was keep her clean and wipe the foam off her bluish lips with a cool, moist wash cloth. She never opened her eyes again. A strong, sweetish odor of decay emanated from her. A few times she moaned. My mother and I took turns the next day watching by her bedside and in the evening the pharmacist and his wife came again. This time they did not leave. Death was imminent and we all knew it.

We talked in whispers, gathered around the shaded lamp in a corner of the room. Frau Lange kept asking my mother's forgiveness. She had meant so well. In response, my mother lightly patted her arm a few times. Herr Lange kept falling asleep. He would snore a little, awake with a start and guiltily look around to see if anyone had noticed.

Toward morning the breathing changed and became harsh and irregular, and when the first gray streaks showed on the horizon, the woman died.

Mara Nothing. She had died, not in the hell hole, but in a clean room, between clean sheets, with four sad and silent people holding watch. Somebody had stroked her hair a few times during the night, somebody had cried for her, just a few quickly stifled sobs. Did it matter? Maybe it made no difference at all. Maybe it did.

* * * * * * * * * * * * *

On a cold and drizzly November evening I answered a knock at the door and admitted an oddly matched couple into the hall. The woman was carrying a well-covered bundle in her arms; the man, who was half a head shorter than the woman, carried two large suitcases. The bundle turned out to be a baby, no more than a few months old. The woman was in her thirties, plump and red-haired. The man looked older, wan and exhausted, and when I took his damp coat from him a rather prominent hunchback was revealed. The introduction in the dark hall was short and inconclusive; upstairs in the warm little sitting room the man gave a more detailed explanation of their sudden presence. Our surprise seemed to discomfit him considerably; he seemed embarrassed and upset.

"Herr Benneman never called or wrote to you?" he asked more than once. (Herr Benneman was the publisher.)

"Never," said my mother, not unbending a bit. I went into the kitchen to see if I could revive the fire to the point of brewing a bit of ersatzkaffee; our guest's acute discomfort began to spill over on me. When I returned with the two cups, my mother's expression was less perplexed but, if possible, even more displeased.

She remembered our visitor now; he was our landlord's editor-in-chief. The high, domed forehead loomed over his owlish, intelligent eyes. He looked ill with fatigue and spoke in a low, diffident voice.

"Rosalind," (a quick glance toward his red-haired wife) "had been my dear friend and hostess for a long time. When conditions became increasingly difficult we decided to marry. The baby . . ." (a little apologetic smile), "came as a complete surprise. We were greatly worried . . . the constant air raids, the cold shelters . . ., never a full night's sleep. Rosalind is fully occupied with the baby without having a cantankerous husband around who keeps irregular hours and is useless around the house." Another painful facsimile of a smile.

"Anyway, Herr Dr. Benneman offered us, that is, my wife and child, a refuge in his—in this house for the duration of the war. I had no idea that he did not contact you. Rosalind and I would be very grateful for your kindness. Wouldn't we, dear?"

Rosalind—who had been looking around the room with open curiosity—obviously thought that enough palaver had been exchanged. She turned her full, white face with the dark raisin eyes toward my mother.

"I would like to change the baby," she said coolly polite, "and I am very tired. Would you show us to our room, please." I caught my breath. This will not do at all, Rosalind, I thought.

"You don't have a room here—as yet," said my mother doing Rosalind one better in cold politeness. "I will have to see where I can place you and the child."

At the tone of my mother's voice, the expression in Rosalind's doughy face changed as if somebody had plugged in an electric current. Her languid, almost bored features became alert and cunning. She leaned back in her chair and once again looked around the room, this time with slow, impudent deliberation. And then she looked at my mother. The message on her face could not have been clearer if it would have been spelled out with black paint on the white wall: We are here as guests of my husband's employer, not yours!

I could read my mother's answer in the icy stare she directed at the young woman: Take care! it signaled, or—your husband's employer notwithstanding—you will be out on your ears!

"His hostess, indeed!" said my mother wrathfully to me that night. "She was his cook! I remember Benneman telling me about his chief editor's misalliance. She threatened to quit and he went into a panic and married her. And the baby came as a surprise! I am sure it did, to him. She would have been about as surprised at finding that she has a thumb on each hand!"

The wan, little man fled; his coat barely dried, on the early morning train. Rosalind and the baby stayed. They moved into the smaller of the two pub rooms where the sick woman had lain. It was cold now, and Rosalind applied for food — and wood rations, but there was a waiting period before the coupons were issued. In the meantime, my mother had to grit her teeth and lend her some of our wood rather than have her underfoot in our crowded family room upstairs.

"I expect to get my wood back when you receive your ration," my mother told her, "we don't have enough ourselves to see us through the winter."

Rosalind took the wood without a thank-you. After all, my mother had made it clear that this was not a present. My mother responded to this new insolence by checking the room downstairs for cleanliness when Rosalind was out one day. Finding it wanting, she placed a broom, dustpan and dust rag prominently in the middle of the room. Rosalind promptly returned the equipment by leaning it against our kitchen door where it would drop on the first person who opened the door from the inside. My mother told her that she would have to furnish her share of newspaper squares for the outhouse. Rosalind shrugged her plump shoulders and said she thought rather not, seeing that she wasn't interested in reading newspapers and did not have any. My mother, driven to more severe measures, removed the umbrella from its corner in the front hall. Miss Milktooth on the third floor took this as a personal insult and loudly invited Rosalind to come up for some peppermint tea and cookies.

Rosalind told her appreciative third floor audience that my mother had requested she keep the baby quiet between two and four in the afternoon, which, she said, forced her to sit, on bad days, for two hours in the post office with the baby. Miss Milktooth said she was shocked and hoped that other Christian people would be too.

The wood was approved and we saw the first load arrive and the older Einfalt boy stacking it under Rosalind's window. My mother got ready to go down and ask for her share of the wood.

During the whole squabble I never knew if I should laugh or cry. It began to affect my stomach a little. By now, none of the women would speak to my mother, and at times I had to carry messages back and forth that were rather acidic and were difficult to tone down into civil communications.

"Don't ask for the wood back just yet, Mutti," I suggested with some trepidation, knowing that I was treading on thin ice, indeed. "She owes us a good bit. If we take our wood now, what is she to heat with? We would just have to lend it back to her."

My mother grumbled but could not refute the logic of it. A week later Rosalind announced that she was moving in with Frau Einfalt and her family. When my mother returned from a trip into town, Frau Einfalt, her son and sister were just carrying the last of Rosalind's wood up to the third floor. My mother stormed into the kitchen.

"Did you see what they are doing?" she furiously asked me.

"Now, thanks to your interference, we will never get our wood back!" She was right, we never did. And I never could quite figure out where we had gone wrong in this wood business.

"Well," said my mother grimly, "you are doing the splitting. Good luck!"

The wood came in large round logs and had to be split into smaller pieces before it could be used. I did the splitting and it is nothing I like to remember. I never really learned how. I would balance a log on an old tree stump that was used for this purpose, and give it a mighty whack with the ax, and though I felt my aim had been good and true, the log would just move over a little and then roll off and the ax would be buried deep into the tree stump. I sometimes needed the help of the Einfalt boy to extract it. If I did catch the log off guard and it was not paying sufficient attention to our game to move over quickly enough, it would actually split, but at least one of the pieces would always be airborne and sail through space in directions that could not possibly be predicted. It was one of the minor miracles of that year that I never got my head knocked off during those wood splitting sessions and never killed anything that happened to pass by our house at the time.

* * * * * * * * * * * * *

It must have been early December when a letter arrived from my mother's lawyer in Berlin. Herr Dr. Pringel had been my mother's adviser — inasmuch as anybody could advise my mother — and staunch defender against unreasonable tenants and other exploiters of widows and orphans in the courts of law and justice. Now he turned to her for help. It was a long, moving, handwritten letter.

"I am writing to you as a father and husband," wrote Herr Dr. Pringel, "I do not know where else to turn. Berlin is fast becoming a powder keg. We see the handwriting on the wall. How long can it last? Food is becoming scarcer all the time. My wife has been delicate, as you know, since the birth of the twins. She is wasting away under the present conditions here. The twins, nine years old, are still lively and healthy, but nightly their lives are threatened, as are ours, of course.

We must leave the city and what better course can I take than to appeal to your generous person whom I, in my modest way, have been proud to assist so many times . . . (and for less than the going legal fees) . . ."

My mother was a practical person. She was moderately moved and flattered by this appeal. She could, also, foresee her financial resources drying up within the near future. Besides, it did not do for the furniture downstairs to stand all winter in freezing temperatures.

So she wrote back to Berlin that, under the pressing circumstances, she would open her house to them and might be able to let them have two rooms and kitchen on the first floor. She would have to charge them an appropriate rent, of course, but that, surely, was a small consideration. The appropriate rent, it turned out, was appropriate for Berlin, not for a little town in Thuringia, but she did not see how this would make any difference.

The Pringels arrived a few days later. They had been ready and packed, awaiting my mother's answer.

"My dear, gracious lady," said Dr. Pringel, bending low over my mother's hand, his voice ringing with emotion. He was spearheading the little group pressing into our hall. Somehow there were more of them than we had anticipated, more people, more luggage, more occupied space.

To begin with, there were two women instead of one. They seemed both about the same age and were both extraordinarily thin. One of them, her hair and face so colorless that she blended right into the silver fox she wore, gave us a brave little smile; the other one was dark and wiry and, after a quick daring glance through the open kitchen door, began to count the pieces of luggage.

"We brought Gertrud, our dear, invaluable friend and housekeeper along," explained Dr. Pringel, following my mother's puzzled look. "We knew you would not mind."

We didn't mind. That is, I didn't. She and I were to share the tiny upstairs kitchen, since the downstairs kitchen proved totally impossible during the winter months, and I don't remember a single argument. She, too, of course, eventually ceased talking to us, but that was still in the future. Right now graciousness and gratitude enveloped all of us like a pink, perfumed cloud. The pink cloud, however, lost some of its hue when my mother produced and explained the (hidden) umbrella to them.

"We did not *know*!" said Dr. Pringel, his smile growing visibly pained. His wife's smile vanished altogether. Her hand, ever so slightly, reached toward the hall table for support. The twins, two beautiful, curly-haired, blond boys of nine, thought it a huge joke.

The luggage was moved into the rooms and everybody followed. The invaluable Gertrud cast an experienced eye around and immediately discovered a hole in the curtains. I saw her throwing a meaningful glance at her mistress, but her mistress had collapsed into a chair and was covering her eyes with one gloved hand.

The Rock Cellar was now crowded beyond capacity. My mother, who had originally set up housekeeping with little Einfalt and her two children, now found herself heading a motley crew of seven women, six children, and one man, most of them in open mutiny and the rest progressing speedily toward it. Frau Pringel, never the life of the party, was the first casualty. We hardly ever saw her. All necessary tasks were performed by the efficient and tireless Gertrud. When it turned out that the kitchen downstairs was absolutely worthless in winter, my mother permitted Gertrud to cook on our stove upstairs provided she brought her own wood. Shortly afterward, Herr Dr. Pringel ascended the stairs to pay us a formal visit.

After a few pleasantries he cleared his throat and, with a light wave of the hand and a hearty little chuckle, dismissing what he was about to say as almost too insignificant to mention, he mentioned it anyway and said that the rent, obviously, would need some adjustment now that there was no kitchen included.

My mother's face registered nothing but blank astonishment.

"But, *lieber Herr Doktor*," she said, "what it does mean is that we will have to give you space in our own kitchen, which will put us to much greater inconvenience than letting you have the big kitchen downstairs. I do not understand where the rent adjustment comes in."

Momentarily shot out of the saddle by this kind of logic, Dr. Pringel cleared his throat again and continued, this time without the hearty chuckle, "We had no idea that we would have no bathroom!"

"That's war for you," said my mother sympathetically.

Dr. Pringel got up from the chair in wordless indignation. But he could not leave in total defeat; he fired one more parting shot before he stalked out of the apartment.

". . . and there are holes in the curtains," he all but hissed at my mother.

My stomach contracted knowingly almost before my brain spelled it out. This would be *IT* as far as my mother was concerned. Herr Dr. Pringel, Esq., had done the unforgivable: He had crossed the line of good taste.

Katja, firmly anchored in her corner by the tile stove, needles clicking, head nodding wisely, was staunchly on my mother's side.

"Zey are such little ants. Zey crrawl in here — zey vill crrawl out again ven ze time comes. Zey are of no consequence. Nah?" My mother used to listen to Katja's philosophical meditations with mixed feelings. She herself had given similar comfort to many people, but she was never very keen on having her own advice served back to her.

* * * * * * * * * * * * *

It would not be a fair account of events if I did not stop here for a moment to comment on the situation. We were by now fifteen people crowded into three small rooms (the only ones properly heated), not for a weekend or even a fortnight, but for the duration of a long cold winter. This comedy-drama which took place during those months in the Rock Cellar was reenacted — with variations of script and characters — in every house and apartment in Germany where too many people were forcibly crowded in too small a place for too long a time. I have never heard of a single friendship forged between natives and refugees during those years of forced togetherness. It was the natives and landlords who commiserated with each other over dirty bathrooms, poorly washed dishes, careless usage of light and heat, badly treated furniture, and lack of gratitude. The refugees found comfort in each other against unsympathetic and heartless treatment, exclusion and loneliness.

"Connections" was now the most important word in everybody's vocabulary. Without connections it became daily harder to make ends meet. Refugees, usually, had no connections; they were strangers, stranded in alien territory, without allies or friends. They had to start from scratch and there was little time or chance to form alliances and contacts that would assist them in the process of survival.

My mother's talent for making friends and, against all odds, for finding and cementing connections, bordered on genius. Although by definition a refugee, she was, by circumstances, a landlady. She had connections with the local mill (hence the supply of cream of wheat.) She made a friend of the baker and we seldom lacked bread. The butcher's wife beamed when my mother appeared in the doorway. The butcher had a very pretty, rosy-cheeked daughter who helped in the shop. She had only just finished school, having had to repeat two classes in the process. My mother just happened to have in her handbag a few pictures of her three good-looking, eligible sons. The pharmacist and his wife had become good and true friends. They were enthusiastic participants in my mother's cultural evenings through which Frau Lange listened, enraptured, and Herr Lange slept. Three of the four factory owners and their wives had adopted my mother as a worthy and valuable cause, an incredible feat in itself, since there was a good bit of social jealousy among them. Most of those people remained my mother's friends long after the war ended and she returned to Berlin.

The one sore point with my mother (and one she found incomprehensible) was that nobody ever thought of offering her the use of their bathtub.

"They *know* that we do not have a bathroom," she would say in puzzled exasperation, "Wouldn't you think that one of them would get the idea of offering us their tub once in a while?"

She never forgot this one blind spot in her friends' thoughtfulness. Years later, when she was living again in her apartment in West Berlin and any one of her friends who lived in a cold water flat in the East would come for a visit (before the dividing wall went up) she would draw a full bath for her. While her visitor soaked in the steaming tub, my mother would set the tea table, smiling to herself while going about her task, imagining her friend's pleasure.

Chapter 17

Our nearest neighbors, at the bottom of the hill, was a family named Bossier. The Bossiers owned one of the four factories, but, like all but one of the other factory owners, they lived in a row house, side by side with their workers. The Bossier's sons were soldiers, gone since the beginning of the war. Their daughter, Margarete, had taken her brothers' place in the factory, learning the trade by working her way up through every phase of the labor process. From her mother, Margarete had inherited the short, square body and the slightly bulging eyes, from her father the rosy complexion and cheerful disposition. My mother, who liked Margarete, used to deplore her lack of beauty and was certain it would keep her from finding a husband. A number of other people shared her opinion. The war pressed on and Margarete was not getting any younger. She fooled everybody. Shortly after the war she met and married a refugee soldier who had lost a leg to the Russian winter. They went to West Germany, with the help of the Marshall plan, and they started their own hemp factory as well as a family of lively kids, some of them with slightly bulging eyes, which did not seem to bother either them or their parents one bit.

Herr Bossier was a large, well-built man with snow-white hair and a kind and generous heart, which, his wife felt, had to be curbed once in a while before he got into trouble with the authorities. It was Herr Bossier who would beckon to me when I came past his house pushing the baby buggy uphill. Making sure that his wife was at a safe distance, he would quickly put a few skeins of yarn under the baby's blanket. The yarn was not fine and had not been intended for baby clothes. It was earth-colored, all shades of brown and black, but under Katja's clever hands and busy needles, it would be turned into smart little suits for Bertel who was fast outgrowing his blue little baby sweaters.

The baby was the one great source of joy in our lives. During the first months he had cried a great deal. Since in a small town everybody knows everybody else's business, I was the recipient of a wealth of well-meaning advice. It was the first time I met up with samples of genuine folklore, kept alive from one generation to the next in the woodlands of the heart of Germany.

"Your baby cries so much because you cried when you carried it," I was told.

"Did you bury the gown you wore when you gave birth? Ah, dear, you should have buried it on the third day after the baby was born."

"Invite the baby's godmother and have her sit beside the crib for three days. After that, send her home. She will take the crying with her."

"What you need is a good night's sleep," said my mother, and she packed me off to an inn two train stations away from our town. I went to bed at eight that night and slept for twelve hours straight without the slightest effort.

"You are probably starving your baby," said the gray-haired woman pediatrician at the county seat. She didn't have time to pull punches, her waiting room was overflowing. "Give him carrot juice and strengthen the formula!"

And so Bertel stopped crying. He always was a beautiful baby; now he became a happy one. He did not so much change my life as shift its focus. As long as you are childless, your own two sturdy feet are your center of gravity. How, then is it possible that this center can move so quickly to this tiny, pink creature you don't even know very well as yet? From the moment of the baby's birth, you will regard almost anything in terms of how it will affect not yourself but your child. This becomes so completely ingrained in time that it will be part of you and cannot be unlearned once your child is grown up. All you can hope for then is to learn to control this instinct, which is best done by biting your tongue or counting to one hundred before you speak.

* * * * * * * * * * * * * *

Those last months before the end of the war should be a bleak black spot in the tapestry of my memory. That there were bright and joyful moments was largely owing to Bertel's happy and normal development. Food got scarcer, and so did wood. The war news was frightening. There were few of us who did not realize that we were ruled by a madman. We seldom heard from my brothers. Dolfi had been drafted; Wolfgang was being swept back with the field hospitals to the interior of the country. Christmas 1944 was approaching. Our sixth war Christmas would also be Bertel's first, and this is the way we wanted to look upon it. The little boy should see the light of a candle, a branch of evergreen, a toy. He was aware of so much now. He was shy with strangers but became increasingly aware of other children. Whenever he caught a glimpse of the Pringel twins he trembled with excitement, smiled, wiggled, and tried to catch their attention. The twins, brainwashed by the invaluable Gertrud, I suspected, would sail past him, nose in the air, without so much as a glance in Bertel's direction, and I would gather my devastated baby in my arms and could have cheerfully strangled those two angel-faced brats.

Whenever Dr. Pringel met me in the doorway or hall, he would stop and open a conversation with me, which by now made me very uncomfortable. Returning from town one day, I had entered the hall and found him standing on his tiptoes on a chair counting the glasses of canned fruit and vegetables my mother kept on top of the hall closet. He had weathered his embarrassment very nicely. I was still working on mine. Also, his conversation usually did nothing to put me at ease.

"Two geese! Two geese we had last Christmas, Frau Eva," he said to me one evening, his voice plaintive, his eyes behind the glittering spectacles resting reproachfully on me.

"And what do we have this time? Nothing! Not even a roast!" He lifted his folded hands into the air as if to call on heaven to be witness to this outrage.

Since most people had not even seen a goose since the first year of the war (of which he must have been well aware), I could only marvel at so much nerve but was at a loss for an answer. I knew that much of the

Pringels' wrath was rooted in envy of my mother's "connections," but not even Herr Pringel could assume that those connections would produce a goose for us at Christmas.

What my mother did produce, however, was a goat. She came walking up the hill one day pulling a little white baby goat behind her on a rope. Actually they took turns. Sometimes the goat would jump ahead and pull my mother. At other times it would stop and push its soft pink nose into a few grass tips along the ditch, and my mother would have to forcefully set it in motion again. The little goat would then playfully skip around my mother's legs a few times and get her hopelessly entangled in the rope. I was standing in front of the house watching their progress up the hill and holding Bertel who was squealing with fear and ecstasy.

"What are you doing with this animal?" I asked my mother in amazement.

"It's a goat. Our goat," said my mother, not blinking an eyelash.

Good Lord, she found it! I thought wildly.

"Our goat?" Unconsciously I looked down the road. I suppose I half expected to see a farmer in hot pursuit of the animal.

"Where did you get it?"

"I traded it." My mother was busy disentangling herself once again from the rope around her legs. Bertel struggled to free himself from my arm to reach the beautiful little creature, which was trying to nibble on his shoelaces.

"Traded it for what?"

"For a pair of shoes," said my mother not very distinctly.

"We'll put it in the shed behind the washhouse," she continued, more forceful now, and beamed down at the little goat. "Just think of the fresh milk we will have one day! Did you know that goat milk is much healthier for babies than cow milk?"

"A pair of old shoes? A goat? A whole little goat?"

"Well . . . not shoes exactly. Boots."

"But we don't have any boots, " I said, dumfounded.

For the first time my mother looked at me directly, her eyes shooting daggers.

"Are you siding with my enemies again?" she asked coldly.

I knew my mother would not be cornered. She was the master of the flank attack. But I had not meant to corner her. All my questions had been asked in good faith. The blow of her accusation struck me swift and unprepared. For a second, everything swam in front of my eyes. I clung to the baby in my arms, trying to regain my bearings.

There had been times when the effort of keeping peace in our house had drained me emotionally and physically. I failed to realize that my mother had not asked me to keep peace, did not need peace, and was not suffering from any physical discomfort caused by the absence of peace.

My mother, for her part, could not fathom a human being who might be unable to function in an atmosphere of dislike and strife. Secretly, she interpreted all my conciliatory efforts as disloyalty toward her. Confronted by this sudden realization, I remained mute with shock.

My mother saw that she had gone too far. She did not in the least hesitate to wing a body, if necessary in midair, whenever she deemed it essential for the continuous and rather exemplary equilibrium of her own mental state. Looking at my dazed expression, she perceived, however, that she had not so much hurt me as harmed a fundamental structure in our relationship and thus was in danger of getting hurt herself. For a moment she looked frightened.

Retracting or apologizing was out of the question, but for a few weeks afterward my mother seemed more mellow and less rash in expressing her displeasure.

In any case, this short encounter ended all interviews about the origin of the new little member of our household. It was our goat now, residing in a shed behind the washhouse and being visited, petted, and pampered by all but Frau Pringel who wouldn't have known in which direction the washhouse was anyway. We could not feed it with refuse from the kitchen (there never was any) but we had plenty of hay saved from the backyard.

* * * * * * * * * * *

I wonder if there are still people who know what a washhouse is? The washkitchen (as it was called in Germany) was a sort of halfway house between the flat stones of the riverbanks and our modern laundry rooms, enameled in matching colors.

There were no washing machines when I was young and no dryers. Every house had either a washhouse attached to it or a large washkitchen in the basement, full of zinc and copper tubs, long wooden poles, and a wood-burning stove. Every city family had its own washerwoman, who would appear once a month, regularly as clockwork, only to disappear again for two days into the steam and darkness of the washkitchen. Her hands would always be very clean, very soft, and slightly rippled, and as a little girl I used to wonder if there was chance that they would dissolve, one day, completely. Her midday meal would be carried down to her, and in the afternoon she would be served a tray with coffee and a sweet roll. Sometimes I would tag along into the basement and with bated breath peer through the open doorway.

Wrapped in a gray smock, a few damp strands of hair escaping over her cheeks and eyes, the woman would be perched on a high, wooden stool in the depth of the misty cave. Like a plump, elderly swamp queen, she sat there and spooned her soup with soft, shapeless hands while the white steam rose from the mysterious cauldrons around her and the air was heavy with the rich, astringent odor of laundry soap.

The reality was less romantic. Those washerwomen worked long, back-breaking hours in health-threatening conditions, five or six days a week, for little money. They always had families to support, which prevented them from working as live-in maids or cooks, whose working conditions in Germany were regulated by social laws and the general patriarchal system practiced in every German household worth its salt. Washerwomen were considered outsiders and benefitted from neither system.

Washhouses in the country were a different matter. They were sheds, above ground, sometimes not even attached to the main house. All through spring, summer and fall the door leading to the outside would stand wide open, permitting a free flow of visitors and a quick chat with all passersby. The country washhouse had neither the mystery nor the misery of the city cellars.

In the city the clothes would all be hung on long lines strung across the basement ceiling; summer or winter made as little difference to the woman who worked there as to the mole underground. In the country, hanging the wash on a mild spring morning was the happiest part of the day's work. In late fall or winter, though, one might well think longingly of a heated basement room. There was no way I could hang up a baby's shirt or get hold of the corners of a diaper wearing gloves, and often, long before the basket was empty, my fingertips turned blue and numb and had to be warmed inside the sleeves a while before I was able to continue. On those days the wash did not so much dry as freeze stiff so that taking it down was like removing pieces of cardboard from the line. To manage those pieces, I had to use a kind of karate chop right through their middle, which bent them to the size of the basket.

At the Rock Cellar we had no washerwoman, of course. The whole process had to be simplified. The starching of the laundry had long since fallen by the wayside. So had the second boiling of the laundry in clear water. But the nightly soaking, the boiling in soap water, the scrubbing, rinsing, and wringing were all still the same, as was the hanging on the line between trees, winter or summer. The diapers had to be done every second day, and at least once a week they were boiled. Wood was scarce and the soap was very bad. In fact, it could hardly be called soap anymore. We were given rectangles of hard, gray clay that had some properties suitable for friction. Scrubbing or dropping them accidentally on the floor did not hurt them; what those so-called soap squares really could not tolerate was water. If they touched water for longer than a few seconds they began to disintegrate into a thick, sluggish, gray mass. We washed ourselves with this gray clay and we scrubbed our laundry with it. Rinsing became the hardest job, because often the clay would stick to the clothes like chewing gum.

* * * * * * * * * * * * *

It all seemed to matter less and less as the war came closer. My oldest brother, Wolfgang, a young, inexperienced doctor, was now working around the clock in a field hospital to the east of us. We did not know where. My youngest brother was a soldier in the west. We did not hear from either of them anymore. Every evening, Herr Dr. Pringel walked solemnly up the stairs, through the kitchen and into our family room, where my mother was busy soundproofing the walls by hanging blankets over doors, windows and air shafts. The door was locked behind him. He sank into a chair in the corner remaining in semi-darkness. I sat in the opposite corner. My mother sat at the table beside the shaded lamp, and began turning the knobs of the little radio. We were listening every night to the Allied newscast in German. Listening to foreign war news had been declared high treason with a subsequent death penalty. I don't know how many of our countrymen were doing the same thing at the same time, but there must have been millions. Nobody spoke to anybody about it. We did not even discuss the news among ourselves in that little room. Dr. Pringel shook his head at times and sighed. My mother barely suppressed her exclamations of fears, hopes, and fury. Her official name for Hitler had long since changed from "this numbskull" to "the thug." When the broadcast ended, Dr. Pringel got off the chair, bowed a polite good night to my mother, and left. It was the daily hour of truce between my mother and him, united in disgust and anger against the senseless prolonging of killing and dying. In the morning they would resume their private war again.

If the foreign news was never discussed or quoted, rumors were rampant. Our own newscast long ago had ceased to give us any comprehensive or trustworthy information. We did not know what was really happening either to the east or to the west of us, nor in the south, for that matter. Living in "The Green Heart" of Germany, we did not know from which direction the first bullet into this heart would be fired.

The last men in town between sixteen and sixty had been called to arms and, under the command of two sergeants, had marched past our house toward the east. They were marching along in a confused column, wearing civilian clothes and carrying shopping bags or small bundles with their private belongings. A little girl in a sweater that was much too big for her was running and skipping alongside, waving and shouting: "Good-bye, Grandpa, bye-bye, Grandpa!" all the way up the hill until one of the sergeants turned and chased her back. There were still a few people who talked about a wonder weapon, but nobody paid any attention to them.

In early spring, some brown skinned men appeared at the Rock Cellar, spade in hand, accompanied by a German official. The official told us that the men were supposed to dig a second exit to our rock tunnel which would then be used for a general shelter for the population of the town.

The official inspected the cellar and pounded, poked, and measured the hill behind our house. He staked out the spot where the men were to do the digging and disappeared. We never saw him again. The men, however, three or four of them, appeared every morning at seven with their shovels and spades and left around five in the afternoon.

Spring came early that year. The spring of 1945. It was the earliest, warmest, most beautiful spring imaginable, a truly compassionate gift that heaven sent our way. Every morning we would wake up to a cloudless blue sky and a gentle wind from the south. Spring flowers, young leaves and blossoms unfolded in front of our eyes. The brown skinned men made themselves at home under the apple tree. They stretched out on the young grass, their heads pillowed by their folded arms, and smiled into the blue sky above them. They would sit with their back against the tree trunk, whittling, whistling, or playing cards. Whenever I appeared with my basket I was in for a good-natured ribbing. One of them, I remember, always held a violet between his lips, chewing on its stem. The spades were resting, undisturbed, nearby. The hole they had dug was about the size of one of our laundry tubs and never got any bigger. Nobody seriously believed that an exit could be dug by hand through the rock under the hill. The foreign newscast said Berlin was about to be taken by the victorious Red Army. The Americans were heading toward Thuringia. Our war was coming to an end.

Chapter 18

History was planting her heavy footprint on my country. I am not a historian. I am not about to carve historic events irrevocably into slabs of granite. All I want to do is tell what happened in those spring days of 1945, what I felt and experienced in a small town in Thuringia and, more exactly, in an old house on a hillside which was called The Rock Cellar.

I am aware that staggering events took place not just in Germany but around the globe. We know now that decisions of such magnitude were made at the time that—should they turn out to be erroneous—they would cast their long, dark shadows over the rest of the century.

The German war news had ceased to make any sense. Neither did we believe everything that was told to us at our secret radio sessions at night. We did grasp that it could only be a matter of days until the war itself would roll over our town. Everything slowed down to a snail's pace. To say that we were paralyzed by fear would be wrong. Our lives seemed to have come to a standstill. An idleness born out of a deep lassitude, a lassitude born out of an overwhelming sense of futility, had taken hold of us to the point of paralysis. It is difficult to describe this feeling. How can I find a parallel to which one who was not there might be able to relate? Have you ever tried to rake leaves in the face of a storm? Sooner or later you will lay down the rake and say: "This is senseless. I will try again when the storm has blown over and I can see what might be done."

We did the essentials; we got up in the morning, got our rations (which the merchants doubled in view of the approaching disaster), prepared meals, washed, and went to bed. As for the rest of the time, we sat on the hill in the sun taking comfort from the larks in the sky, the baby's cheerful attempts to eat the dandelions around him, and the serene clicking of

Katja's knitting needles. The factories were closed. Our gypsies had disappeared. The shopkeepers barred their doors.

The town stopped breathing.

When I climbed down the steps with the baby for his midday meal I saw a soldier sitting at the roadside next to our house, rubbing his sore feet. Soldiers had walked before up the hill and past our house, but for a few days now there had been none.

I stopped and looked in the blank, gray face.

"Where are they?" I asked.

"Right behind me," he said. Then he leaned back into the grassy bank and closed his eyes. When we came out of the house a couple of hours later, three more soldiers had joined him. They had lost their battalions and their buddies and with them lost all sense of direction and purpose. They had started to walk east to find some unit that would take them in. They had walked fast at first, and then slower, dragging their feet through villages and little towns where nobody could tell them where the German lines were. At the last house of the last town they had finally realized that they were walking straight into the Russian guns.

Sweeping leaves in the face of a storm. They, too, had put down their tools and decided to wait it out. My mother and I went back into the house to revive the fire and boil potatoes. There were more than a dozen soldiers when we carried the steaming potatoes, peelings and all, out to them on the grass bank. In a large pitcher we carried the brown liquid we all drank, the unlovely ersatzkaffee. They slept on the floor in the hall. In the early afternoon of the next day, the last of them arrived, running or limping up the hill. They told the town's people that the American tanks would arrive within the hour. The younger soldiers were plainly scared. They had been told too often that they would all be shot. The older ones seemed grimly resigned. A few of them, in a sweep of bitterness and disgust, tore off their medals and hurled them into the ditch. My mother paid little attention to such futile gestures but they stunned me. Days later, when the tanks had gone, I went down and hunted for the medals by the roadside. I found a few and cleaned the dirt and grass off them and hid them. I could not have explained what made me do this. I think it was a nebulous idea that one distant day one of the soldiers would return to look for his Iron Cross. They were not given for burning down resisting villages or for massive bombings. For those deeds grander medals were bestowed by appreciative governments the world over. These were simple black crosses, given, perhaps, for silencing a death-spitting machine gun or for dragging a wounded comrade out of the line of fire, for overcoming, momentarily, the two strongest emotions in us: fear and survival instinct, in order to help others. Soldiers, friend or enemy, knew this, I think. My mother kept my brother Peter's picture on her desk and, on a piece of black velvet, his Iron Cross beside; and, though American, French, and Russian soldiers were soon to stomp through our house for many months to come and though all of them looked at the medal and some of them touched it lightly, I saw no hate in their faces and nobody took it from us.

In town, a hasty conference took place between the few remaining men. How were they to let the on-rolling tanks know that this was an open town which would make no attempt at defense? It was rumored that the Americans were well aware of the German propaganda campaign which had challenged every house in every town and village to become a fortress against the enemy. The Americans, so close to victory, were loath at this point to lose even a single man and would, if their suspicion was aroused, just as quickly deck a town with artillery than to test its intentions.

Somebody, it was decided, would have to walk toward the tanks and deliver the message. There was, however, no guarantee that this lone messenger would not be shot first and recognized afterward as having been harmless. (To send a woman, who would have been a great deal safer under the circumstances, was unthinkable. We were still a quarter of a century away from the great Equal Rights ideas. If word got around that a town had permitted a woman to meet those tanks, its men, old and decrepit as they were, would never have been able to lift their heads again.)

The parson, a tall, elderly bachelor, volunteered to undertake this precarious mission. Accompanied by anxious looks and fervent prayers, he set out with long, firm strides, never looking to the right or left along the tree-lined, dusty country road. He walked all the way to the next village, where he learned that the Americans had passed hours ago. Foregoing the open road, they had chosen to approach our town from both sides across the fields. So the parson got a drink of water and marched back without ever meeting a single soul but the birds in the trees, a grazing deer, and a few munching rabbits.

By now we had more than twenty soldiers in and around our house. This was not good. None of them had kept his weapons but all of them wore uniforms. A house at the edge of town, called the Rock Cellar, with two dozen German soldiers wandering in and out, might signal all the wrong things to an approaching enemy. When I realized this, something very close to panic overcame me. We were all in a precarious state of nerves. I grabbed the white sheet off my bed and hung it full-length out of the second floor window where it could be seen from the bottom of the hill by anybody approaching by the road. Quite reassured by this solution I came walking down the steps again when I saw my mother entering the hall in great agitation.

"What did you do!!" It was not a question but an outcry. "Pull the sheet in, child! Quick, pull the sheet in!" She ran ahead of me up the steps. Together we gathered the sheet back into the room.

"But *why*? Why not let them know that . . ."

"Do you realize what will happen to us if this town is taken back by German troops even for one day—and the S.S. hears about our sheet?!"

My knees buckled under me. The thought had never occurred to me. I sat down on the bed, trembling and hugging the crumpled sheet.

"Let's get the soldiers into the house and into the cellar," said my mother. "We will leave the door open—no hiding—but no soldier is to come forward until we have a chance to speak to some Americans. That's all we can do."

The soldiers went willingly enough; the door was left open. The rest of us gathered in a group at the side of the house; the Pringels, closest to the door, poised for flight back into the house; my mother, outwardly calm and in control; Katja, for once without her knitting, towering over all of us, clearly curious and enjoying the excitement; and I, with Bertel in my arm, still trembling a little when thinking of that blasted sheet in the window, standing between them. The Einfalts were standing behind us. The older boy was clinging to his mother, who was crying quietly; the younger one was holding on to his aunt's hand and serenely chewing on a handful of raw spaghetti. Rosalind was bringing up the rear holding her baby and trying to look as if she couldn't care less. That's how we stood, wordlessly frozen to the ground, as the first huge tank rolled slowly past our house.

The feeling I remember most is one of tremendous relief. It was so strong that I had the insane desire to wave. I know, everyone but the children felt the same way. Understand me right, this feeling had nothing to do with politics—not yet. It was the release of a tension that had lasted too long and had become nearly unbearable. In this urge to wave to those first American soldiers there was an element of gratitude for ending an untenable situation.

Within an hour, one of the tanks rolled into the space between the hill and the side of the house. To the officer who approached us, my mother said politely: *"Wir haben Soldaten im Haus, die sich gefangen geben wollen."*

Frowning, the officer shrugged his shoulder.

"We have soldiers here," I said, trying out my miserable English for the first time. My heart was pounding in my throat, "They have no arms." I did not know the word for surrender.

Thank God, he was not stupid. He understood what I was trying to say. He and his men went into the house and came out with our soldiers. There were so many of them that he ordered the ranking German soldier to form a column of two's and, accompanied by two American soldiers, they began their march to prison camp.

The tanks moved no farther that night. They were so far ahead of their supplies that they stopped in our town to await them. For nine days they stood in our yards, partly sheltered by our houses while leisurely shooting each day a few rounds into the next village. We had no way of knowing if there were German troops in the next village or if there would not be a sudden concerted counter attack. We heard many shots fired in the night and we felt that our beds were not the best place to be. Our house, standing on the east end of town, would be the first target in any counter effort. So we dragged our mattresses into a corner behind the kitchen stove which was the safest place we could think of, and the three of us slept there on the floor in the kitchen for the next nine nights.

During the day we stayed inside the house. For the first time we saw some small German strafe planes, flying low, aiming swift rounds of machine gun fire at the tanks parked in the alleys and alongside the houses. Eventually, I had no choice but to make my way to the washhouse to take care of the diapers and baby clothes. I remember running close to the house, holding the bucket in one hand and in the other the large metal lid of the biggest of our washtubs like an ancient shield between me and the open road. Later, my brothers would tell me that a machine gun from a strafe plane would have pierced my wonderful shield like a piece of swiss cheese, but I didn't know that at the time and it helped being optimistic.

We didn't talk to those first Americans. They were busy with their war and we were busy staying out of their way. When the supplies caught up with them, they took their tanks and guns and moved on. The next contingent moved in and the town's occupation began in earnest. Only then did the people finally meet their conquerors.

* * * * * * * * * * * * *

We knew too much—and much too little—about each other. Somebody said once: "Ignorance ain't knowing nothing. It's knowing a lot that ain't so." For years now, both sides had been thoroughly brainwashed. One's inner attitude depended entirely on how much of it one had believed and how much rejected. Still—the situation was uneven, to put it mildly. We knew we had been lied to a great deal. We did not know what had been found inside the concentration camps. The Americans felt that they had been told the truth and they had seen or heard about the concentration camps. The two atomic bombs had not yet been dropped. We were a great deal more monstrous in their eyes than they were in ours.

We would have liked to see them as our liberators. But five and one-half years of bloody war and the deluge of scare propaganda with which we had been relentlessly flooded, prevented an open trust. Besides, there was little encouragement in the beginning. The soldiers were under strict orders not to fraternize. That this order had to be sternly repeated and repeated so many times says a great deal about human nature. Indoctrinated hate is, at once, a wholesale and a second-hand emotion. When the middleman is eliminated and replaced by first-hand encounters, we find ourselves wondering how we could have been persuaded to adopt such strong emotion so readily and without questions.

* * * * * * * * * * * * *

The first wave of occupation forces arrived determined to go into the pages of history as a civilized and disciplined conquering army. That did not exclude a certain amount of strutting and a fine show of moral superiority. This has nothing to do with either morals or being superior; it is simply an unconscious response to the fact that one is better washed, better clothed and better fed than the other fellow. It is dormant in all of us and a chronic affliction of all occupation forces. It is not incurable, though, and is rather easily overcome by a few insights and some native intelligence.

This sentiment, however, while still fresh and intact, is of considerable assistance to occupation officials who have to deal with such unpleasant tasks as penalizing offenders against the imposed curfew or sentencing civilians who are caught stealing food. Most assuredly it sustains those whose job it is to requisition houses for the military. Going around ordering families out of their homes all day and feeling rotten about it all night would be bad business indeed.

"The poor people!" my mother commiserated. "Isn't it awful? And did you notice that they are taking all the nicest houses in town?"

"Well, so did we in Athens," I said, thinking of the Admiral's marble mansion.

"Always contradicting!" said my mother irritably. "You know very well what I mean. It isn't the same."

I wasn't being contrary. I knew what she meant. But I had, at one time, been on the other side of the fence. And there were quite definitely similarities.

My brother Wolfgang told me once that during the French campaign he and two other soldiers had quarters in a cottage on the edge of a little French town. The cottage had been vacated under the same circumstances and the owners had disappeared. Wolfgang was twenty, then, and the other two soldiers were not much older. They stayed in the cottage for ten days or so and got quite used to it. After a while they began opening a few of the home canned goods they found in the basement, which greatly enhanced their dreary rations. When they had stayed there for about a week an elderly couple appeared at the door. They were the owners of the cottage.

The three young men were mortified because, my brother said, they had not washed the dishes for a few days and they were stacked, dirty, on the kitchen counter. The old couple walked through the rooms and began to cry. The boys thought this was on account of the canned goods they had eaten and they felt bad about it. But it turned out that the two old people were crying because nothing was broken or ruined or stolen and even the beds were made.

Chapter 19

Our first Americans seemed creatures from another star to us. They looked different. They were rosy-cheeked, loose limbed and incredibly clean. They looked as if they washed themselves all the time, and not with pieces of gray clay. They walked silently like cats on leather soles rather than in hobnailed boots. They were loose limbed and athletic looking but they seemed to have peculiarly well rounded posteriors which gave them a very different build from German men. Weeks went by (it took a while to get a closer look) until I discovered that this strange shape was the result of two back pockets in their trousers in which they seemed to carry most of their movable belongings. I had never seen a man with as much as a paper clip in a back pocket, let alone a comb, billfold, pocket knife, handkerchief, family photos, and the last letter from home.

Within a short time we noticed other wondrous things. I came home one day and told my mother that I had seen American soldiers playing ball. Not soccer or tennis (there were no courts in town) but catch-and-throw as only little girls did in Germany, and that, furthermore, they were using a large brown bag, pulled over one hand, to catch the ball. I don't think my mother quite believed me until she saw it with her own eyes. They kept this childish game up for hours and seemed not the least bit embarrassed to have the town's people watch them. They treated their army gear with friendly contempt, not unlike children who are a bit bored with their everyday toys. Soldiers, who came to sun themselves in our backyard, kicked off their shoes and socks in any direction, sunk back into the grass and wiggled their rosy toes contently in the sunshine. I had never before seen a man kick off his shoes. More astonishing yet: One day a soldier, telling me that he was sick and tired of war, gave his helmet, which he had thrown to the ground, such a mighty kick that it flew deep into the raspberry bushes. To say that I was stunned would be understating it. I think I expected a carload of MP's to come rushing up the hill and drag the soldier off to be court-martialed.

The town's children, quick to sense a kinship, often followed the soldiers around as if they were so many pied pipers. Walking through town on a warm June morning, I saw a group of children shouting and dancing in front of one of the occupied houses. Soldiers were leaning out of a second floor window laughing and shouting back at them. One of them, with a great swing of his arm, threw a handful of candy at the children, who wildly scrambled all over each other to get their share. Back under the window they went for more. An arm appeared again, but this time to pour a pitcher of water over the kids. Squeals of mock terror, flight, laughter, return, and another handful of candy came raining down. It was obvious that both parties were delighted with this game. It reminded me of tricks my brothers played on each other, only that they had been less generous with candy. Unfortunately, those soldiers were as generously thoughtless with other rations as well. We saw many a half emptied can of food carelessly thrown away and it took all our pride to walk by and not pick it up and take it home. Only cigarette butts transcended this pride, and I often turned my head away in embarrassment when I saw a German man bend down furtively to the pavement.

Even their mischief had an aura of innocence, or at least a lack of basic evil about it, which seemed remarkable to me. The only shots heard within the town during that time were fired by a soldier very much in pursuit of happiness (clearly his inherent right). Our neighbors, the Bossiers, had a maid who in every respect qualified for Benjamin Franklin's requirements for the perfect domestic. "*Let thy maid servant be strong, faithful, and homely,*" Franklin advised.

This young woman went into town one day, straight into the arms of an American soldier who had recently sampled some liberated bottles of native wine and was now in search of happiness. He grabbed her by the wrist and told her that he loved her. She squealed and ran. So did he. She ran faster but he had the longer legs. She reached the front door of her home just as he caught up with her. Herr Bossier hearing the screeching, opened the door, grasped the situation and, immediately afterward, the girl's arm. But the other arm had been gripped by the soldier, who now began waving his pistol about. Herr Bossier did not much fancy the sight of a gun in the hands of a tipsy soldier, but, being a patriarch of the old school, he saw his duty in protecting the young woman given into his care. Gun or no gun, he would not let go of her. The tug of war lasted a few minutes and then Herr Bossier, who was old but sober, gave one mighty pull and the girl flew into the house. The door was slammed and bolted in the soldier's face. Enraged, the thwarted pursuer fired a few shots into the bottom of the door, after which he turned and lumbered back to town where he got a cool reception from his own MPs. The girl became somewhat of a celebrity and thereafter enjoyed a great deal more attention from men of all ages.

It was only a few days after this incident that Dr. Pringel and I had our own encounter with a gun in a drunken man's hand.

I was standing in our first floor "summer kitchen" which we were sharing with the Pringels at that time (I forget why; maybe because they had been sharing ours all winter). I was washing dishes in a pan of luke warm soda water when I heard the dreaded familiar sound of Dr. Pringel's approach. He had a way of rubbing his bony white hands together when setting out toward a challenging task that sounded like the wind going through dry leaves on a late November day. I could hear the faint rustling of it before I heard his footsteps.

He was approaching, I knew, to present "his side of the story." I already knew his side of the story. I had heard it so often that I could have prompted him had he ever gotten stuck with it, but he never did. There were three parts to it: (1) How wonderful he, Dr. Pringel, had been to my parents for many years, ever since the days when I was a babe in rompers; (2) what a piece of cake the war had been for him and his family when they were still living in Berlin, and (3) how dreadful life was now under the inhospitable roof which my ungrateful mother provided for them. During the last part, he seldom failed to mention the torn curtains. I don't know why he didn't set the invaluable Gertrud to mend them if they bothered him so much. I suppose it was his last and finest trump card, the one visible proof of how fate and my mother had wronged him.

Usually he waylaid me with his story when he thought me alone. When he caught me in the kitchen, I would often find means of escaping even if it meant allowing the water to get cold in the pan. After listening a while to Part I, I would suddenly drop the dishrag, unfocus my eyes, cock my ear toward the ceiling, and assume my: "Hark! The baby!" expression.

"I don't hear anything," Dr. Pringel would say extremely annoyed, but with an apologetic smile I would rush past him, up the stairs and into our room where Bertel would be sleeping peacefully in the crib and the furious rustling downstairs could not be heard any longer.

This time, however, it would not do. I was sure Dr. Pringel had seen my mother, with the baby tucked safely in the buggy, depart for town. It meant that I was in for the unabbreviated version of the tireless doctor's three-part story. We had just about reached the Christmas geese in Part II when the front door was pushed open rather violently and a very long, very thin American soldier staggered into the house. He spotted us through the open door and hurled himself through the dim hall into the kitchen. He was obviously drunk; his sloppily buttoned shirt, bloodshot eyes, and unsteady motions boded us no good. No sooner had he joined us when he pulled out his gun, brandished it wildly at us and screamed:

"Stick up your hands!"

"What did he say?" asked Dr. Pringel. He looked green and appalled. He knew Greek and Latin and a smattering of French but no English. Mine was anything but good.

"No jabbering! Stick up your hands, you filthy Krauts!" screamed the soldier, pointing his gun at each of us in turn.

"He wants us to put our hands up. I didn't understand the rest," I reported truthfully. Dr. Pringel's arms shot in the air and, as the tipsy gun whirled on me, so did mine.

Never before or after did I have to hold my hands above my head. It's an extraordinary sensation. Something inside you very strongly objects to this position. It means helpless surrender, not to somebody morally, mentally, or even physically superior to you but to somebody who has the upper hand only by virtue of holding a coarse piece of metal in his hand that could snuff out your life in a second. It is frightening, infuriating, and humiliating. It pits your pride against your common sense. I really can see only one good reason for putting a person into this position: if he or she was threatening to harm another human being. I can think of no other excuse, then or now.

Luckily, common sense prevails most of the time. Dr. Pringel and I, in rare harmony, stood rooted to the cold stone floor, our hearts hammering in our throats, our eyes watchfully on the unsteady waving gun. Dr. Pringel's teeth were chattering like muted castanets. For somebody who stalked about on felt soles this man had a lot of audible emotions.

Now that he had us standing there with our arms up in the air, our visitor was not quite sure what to do with us. For one thing, though, we were to listen to him. His main grievance, it seemed, was to be there at all.

"You and your goddamn country," he began shouting at Dr. Pringel, "I wouldn't have to be here if it wasn't for you! You started this goddamn war and you lost it and now see where it got you!"

"What is he saying?" asked the pale doctor nervously.

"I don't really know," I whispered helplessly. Drops of dishwater were running down my arms and into my armpits, tickling me remorselessly.

"I think he said that you started the war."

"*WHAT*!" exclaimed Dr. Pringel, dropping his arms in profound shock.

"Hands up, you lousy Kraut!" screamed the soldier.

Herr Dr. Pringel's hands went back up into the air.

"The man is totally misinformed!" Dr. Pringel's spectacles sparkled with indignation. "Have the goodness to tell him that it is well known in certain circles that I was intellectually and morally adamantly opposed to . . ."

The soldier let out such a stream of words that I could not make out anything at all except for numerous goddamns.

I was the only one facing the door and the only one who saw my mother entering the hall. With one glance she seemed to take in the unpromising scene in the kitchen and noiselessly backed out of the door again.

Our visitor was gradually running out of steam. His gun dangled loosely in his hand, not pointing at anything or anybody in particular. Cautiously, I began scratching my arms, then dropping them altogether. When nothing much happened I turned around and continued washing the dishes. The soldier just didn't look like the sort of person who would shoot a dishwashing woman in the back. Silence ensued, during which I heard nothing but Dr. Pringel's teeth clicking. There was a bit of fidgeting behind me and then I felt a tap on my shoulder.

"Want to see some pictures?" asked the soldier.

I spun around, startled, not at all sure of what I had heard. The soldier's eyes were still bloodshot and his breath had not gotten any better, but gone was the threatening stance. There was a look about him that I thought I recognized.

"Why, he is nothing but a very young, very homesick boy," I thought surprised. Somebody had trusted him with a gun and somebody else with too much wine.

"Want to see a picture of my kid brother's graduation?" he asked. His face was eager and friendly as he dug around in his back pocket.

I did not know what a graduation was. "Kid" sounded like "Kind" the German word for child. Probably a brother younger than he. He obviously wanted to show me some family photos. I wanted to say something like: "By all means. I'd love to see your photos!" but my English did not cover such gracious phrases, so I just said: "Yes, please." And to make up for this lack of amenity I smiled a little at him. The kid brother's graduation picture turned out to be a photo of a gangling teenager with a big, bashful grin on his face. He was slouched against some sort of a pillar and, for inexplicable reasons, he wore a large parson's robe and the head dress of a chancellor of a university. Possibly, he was on the way to a costume party. I found myself marvelling how his mother had gotten him into this peculiar outfit. No wonder he looked so embarrassed.

His big brother, standing right beside me, seemed to find nothing astonishing in this strange appearance. He kept gazing lovingly at the much handled little snapshot. I was nodding and smiling and digging deep into my vocabulary in an effort to put a pleasant sentence together when the front door swung open wide and noisily, admitting two husky MPs. Behind them hovered my mother's anxious face. At the uncompromising sight of his two countrymen heading purposefully toward the kitchen, the soldier turned a shade of green, steadied himself with one hand against the kitchen table, and threw up. I only just got my legs out of the way. Far from being moved by this unfortunate turn of events, each MP grabbed the ailing young man by one arm and unceremoniously marched him down the hall and out of the door.

"Well I never . . .!!" said Dr. Pringel weakly, dropping his numb arms.

"Are you hurt?" asked my mother.

I shook my head. My mother glanced briefly at the floor, shrugged her shoulders as if to say: "What next!" and left the kitchen. I heard her carry the baby upstairs. She was postponing all questions until we would meet in more pleasant surroundings! Dr. Pringel, too, had disappeared suddenly and soundlessly on his felt soles. Not even a rustling of hands was heard.

I made a face at the kitchen door through which so many had escaped so swiftly.

"Cowards!" I said. "Ninnies, bullies, traitors . . ." my German was not as easily exhausted as my English. And as I went for mop and bucket I thought that just once I would like to manage to be the first one out of a door.

The homesick young soldier was not the only uninvited visitor we had during those days. Many times there was a knock at the door and men in uniform demanded to search the house. With a great deal of scowling and severe looks we were questioned about the possession of weapons: Guns? Luegers? Maybe a Hitler Youth dagger or camping knife, preferably with a Nazi insignia on it? When I finally found one of the latter and tremulously turned it over to the very next patrol, I noticed their beaming faces and one of them gave me a very nice "Thank you," which aroused the first, faint suspicion in me. We were new to all this and had no idea what to expect, but I had never heard of a soldier saying: "Thank you" to an enemy who was handing over his weapons. When, eventually, we discovered that there was a great deal of private enterprise going on, I was very sorry that I had been in such a hurry to get rid of the cursed thing. We could have traded it a few weeks later for soap or powdered eggs.

I held the same regrets for a beautiful little pistol with a handle of mother-of-pearl inlay that turned up in the lowest and most swollen drawer of an antique chest in our living room. The two sergeants who made me pry open the old chest were of the imperious kind, ordering us about rather than asking politely. They were the first Americans who insisted on seeing the contents of the chest. The bottom drawer was stuck as if glued and I had to go down on my knees trying to inch it open. When I happened to look up unexpectedly I saw the two sergeants grinning and winking at each other. By that time I had broken two nails and cut my thumb and that grin was all I needed. I had had my misgivings about all those official search parties for a good while now. I scrambled to my feet.

"You are crizzy!" I furiously snapped at them. They looked baffled.

"What?" they asked, practically in unison.

"You are crizzy," I yelled, defiantly, my heart racing.

"You mean: crazy?"

It's one thing to defy death, quite another to hurl "The Supreme Insult" into your enemy's face only to have him correct your pronunciation! I was devastated. They were greatly entertained. Immediately, though, they became once more the scowling conquerors.

"Open the drawer, Miss!" It sounded threatening.

So I went back on my knees and after a while I had worried and coaxed the old drawer open. It was full of mementos, yellowed newspaper clippings, old pictures, ribbons, and far back in a corner was the little pistol. Not even my mother remembered it. The sergeants were delighted. They all but congratulated each other on their cleverness as they took turns playing around with their precious loot. They were still admiring it when they walked out of the house accompanied by my warmest wishes and hopes that they would bloody each other's nose before the day was over by way of determining who would keep it.

I knew I had been taken again and was determined that this would be the last time. As it turned out, there was no need for this fierce resolution. After the first troops left, a more permanent occupation force moved in and thereafter any uniformed visitor at our door was more in search of a friendly face than of daggers and guns.

Our experiences in the Rock Cellar with those first troops were not isolated cases. A pattern of the same mixture of mischievous, irresponsible, and good natured behavior could be found in almost every house that soldiers entered or occupied. When the town's coffin maker, a man named August Schneider, moved back into his home after it had been occupied for two weeks, he found the house in good order. On each of the three coffins in his workshop rested a pack of cigarettes; a little note had been attached to one of them, saying: "Thank you, Schneider."

The wife of the town's haberdasher was not so lucky. She found her dresses in the bedroom closet still hanging orderly side by side but each one had been cut from top to bottom, the full length of it. In her little girl's nursery, on top of a picture book, lay four candy bars.

On many bathroom mirrors, messages had been written with toothpaste, apparently a favorite pastime of the Americans and one, until then, unknown in Germany. The messages did not vary greatly, "Heil Hitler" was the most frequent, winning hands down, followed by "Hitler is dead!" "Hi, there" was a close third. A few said, "Thanks" and a number of them made some unflattering reference to a certain person named "Kraut," completely mystifying the returning occupants. None of us knew what was meant by this. It was finally decided, more or less by consensus, that it might have been the name of their commanding officer.

* * * * * * * * * * * * *

With the arrival of the second occupation contingent, a structured administration was attempted and some semblance of badly needed order and routine reestablished.

No—not re-established. Cancel the "re."

Anything that had been—most particularly anything that had gone under the label of law and order—was to be eradicated, changed, or at least purified.

I have always thought it amazing how, in the course of this century, the forces that are and the powers that would be in Germany have fallen all over each other to liberate the working classes. There was, to begin with, the revolution that ended the first world war and freed the socialists and workers from the imperialistic oppression.

A scant fifteen years later Hitler proclaimed, at long last, the true equalization and liberation of the working classes. Now the Americans were proclaiming the Great Freedom for the Oppressed, and right around the corner, the Red Army was getting ready to rush in and, once again, liberate the German workers, this time not only from their middle class oppressors, but also from the Americans.

The first post-war liberation I witnessed took place in our own house and involved such unlikely heroine as our little Einfalt.

She must have lain in wait for this moment. When my mother stepped into the entrance hall one morning, Frau Einfalt (wearing an old house robe as a visible signal of rebellion) was standing on the stairs halfway between the third and the second floor, ready to do battle. Either little Einfalt was a ventriloquist of some talent or she had considerable help from an invisible prompter behind her. We seemed to be hearing everything twice, once in a whisper and immediately after in Frau Einfalt's tremulous voice.

"I want youse to know, I won't come down no more," she announced, her little white rabbit face looking down at the back of my mother's head as if peering into the barrel of a gun, ready to perish for her cause.

"What nonsense," said my mother, straightening her hair in front of the hall mirror. "Get dressed and come down around eleven. And start with the hall, please. It needs sweeping."

"I won't do nothing!" it whispered from the background and "I won't! I won't be coming down to do nothing," rasped little Einfalt obediently.

My mother turned around and looked up. "May I remind you that you have a contract," she said severely.

A moment of silence. Then a whisper: "I'll pay your whole stupid rent . . ."

"I'll pay the whole rent . . ." said Frau Einfalt faintly.

"Youse can clean up after yourselves from now on," whispered it out of the darkness. But little Einfalt was spent. Her voice had died on her. She pulled her robe tightly around her and prepared for retreat.

Presently she was pushed aside with a hefty shove and a rosy, round face appeared around the corner of the stairwell.

"Youse can clean up after yourselves from now on!" screeched Miss Milktooth. "Clean your own filthy hall!"

I thought that last remark was rather unfair considering that it was their two boys and the twins who tracked in all the mud after playing at the creek below the road. But there would be no use arguing the finer points. Great principles were involved here, and common sense and great principles are rarely on speaking terms.

My mother, with a short: "We'll see about that," walked toward the kitchen. I followed, throwing one more curious glance up the stairs just in time to see Rosalind's triumphant face peering over the bannister.

The next liberated crew who happened to drop by were our tunnel-digging friends. There was nothing threatening about them. They were singing and hollering as they strutted up the street with some of their buddies, proudly pointing out "their" hill and "their" tree. The youngest one who had always chewed on a violet, gave me a little wink out of the corner of his eye. They were careful, though, not to steer their friends too close to the spot of their endeavors, the little spittoon of a hole they had dug during all those weeks of "hard labor."

A wave of labor camp occupants flooded all over town with a great show of joy and victory. I can't say that the townspeople were unduly worried. It was just one more troublesome aspect to cope with. I don't remember a single hostile incident provoked by either side. After a week or so, when the wave of celebration had crested and worn itself thin, many of the camp inmates who had worked in homes or on farms began visiting their former employers—perhaps out of genuine attachment or out of sheer habit; most likely because they simply did not know what else to do with their time.

Katja swept into our house, pleased and excited, but soon after sat, as she had done during all those past weeks, again in her garden chair in the backyard, knitting and minding the baby.

There came the day when the Americans announced that all displaced foreigners residing in the former labor camp would be processed and repatriated as quickly as possible. The reaction was not entirely what their liberators had expected. There were many happy and excited faces, to be sure, but there was also a great deal of uncertainty and, when the message had sunk in, there was some real panic.

One of those who went into shock was our own Katja. This serene, majestic woman who had kept a cool head through the most bitter and harshest of times, now was almost irrational with dread. It took all my mother's persuasive strength to calm her down sufficiently to consider some of her options.

This scene was repeated with small variations in many families. Ukrainian maids clung to their German mistresses like frightened children, and the good women, helplessly, tried to calm down the weeping girls with hopeless promises of future visits.

The American officials, who had worked hard to set this repatriation process in motion, were totally bewildered. They were sure that there had been some misunderstanding.

"You are going home," they kept reassuring their distressed charges. "You don't understand: We are sending you home!"

But that was precisely where some of them did not want to go.

There were those however who were homeward bound with grim resolve and desperate determination. It would need all of this and more to get them there. Refugees from Hamburg and Bremen, from the industrial Ruhr area and the heavily bombed cities along the Rhine, realized that the war was over in their part of the country, and with that realization the thought of even one more week in exile became unbearable. They would rather walk hundreds of miles in broken shoes and on bandaged feet and face the possibility of a burned out home when they arrived than to cook one more meal in a kitchen where they were not wanted, under a roof that had barely tolerated them.

It was during this first unauthorized wave of repatriation that two women—pulling a wagon with a child—knocked at the door of the Rock Cellar. They had stopped an old man on the street to inquire if he knew of anybody who might serve them as interpreter, and he had directed them to our house.

I never knew the old man's name and he never knew the chain of events he had set in motion simply by pointing out our house to the women.

After our first lamentable meeting the lieutenant in charge of the town's affairs had taken the women to headquarters where their request for a highway pass was flatly turned down. The women had trudged on anyway, across fields and woods, avoiding the open road. And the stern lieutenant had appeared at our doorstep the next day, meekly asking for German lessons.

The weeks that followed—those few weeks of spring and early summer in 1945—seem, in my memory, all steeped in a soft hue of peace and promise. No bombers were droning in gray skies above our heads. No bellowing flak or artillery sent chills down our spine. Our nights were blessed with uninterrupted sleep. Our days were filled with the simplest task of living. Every afternoon the lieutenant with the steel-rimmed glasses—armed with a dictionary, pad and pencil—doggedly marched up the hill toward the Rock Cellar, deaf to his comrades, chaffing and his superior's admonitions.

Bertel squealed with delight as soon as he caught sight of him. Katja proudly beamed at him as if she, personally, had produced this young man to bring cheer into the lives of her friends. My mother greeted him with cautious friendliness. She appreciated his efforts to converse with her in German. Her senses registered good manners and good breeding. Her intuition told her that here was a decent human being. But her pragmatic mind determined that there was no future in this attachment, and she was hoping that I knew this, too.

It must have rained at times during those weeks for the trees and bushes were green, the road was without dust, and the air was sweet with the blooming meadows around us. But I don't remember any dark skies or bleak, wet days. Our lessons always took place on the grassy hillside at the back of the house. When one afternoon, leafing through my pupil's homework papers, I came upon a sentence (written in rather tortuous German): "Can I have a picture of the prettiest girl in the world?" I was quite ready to believe that there never had been a spring as lovely as this one.

* * * * * * * * * * * * *

There was a steadily growing movement of people all around us and the Rock Cellar was no exception. Katja was no longer with us. Our "Brremen" had literally sailed into the sunset. After weeks of tears and terror, the lieutenant had managed to transfer her officially from an eastbound group of foreign laborers to a group that was sent west to a camp for political refugees and survivors. When she came to say goodbye, she was all hope and smiles. At the camp, as we learned later, she had reverted to her old level-headed self and even took up her daily exercises again. After careful evaluation of her fellow campers she began to pursue an elderly Polish Jewish gentleman, one head shorter and fifty pounds lighter than herself, who had relatives in the West Indies. This was about as far removed from the reach of the Red Armies as Katja could imagine. Her affection for the gentleman grew in equal proportion to his prospects of emigrating and joining his cousins on those distant islands. When he finally set sail for the New World, he took his large and beaming bride along with him. But that was still in the future. We had our hands full dealing with the day-by-day emergencies. Little Einfalt threatened to leave, and leave she did, eventually. My mother was not unduly disturbed by this departure, but she did miss the rent. The fair Rosalinde, one bright June morning, packed all her belongings in the baby buggy, placed her baby (which, I am happy to report, was straight limbed and healthy) on top of it, and set out, by foot, toward Hannover.

My mother's trip to the city, as I said, had to do with business, such as it was. We had had no news of our landlord for months now. My mother, for all practical purposes, was in charge and possession of the old inn. The banks were closed; all government payments and pensions had ceased, there being no government. In other words, we had no money and no income other than the rent from the Pringels. We were more puzzled than panicked by this situation, but it was a problem we could no longer ignore.

My brother Peter had made a testament leaving everything he owned to my mother. As it turned out, he did have a savings account placed with the German Postal organization, one of the many services the German post had always provided. Inexplicably, those were the only accounts not frozen.

My mother was in possession of my brother's testament but not of the number of his savings account, and without it she could lay no claim to the money. It was when we were most perplexed by this impasse that I remembered the check Peter had given me as a present when he visited me during my student days in Munich. I had never cashed it. This check would surely have been written on his postal account if only it could be located. Four years had gone by and our world had been turned upside down since then. I still think of it as a minor miracle that, after a long and tenacious search, I actually found the check. The number was printed on it. It was the key to the account which was to pay our grocery bills and wood rations for quite a long time. There was nothing else to pay, since nothing else was offered.

Some time during the early days of my mother's stay at the Rock Cellar our landlord had sent a large parcel to her for storage and safekeeping. One day in June, when our resources were approaching their lowest ebb, I found my mother busy prying the lid of the box open with an old kitchen knife. She did not look the least bit guilty when I entered the room unexpectedly. She explained to me that this box had been meant for emergencies and that Herr Benneman had been in no way explicit about whose emergencies he had in mind, and if we were not in the midst of one she would like to know who was! The box, it turned out, was filled with cartons of cigars. My mother began to use them so judiciously and traded them so carefully that they lasted all through winter. I was not living at the Rock Cellar any more when she lifted the last of the cartons out of the box. She told me that underneath it she found a scrap of paper. Scribbled on it in the publisher's handwriting were only four words: "Well, then, goodbye!"

"See," said my mother placidly, "he knew."

Even at that time my mother had no idea of the grim double meaning of her complacent comment. Months later we learned that the publisher, our friend and benefactor, two days before the Allies reached Hannover had taken a small handgun out of the drawer of his desk, and with the same deliberate precision with which he had handled all his affairs, had used it for the first and last time in his life. He was childless and left no one but his young widow who, for the time being, seemed to have vanished from the face of the earth.

The cigars were a staggering windfall for our little household. They were on my mother's mind (if not on her conscience) almost day and night.

It was not long after their discovery that she set out to strike the boldest bargain yet. She left early in the morning, keeping, as always, her own counsel. Toward noon she came straggling up the hill carrying a large box that seemed to have a life of its own and constantly threatened to slip out of her hands. After she deposited the box with a hefty thump on the tree stump outside the house, I cautiously peeked into it only to look straight into a small, yellow eye peering malevolently back at me. It was a large hen cowering, frightened and distrustful, at the bottom of the box and hiding under her honey brown wings half a dozen excited and restless chicks. This time I knew better than to ask: how, where, and whence? It was decided that they, too, would go behind the wash kitchen, into the empty doghouse, which we now closed at night with an old burlap sack.

So far, our little menagerie had been all promise and no action. The little goat was eating mountains of hay and growing by leaps and bounds, but having not yet been bred and given birth to a kid, there was of course, no milk. And the hen was fully occupied with her chicks and was not about to add to her strenuous family by laying eggs.

"But just wait," said my mother hopefully, "one day soon we will have milk and eggs. We'll only have to make sure that nobody in town knows about it."

That would have meant the loss of most of our ration cards, such as they were. Since we could buy no chicken feed, my mother persuaded one of our liberated workers, who were still hanging about, to fence in a large scratching place for them. It would have worked out very well, I think, but on the fourth night, the fox got into the doghouse and ate all the chicks. The hen, who had barely escaped the massacre, went into shock. When we finally found her she was sitting on a branch up in the oak tree beside the front door and refused to come down. From then on she lived there. She would come down only to feed when she thought nobody was around and the slightest footstep or crackling of a twig on the ground would send her fluttering back into the tree. There she would sit motionless, just clinging to her branch, with a glazed, wild look in her yellow eyes.

Weeks went by and even my mother became somewhat discouraged with her farm projects. If there had not been some secret misgivings in her mind about the roasting and eating of a mentally ill chicken I am sure she would have had me catch it, never mind how.

In the middle of June my brother Dolfi came home from prison camp. He did not know we had gotten word already that he had survived. So he stopped first at a house in town, because he was afraid of what it might do to my mother if he should suddenly and unannounced stand in our doorway. He asked a boy who lived there to walk up to our house and tell my mother that a young man had stopped at their place who would very much like to come and visit her if she would offer him a bowl of hot cream of wheat. Everybody in our family knew that Dolfi was crazy about cream of wheat porridge; it was a family joke. The boy came up and delivered his message and we knew what it meant. We were standing by the door when Dolfi came running up the hill. I was overjoyed to see him. He was still my little brother, even though he was now a head taller than I.

I was concerned, however, what he might think and say when he discovered that an American was coming to our house every day to see me. The treatment in the overcrowded prisoner-of-war camp had definitely been of the nonfraternizing kind. But there was no need to worry. Dolfi just beamed and shook hands with the lieutenant. He wasn't mad at anybody. He was just happy to be home. He was still growing a bit and always terribly hungry. His uniform was a malodorous rag. He looked like Tipsy the Tramp, and my mother had to dig deep into her miracle chest to find some clothes for him.

As soon as I was alone with my brother I asked him how it had been when he was taken prisoner, and did he have to hold his hands up over his head? My own experience was still very much with me. I suspect that it had been more traumatic than I realized at the time and I had not resolved it yet.

Dolfi told me that when his unit was overtaken he hid in an empty rabbit cage at an abandoned farm. An American soldier saw him and stood there with a gun and made him climb out and walk in front of him. He was told to put up his hands, so he folded them behind his head and walked ahead and whistled. I don't think he whistled very loudly, but it was his way of dealing with the situation. He was lucky; the American must have seen that in spite of his size and stripe, this was just a kid whistling in the dark and he didn't push him around or tell him to dig his own grave or any such thing as happened once in a while when soldiers got a little victory drunk.

After Dolfi was with us for a few days and rested and cleaned up and had his turn trying to coax the chicken down from the tree (the poor thing just gave him the evil eye and hopped a branch higher), he walked to the next village and got a job on a farm, because there was no way my mother could have fed him.

This all happened in June which was another beautiful month, and a semblance of order and routine had settled over the town, when out of nowhere a frightening new rumor sprung up. The Americans were leaving, the rumor had it, and the Russians were going to occupy the town. This seemed so ridiculous and farfetched that the town's people were inclined to discredit and ignore it. But the rumor refused to die. It became bleak reality one morning when the lieutenant faced us with the terrifying news: "We are leaving. The Russians are coming."

Three days later the American uniforms had disappeared. The last to leave was my lieutenant. At my last glimpse of him, he was sitting in his jeep beside the driver, roaring down the hill heading west.

Chapter 20

For a few days we lived as if suspended in a vacuum. No guns, no jeeps, no soldiers, no curfew or regimentation of any kind. The people who had been evicted drifted cautiously back into their houses and began cleaning up after their untidy tenants. A vague but deep and real sense of fear hung over the town. We had heard no official report and had seen no printed word of the events that had taken place in the rest of the country, but the tales that the east winds had carried to us had been grim indeed.

On the fourth day, one of the factory owners (the one whom the Americans had made temporary mayor of the town), gathered a number of friends in his house. No food or drink was offered but there was music, the great abiding solace of many of my countrymen. Piano, violin, Brahms and Schubert's Lieder . . . for a few hours at least the faces around me seemed redeemed and released of their cares and sorrows.

I had to leave early, Bertel had been left in the hands of a rather young babysitter. Our host accompanied me to the door.

"I do not wish to alarm you," he said in a low voice, "but I have gotten words that the first Russian troops have arrived during the afternoon. I want you to be prepared."

I crept out onto the street and hurried through town, keeping close to the walls of the houses. I did not want to be noticed or to raise any kind of a stir. I did not see anybody, neither friend nor foe, and when I reached the Rock Cellar I was out of breath and felt relieved and slightly foolish.

The occupancy did not really begin until the next day. The Russians moved into a ghost town that ominous June morning. The streets were deserted. The windows were closed and the curtains drawn. Sick with apprehension, yet filled with morbid curiosity, the families clustered behind a crack in the curtains to catch a glimpse of the legendary Red Army. What we beheld that morning was a sight as fantastic as it was unexpected. I doubt that anybody who saw it ever forgot it.

They came from the east, passing our house on the way into town. The first dozen vehicles were small open cars carrying stony-faced officers. They were followed by trucks rolling downhill with screeching brakes on monstrous wheels designed for thousands of miles of Russian spring mud. Behind the trucks came the soldiers. During their long trek through a defeated country they had mounted themselves, each one, as it seemed, to his own taste and resourcefulness. Scores of men were pushing bicycles. It was soon apparent to us that they did not know how to ride them but, judging by their proud and happy grins, they had great hopes for the future. In the meantime they used them as carriers for their gear. Many of the bikes were low on air in spite of air pumps fastened to their frames. Every yard of bumpy road was increasingly ruinous to the irreplaceable tires, a fact that made us cringe but to which the genial owners seemed totally oblivious. As they passed our house they had their hands full keeping the loaded bikes from rolling out of their grip. They were not always successful, and when a bicycle tore loose and shot down the hill, crash landing into the first obstacle in its way, it was greeted with great rounds of applause by the rest of the soldiers, although we could not tell if they were cheering for the bike or their buddy.

We saw countless little Volkswagens which, very likely, had run out of gasoline many miles ago. Their transportation was a triumph of teamwork. Half a dozen soldiers would get behind and around them and patiently push them up the long, weary mountain roads. At the top of each hill everybody nearby would jump into the car in one mad scramble; the one closest to the wheel would be in charge of the steering and down they went, shouting and waving at their fellow soldiers, who wisely jumped into the nearest ditch whenever they heard one of those joy rides coming.

Dozens of wagons rumbled by, mostly farm carts but sprinkled in between were horse-drawn hearses, which were stripped of their coffins and some of their doleful trimmings and were merrily rolling along on their rubber-tired wheels.

All of those carriages, outfitted with chairs, sometimes a table and almost always a sofa, were crowded with buoyant soldiers, many of them singing to the tunes of a mouth organ or harmonica. (It became increasingly clear that red plush sofas enjoyed great popularity, and sometime during the day I went downstairs and helped the Pringels cover our red sofa in their living room with a bedspread.)

Every conceivable and inconceivable vehicle rolled by our window that day while we stared through the curtain cracks, too fearful to laugh, too amazed to move, mesmerized by this incredible spectacle.

In the evening, the Russians moved into the barracks just outside of the town.

I don't think anybody slept very much that night. The warm, dark summer air was filled with strange and frightening sounds: calling and shouting, commands, sharp as the crack of a whip, shots fired aimlessly into the night, singing that began and abruptly ended and the long, eerie howling of the aroused dogs at some nearby farms.

It must have been around six in the morning—my mother was up and dressing—when she chanced to look out of the window. Instantly, her face froze in terror. Two Russian officers were walking swiftly up the hill heading straight toward our house.

The next few minutes were spent in such a frenzy that I have barely been able to sort them out in my memory. I know that I had never seen my mother so frantic. In a matter of seconds she had pulled me out of bed. I was wearing a pair of pajamas that belonged to one of my brothers. The sleeves and pants were much too long for me and I kept stumbling over them. My mother had taken hold of my arm in a vise-like grip and, half coaxing, half scolding, (". . . Hurry! Hurry! What's the matter with you . . . have you forgotten what happened to the young women in Berlin . . . Hurry, for God's sake! . . .") She pulled me across the living room and pushed me into the bowling alley. Behind the door, to the left, stood a large chest and my mother ordered me to hide there. By that time her panic had so completely infected me that without further protest I crawled behind the chest and crouched low on the floor. My mother threw anything near her on top of me: Newspapers, old rags, straw and rotting apples. She left me like this, slamming the door shut, and rushed downstairs to unlock the iron bar at the front door where the knocking in the meantime had turned into a ferocious hammering.

It was frightfully hot and dirty behind that chest. I strained my ears for any sounds from below, but all I heard was the pounding of my own heart.

The idea that I might be sharing those close quarters with a spider web and that, at the very moment, some large and indignant spider might be climbing somewhere over my pajamas made me almost physically ill, and I had just about decided that anything would be better than that when I heard heavy footsteps in the living room.

The Russians, as we were about to discover, used a certain tactic in searching houses. They came very early in the morning, forced a quick entrance, and demanded to know how many people, male and female, were staying at the house. Once they had gotten that information from some tremulous occupant they proceeded to look into every room and count the beds that had been slept in. I say had been, because certainly nobody was still in it once they began their search. If there was one unmade bed unaccounted for, no explanation was accepted.

Thus it happened that my mother was found out and the hunt was on.

I heard them enter the living room and clatter about. A short pause and then the door to the bowling alley was slowly opened.

A long silence ensued, which was much more unnerving than all the previous pounding and stomping, and then one of those rotten apples on top of me rolled down to the floor. It gave a soft, gentle thud, but for all its effect the house might have come down about my ears.

"*Du, hinter das. Komm hier!*" (You, behind that, come here) said a heavy voice in slow and accented German.

There was no use pretending that I was not there. Slowly I emerged from under the assorted garbage on top of me and faced the voice and its companion. The sight was most disheartening. They were two rather stocky men. The older one, who had spoken, was much heavier than the other. His face looked pasty; he had a broad nose and a thin mouth, and his eyes, which were almost colorless, were cold and suspicious. The younger man was not quite as fearsome looking but, except for a short flicker of interest when I first made my appearance, his face remained entirely expressionless throughout the whole time.

Never had I seen two gloomier looking fellows. The surprise, however, seemed mutual. They, apparently, had never seen anything quite like me, either.

My face was hot and flushed and streaks of dirt and perspiration were running down my cheeks. My hair was covered with straw and large strands of it were hanging down over my nose. The sleeves of those confounded pajamas dangled down toward the floor and I was trying to hold on to my pants.

After we had regarded each other for a while, silently and with mutual distrust, the older one spoke again, sharply, in German:

"Why you behind there?"

Now there was a question I was not prepared to answer. By now I was frightened enough to expect almost anything, but not to have to explain to those two gentlemen why I had been on my hands and knees behind that stupid chest. What on earth was I to say? Where was my mother when I needed her? (My mother, as it turned out, had not been permitted to enter the bowling alley with them.)

For a second I thought of playing the family halfwit. Or else falling down in a dead faint (I always consider this as my last option) but it would take a good deal of stage presence for either one of these performances and I just didn't have it in me at that moment.

"Why you behind there?" asked the horrible man again, louder.

I had heard him very clearly the first time.

"I was looking for something," I mumbled.

"You look for something what?"

But I had all I could take.

"For my slippers!" I yelled and, holding up my pajama pants with both hands, I simply ran past them through the living room into the hall.

I was certain that they would shoot me. And so strong is the power of imagination and so shaky were my nerves that I could almost feel a bullet hit me between the shoulder blades.

In reality nothing much happened. The two officers thundered behind me into the hall. The younger one wrote something into a little book and they started down the steps. In the doorway the older one turned once more toward my white-faced mother. Shaking a finger at her, he grumbled: "Lie not again, woman. No good!" And they were gone.

There were many more searches during the weeks that followed but I would never again hide behind that chest or any other place for that matter, not for the devil himself!

The incident might have been closed (though never forgotten) if it were not for one brief encounter on another occasion.

I was standing in line in front of the town hall some two weeks later. The Russians had issued a harsh order—one of many in those days—that each woman between fifteen and fifty was to go through a medical check for venereal disease or she would receive no ration cards. There were only two doctors left in a town filled with women and only two days were allowed for this procedure. Although the examination was as short as it was unpleasant, we had to wait in line for hours, silent, resentful, and hungry.

When finally my turn came I found the doctor sitting on the only chair in the bare room staring vacantly into space and mopping his forehead. He gave me a quick, wry nod of recognition and, pointing with his chin toward the door, he said:

"For heavens sake, get out of here." And gratefully I fled.

Once outside the room a plump Russian woman in uniform stamped the back of my left hand and I joined the next line, waiting for my ration cards.

Russian soldiers and officers went in and out of the town hall. Suddenly one of them stopped near our line and called:

"You! Woman in blue dress, come here!"

There was only one blue dress any place around and that was mine. Besides, he was looking straight at me. In the feeble and somewhat uncharitable hope that he might settle for another dress once I was out of sight I tried to shrink back into the crowd. But the crowd would have nothing of me. Immediately, there was an unfriendly little vacuum around me. And just in case I still hadn't gotten the idea, many hands were pointing at me and the women whispered:

"You! He means you!"

I walked toward him as slowly as I dared, and just before I reached him I recognized him. He was one of our two Russian visitors that first morning. The silent partner. His face was as expressionless now as it had been during our first meeting. I began to wonder if I would ever see my family again. Right then he spoke.

"You find slippers yet, eh?"

And suddenly and entirely unexpectedly he smiled, a friendly, conspiratorial smile, as if he and I shared a neat little secret together.

* * * * * * * * * * * * *

"We" were still we, the town's people, only a great deal more apprehensive than before. But "they" were now the Russians, and the house searches and curfews and orders began all over again, only in a different style and with different goals in mind. It was not very long that one surprising fact emerged: many more Russians than Americans knew a smattering of German. None of us knew a word of Russian, though, and communication remained difficult.

The Russian quartermaster's men went through town and marked most of the same houses as the Americans had for occupancy. Nobody considered the Rock Cellar, which was, as always, taken for a pub. The families hastily packed a few of their belongings and, once again, vacated the premises. At nightfall the Russians moved into the houses, sat down in the kitchens and dining rooms, and waited for somebody to show up and cook their dinner. Of course, nobody came. The next day they went around looking for their absentee landladies. It turned out that they had no intention of staying in those houses by themselves. So the families moved back into their homes dragging their feet a bit, not knowing what to expect or whether to laugh or cry. From then on they cooked and washed for their Russian tenants and made their beds and tried to persuade them to throw the used newspaper squares into the toilet bowl and not the bathtub.

At night, the Russians would sit around the kitchen table with "their" families, pour vodka into glasses and flower vases, and make them drink toasts to the great Russian victory and to Hitler being kaput. They brought their rations to the house and the women would cook for them and feed their children a little on the side. When the Russians had a lot to drink they would sing and get very homesick. The children were put to sleep on cushions on the floor but the grown-ups were to stay with them and be family.

There were incidents, of course, but not as many as we had expected. I remember one of them quite vividly. The Russians had immediately demoted the mayor (he being a factory owner) and set up another one, which did not mean that his house was unoccupied. One night the couple had gone to bed and the soldiers in the kitchen just drank and sang and got more inspired by the minute. They began playing the gramophone and decided to dance. They moved the furniture out of the way and then discovered that they had no partners. So up they went to the bedroom and requested the mayor's wife, a placid little woman in her fifties, to come down and dance with them. The lady hid under the bed covers, and the mayor bravely blocked the bedroom door, only to get pounded for his troubles. The wife, to save her husband further punches, climbed out of bed and agreed to come. She was triumphantly escorted, in her nightgown, down to the kitchen where she danced with each of the soldiers until, one after another, they were too drunk to get up from the chairs and she could safely make her exit and run up and look after her bruised husband.

The officers who had appeared on the first morning were not the only Russians who came uninvited. There were many more. I used to divide them roughly into three categories: The official visits, the semi-official visits, and the drop-ins. They all had one thing in common: They used the butts of their rifles to knock at the door and they were people of exceedingly short patience. When my brother was home, he would run down the steps and open the door, ducking immediately to the side in case the last swing of the rifle butt should meet up with his skull. When my mother or I opened the door the last swing was more likely to be arrested in mid air, which did not mean that the visit was going to be any more pleasant. The Pringels never opened the door, even though they lived on the ground floor and had the shortest route. Instead, during the first days, they would come flying up the steps, the delicate Frau Pringel as nimbly as the twins, and crowd into our kitchen, where we would usually be waiting. Hiding behind a locked kitchen door would only have meant another wood splintering hammering. We would stand in the open doorway, my mother and I vaguely in front, sometimes carrying Bertel, the twins peeking around us on either side (not exactly scared out of their wits, I might add). Behind them, one hand protectively on each boy's shoulder, her black bird's eyes daring the enemy to lay hands on either of them or her, for that matter, stood the invaluable Gertrud; and behind her, as far back as the kitchen would permit, which was not very far, hovered the two Pringels.

The official callers would mostly come very early in the morning or after dark at night. They would ask a few questions in German: "Was this everybody who lived in the house? Were there no more persons any place in the house or absent at the time?" Then they would push us aside and walk into the next room and the search began. They were always searching. They did not believe anybody or anything; they breathed mistrust. We never did figure out just what it was they were trying to find. Weapons? Kitchen knives? Uniforms, explosives, stolen caviar? *Mein Kampf*? Mainly, I think, they were looking for people. At that time we knew very little of the bunker in Berlin, of Hitler's supposed suicide and Himmler's disappearance. Maybe they were truly hoping to find one or the other harbored in somebody's house in just such a little forlorn town as ours. The fact that the Americans had combed our homes already for weeks on end and that we would have to be totally insane to hide a well-known Nazi criminal under our bed or in any of the creaking old cabinets around the house never seemed to enter the picture.

What did enter the picture, however, was our growing conviction that they had begun to look for young males who had come home from the war unscathed. After they had shown repeated interest in my brother's whereabouts we were taking no more chances. When such a search team appeared during one of Dolfi's visits to us, I developed some slight mechanical trouble with the opening of the front door while my mother helped him climb out of a second floor window.

There was no doubt in anybody's mind as to the purpose of the semi-official visitors. It was all rather businesslike and fully understood by both parties. Radios, watches, small clocks, and cameras were the main objects of their search. Eventually, all telephones were taken. In some houses a rather painful removal of a bicycle or two took place, which were our only means of transportation. By now we were either totally stripped of all those things or else had them so well hidden that they could not be found. However, hope springs eternal. The semi-official visits kept up for a long time and were only reluctantly abandoned.

The drop-ins, now, were a different sort altogether. They came around at sunset and wanted nothing but to drink their vodka in friendly company. They were homesick young boys, and for me it was the same kind of experience the third time around. They were sick of war, sick of the barracks, and sick of each other's faces. They wanted a house, a kitchen, a family, and vodka. They all thought we were an inn and it was difficult to make them understand that we did not sell vodka and had none hidden. Eventually they caught on and brought their own bottles. The idea of their visit was that we would join them in a party. My mother told them that we had no glasses. That's how I came to know about the flower vases. They just dumped the flowers out of the vases and poured vodka into them. In the end, my mother produced some glasses because drinking vodka out of an old flower vase was just about the pits.

They wandered through the house, talked, and asked questions in Russian. They touched things, shook their heads, and looked at framed photographs. They often picked up the Iron Cross medal beside my brother's picture, looked questioningly at my mother, and put it gently down again. They picked up books and peeked inside. One day they happened to pick up some of my father's books and my mother said: *"Mein Mann! Artista!"* and she tapped first the book and then her own chest energetically. It was

truly an inspired move. Their faces were all wonder and awe. They picked up more books, holding them toward my mother:

"Dein Mann?"

She nodded vigorously, and after that they treated her with great
respect. From that day on my mother always had some of my father's books
within reach, and when our drop-in visitors appeared and began their
rounds those books were the first items she showed them.

My mother, I should say at this point, became an absolute expert in
handling those young men once she realized that she had only to be her
own self, this rather splendid mixture of Mother Earth and Grand Duchess
of Talliho.

When I came back for a visit after I had left town that fall, our staunch
old friend and neighbor Herr Bossier said to me: "We often worry about
your mother being alone there with the child, but it is amazing how she
manages. You might find this hard to believe, but my wife and I have seen
soldiers stomping into that house, hollering for vodka, and we were holding our breath and praying for your dear mother. And after five or ten
minutes we see those same soldiers come out again, each one with an apple
in his hand. If my eyesight were better, I would swear they were looking
sort of dazed."

"I believe it," I said.

I remember one late afternoon, when Dolfi came upstairs with some
drop-ins. Two young Russians who were hollering for vodka, what else?
My mother was cooking supper. She used wood sparingly for that and had
a small fire of twigs going over which she stirred a pot of gruel. This was
always the same ghastly brew: she would throw a handful of full grain into
boiling salt water and stir it until the grain swelled and opened and thickened into a slimy soup. Only then did she consider it fit for human consumption and ready to render the ultimate nourishment. For all I know
she might have been right with this but it was pretty awful.

The two Russians came into the kitchen and looked around, at my
mother bent over the stove, and at the baby and me sitting at the kitchen
table.

"Vodka," they said but this time with a notable lack of conviction.

"Oh, bother." said my mother. "Not again." She'd barely turned her
head.

"Vodka, woman!" said one of the soldiers in German, asserting himself.

"Ach, do sit down. You are forever underfoot," said my mother cross-ly. "Sit down! There!" she ordered sternly, pointing with the wooden spoon at the stool and the top of the little stepladder in the corner. The Rus-sians understood no German but they always understood my mother when she talked to them like this. They sat down where they were told. My brother leaned against the door frame and we all waited in silence. My mother peered into the pot, declared the gruel done, and pulled it off the fire. She handed out soup plates and spoons, one to each of us including the two soldiers who obediently held on to theirs. With a big ladle she slapped two scoops of the gruel into each bowl, the last one for herself. We nodded at each other (that being what was left of the prayer we used to say before each meal) and started eating. So, after a moment of hesita-tion, did the soldiers. They ate very slowly. Their faces were a study in bleak politeness. My brother gulped his food down hungrily; my mother ate stoically. Bertel, who was the only one who had milk poured over his gruel, hummed while I fed him, as he always did—hummmm . . . like a wordless little song, and I, as always, tried not to gag. It felt good once it was past the tastebuds down in the stomach. My mother got up, took the pot and ladle and approached the table, obviously bent on giving out a second helping. All politeness gone, the first Russian covered his bowl with both hands.

"*Genug, Frau!*" (Enough, woman!) he said, horrified. The other one followed his example.

"Well, suit yourself," said my mother and handed the rest to Dolfi who scraped the pot clean until it hardly needed washing. The two soldiers put their plates down, nodded toward my mother, and squeezed hastily through the door. They needed no one to see them out.

Bertel's first birthday was approaching and I had been hoarding some rations for that day. It wasn't enough for a cake, but I planned to bake him some cookies. I had saved two eggs and some lard coupons. Flour I had set aside a good while ago, already with the cookies in mind, also a few spoonful of sugar. My mother was not there at the time. She had hitched a ride to a city some hundred miles to the east of us where she hoped to find some traces of my oldest brother, Wolfgang.

Anyway, I was alone with Bertel, and after I had put him to bed on the evening before his birthday I fired the stove and mixed the dough in a clay pot. Half forgotten memories awakened and teased me, of childhood birthdays, of ladies' teas in my mother's parlor, of Christmases long ago, and I smiled a little as I kneaded and patted the golden ball taking shape under my fingers. When I lifted the bowl to spread a towel on the table in preparation to rolling out the dough it slipped out of my hand and fell on the floor.

The clay pot shattered into a hundred pieces, scattering all over the kitchen. For a minute I was too stupefied to take in the finality of the disaster. It had taken weeks to save up all those ingredients, and in one second my golden ball lay there on the floor, shapeless and pitiful, large pointed splinters like ancient darning needles sticking out from all sides.

After a while I lifted the dough carefully into another bowl and began picking out the splinters—first the ones on the outside and then digging slowly into it. Wherever my fingers probed I felt sharp little pieces buried deep inside the soft mass. There seemed no end to them. I cautiously put a bit of dough into my mouth and felt it crunching between my teeth. The story of Lucretia Borgia rushed to my mind, the beautiful daughter of a wicked pope, who had killed troublesome lovers by mixing ground glass into their food.

It never occurred to me to throw away the dough. You might have a hard time accepting this, but there are many things that can be comprehended only within their own time and circumstances. We had eaten fermented vegetable soup, smelly meat, frozen potatoes, and moldy bread. We had drunk juice made out of rotting and wormy apples and milk that had soured from lack of refrigeration.

We never threw anything away that was meant to be eaten.

I baked the cookies that evening, tears of frustration running down my cheeks. I did not care where they landed. I knew that the baby would never eat a single one of these cookies. Neither would I share them with anybody else. I would have to eat them all myself.

During the following week, whenever Bertel was tucked in for the night, I would eat one or two of the cookies. The kitchen would be only dimly lit by the glow of the dying summer day. I wanted nothing to distract me. Sitting quietly on the chair I would chew each bite a few dozen times with great concentration. When I could hold on no longer and started to swallow by sheer reflex, I thought of the beauteous Lucretia and her finely ground glass and my throat would close and the bite resurge and I would chew some more. The first time I did this I cried again, out of grief and disappointment but also, I suspect, because of a certain amount of panic. I wondered if I would die and how much it would hurt.

After a few times when nothing happened, not even a stomach ache, I would just sit there in the silent darkness, resigned and half asleep, like any of those patient creatures in pastures around town chewing their cud in the night.

I did not see much of the Pringels while my mother was gone. Dr. Pringel had ceased to waylay me. He probably would have given a great deal if he could have made me forget "his side of the story," especially things like the two Christmas geese. He was mortally afraid that somebody might start a rumor that he had been a capitalist. The truth is that I do not remember anything drastic happening to any one person in our town. There was no outright looting, raping, or shooting. The Russians had come relatively late to us and much of their fury had been spent. The factory owners, of course, were immediately dispossessed and the workers "liberated." The owners were to work from now on side by side with their workers. This was not as big a deal as the Russians had meant it to be. The factories were small and every one of the owners had learned his trade from the bottom up. So, this not making much of a splash, the owners were soon put back into administrative positions, along, of course, with a substantial workers' council.

The Russians located the few known communists who were still around and made one of them mayor of the town. The new mayor was bursting with pride and reform ideas, but after the night of the dance he became sulky and when his bike was also "liberated" by one of those semi-official visitors he turned sour and got into some lively arguments with the Russian town commandant.

The little farmers—there were no big ones around—were the ones who suffered most. It seemed to me there was much that was contradictory in the communist theories and the way the Russians dealt with the small farmers was, possibly, the largest contradiction. (This was more than forty years ago, and time has surely borne this out.)

Immediately after occupancy, the Russians ordered a two-hour change into summer time. Farmers got up at 5 o'clock anyway; this meant that they were to get up at 3 o'clock every morning. It was still dark then and no work could be done around the farm or in the fields. None of the animals went along with this new order, not the goats nor the cows nor the chickens. Cleaning the stables or milking at that early hour was out of the question.

Big trucks came around and confiscated farm machinery, on which the farmers were more than ever dependent since all the young men were gone. And then one morning, around 6 a.m. Russian summer time (4 a.m. God's time) the big roundup of cows began. We saw them being herded through town later in the day, running off into side streets or pushing through fences into the gardens while Russian soldiers were swarming around them swearing and punching at them with the butts of their rifles. None of them really seemed to know what they were doing. I could not imagine how they intended to transport this chaos of men and animals a thousand miles east into Russia. I need not have wondered. It was all over in twenty-four hours.

Around four o'clock the next morning, between our town and the next village, the disoriented animals had stampeded and invaded the clover and lupine fields along the road. We did not see them die but we heard much about it: how they gulped down the greens which were heavy with dew, how they ate and ate until they could hold no more, and how their bellies swelled and became huge balloons. They had lain, stricken, in the fields, their deep moans of pain filling the dawn until they fell silent, one by one, and lay there with glazed, broken eyes, and the only sounds were the cursing and kicking of the Russian soldiers.

Well, the cows were dead and no kicking would get them up and about again. They had to be butchered on the spot, or even the meat would be lost. It was all pretty bloody and gruesome and completely senseless which somehow made it worse. It is easier to deal with a disaster when one can, at least, comprehend it. It made the food rations still smaller, but it was the irrational execution of it all that was most frightening to the population.

* * * * * * * * * * * * *

It was around that time at the Rock Cellar that Mother Nature asserted herself. One afternoon we heard a great deal of cackling and commotion on the side porch. I ran out to investigate and discovered that our mad chicken had come down from the tree and was sitting in a box filled with old rags. When she saw me coming she fluttered away under shrieks of protest. In the box, between the rags, lay a small brown egg! Well — finding the Hope diamond could have hardly excited me more. I picked up the egg and ran into the house to share the stupendous news with my mother, and we both inspected the site of this amazing event. The chicken was crouched up in the tree again, looking as mean and mad as ever. The same thing happened the next day at just about the same time.

Two eggs in two days! We looked at each other in breathless wonder.

"But why is she making all that noise?" asked my mother.

"They always do," I said from the depth of my vast farm experience. "It's a special kind of cackle. I think they are proud of their accomplishment."

"Well," said my mother firmly, "we can't have that. Sooner or later everybody in town will know that our chicken is finally laying. The next thing we'll know, we will have to take the eggs to the town depot or else lose our ration cards."

There was truth in that, and now we were both at a loss as to what to do. However, this was never a lasting condition with my mother.

"It's really quite simple," she said, her face brightening. "You will have to prevent her from cackling."

"I . . . *what*?"

"Well, you just told me they make this particular racket only after the egg is laid. So you just wait until she is done and then keep her from cackling."

"How?" I was exceedingly doubtful.

"Use your head," said my mother loftily, and the matter was closed for her.

What I did use was a dusty old potato sack. The chicken would not come down as long as she saw me loitering about, so I would hide and wait. Pretty soon she would come flying down, strutting around the rag box a few times, clucking and pushing her head back and forth. Presently she would hop in, settle down and gaze determinedly into space. As soon as she moved again and got all flustery and began to stretch her neck, I would jump at her and put the sack over her head. The proud cackle would turn into a muffled, terrified squeaking. I would carry her under the tree and release her, and she would fly straight up onto her branch, her moment of glory squashed and gone. Poor little thing! That was no way to coax a mentally unbalanced chicken back to sanity.

I did not have to do it often, thank heaven. After a few days, whenever the chicken saw me rushing up with my potato sack poised in midair, she would squawk and flutter off the box and back into the tree of her own free will. I would pretend to tidy up the porch a bit, drop the warm egg into my apron pocket, and leisurely stroll back into the house. It was fortunate that Miss Milktooth had long since departed. She would not have been fooled for a minute. The Pringels were city people. I am sure that if they ever observed this strange maneuver, they thought we had decided to eat the chicken after all and that I was trying to catch it every afternoon around five o'clock.

* * * * * * * * * * * * *

Fall approached, and it became apparent that Dolfi and I would have to go back to Berlin. The baby would stay with my mother. The city just then was no place where a fourteen-month-old child could survive. I would have to find work; Dolfi would have to continue his education. The parting with Bertel was inevitable and the heartache only tempered by necessity and our determination to be back for Christmas, come hell or high water.

On a misty September morning, around seven Russian time (five o'clock by cows and chicken standards), we were standing ready and waiting in front of the Rock Cellar. There were three of us, Dolfi, myself and Regina, a refugee friend who had spent two miserable and homesick years in our little town and was eager to return to Berlin. The sky was a soft gray, barely light, when a creaky old pickup truck pulled up in front of the house. It was empty. The driver was going into the Halle area to load coal.

The transaction between us and him was swift and simple: two large pre-war cigars and one bag of guaranteed non-wormy apples. I don't know what Regina gave him; people did not often ask each other that question.

"Room for only one in the cab," said the driver. "The other two will have to ride in the back."

Regina, who said she was inclined to fall carsick, got into the cab, and Dolfi and I climbed into the truck bed and settled down with our backs propped against the back of the cab. We all had packed a minimum of luggage, since we had no idea what our travel might involve—how many obstacles we might have to overcome and how much of it we might have to do on foot.

We did, eventually, have to do some precarious walking across a kind of jungle bridge over the Saale River. The trip turned out to be very different from what we had expected, a kind of Alice-in-Wonderland adventure, but the story of it belongs to the next chapter of our lives, the one still ahead of us rather than the one we left behind. When the truck rattled out of the sleepy little town, up the long road toward the hills and forest of Thuringia, it started to rain, fine warm drops falling gently out of the soft gray sky. The large trees on both sides of the road came rushing up over us from nowhere, nodded the golden tips of their branches over our heads, goodbye, goodbye, God's speed . . . and faded down the road. How odd that I should remember the raindrops in my hair that morning or looking idly at my hands and wondering when and how I would be able to wash the coal dust off them. I remember the feeling of my brother's reassuring shoulder beside mine. He sang a little and I hummed along, softly, so I would not throw him off tune.

Regina in the cab fell carsick anyway and threw up into her hat. Dolfi and I were rattled around a good bit and got a little wet around our shoulders and legs, but the sense of a beginning was strong and thrilling in all three of us, and we were scared and curious and full of expectations.

PART VI

1945-1946

Berlin

The Aftermath

Chapter 21

It was late afternoon when the truck deposited us at the west bank of the river Saale and drove on toward the coal mines. The rain had stopped and the air was warm and moist. Each of us carried some cumbersome bags and parcels and Regina carried her hat in one hand.

"Do you think it can be washed?" she asked hopelessly. The bridge to Halle across the water had been destroyed and a sort of monkey bridge hammered together. With every step it weaved precariously from side to side and it took all our concentration not to lose our balance. Regina threw her hat into the river and hung on for dear life. It would be years before she would be able to buy a new one.

Parts of Halle had been bombed and burned and landmarks had disappeared. Regina, who was divorced and attractive, had a friend, an old suitor, living in town. She had turned him down a number of times during more prosperous days but, as she blithely assured us, they were still the best of friends and so we intended to spend the night at his place. Miraculously, she found her way to his apartment house, which was still standing. We hesitated at the entrance; some lingering shreds of pre-war breeding and courtesy made us wish to turn around and walk away. We had no illusions about our reception. If there was anything in those days that people dreaded almost as much as drunken soldiers at their doorstep, it was a visit such as we were planning. Nobody wanted to answer a knock at the door to find a group of scrubby travelers standing there, knapsacks on their backs, a dilapidated suitcase in hand, and a hopeful smile on their unwashed and, alas, familiar face. This was the stuff of which nightmares were made. The urge to slam the door shut before any mutual recognition took place was overwhelming and the old suitor was no exception. It didn't help the situation that Regina had two equally seedy-looking strangers with her — three more people when there was barely shelter and food for one.

"Dear Alfred!" cried Regina, who had read his face very well and stepped nimbly past him into the dark hall. "Dear Alfred, how are you?" And Alfred, who had felt better before he opened the door, resigned to the inevitable. There would be no food, but we could stay the night.

Our next immediate destination was the garage from which all authorized transportation vehicles left the city. There, with maximum speed and minimum fuss, two black cigars changed hands and the dispatcher sent for the driver of a truck that would leave in the morning, loaded with hospital equipment, in the direction of Berlin. Two more cigars went as down payment to the driver who promised to pick us up at a certain street corner.

We were standing at daybreak at the appointed corner nervously awaiting our ride. When the truck finally approached, almost an hour later, it gave no indication of slowing down.

"He's not going to stop! . . . He's going right by us!" Regina and I yelled. Dolfi stepped off the curb ready to jump on the running board. With a shrill sound the driver hit the brakes and we picked up our bags and parcels and ran toward the truck. The driver got out of the cab, he did not look friendly.

"Dunno if you wanna ride in it," he muttered. "It's pretty full." We did not move, so he shrugged his shoulders and opened the doors. He had not exaggerated; the truck was loaded almost to its roof with mattresses. There was only a narrow space left right behind the doors.

"You can't sit there," said the driver, following our hopeful glance, "I hafta pick up another load."

"We'll ride on top of the mattresses," we said, and at once we climbed up, one after another, Dolfi giving us a lift from behind and handing up the parcels and bags. There was not enough room to sit, so we tried lying on our stomachs, propped up on our elbows. We had barely shifted into a comfortable position when the truck stopped again. The doors were unlocked and the driver's face appeared in the opening. He looked wrathful and entirely uncompromising.

"I ain't taking you," he said. "It's not permitted. You hafta get out and that's all there is to it."

"Who say's it's not permitted?" asked Dolfi, lying on his stomach and glaring down at the driver.

"Them. The Russians. Them in there," said the driver, pointing at a large building behind him. "That's their headquarters and I can't haul nobody without their permission. So out you go!"

None of us moved; our minds were racing through our options.

"I am going to get permission," I said loudly. "You stay here and wait."

I rolled by the speechless Regina, past my brother, whose face was one big question mark, and climbed down off the truck. Without wasting a look on the nonplussed driver, I marched across the street and through the main doors of the building. My heart was beating wildly; I had not the foggiest notion what I was going to do. Once inside the building I saw that there was little cause for alarm. Soldiers, officers, and civilians swarmed in and out like a beehive and nobody paid any attention to me. I sat down on a bench along the wall and waited. When five minutes or so had gone by I went out and walked back to the truck. The driver was still standing beside the truck looking more apprehensive now than mutinous. Regina and Dolfi, who had cautiously stayed where they were, hung over the edge of the mattresses in breathless suspense.

"Help me up, Dolfi," I said calmly. "I talked to one of the officers in charge and he said it was perfectly all right as long as it did not interfere with the route or cargo."

"I don't believe you," said the driver, sounding a good deal less belligerent than before. I turned my head and looked him unblinkingly into the eyes.

"Go in yourself and ask," I said, shrugging my shoulders. It's a Captain... Captain Dostoyevsky..." (It was the only Russian name I could think of in a hurry.) "Third or fourth door on the left. First floor. And don't worry," I added maliciously, "I didn't mention the cigars."

For a second the driver looked like a terrified little boy. Then he slammed the doors shut, climbed into the cab and drove on.

"What happened?" asked Dolfi.

"Did you really . . .?" whispered Regina, awed.

Sinking back into the mattresses, I put on my most inscrutable face. And as we rolled slowly over the bumpy city streets, I lay on my back, staring at the stained ceiling above me, and wondered if I wasn't my mother's daughter after all.

We stopped one more time when the driver took on the second load. It consisted of two large boxes and a girl—barely out of her teens—who accompanied them. Wordlessly the driver deposited them inside the truck and we were on our way to Berlin.

Immediately we began to strike up an acquaintance with the girl who was crouching on the floor beside the boxes.

"What's in them?" we inquired.

"Candy," said the girl. "Hard candy, for some Polish hospital near the border."

Candy?! Yes, two large boxes full of hard candy, the kind that are called bonbons in Europe. None of us had seen or tasted a bonbon for years.

Like lightning Dolfi descended and joined the girl on the floor. There was hardly room for the two. He scrutinized the boxes, which were securely tied with string.

"Can you open them?"

"No!" cried the girl anxiously. "Don't touch the string. They know how it was tied."

"Maybe there's a hole somewhere," Dolfi said. He poked a bony finger into a corner. "See, there is one."

"Where?" The girl was doubtful.

"Here," he said, poking his finger deeper into the box. "It probably got damaged loading." He pulled out a bonbon and handed it to the girl, who shrank back.

"Well, take it! It could have fallen out on its own," he said. The girl took it hesitatingly, still looking unconvinced. Then Dolfi threw a bonbon to Regina and me.

It was a long ride from the city on the Saale River to Berlin, not as the crow flies, but as the neglected, ill-repaired country road wound its way through the fields and villages. It was dark inside; the only light came through the cracks around the doors, but the truck was a drafty old thing and the air never got stuffy. We could not sit up; it was either on the stomach or flat on the back. The girl had long since joined us on top of the mattresses and we were talking and laughing and sucking bonbons in between to refresh our spirits. We were not greedy; we did not want the girl to get into trouble. We took no more bonbons than could have legitimately dropped out of a small hole, and Dolfi made sure that it looked like a natural tear in the poor material of the carton.

It was the most unlikely ride I ever took in my life; a moment of pure, unadulterated fun in the midst of a terrible and uncertain time.

Our driver, who had been so troublesome in the beginning, somewhere along the road had a change of heart; to our amazement, he took us directly to the door of our apartment house in the west of Berlin. This was such an unexpected bonus that we gave him two more cigars, although our supply was nearing the end.

We had spent most of the day horizontally in complete darkness and, standing up straight in the daylight, we needed a few seconds to get our bearings. What we saw was heartening: our neighborhood was still standing. The little park across the street was an unkempt jungle of bushes and weeds. The benches were gone, presumably used for firewood. The bakery on the corner had cardboard nailed across its show windows but seemed open for business. The linden trees still lined the street, alive with autumn colors. Deep pockmarks caused by flak splinters and artillery dotted the walls of our house. The front door was broken and the windows were boarded except for one small panel of glass in each one to let in some daylight. The tiles in the entrance hall were cracked, the stairs were without carpet and very dirty. Our apartment door, which had been blown into the living room during one of the air raids, was loosely attached to its frame again. During the same attack that had totally demolished two other apartment houses nearby, the wall between the two bedrooms had fallen down. Fräulein Pritts had swept away the debris and now occupied this particular space.

Fräulein Pritts, it appeared, was at present our tenant, although she did not see it that way. She had walked away from her own burning apartment with little more than she was wearing and had been told by the block administrator to move into our vacant rooms. It was there that she lived through the horrors of the last days of war and the first days of occupation. She had carried buckets of plaster down the stairs, replaced the doors, and cleaned the bathtub after marauding soldiers had used it to relieve themselves. She had not run off and let other people carry the burden, she said, and she regarded herself by moral and divine rights to be the mistress of the few empty, sooty rooms that used to be our apartment. In a long, straight robe that years without soap and hot water had given the hue of antique gold, she stood in front of the kitchen door, her arms folded across her chest, long gray tresses falling over her shoulders, and her fierce blue eyes watched every movement of ours. Her lips moved soundlessly, murmuring ancient curses upon our heads. A virginal priestess guarding the temple of Vesta against barbarian intruders.

We had no intention of disturbing the lady in her holy fervor. All we wanted was to use the bathroom and find a place to sleep. It was too late for Regina to make her way to her own house. We shared the last of our food and took inventory. There were two metal folding beds with army blankets as mattresses. The dining room still held the couch, two chairs and a massive table that had been left behind. Each of us had carried a blanket and a sheet in our luggage. Dolfi began to pile stuff on top of the metal springs of one of the cots: rags, old newspaper from the basement and some shredded coconut runners he swiped from the hallway. He rolled up his jacket for a cushion and was settled for the night. Regina and I opted for the narrow couch. The couch looked bedraggled, but so did we and it did not take us long to accommodate ourselves to its sparse comfort. As long as we could keep our feet out of each other's face and hair, we were in good shape. We felt that the day had been surprisingly successful; we had gotten on very well indeed. Tomorrow we would arrange ourselves with the militant Fräulein in gold and thereafter tackle each hurdle as it came along. Tonight we slept.

Chapter 22

We had lived in Thuringia without newspaper, radio, or telephone, cut off from the political and military news of the world around us. Now that we had left the shelter of the small town, all the tales of horror seemed to close in on us at once.

As with everything else I have said here, I can only speak for myself in this matter. It was in the fall of 1945 that I saw the first pictures of Jewish mass graves and read the first statistics of German concentration camps. You cannot "deal" with this kind of monstrous information. Dealing is done on an intellectual level. All my initial reactions belonged to the passages of death. The mind races like a trapped animal through every possibility of escape.

Disbelief . . . had Hitler not shown us the pictures of a German peasant family in Poland, their tongues nailed to their kitchen table? And were we not now told that those pictures had been fake?

Denial . . . it could not have been all Jews. Were there not mass graves all over Europe? But another picture was fighting its way into my consciousness: a train filled with human beings — body pressed against body — of white-faced, silent people. There had been no Madagascar for them, no Polish farms, after all.

Anger, furious, impotent rage . . . How could they have done this to them? To us?

And the most unbearable thought of it all: this had been done by people who spoke my language, by people who had been children, once, and gone to German schools, playing cops and robbers in the school yard, as we had done, eating their black bread and lard sandwiches during recess, sleeping under featherbeds at night, and celebrating Christmas under the candle light of German Christmas trees. What had turned them into monsters? How had they walked in the midst of us without the mark of Caine on their foreheads?

It was in the same fall of 1945 that we heard of the burning of Dresden where rings of fire bombs had been thrown around refugee camps only weeks before the end of the war. And gradually at that time we were learning of the effects of an atomic weapon that had been used to annihilate two cities at the other side of the world.

I think it was the very number of the dead that spun it into the abstract, the inconceivable, for me. Who can really grasp a million light years? Months later I read one evening in an American newspaper a detailed account of a hotel fire in a small town in Ohio in which seventeen people had died. I did not know where Ohio was, but seventeen people burning to death, this I could grasp. I cried myself to sleep that night, endless, inconsolable tears, wept for seventeen trapped and burning people . . . and for the millions of others who had perished all over the world in the wake of that terrible war.

"How could you have lived a fairly content life under those circumstances?" I was asked once by an analytical, intelligent person. "Content" is surely the wrong word, but I understood her question. How could you have gone about your daily tasks, just then, she was asking, working at your job, worrying about a leaky little cookpot and your frostbitten toes, fretting about rations, laughing with your friends, enjoying a sunny day and sleeping at night under your blanket, coat, newspaper . . . whatever, without nightmare, with no terrifying visions haunting you and keeping you awake?

I believe every one of us, my questioner not exempt, had sooner or later to deal with that question. My own answer was very simple: I ran. With my eyes closed and my hands over my ears, I fled into the day-by-day struggle of simply getting on with life. It was a heedless, headlong, sanity-saving flight, away from all mental images of Jewish mass graves, of burning refugee camps, of cities that had been wiped off the face of the earth. Away from the knowledge that every time I climbed over the rubble of my own city I stepped over the bodies of men, women, and children still buried underneath it. Away from stories of single fates of such terror and proximity that it did not bear thinking about.

I have never believed in the concept of collective guilt. Hitler believed in "Sippenhaft," guilt by blood ties, and he mercilessly acted upon it. Guilt for crimes against humanity as well as for cruel and unusual punishment meted out to fellow human beings should be placed on those who conceived them, approved them, ordered them, executed them, and applauded them afterward. And there it should remain.

Collective horror, grief, sadness, and hope is a different matter.

* * * * * * * * * * * * * *

Germany, in compliance with the Yalta-Potsdam agreements, was divided into four occupied zones (Russian, French, English, and American), each zone claiming one-fourth of the country's capital, Berlin, as its sector. On paper, these zones and sectors were to be treated with complete equality; in practice it did not work out that way for a single day. Each occupation force had its own ideas on how to administer occupied territory, although the three western allies kept, by and large, to the official wording of the agreement.

As to the population in the city, the Berliners themselves, they now lived side-by-side with their conquerors, the sun rising and setting for them at precisely the same moment and the same clouds rolling over their heads at night. But that was where all resemblance ended; they might have lived on different stars for all the rest of it. We did not share the weather with them, for *their* houses were heated. Their food and drink were different; all water was carefully boiled for them before consumption, while we drank whatever came out of the pipes. We did not even share the daylight with them, since our windows were boarded and theirs were not.

The "OFF LIMITS" signs that sprouted up overnight in almost every undamaged corner of the city, are still a prominent memory for the people of Berlin. In fact, those were the only two English words many of them ever learned. They were printed in large letters and marked all the residential areas, parks, concert halls, movie theaters, beaches, swimming pools, and restaurants into which no Berliner was permitted to set foot. No fraternization was allowed. In our small town in Thuringia a sort of melting process, an intermingling of lives, had already begun to take place. There was little of this in Berlin. Few segregations of the ruling and the ruled had ever been more effectively spelled out and observed than it was in Berlin during those first postwar years.

There had to be, of course, communication of some kind. The commandants of each of the four occupation powers dealt with the mayor of the city and the heads of the separate city councils. Each occupation force licensed one newspaper, printed in the German language and written and edited by German newspapermen. Each of those papers was earnestly intent on teaching the population democracy while, at the same time, cautiously testing the waters of free speech themselves.

Dolfi and I read three of the four daily papers and afterwards used them to wrap our feet in the evening or for additional covers at night. They printed no ads or private announcements. Since few people had a radio, few a telephone, and mail service was still non-existent, the people of Berlin had to find their own way of communicating with each other. What the drums were to the jungles of Africa, the corner trees of each city block became to the Berliner. Slips of white paper, dozens of them, were tagged onto each of these trees, every paper carrying a message to a fellow citizen. It was through this tree-communication system that I eventually traded a painfully saved loaf of bread for a non-leaking cookpot. And it was through a slip of white paper stuck to a corner tree a few blocks away that I, or rather Dolfi, found a job for me. The slip said that teachers for elementary schools were desperately needed and would any non-Party member with Abitur please apply to the nearest school district. I applied and thus got acquainted with the unforgettable *"Fragebogen,"* the allied questionnaire.

For Dolfi, finding a job had been just a matter of showing up. Young men with all their limbs and senses intact were the rarest of all commodities. Within two days he had found work as a roofer. No denazification was necessary. If a young man wanted to risk his neck crawling on top of the shattered city roofs, his former or present political inclinations were of little interest to anyone.

A teacher was a different matter altogether. I had to undergo, together with the vast majority of the population, the all-embracing, wondrous process of denazification.

America's civil service apparatus is small compared to that of most other nations. Although here, too, the government is the largest employer, it is much less pervading and powerful than in many other countries. If the government happens to be a dictatorship, its power is practically unlimited.

Unlike in communist countries, where party membership is a hard-earned privilege, the Nazi government expected its civil servants to join its ranks unquestioningly. Many did so willingly, either out of idealism or being career-oriented. Others chose to do so as the road of least resistance. They joined the party, paid their dues, and kept the party button (called "bon-bon" by the Berliners) in the drawer with their socks (for quick availability). Some escaped the heat or thought they could by joining small, less conspicuous organizations.

(Here I have to get something off my chest, irreverent and irrelevant as it might seem: In all the years of living under Hitler, I did not hear ordinary people saying "Jawohl" or "Heil Hitler" to each other as often as in a single Hollywood movie supposedly depicting life in Nazi Germany).

All members of any kind of organization, as well as anybody who had held a responsible job anywhere, could not return to work unless sifted, judged, and purified by the denazification process.

The core of the process was "*der Fragebogen*." The questionnaire was compiled and prepared with the understandable intention of separating the sheep from the goats. One hundred and thirty-one questions whose answers would be, to quote a prominent English newspaper at the time, "a window in that dark, sinister, skeleton-laden cupboard that is the German mind." Not a promising beginning. Nothing to build mutual trust on. The questionnaire, in fact, was a great deal more sinister than many of the people who had to fill it out.

There were such questions as:

"List any title of nobility ever held by you or your wife, or your or her grandparents."

"What religious preference did you give in the census of 1933?"

"Did you ever sever your connection with any church? Give detailed reasons for it."

"Any travel? When? Where? How long? Was the journey made at your expense? If not, who paid for it?"

"Name persons or organizations visited during those travels."

"List foreign languages you speak and indicate your fluency."

"Show the source and amounts of your annual income from January 1, 1933, to date (1945)."

"List on a separate sheet all titles and publishers of all publications from 1923 to the present, written whole or in part or compiled or edited by you."

"List all addresses, speeches, and talks given by you; list subjects, audiences, and dates."

"With the exception of Winterhilfe, have you ever given any contribution to any of the above listed organizations . . .?"

"Have you any relatives who held any rank or position in any of the 56 organizations listed above?"

Fifty-six organizations were named, the Party itself being Number 1, of course, down to nurses, funeral directors, and vacation clubs. Escaping all of them had been virtually impossible. We remembered or hoped to remember everything we had joined over the years, but relatives were a different matter. Which brother, aunt, or cousin had belonged to what organization was not often a shared knowledge.

Not the worst people balked at this ordeal. Can you imagine a U.S. citizen being compelled to account for every step taken, every political word uttered in public, during the last twenty years? It was the small-time Nazis, those who had made everybody's life miserable with their watching and snooping, who slipped through the "infallible" mesh of the questionnaire like smooth little eels, while stout anti-Nazis (like my mother, for instance) in turn agonized or hotly objected.

The majority of people, well primed by a twelve-year Nazi regimen to expect and suffer limitless invasions of privacy, sat down and meekly started scribbling in the answers and what they did not remember they made up. For them, as one astute allied observer remarked, "it was just one more affliction that, too, would pass."

Although it was an integrate part of German law before Hitler's time, none of my generation had ever heard the words "innocent until proven guilty." I had no idea that there were countries where this concept was the premise of a judicial system. We had been raised within the narrow confines of an absolute government, our political thinking at all times shadowed by the fears of the old Russian saying: "Before God and the Czar we are all guilty."

The questionnaire, which we were now facing, was simply a continuation of it.

The British were the first to realize the futility of the questionnaire procedure. Nobody but saints would emerge untainted when all the questions were answered. Very soon, the English authorities concentrated on two basic questions: "Were you a Nazi big shot?" and "Were you in the SS?" If the answer to both questions was "no," a stony-faced Englishman would hand out work permits. Never wasting time or smiles on the former enemy, the unspoken message was "Back to work, mister. Back to your post as subway conductor, bus driver, surgeon, pharmacist, teacher, traffic cop . . . We are not going to do your bloody jobs for you."

It was the Americans who wanted pure minds and pristine hands only, and of those there were precious few around. Saints had been turned into martyrs with an appalling efficiency in Nazi Germany.

Gradually, out of the population of Berlin, a certain elite began to crystallize. Those who lived in the American sector and worked in the English sector were the fortunate few who were a step and a half ahead of everybody else. They were the ones to be congratulated and envied. They were back at their jobs (English sector) and their ration cards would be honored at the proper date (American sector). The Americans were unfalteringly conscientious in every aspect of their administration. If this meant an interminable delay of work permits while processing the questionnaires, it also meant that the flour designated to their sector would be delivered to the bakeries punctually and at the right amount. Nobody claimed that this was one of the English authorities' priorities. The French were hungry themselves, and the Russians, as in all other affairs, marched to their own drummer.

Chapter 23

My mother always believed that our tenant, Roswitha Pritts, had taken her little silver sugar bowl. Forty years later, in her testament, when she designated her silver tea service to one of us, she wrote: ". . . all but the silver sugar bowl which was stolen by Fräulein Pritts."

Dolfi and I were never entirely convinced of it. Not that Fräulein Pritts was not as hardy and ruthless a survivor as the best of them. But when one stole in those days, one took firewood and bricks, an old stove pipe, a piece of rope, or maybe a head of cabbage if one could get away with it. Little silver sugar bowls were entirely useless. I doubt that she could have gotten as much as three slices of bread or one red apple for it.

The postwar years went through the cities of Germany like a barbed-wire broom. The laws of survival were harsh. They required qualities that were at once hard as nails and fluid as mercury. It meant to be resourceful and imaginative, to be cunning, tenacious, and watchful. It meant to be able to be at the grocery store within an hour of the arrival of the supply truck with valid food stamps in your hand, and never, never to be the last one in the bread line. It meant not to gulp down your food in one greedy meal, no matter how hungry you were, but to save some for a later, more desperate hour.

We were hungry now. Not the way you are hungry after a tennis game or a long hike and might rush to the ice box or the pantry shelf to look for a snack to tide you over until the next meal. There was no ice box and the pantry shelf was empty and covered with dust and crumbled plaster. Neither was there a planned next meal. Whenever our food stamps were called, we stood in line and hoped for the best. Whatever we took home was prepared and stretched over forty-eight hours, sometimes even three days, until the next food stamps were due. We would keep small chunks of bread in our pockets and break off a bite at a time, in the subway or at work or before going to bed at night. Hunger can keep you awake. It is a very real pain, a hot ache in the region of your stomach, and this burning and gnawing away at the stomach walls and innards was now with us most of the time.

Survival required that you keep moving to keep your circulation going in an unheated room when the temperature would drop below freezing for days at a time, until all you wanted to do was to crawl into a corner and die. Surviving—first and last—meant hanging on to a stubborn, childlike, unshakable faith that tomorrow or the next day or, perhaps, the spring after, the nightmare would end, the world would be brighter, and life, at long last, would be better, perhaps even joyful.

The very old and the very young, the timid and the very honorable, who possessed few or none of these requirements were badly off indeed. And when the second winter came around, which was the coldest winter of the decade, and the homes were still unheated, they were gone, swept away, having left a world that could not, and would not, sustain them.

Roswitha Pritts of the undetermined age and mysterious livelihood would not be swept away. She had been—no, she was, she told us—an actress, though presently without engagement. She was a slender woman of medium height; her face was unlined and of a smooth, pink complexion. I don't know what color her hair had been before the war did away with cosmetics and hair dye and tens of thousands of women turned gray overnight. Roswitha's hair was iron gray, long, strong and wavy; she often did not bother to put it up but let it flow freely over her shoulders and back. Her eyes were of a stark cornflower blue. She never smiled, but when she stood in the kitchen, her arms and eyes turned toward the ceiling to call on heaven to be her witness, I could see that her teeth were nice and even. I should add here that I never really knew to whom she was addressing herself up there, for she was an atheist and in the new democratic city government she was the Communist delegate of our district.

I believe that she hated us with all the frustrated fury of the dispossessed. There was nothing personal in this hate, at least in the beginning: we were young and seemingly healthy, we were members of the bourgeoisie and therefore the natural enemy of the working class, and we were the rightful owners of the place—a fact which we never brought up but she often did by her furious denial of it. Later on, after we had listened to her tirades with patience and forebearing and her hate threatened to run thin, she boosted it with more particular reasons. She hated us for using the kitchen and the bathroom, for having a higher food ration quota that she did, and for the sound of laughter that sometimes came from our room. Most of all, I think, she hated us for discovering who the mysterious visitors were whom she received at the door after nightfall and quickly led into her room. They would remain there for half an hour and then leave, as stealthily as they had come, often with a rolled-up paper or chart under their arm. For Fräulein Pritts, avowed disbeliever, card-carrying member of the Communist Party, and delegate to city hall, drew and read horoscopes for a living. She never admitted it, but she could never completely leave the stars out of her cheerless diatribes. They enabled her to prophesy dismal futures for her enemies.

Closing my eyes and letting my mind drift back to that fall and winter, I see myself standing in the dingy little kitchen with the chipped paint and boarded window, bending over the old stove that would give us cooking gas for precisely ninety minutes every day which had to be shared between the occupants of each apartment. Fräulein Pritts had finished her meal by then and it was my turn now. At our arrival I had found a single cookpot, a little brown thing with a tiny hole in its enameled bottom and in that I cooked all our meals. The pot kept leaking, a thin little drop at a time, which I would try to catch before it extinguished the gas flame underneath. This happened sometimes when I became too engrossed in Fräulein Pritts' performance. She would stand in the middle of the kitchen, wrapped in her dusky cocoon, her hair undulating around her shoulders, her arms gesticulating, her face turned toward the ceiling, and dark prophecies would flow from her mouth in her well-modulated actress voice. They all concerned her enemies, in which ranks Dolfi and I figured prominently. Strangely enough, though, her number one target was a young girl whom she had never seen and would never meet and who, most assuredly, knew nothing of this sinister Cassandra in the dreary little kitchen in far-away Berlin.

"Elizabeth of England," she would cry, "Ha! She fancies herself to be queen one day. I will tell you now in truth" (verily I say unto you?) "With an Elizabeth it began and with an Elizabeth it shall end!"

At other times her voice was more mellow, her face took on a trance-like expression and she almost sang toward the ceiling:

"He will come! He promised! He promised to come and take me away from my enemies and life will be beautiful again. You can laugh and sneer" (I never sneered, I was much too spellbound) "but I know what I know. One day he will come back and take me with him and you will all be left behind to rot."

I took my leaking pot and two plates into our room and sat down with Dolfi to eat.

"Did you hear her?" I whispered. "Who does she mean by that? Jesus? I thought she was a Communist?"

"Remarque," said Dolfi with his mouth full.

"Remark what?"

"Not what, who," Dolfi said, trying to chew and swallow more slowly. "Erich Maria Remarque; the guy who wrote *All Quiet on the Western Front*. She knew him before he left Germany. She says they were in love. You know how she makes things up."

While I was the fascinated recipient of most of Roswitha Pritts' fantasies and prophecies, Dolfi's dealings with her were more on the practical side. They negotiated over the endless stream of frictions which such unwilling togetherness is bound to produce. Consequently, she loathed him just a bit more than she did me. These negotiations usually took place through a crack of the door to her room. She never permitted either of us inside. During their arguments she was every bit as eloquent as in her kitchen performances.

"I don't understand it," Dolfi said, "she bawls me out but she never looks at me. She always looks into the corner behind her door. I don't know what it is about that corner, but the more she stares into it, the more grandly she carries on."

This was to remain the last of Roswitha Pritts' mysteries and was not solved for many months, not until the following winter when Dolfi mentioned it in one of his letters.

"I finally managed to take a quick step into her room," he wrote. "I had to find out what it was about that blasted corner that inspired her so. We should have guessed it. She has a large mirror there, hanging right behind the door."

There came one evening in late November that seemed to be different from the others. I was standing as usual at the stove, peering into the pot and wondering if adding more water to the stew would make any difference; Fräulein Pritts had not yet left the kitchen. She was sitting quietly at the kitchen table gazing dully at the cracked wall in front of her. This, of course, was rather unusual. I figured that she had, most likely, miscalculated her ration and had eaten very little that night. It happened to all of us. Her elbows were on the table, her face rested in her hands and she was whispering to herself. The words were familiar enough but the voice was different, small, lost, desolate.

"He promised! He promised he would come . . ."

She paid no attention to me and I turned to take a long look at her. What would she have been like — then . . .? Her long, wavy hair would have been blond and soft, her fine skin glowing with health and youth. Those startling blue eyes might have sparkled with joy of life instead of indignation. I had never seen her smile — she would have been very pretty, beautiful even, when she smiled. I had no idea what roles she had played in those days, but she certainly had known her way about in the world of artists and actors.

When she looked up I quickly turned back to the stove but I could not shake that vision. It was still occupying my mind when Dolfi and I were eating our watered down supper. Suddenly, an amazing thought struck me.

"You know what," I said to my brother, who quite obviously didn't know and was unprepared for what was coming.

"I believe her. I don't think she is making it up."

We were always suspect in Fräulein Pritts' eyes. Just how suspect I found out rather unexpectedly one winter night when Dolfi and I were entertaining a few guests. Entertaining at that time meant sitting on the beds wrapped in our winter coats and blankets and talking up a storm. Nobody expected to be served food or drink. Talk was enough. I remember that one of our guests had suggested we try a seance or a table knocking. None of us had ever been present at one, but we knew it involved the touching of hands. This meant we had to get our hands unwrapped and after a while they turned blue and stiff and that was the end of that. The seance was broken up prematurely and the hands speedily returned under the blankets.

Dolfi got up and began walking around the room, edging ever closer to the door. There was nothing unusual in this; stomping about was one of the ways to keep warm. We were still giggling about the aborted seance when Dolfi suddenly pulled the door open and in tumbled Fräulein Pritts.

She had been crouched against the door, listening at the keyhole. Nobody laughed; Dolfi looked like a magician who had finally managed to pull the rabbit out of his hat, and the rest of us were much too surprised to do anything at all. Fräulein Pritts scrambled off the floor, gathered her robe around her and walked out with as much dignity as she could muster. I honestly don't know what she expected to hear. The era of political spying and denouncing was over; it had come to a fiery and horrendous end. We, the young generation, raw newcomers to the concept of democracy, were to be introduced to a new political scene. Wasn't Fräulein Pritts an elected member of this new democratic body that was to be our teacher and guide? This definitely did not include listening at keyholes.

It is true that the political joke, the black humor of the underdog, was emerging from under the rubble, alive and well, and peering irreverently at the powers that be. But that was to be part of the freedom of speech that we were being taught, not a criminal offense.

I wonder if she was not drawn to the keyhole simply by the sound of cheerful voices. She knew we were as hungry and cold as she was; where, then, did the cheerfulness come from? What was the reason for the laughter?

She never forgave Dolfi for this incident. She bided her time. And when she caught and tripped him at last, it was with all the penned up vengeance of many months of waiting. She caught him in the only possible trap: hunger. After I had left Berlin, the temptation to hang on for awhile to my food stamps was too much for him; he took the double ration cards that were handed to him, without protest. On the day she was sure of it, Roswitha Pritts denounced him to the authorities. There, now, was an offense to be severely punished. He was told that the illegal food stamps had to be paid back; a certain amount would be deducted from his own ration every month, which would leave him with precisely enough to starve slowly. There seemed to be no choice but to give up his studies and his job and return to the little town in Thuringia. But where there is a dilemma, there is a solution; not for nothing was he Lucie's son. He found his way to a Catholic hospital and told the nuns the whole story. And without fuss or conditions, these good women fed the grateful young culprit one warm meal a day from the meager scraps of their kitchen. It was enough to keep him alive and going until his full rations were restored.

Once I inquired about Fräulein Pritts in one of my letters to my brother. It was during the second winter after the war, the one that was said to be the coldest in people's memory, and there was no heat yet in any of the houses in Berlin. Fräulein Pritts had grown very quiet, Dolfi wrote, and he did not see her very often. But once in awhile, at night, he could hear muffled sobbing coming from her room.

Chapter 24

The Baroness von Benturnet had been persuaded to come out of retirement to open up and head one of the city's larger elementary schools for
girls. It was her duty, a desperate city administration told her, to help those
children get back to school.

Adelhaide von Benturnet knew all about duty and honor. Descendant
of French Huguenot and Prussian aristocracy, she had absorbed those two
chilly virtues with her mother's milk. Perhaps that was why her blood ran
so blue in the fine veins under the white skin of her temples and why she
never had to lower her steely blue eyes before anybody. She had been the
headmistress of elementary schools for many years and had gone into retirement before the government's invitation to its civil servants to join the party
had turned into relentless pressure.

Staffing a school in the summer of 1945 was not easy. The school administration appealed to other retired women teachers and searched the
city eagerly for young people like myself, who had a good educational background and had never held membership in a major organization. Lacking
entirely was the age group in between. All the active teachers had been
dismissed by the occupation forces and were now undergoing the snail-
paced denazification process. (It would be years before Eagle-Eye Arns,
our peerless village school teacher, would be reinstated.) The children
could not wait that long.

I had two interviews before I started my teaching job. The first one
had been with the district superintendent of schools, a former school administrator who had been, like the baroness, coaxed out of retirement. The
old gentlemen was delighted to meet the daughter of one of his favorite
authors. Walking back and forth the length of his office, he shot questions

at me, waved his arms and pulled at his thin, gray hair describing the sorry education situation. At the end of the interview he designated a school for me, shook my hand, and sent me on my way, accompanied by an enthusiastic note addressed to my future headmistress.

My second interview was with Fräulein von Benturnet. She must have been close to seventy at the time, serene, fine-featured and slightly intimidating. The same might be said of her interview with me. I handed her the letter; she invited me to sit while she read it without a single change of expression. After I knew her better I blushed to think how inappropriate she must have considered her superior's enthusiasm prompted by my father's name. But if she disapproved of this sort of partiality, at least she did not hold it against me. Adelhaide von Benturnet was nothing if not fair. She talked objectively and to the point. Under the guidance of a mentor I would teach a fifth grade class, self-contained, all subjects except music, art, and gym, which were not yet on any curriculum. My mentor would be one of the older teachers who carried a full teaching load herself but would try to attend some of my classes. As often as possible I was to sit in on my mentor's lessons. To free the young teachers to do so, the Baroness herself would take over one of our classes at times. There was an unfortunate lack of books, paper, and pencils; utmost economy was recommended. A full lesson plan for the day was to be submitted in writing to my mentor as well as a follow-up report on each hour: did the lesson go as planned? If not, state the reasons.

The interview closed, she led me through the empty halls to my future classroom. With measured friendliness she introduced me to the children as their new teacher, and—without wasting any time on a word of cheer or admonition—she left us to each other. Twenty-eight pairs of eyes were gazing at me in silent expectation. No preparation, no experience, no angel from heaven rushed to my aid. It was sink or swim: ready . . . set . . . *teach*!

"Good morning," I said, my valiant attempt at cheerfulness sounding more breathless than breezy in my own ears, "Why don't we start by you coming forward, one at a time, and writing your name on the blackboard for me."

I still think of my class, my fifth graders (who would now be all married, middle-aged women) with a great deal of affection and gratitude. In no time at all we were a team. It would be years yet before it became the vogue for students to look poker faced and bored, before it was considered "not cool" to volunteer for an answer. Those girls were with me from day one. They saw me through the uncertainty of the first hour and through the exhausting first week. They helped me through harrowing arithmetic lessons when a few of them grasped the problems quicker than I did. And they were on my side, in a body, when the last two benches were occupied by a silent, unsmiling evaluation committee.

Without this small army of true-blue friends it would have been heavy going for us young teachers. More than half of the faculty was the age of our grandmothers, but there was nothing grandmotherly about them: gray-haired spinster ladies, every one of them, teachers of the old school, correct, polite, distant. There was never a joke, an encouraging word, a friendly arm around our shoulders. Missing completely was the mother generation, the women closer to our age, who might have had some memory of their own frustrating first months in a classroom.

My mentor was one of those women whose hair, skin, eyes, and rimless spectacles were all of the same color. She was a superb teacher; sitting in one of her classes was an inspiring experience. She never rushed the children—she guided them slowly, methodically, patiently—yet her lessons never dragged. Each lesson plan was a marvel. It never seemed a minute too long or a breath too short. My own lesson plans were only slightly short of disastrous. Either they were not long enough and I would find myself with my prepared material exhausted and seven interminable minutes to go, or, more often, I got so side-tracked that by the time the bell rang we were not even three-quarters of the way through the projected outline.

None of the older teachers ever pointed out the fact that there were forty years of experience separating us which could not be bridged in two months. When my mentor sat in on my classes, I was so nervous that my hand trembled when I used the blackboard. At the end of the hour, just before the bell rang, she quietly rose and left the room. This was neither a positive nor a negative sign; it was simply protocol. She would hand in a written report to the headmistress, who would call me into the office if the report warranted it. I knew that, yet I never got used to these silent departures.

When I finally was called into the office, it was not for my deplorable lesson plans.

Two of my students, lively, likeable ten-year-olds, came to my desk after class one day. Their mothers were taking them to a children's theater matinee that Sunday; they said they had asked their mothers to get an extra ticket for their teacher. Would I please—"oh, please"—come with them and their moms to the theater? I said I would be delighted. I loved my class; I was hourly, daily, struggling to do right by them; any show of trust and affection was manna from heaven.

That it would be a trip to the theater was an additional bonus. Most of the theater buildings had been destroyed. A few of the undamaged ones were off-limits. But Berlin without theater was unthinkable; the population thought so, the actors thought so, the directors thought so. In large basements makeshift stages had been erected; benches were grouped around them in semi-circles. (It was discovered that Shakespeare's dramas were ideally suited for this improvisation since he had written his plays for just such a setting.) That Sunday morning I met the girls and their mothers in the city and I remember the day as a happy, harmonious outing.

Two days later I was called to the office for the first time since my arrival at the school. The Baroness was sitting behind her desk, straight as a rod, outwardly calm, but her face boded no good. She did not invite me to sit down.

"Did you accept an invitation to the theater by one or more of your pupils?" The steely blue eyes bored into my face.

"Yes." For some inexplicable reason my heart started pounding.

"Did you pay for your own ticket?"

"No, their mothers had gotten the tickets and . . ."

"How dare you accept such an invitation!"

I was dumfounded. Rarely, if ever, had I been face to face with such deep, controlled anger.

"Why? Why should I not have gone with them?" I was completely at sea.

She got up and walked to the window, turning her back on me. The silence was terrible. It seemed to indicate the enormity of the transgression of which I was still ignorant.

Then Adelhaide von Benturnet turned around and spelled out for me one of the basic rules of Prussian-Huguenot ethics.

"By accepting this invitation—an invitation, gift, or favor of any kind—you indebted yourself to the student. If the child's grade in any subject might be in question—might, in an extreme case, lie between passing and failing—this indebtedness would undoubtedly influence you. It might, in fact, consciously or subconsciously, become the deciding factor."

I could see her point; I understood what she was saying. But I felt I had to make one small attempt in my defense.

"Those were my two best students . . ."

A withering look from behind the desk stopped me.

"That has nothing at all to do with it," said the Baroness.

The faculty room was about as jolly as a third-class waiting room in the outskirts of Berlin. The impression was reinforced by the fact that we now kept our winter coats on all through the day. When the headmistress entered the room one particular November morning her face was brighter than usual, she had exciting news for us. The Americans had initiated a school feeding program for children, she told us. Every noon, a mobile soup kitchen would come around; the hot soup would be delivered in large containers. Each child would be supplied with a bowl and spoon and, room by room, they would line up and be given a bowlful of soup. The teachers would take turns supervising the children and ladling out the soup. However — the Baroness' voice was cool and unemotional — no teacher was to partake in this meal. The authorities had been very explicit on this point. "Not a single spoonful," said the Baroness. A teacher breaking this rule would be severely reprimanded or even dismissed.

She turned to go, stopped, and faced us once more.

"Not only would the teacher suffer the consequences of breaking the rule," she said, "but if the American authorities would learn of this infringement, the entire school feeding program would be endangered."

Having thus marshalled forth those two battered vigilantes, duty and honor, in every faltering conscience around her, she departed, leaving us wrapped in our coats in a room that seemed rather colder than before.

Doing soup kitchen duty became the most dreaded task of the week. Homer's gods knew what they were doing when they condemned Tantalus, an offending mortal, not only to be imprisoned without food or drink in all eternity but to be chained within the sight, sounds, and smells of their own dining feasts. There wasn't a teacher among us who was not going through purgatory, bending over the kettle for an hour, breathing in the warm savory smell of the soup while ladling it out to two hundred children.

* * * * * * * * * * * * *

When my brothers and I dissolved my mother's Berliner household some forty years later, one of us pulled from the depth of an ancient cabinet an amber-colored glass bowl and Dolfi's eyes met mine with a smile of sudden recognition. The bowl was meant for desserts or fruit and my mother, not anticipating much of either, had left it behind when she moved to Thuringia. I much preferred it to the leaky pot when serving or storing food.

We both had come home late that day—the day we both remembered looking at the amber bowl—Dolfi had begun evening classes at law school and I had to attend seminars three days a week after school hours. Either for that reason or else because I had miscalculated our rations, there was no food in the house. There had been a slice of bread in the morning and not much on the day before.

"There's got to be *something*," said Dolfi, wildly opening drawers and cabinet doors, "anything at all. Aren't there some old canisters around from before we moved? We might be able to scrape something from the bottom."

We did, at long last, find a tin box filled with grayish-white powder. I cautiously tasted it with the tip of my finger.

"Starch," I said, tentatively.

"Can one eat it?"

"Well, it's not poisonous, if that's what you mean. It's used to thicken stuff."

"Good!" Dolfi said, his face lighting up. "Just thicken water."

I filled the cookpot with water and when it boiled I began to stir in the starch. A glassy mass evolved. It occurred to me that, if I would stir in some of the brown grind that passed for ersatzkaffee, it might at least not look quite so disgustingly like the stuff we used to starch collars and cuffs with in the old days. In a cracked little egg cup I had seen a few ancient saccharin tablets and those, too, I dropped into the pot. Then I poured the thick, brown mass into the amber glass bowl. It soon cooled and jelled in the unheated room. Dolfi drew a line with his spoon through the middle of the bowl. "Half yours, half mine," he said. Holding our plates close to the bowl, we balanced some of the wiggly stuff onto them. I swallowed the first spoonful quickly and the second before I had time to think of the taste of the first one.

There was no warning nausea, not even time to say "Yakh!" My stomach acted all on its own. It contracted with such sudden fury that the glutinous mass shot back up into my throat.

I clamped my hands over my mouth and ran out of the room. As I bent over the toilet bowl, my stomach now was in full revolt, heaving with painful contractions that forced me on my knees onto the floor. Eventually it brought up burning gall that drove tears into my eyes. I don't remember how long it took until I regained control over my protesting insides. I rubbed the cold sweat off my face, rinsed my hands and returned to our room. My eyes were red-rimmed and I was shaking. Dolfi was still sitting where I had left him. The amber bowl in front of him was half empty.

"Do you want your half?" he asked, trying to sound uninterested. When my hand flew to my mouth in wordless response, he gulped down the rest.

With nothing more in my stomach than the night before, I went to work the next morning. And with something bordering on total panic I saw my name on the list for the soup kitchen that day.

* * * * * * * * * * * * * *

The evaluation committee descended upon me and my fifth graders unexpectedly. The rule said that twenty-four hour notice had to be given to the teacher. " . . . but," said the Baroness, "I should like you to waive this rule. The committee has arrived and Fräulein M., who is scheduled, is ill. The committee will take into consideration that you will teach without previous notification." I'll just bet, I thought grimly. However, there was nothing to be done but politely consent.

I had precisely two minutes to prepare my students.

"Those people, who will be sitting in the back of the room, will be here to see how you and I are doing," I told them. "Do your best, girls. Don't let me down."

And then the troops filed in.

My lesson plan was not applicable since it was to have been mostly written work. I had to improvise. I chose a poem, a golden oldie of my own and my parents' school years. It talked about *"Heinzelmaennchen,"* benign little house elves who, long ago, used to come in the night to help the poor people finish their work. They went to the aid of the cobbler, the tailor, the baker, and the wine cooper. It was a wonderfully long poem and the children had never heard of it. So we went through each verse, each trade together.

"Have you ever wondered how a loaf of bread is made? A pair of shoes?" Those were war children in front of me and the questions were not simply rhetoric.

The lesson was lively; there were questions, answers, and an eager show of hands. Experiences were remembered and recounted. The hour flew by.

Within a week any audited teacher was called before the headmistress and handed a written evaluation to be signed — or not signed — by her. Written objection to a bad evaluation was permitted and a hearing would be granted to the teacher.

Inscrutable as always, the Baroness handed me my evaluation. However, I had been invited to sit. Somewhere, at the bottom of an old chest, I still have the paper, yellowed and brittle by now; it had been given to me when I left with the rest of the documents.

"The committee is aware that it observed an inspired teacher," it said. "She carried her students with her with an enthusiasm that was quite obviously contagious . . . Although there seemed to be a certain lack of structure, neither the children nor the teacher seemed to be put off by this . . . She has to be careful not to be carried away to the point where . . . she answers her own questions . . . When the bell rang at the end of the lesson, a distinct *'Ooch, schade'* (Aw, shucks) was heard from some of the children. The committee thinks this worth mentioning since this was a unique experience for each one of its members."

I did not dare look up from the paper. I was so happy, I could have bawled.

"Do you wish to object?" asked the Baroness.

"No. Oh, no!"

"Then sign, please. Well," said the Baroness not unkindly, "we will have to do something about this."

What was she talking about?

"Your mentor, also, has complained about the lack of structure in your lesson plans. I have decided to transfer you to our special class of second graders, the slow learners. It will necessitate more meticulous lesson preparations."

And so, on the following Monday I walked down the long musty corridor to the last and darkest of the rooms where twenty slow learners were fatalistically awaiting the arrival of yet another new teacher. They did not think their classroom particularly gloomy; their homes were more dreary than this. None of the children had a father living at home. Some of the men had been killed, some were prisoners-of-war and some missing in action. They lived with their mothers or grandmothers or with people of whom they were not sure who they were. They believed everything I said. If I had told them that it had been discovered that it was not the sun but the moon that was shining on us during the day, they would not have questioned it for a moment. They listened attentively, they copied diligently from the blackboard; they just had trouble remembering. Nobody at home had time to go over their homework with them. All the mothers worked; the grandmothers and "aunts" queued up at the grocery stores. Our school books were a mess. Since there had not been time to compile and print new "readers" for the beginners' classes, the old readers had been returned to the schools, dotted with blobs of printer's ink. "Inflammatory" words like soldier, flag, marching, fatherland, victory, future, and honor had been blocked out. Often I could not even guess what had been under the black smear.

Some of the little girls were chatty, some had become so introverted that they never spoke at all. It was one of those withdrawn ones that was standing beside my desk one day, obedient, unresponsive, while I was trying to explain a simple sentence to her which she was to write on the blackboard. Her eyes never left my face, but there was no flicker of comprehension in them. I am not getting through to her, I thought; I can't waste all that time on a single little waif from another planet who refuses to join us here in the real world.

"Sit down, child," I wanted to say. Instead I said, "Would you like to sit on my lap?"

The girl became electrified, then rigid. Her eyes widened.

An almost inaudible "Yes."

I lifted her up on my lap, put my arms around her and felt the tense little frame relax against my body. Her head rested in the hollow of my neck; her hair smelled pathetically of dust and musty linen; at the same time there was a scent of very young children about her.

Nineteen pairs of eyes gazed at us in hushed wonderment. Abstractedly rocking the child, my eyes scanned the lesson plan on my desk; we were already limping hopelessly behind schedule. I was to explain each unexpected delay, each crack in the structure of the lesson plan, in my follow-up report, and I was wondering how this turn of events would look to my mentor. Well, I would think of something. I rocked her a while longer then I gave her a little goodbye squeeze, slipped her off my lap, and turned her in the direction of her seat.

"Me, too," said a small voice from the other side of my desk.

"Me, too," echoed half a dozen voices all through the room. I was about to get a first-hand lesson in the hazards of setting precedents.

There was no way out; perhaps I didn't even look for one. I got better at organizing those hugging sessions than I ever did at doing lesson plans. At least once a week, each child got a turn sitting on my lap, unhurried and as long as was needed. Although nobody ever entered the classroom unannounced, I never lost a feeling of panic when I heard steps echoing along the hallway. The vision of the headmistress opening the door and finding one of her teachers hugging and rocking a child on her lap made my hair stand on end.

* * * * * * * * * * * * * *

The two-hundredth anniversary of the birth of Pestalozzi, the great Swiss educational reformer, fell into that winter. The schools were ordered to celebrate this event. The headmistress told the teachers that each class was to contribute something toward the celebration: a skit, a song, a reading—it was left to the teacher. I could not think of anything my slow learners might successfully present. The whole thing kept slipping my mind; there seemed to be lots of time to worry about it. And suddenly it was almost upon us and we had nothing to offer.

So a few nights before the great event I sat at the table in our room, bundled in newspaper and blankets to the tip of my nose—even the ink in the inkwell was frozen that night—and tried my hand at a poem. If my children were to understand and recite it, it had to be done in the simplest possible terms: artless, plain, but not moronic.

Dolfi kept stomping around the room, slapping his arms, asking questions and being sociable, all in the pursuit of keeping warm. I yelled at him to be quiet. We sometimes got on each other's nerves like that.

"Good grief," he growled, "what's the matter with you? It's just a stupid little poem, not a matter of life and death."

"That's easy for you to say," I said miserably, "You are not unstructured. I've got to get this done. I don't know how I am going to pound this into their heads, anyway."

In the end I managed by selecting eight undaunted little girls, giving them two lines each, and, by standing behind them, smiling brightly at the audience and poking an invisible finger into the back of each child as her turn came, they all spoke on cue.

It was about three months later when I was called for a third time into the front office. The Baroness looked more animated than I had ever seen her.

"Your Pestalozzi poem has been accepted for publication in the new "readers" for the elementary schools of Berlin," she said. "Our school and you will be given credit." She was smiling now. "I congratulate you."

"Thank you, Fräulein von Benturnet," I said. Since there seemed to be nothing more to add, I returned to my class. Our headmistress had never shared either joy or grief with us, and I knew of no way now to share my elation with her.

Chapter 25

In November I wrote a letter to the lieutenant. The words I used were
as simple and straightforward as I could manage in a foreign language. But
there was nothing simple about either the writing or the mailing of the letter and it took most of the month to accomplish this. I had only a few free
hours during the week and then I was not always ready to pick up paper
and pen. Sometimes the cold seemed to numb not only my fingers but the
process of thinking as well. My written English was precarious, and often,
laboring over a sentence structure, the seeming futility of writing the letter at all would overwhelm me. I did not know where the lieutenant was.
Had he been sent to the Far East? If so, had he survived the last days of
the war? How was I to mail the letter once it was written? He had given
me his home address; if, indeed, the letter ever got there, would not his
relatives take exception and refuse to forward it? And if, against all odds,
it did reach the lieutenant, how would he receive it? Would he hastily, joyfully tear it open, or would he push it aside for a while, postponing the
opening, dreading a little what it might say? The bond between us that had
appeared so indestructible under the blue summer sky in Thuringia seemed
very fragile now, many months later, in the chilly, dark room in Berlin.

I was staunchly resolved that there was to be no complaining. Since
almost anything I could say about our daily living might be construed as
complaint or reproach, I would steer clear of details. I would take nothing in our relationship for granted, presume nothing; there would be no
reference to our last meeting. He was to have all the room needed to
withdraw honorably behind the lines of a cordial friendship. I talked of my
work in school and of the children, of Dolfi's roofing experiences and of
our resident Communist who read the stars. In the end the letter sounded

so carefully phrased and distant that I tore it up and wrote a warmer, more personal one. "I miss you," I wrote at the bottom of the page, and, thinking it too compelling, I tore that one up, too. "I missed you after you left," I wrote instead.

The letter, closed and addressed, remained in my coat pocket for many days. Mailing it presented another almost unsurmountable obstacle. There was still no mail service in Germany. I would have to trust an American soldier to forward it. Approaching a soldier with this request would not be very difficult. On the contrary, on weekends or during early evening hours one could find a group of hopeful uniforms on every second or third street corner doing their winsome best to strike up an acquaintance with a German girl.

"Fräulein, wo gehst du?" and "Fräulein, willst du Nylon?" were the opening lines well known to every young woman in the American sector. Everyone of those amiable, underaged, would-be Sybarites might have been delighted to have me walk up to him with my letter. If nothing else, the letter would be his contribution to the general entertainment of his barrack room that night. Neither could I approach the few rather forbidding looking officers who came from time to time to check on the school feedings. (I could just imagine the headmistress's face!)

My chance came one day while I was riding home from work. An American officer, after studying the subway map in vain, turned to me to ask for directions. He looked like everybody's favorite biology teacher, and his tone was neither brusque nor condescending. He addressed me in English and with a matter-of-fact politeness which indicated that he considered me a human being quite on the same level as himself. (It sounds strange now even to me, but the fact is that during this first year after the war, a member of an occupation force addressing a German in an unaffected, civilized manner was as rare as lightning in January.) I showed him his station on the map and he thanked me. With a sudden, frantic resolve, I pulled the letter out of my coat pocket and asked him to mail it.

The letter looked worn and wrinkled and, after glancing at the address, the officer gave me a quick questioning look under which I felt my face turn brick red. "Please, God," I thought, "let him understand that this lieutenant would not have given this girl his address unless he *wanted* her to write to him."

The letter disappeared in the pocket of the uniform.

"All right," said the officer. And then my station came and we were separated. Once again, it was in the hands of destiny.

* * * * * * * * * * * * * *

My mother had given us a list of friends who had lived in Berlin and whose fate she was anxious to know. Public transportation was far from being restored to its pre-war level, and between working and studying we seldom found time enough to hike to distant parts of the city in search of vanished streets and people. The first person we successfully located was our old midwife who had delivered my brothers and me and whom my mother credited with saving her life on at least one occasion. I knew her as a plump, energetic woman with straight, coal-black hair. (My mother used to speculate after each visit whether she had kept her youthful color or simply dyed it.) The woman who opened the door was thinner and her hair was snow white, but she had retained some of her old forcefulness of manner. We identified ourselves and she greeted us with cautious pleasure. There was always an element of anxiety, a secret, unabashed fear of added burden and responsibility when friends tumbled on to each other in those post-war days. Behind her a baby, bundled up like a tiny Eskimo, was crawling over the bare floor, and through the open kitchen door I could see her husband, who had lost a leg, propped up in a chair near the stove. She did not ask us in and we did not expect it. We would be able to report to my mother at Christmas that they were alive and had a roof over their heads.

On a cool, clear Sunday morning we set out to find an elderly couple named Diefenbach, who had been friends of my father's and were of his generation. They had been frequent guests in our house before the war. Herr Diefenbach, a dignified, patriarchal figure, was what used to be called "a man of letters." Writer, editor, journalist, his life had been spent with and around the printed word. Frau Diefenbach I remembered as a small, doll-like, pink woman with an abundance of white curls and very firm opinions on a great many unimportant matters. On larger issues she demurely deferred to her husband. He would discourse in his precise, knowledgeable manner, thought cumbersome only by the young and impatient, while his wife's black squirrel eyes flitted from face to face, demanding silence, exacting loyalty. At the end of the lecture, the faintly triumphant smile on her pursed little mouth always seemed to say "Now then, wasn't that amazing, my dears?"

They lived in a fashionable part of Berlin, near the Kurfuerstendamm, but on that morning we were not able to find their street. Too many landmarks and street signs were gone, and though we knew they lived in one of the streets leading off the avenue, we had to concede that we were thoroughly disoriented.

We were standing at a street corner wondering if we should abandon the search or give it another hour when we saw a young woman walking toward us. She walked unhurriedly, entirely at ease in her surroundings, and she certainly looked as if she belonged there. Her blond hair was short-cropped and covered with a tilted little beret. She wore a brightly colored scarf, tied with great flair, and her full lips were painted a glossy red. In spite of her coat, which was shabby and rather thin, there was an undeniable elegance about her. She reminded me of all the young women—long-legged, beautiful, self-assured—who had strolled down the Kurfuerstendamm so many years ago, before fire and ashes had rained from the sky, changing the face of the city forever.

If anybody would know her way around the Kurfuerstendamm it would be this graceful young creature. Her voice was as pleasant as her smile: no, she did not know exactly which street was the one we wanted, but she would help us look for it. She had been walking like one who was expecting to meet someone but without any great urgency, and now she abandoned whatever plans she had with complete unconcern.

Eventually we located the street and the house. We thanked her and went inside. The house was in bad shape, but by now it was only a matter of the degree of the damage which either shocked or left one indifferent. We quite expected broken stairs, cracked ceilings and boarded windows.

The tarnished brass plaque over the bell still said "Diefenbach," but the bell handle was rusted and would not move. The front door was un-latched and after a moment's hesitation we walked in. The hall was dark and had the pungent cold odor of an abandoned smoke house. The door to the living room was gone. We first thought that the room was empty, but a slight movement on the left caught our attention. In a deep armchair near the window a small, pointed face, framed by untidy white curls, peeked out of a mass of cushions. Two small, bluish claw-like hands seemed to be either playing or praying with a strand of beads which lay on the blanket that covered the rest of her. Dolfi and I went around the chair so that the light of the unboarded windowpane fell on our faces. There we stood, smiling brightly, horribly ill at ease, and wishing that the visit was done and over with.

"Frau Diefenbach, do you remember us?" She looked up without a flicker of recognition in her sunken eyes. Her voice was like cracked crystal.

"Yes, I remember you."

There are situations when pleasant phrases like "How are you?" or "Is there anything we can do?" take on such staggering proportions of phoniness that they simply get stuck in one's throat. Being robbed of all the usual means of social amenities, we were at a loss of how to proceed. Frau Diefenbach herself released us from our discomfort.

"Would you want to see my husband? He is over there . . . yes, just go in . . ." The bluish fingers went on playing with the beads.

We went to the door and walked into what must have been a study at one time. Crumbled plaster, smoke-stained sheets and general dirt covered stacks of books and papers. Stretched out on a daybed was the figure of a man, hidden under a short plaid travel rug. It took Dolfi and me only seconds to realize that this waxen face, covered with sparse gray stubble, that showed above the rug, belonged to a man who had been dead for more than a day or two.

"What are we going to do, Dolfi?!"

"What can we do?" he muttered.

We forced ourselves to remain in the room for a minute to make our retreat look less like flight. Again, Frau Diefenbach came to our rescue.

"It was nice of you to come," she said in her thin, cracked, lady-like voice. "Please tell your mother that Wilhelm is dead. He starved, you know," she added quite matter-of-factly. With this she ceased to take any further notice of us. The faint, hard click of the beads followed us through the door when we left.

"Course, he starved," said the concierge whom we had persuaded to stick her head out of her basement apartment. "He always made her eat whatever there was. Not that there was much to begin with."

"Yeah, yeah," she said in answer to our question. "They know. We reported it. They will come and get him when it's his turn. It's cold enough that another day won't make that much difference." And when we still hesitated she said impatiently "I do her shopping. She don't move out of that chair hardly long enough to get to the kitchen."

The girl was still there when we came out of the house squinting against the blue sky and the wintry sun that slanted over the roof tops.

"It was bad?" she said, studying our faces. "I am so sorry."

We turned toward home and she fell in step with us. She was almost as tall as my brother. As she walked beside us she talked. Her voice was agreeable to the ear; everything about her was unhurried and graceful. Her name was Rita, she told us, Rita Miranoff. She would soon be twenty-one.

She lived with her grandmother, who was part Russian, in a large apartment near the Kurfuerstendamm. There were many beautiful antiques in the apartment. No, her grandmother had never left the city; she had been fortunate, very little had been damaged.

"Tell me about yourselves," she said, and she listened with a naive and disarming curiosity. It took over an hour to get home and she walked the entire way with us. We did not know what to make of this, but she showed no signs of embarrassment.

"Goodbye," she said, smiling, at the front door. "Aufwiedersehen. It was fun, wasn't it." It had gotten chilly and she tucked her scarf closer around her neck but gave no other indication of being cold.

"Grandma must have connections," I said as we climbed up the steps to our apartment. "The lipstick! And the scarf was brand new."

"I wonder," Dolfi said, but did not elaborate.

"Well, it would make more sense if Grandma's connections would come up with a warmer winter coat," I said. "That coat was too thin. She was cold."

And then we forgot about her.

A week later I answered the doorbell to find Rita standing outside in the hall, smiling, the generous mouth painted bright red, the short blond hair windblown.

"Would you like to go for a walk?" she said.

It was cloudy but warmer than the previous Sunday and the three of us walked west toward the suburbs.

"My aunt has friends visiting," Rita said, "so I thought I would visit with you for a while."

"I thought you lived with your grandmother?"

"Well . . . yes . . . but my grandmother speaks only Hungarian and so my aunt comes over quite often to help her."

"Isn't your grandmother Russian?"

"Oh, they all speak a lot of languages," she said lightly.

"But . . ." I opened my mouth. A quick poke in the ribs by my brother stopped me.

Our walk was brisk and short this time; both Dolfi and I had a lot of work waiting for us. Again she saw us back to the door and walked off toward—I hoped—the subway station. This time I could not put her out of my mind so quickly. Something about that bright, pleasant creature had begun to be faintly worrisome.

The weather turned bad that week; the air was clammy, cold, and there had been showers of freezing rain. When Dolfi answered the ring one evening he found Rita, looking wet and bedraggled. She wore the same thin coat and her hair under the little beret was dark with moisture. She smiled at him in her usual manner but could barely suppress a shiver. Dolfi brought her into the kitchen where I was busy stirring the soup of the day.

"I hadn't seen you for a while," she said. Her lips were bluish around the red paint. Dolfi offered her a chair and I peered into the cookpot and hardened my heart. This was our first warm meal that day and the soup was all we had. She had no business coming at that hour. Nobody who wore glossy red lipstick and a brand new silk scarf and lived with a Hungarian Russian grandmother in the midst of undamaged antiques should expect to be invited to a meal.

The soup having been stirred more than sufficiently and Rita still sitting on the kitchen chair, I set out two plates and two spoons.

"You don't mind if we eat, Rita? It's fairly late."

"Oh, no." the girl said hurriedly, "Please eat. I have already eaten."

We both knew instantly that she was lying. I knew Dolfi felt as awful as I did from the slow way he picked up his spoon and looked at his plate. Usually he fell upon his food like a derailed engine.

"Would you like to have some soup, Rita?" It was not easy to wring this out of me.

"Maybe just a little."

Dolfi jumped up and got a plate and spoon. Slowly Rita pulled her chair up to the table while I spooned about a third of Dolfi's and my soup into her bowl. Slowly she filled the first spoon and her hand trembled so uncontrollably that part of it spilled back into the bowl.

"She hasn't eaten all day," I thought, defeated.

She made no attempt to leave and when she went to the bathroom a while later Dolfi and I looked at each other in wordless dismay.

"Let's find out who she is," Dolfi said resolutely. He picked up her handbag and opened it. Nobody dared walking the streets of Berlin without an official identification card.

"Oh, Lord!" he said and then he handed me the card across the table.

Her name was Margot Meier. She was sixteen years old. No permanent address was given.

We could hear the wind going through the bare Linden trees. Single icy raindrops were hitting the windowboards. Rita sat quietly on the kitchen chair while I rinsed the plates. Dolfi rattled around in the spoon drawer in helpless fury.

"Would you like to stay overnight, Rita? We don't really have a bed, just a cot without anything but . . ."

"Yes. I would like that. It doesn't matter about the cot . . ."

Dolfi covered the cot in the former living room with the coconut runners from his cot. "I'll cover myself with my coat," said the girl.

The wind and rain had died down. The temperature had fallen and the room was freezing. As always in nights like this, I could not feel my legs under the covers. Up to my ribs my skin was numb to the touch. Sometimes it took until two or three in the morning before I could wiggle my toes. The door between our room and the living room had lost its glass panes and through the bleak holes I could hear the girl's teeth chattering in the next room. If I was that cold under my blankets, what was it like under that thin coat of hers?

Restless, unhappy, I searched through my scanty knowledge of prostitutes. What dreadful diseases were they supposed to have some times? Could I fall sick just coming too close to her? Surely not if we were both fully clothed. I could not ask Dolfi who, presumably, knew more about these things than I, because she would have heard us.

"Rita?"

"Yes?" She was wide awake.

"Were you asleep?" I was stalling, wanting a few more seconds, a last chance to change my mind.

"No." Tense silence.

"Would you like to come in my bed?"

"Yes." She was off the cot, clutching her coat, finding her way along the wall to my couch.

"Let's put our heads on opposite ends. Put your coat on top of the blankets. Let's see how that works."

She snuggled down, pushing her cold feet against my back; my foot soles rested on hers.

"Good night, Rita."

"Good night."

Unexpectedly, warmth was creeping from her back into my feet, thawing my legs. Her feet against my shoulders ceased to feel like icicles. What an odd situation, how improbable that she should be sharing my bed with me. How many lies had she told us, this clever young woman . . . street-waif, driftwood . . . this forsaken child whose wandering feet rested so quietly now on my back that they seemed to have become part of my own body. She was sleeping; her deep, tranquil breathing was infectious. I had not been so warm in many nights. I began to sift through the jumble of her stories—had they really all been fabrications? But before I was past her grandmother's antiques I, too, was asleep.

We saw Rita a few more times but she never again came in the evening. Having found herself without a protector, with neither food nor shelter on that terrible winter night would have been a frightening lesson to her and she was careful never to let it happen again.

Chapter 26

All along our plan had been to go home for Christmas; home meaning Thuringia, Bertel, my mother, and the Rock Cellar. How we would get there would have to be decided on very short notice. Ostensibly gaining more freedom of movement, we saw new barriers cropping up around us over night like mushrooms after a summer rain. Those barriers were by no means uniform throughout the four occupied zones. As the contention between the occupational powers grew, so did the variety of restrictions, and to what degree these restrictions could be ignored or circumvented depended a great deal on individual courage and ingenuity.

Limited rail service had been reinstated. Westbound trains out of Berlin were run again by German railroad officials stoutly dedicated to reestablishing some kind of order into the system. Once a day a train left from the Russian sector of Berlin to Thuringia and tickets for it would have to be bought in advance. By the time we found out about this, only one vacancy was left. Dolfi, not unduly disturbed, announced that he would travel without the benefit of a ticket.

A picture of Bertel, taken on his first birthday, stood on the desk in our apartment. He had, on that occasion, looked with some doubt upon the photographer and so he looked at me, all through those weeks and months, uncertain and questioning, but I never looked at the picture without a feeling of peace and gratitude. In the north and east of Germany infant death was rampant. To know that Bertel was in good hands, that there were apples, carrots, a bowl of porridge and a piece of bread for him every day of the week, that he played in a warm room and slept in a proper bed, filled my heart with profound thankfulness.

Russia, according to the Yalta terms, had annexed East Prussia and a large chunk of Poland. Poland, in turn, had been compensated with the German provinces of Silesia and Pommern. The Poles, being evacuated from their own towns and villages, packed the German population by the thousands—without exception women, children, and old people—unceremoniously in the few available trains going west. The Russians were speedily dismantling German railroad tracks and shipping the iron trestles to Russia. There was little intercommunication as to which tracks were still intact and which were dismantled, and the refugee trains were often stalled for days on side tracks, awaiting orders to proceed. It was winter, there was no glass in the windows, and very few people had sufficient provisions. The first to die were always the youngest and the oldest in each group. Sometimes fellow travelers would force a half-crazed mother to throw her frozen baby out of the train after it had been dead for some days. Often the mothers would hide the fact that their child had died or else other passengers had given up caring. When those trains finally arrived in Berlin, American soldiers would open the door to find the dead and the half dead all slumped together on seats and floors. After some weeks, the Americans registered an official protest against the conditions of the refugee trains, but nobody accepted responsibility. These incidents were never reported in our new, democratic newspapers, but the knowledge of them could not be kept from the people. As with all other horror stories, I did not want to hear or think about it, but every time I looked at that puzzled face of my little boy I knew that going to Thuringia and leaving him behind there when I left had been the right thing to do.

As our travel date approached I became increasingly anxious. All the uncertainties I had pushed into the farthest corner of my mind surged suddenly into focus. How had they fared back there? Could I be so sure that everything had gone well?

The train had neither sufficient seats nor windowpanes nor anything else by way of comfort. It carried instead—as a first concession to restored law and order—an exceedingly gloomy-looking conductor who was grimly resolved to make the rounds through the congested aisles after each station stop. Dolfi and I sat on the floor boards of the narrow corridor, somewhat protected from the open air by the suitcases and huddled figures of fellow passengers. Every time the unlovely sight of our conductor appeared at the far end of the corridor Dolfi disappeared into the washroom where he would spend the next twenty minutes sitting on the broken toilet seat, having to contend not only with the broken window but with a great deal of wintry draft from below.

One painful detail of our otherwise joyful reunion is burned into my memory. My mother had loyally attempted to keep me alive in the memory of the child, and when she asked Bertel "Where is your Mama?" he ran past me and proudly pointed to a picture of me on my mother's desk. Disconcerted by the tears she saw filling my eyes, my mother hastily gathered him up and pushed him toward me, and I met the same puzzled stare that had looked at me out of the picture in Berlin all those months. Some faint memories though must have lingered in his mind, for he began to respond to my overtures within a very short time, and if I was not yet ahead in his affection of the two people nearest to him, my mother and my brother Wolfgang, I was, at least, speedily elevated to equal status.

At any other time the story of my oldest brother's homecoming would have been stark drama. In this extraordinary year it was but a fleeting episode involving few participants. Shortly after Dolfi and I had left for Berlin, a note had reached my mother, written by one of Wolfgang's colleagues, a young woman doctor. She wrote that he was dangerously ill in a hospital in Halle and that there was nothing they could do for him.

My mother left Bertel, the goat, and the chicken in the care of friends, stuffed a handful of cigars into her blouse, and set out with her bicycle toward the city on the Saale River. It's a long, mountainous road through the Thuringia Forest; I don't know how many days it took her or where she spent the nights. When she arrived in Halle she was not sure where to go. She made the rounds of the hospitals, demanding to see the patients list, wandering halls, and haunting the officials. When she was turned out she reappeared, and in the end she found my brother, thin, feverish, and helpless, mowed down by a rapidly spreading tuberculosis.

Producing black cigars seemingly out of nowhere, she secured a place in a truck bed and found blankets and provisions. She loaded my brother, her bicycle, and herself onto the truck and reached the Rock Cellar before nightfall. On the third floor where little Einfalt had once dwelled, she heaped quilts and blankets on a bed, and there my brother rested throughout the fall and winter months, the clear, cold mountain air streaming through the open window, while my mother roamed the countryside on daily food expeditions. Food now was of paramount importance, and she rarely returned empty-handed. Like a travelling gypsy she bargained, bartered, and coaxed and, if necessary, gathered a few fruits of the land without the assistance of a second consenting adult within sight or earshot. The slight quivering in her stomach had to be attributed to her (never conquered, middle-class) concern at being caught and not to any pangs of conscience. My mother's conscience, enviably sturdy and with a logic all of its own, came through these scouring excursions spotless as a newborn ewe; in fact, there was a certain grim satisfaction, a flicker of triumph in thus besting the rules, society, and fate itself, which, combined, had after all brought on her son's illness and deserved to be defied.

Wolfgang would come down during the day into the warmth of the room on the second floor to read and watch Bertel, but always, after some hours, he returned to his fresh air igloo on the third floor.

When I think of that particular Christmas of 1945 I have a mental picture of Wolfgang lying on the daybed in the family room; Bertel has spread his toys over the foot end of it. A single lamp is sparingly lighting the room, and the brown tile stove is crackling in the corner. A young man is sitting on a chair beside the bed, deep in conversation with my brother. His robust colors contrast sharply with the white, bony contours and deep shadows of my brother's face. The young man is the new village doctor and he comes sometimes in the evening to visit his sick colleague. He had no medication to offer — there being none — no advice or comfort; there is nothing this patient does not know himself about his condition and his chances. He comes out of a feeling of comradeship; he genuinely likes and admires the sick man, and he is in awe of the woman who is keeping him alive.

My mother not only kept my brother alive, she got him back on his feet. When spring came, a pale and shaky but sufficiently recuperated Wolfgang returned to Halle to begin a residency in pathology.

It was not because of fresh goat milk that my brother got well. That playful little goat that my mother hand fed through its nursery days and frisky adolescent months was only one more disaster in my mother's thorny farming career. She was fond of it and spoiled it, her affection being frequently warmed by visions of pails of bubbling fresh milk enhancing the kitchen pantry. However, in order for those bubbly pails to materialize, the goat would, first of all, have to produce a baby goat. So my mother informed herself about these things and when the time came, Agatha was ordered to take the goat to her groom. Agatha, a mustachioed, vaguely middle-aged woman, was my mother's current "domestic assistant." She was slightly retarded and extraordinarily shrewd. She would sweep the dirt not under the rug where my mother was likely to investigate, but under the kitchen linoleum. And when my mother had a visitor or was otherwise engaged, Agatha wiped the plates on the apron across her stomach. My mother never managed to get her to wash the clothes by scrubbing them against the washboard. Instead Agatha "swayed" them; that is, she leaned on her elbows over the tub and gently moved the towels and pillow slips back and forth in the warm water. When my mother bore down on her, Agatha darkly reminded her that she had a weak head and was not to be aggravated. Besides, she said, swaying was better for clothes than scrubbing, everybody knew that; she was surprised at my mother. For the first time my mother, ever the irresistible force, had come upon an immovable object.

The goat groom resided at the other end of town and presently Agatha could be seen wandering through Main Street, dragging the goat behind her on my mother's clothes line. The goat was a social little thing, curious by nature and delighted with this unexpected outing. So Agatha was pulling on one end of the clothes line and the goat on the other while the townsfolk looked through the window curtains and the school children cheered for the goat.

When the first visit did not take, Agatha and the goat were sent for a second try. Nothing came of this, either, and when the matter came up for a third time, Agatha demurred. She wasn't hauling no goat through no town anymore, she said, or she couldn't answer for her nerves. "Besides," she added rather ominously, "that critter ain't human. Even the billy goat don't want her."

My mother put the clothes line around the goat's neck and took her to the vet. The vet was a busy man, but eventually he got around to my mother and her goat. After a short, deft examination, during which my mother gazed out of the window, his overworked, underpaid countenance visibly brightened.

"This goat is a '*Zwitter*'" he said, "a true Hermaphrodite. Very interesting case. Extremely rare; only the second one I have ever seen in my practice."

My mother did not share his scientific delight. She did not want to exhibit the goat, she said, she wanted to milk it.

"Not this one, you won't," the vet said, lovingly patting the head of the animal. He straightened up, suddenly giving my mother a curious stare.

"Aren't you the woman with the crazy chicken?"

Not dignifying this with an answer, my mother dragged the goat home, pushed her in her stall and marched into the house, murder on her mind. If there was to be no milk, there would be meat. Disaffection was the key word here. She fully intended to become sufficiently indifferent to the fate of this undeserving, perverted creature out there. However, when we came home for Christmas she had not progressed along those lines as rapidly as she had hoped; the goat was still alive and peppy and, obviously, had no idea of the disgrace she had brought upon herself.

This was the first Christmas after the war and much of the world was jubilant. We were not part of it. Our country was steeped in trauma, and in stupefying confusion. We had less to eat, less to keep us warm, and nothing at all to give to each other. But the droning of airplanes over our heads had ceased; there was no wailing of sirens at night, no distant explosions to make our blood run cold. And there was hope, and that, at last, we could share with each other.

Our trip back was cold, crowded, and uneventful except for our arrival in Berlin, which caused us some excitement. We found all platform exit gates blocked but one, and that one was guarded by a formidable-looking fellow in uniform. We would have to pass by him, handing him our tickets in single file. Dolfi hung back for a moment, searching his pockets and triumphantly brought forth a movie ticket. I saw no cause for rejoicing, but it seemed to give Dolfi serene peace. He propelled me forward to where the crowd was the thickest and the shoving the most impatient. When he passed through the gate he pressed the movie ticket into the man's hand and walked on. The next passengers pushed through and it took the man a few seconds before he realized that he had been duped. Shouts of "Hey, you—you there! Come back! Come back here this instant!" sounded through the station hall. Nobody paid any attention; the crowd swept on and Dolfi swept right with them.

"Good grief, Dolfi," I said. I was shaking a little. "That was taking a chance. Couldn't you have explained to the man that we had tried to buy a ticket?"

"Sure, and get arrested in the Russian sector?" said Dolfi, and that, being a convincing argument, settled the matter.

The first thing I saw when we arrived at the apartment was a pile of letters stacked on the hall stand. After nine months' paralysis, the German postal service had resumed activity thirteen days before. On the rickety black table in the dim corridor lay eleven letters for me.

I knew the handwriting, the beloved un-European lettering with all the "r's" turned inside out. I knew the capital "G's" and "S's," so unlike the German ones, which always looked to me like swans, sailing proudly across the paper, aloof from the rest of the word. There were eleven letters, one for each postal day.

Fräulein Pritts looked around the corner of the hall, sourly noting our arrival. Her eyes fell on the letters in my hand which she, herself, would have stacked on the hall table.

"Your stars must have entered a very fortunate constellation," she remarked. She sounded bitter but not vengeful. Roswitha Pritts might battle us every step of the way, but she would not take on the stars.

I felt punch drunk, stiff, bone-tired but wide awake and dizzy with happiness. I pulled the desk lamp close to my couch, grabbed my English dictionary and my letters and crawled under the covers. And there, lying on my stomach, with only part of my head sticking out like a turtle, I sorted the letters according to dates and began slowly and lovingly deciphering them, one wondrous letter after the other.

Exactly what had happened? A handful of letters had awaited me on my return from a Christmas vacation. On the surface it had changed nothing. I was muddling through the same daily routine as always. Rushing to catch the subway in the morning and, for the next five hours, trying to unravel the mysteries of spelling and arithmetic to a roomful of stoic little girls. Sitting through tedious seminars, or standing in line in front of a grocery store in the afternoons. At night, wearing gloves — my legs wrapped in blankets and newspapers to coax them back to the land of the living — I was correcting a never ending stream of scribbled papers. It seemed that nothing had changed.

Ah, but it had! Something decisive and wonderful had happened and it changed everything. Those letters had not only expressed love and hope but also an unconditional commitment. As I outwardly went through all the same motions, everything inside me now revolved around those letters. Every single, blessed day another letter was waiting for me when I returned home. The sky was not gray anymore, the kitchen was not bleak. The children were pets and were hugged with new fervor; Fräulein Pritts was to be comforted in her loneliness. The Baroness was a staunch old dear who could not help being what she was, and there was no more doodling of birch trees and bunnies during seminar. When lectures got lengthy I continued my ongoing letter to the lieutenant. For now I would answer him, letter for letter.

The lieutenant was stationed in Wiesbaden. He had been in line for discharge and had promptly reenlisted for another year. He was not about to leave Germany at this point, he wrote. He was assigned to the branch of the military government whose job it was to restore the German postal services. That was no small order. Not only were the buildings missing, but many of the men who had been responsible for running one of Europe's most efficient mail service were dead or had been fired. Another immediate concern was the stamps. All existing postal stamps carried political messages: calls to victory, or worse, Hitler's half-profile. New stamps had to be designed and manufactured. The German post offices had served as a vast saving bank through which bills and wages would be paid. They had run the telegraph services and last, not least, the entire telephone system. To get all this sorted out, restored, and functioning again was a task of some magnitude.

The lieutenant was immersed up to his ears in his new job. He was, in turn, enthusiastic and infuriated; enthusiastic at the progress being made and infuriated at the obstinacy shown on this occasion by the German bureaucracy. It seemed to him that their sluggishness slowed things down entirely unnecessarily. But a German civil servant (in those days) was not sluggish, he was proud. He might be cold and hungry and living with his family in a single basement room, but he knew his place in the hierarchy of the civil service and he would not easily surrender to what amounted to a demotion in his eyes, nor did he wish to be pushed up the ladder two rungs at once.

So the lieutenant had plenty to say about his work in his letters. He also began introducing me to his family, one by one: his younger sister, his aunts, of whom there seemed to be a goodly number, and a single uncle. He talked about his mother who had died when he was away in college, and of his father who lived in the family home alone now except for the presence of a housekeeper. He wrote of the family business, founded by his great grandfather, and how all eyes of the family were looking at him to continue it.

And he wrote about missing us, Bertel and me, about the happy days back in Thuringia and what the future would bring to the three of us. He was the happiest when he wrote about the future; he wrote every day and there never was enough time and paper at hand to finish the letter.

I answered him, carrying paper and pen and my dictionary with me to subway, school and seminar, having to send a letter off, at times, half finished, so he would not be without one the next day.

" . . . This part of the letter is written during recess," I wrote, "but I am not getting on very fast. All my little girls are standing around my desk. They are so curious about you. They know your name. They know that you love me and that I love you; they only ask me that once every recess. They have dozens of questions. What do you look like? Are you very old? Are you an American who has bombs or one who makes soup for children? What am I writing to you? Will we get married? Will we have babies? When the babies open their mouths, will they talk English or German? (What do *YOU* think?) . . ."

" . . . Your family sounds very nice and a bit frightening. I never knew anybody who had seven unmarried aunts. Did they not wish to get married? I only had one cousin when I grew up; he was not married, either, but he had a motorcycle which made him very interesting. Other than my mother and two brothers we do not seem to have any close relatives . . ."

" . . . Why do you ask me if I want to be a Valentine? What is a Valentine? What does one have to do? Do you want me to say yes or no? Explain this quickly to me . . ."

" . . . No, I do not wear lipstick. We cannot buy it. But I think it will not matter a great deal to me and if you do not want me to use lipstick I shan't. So you will not have to worry about red stains on glasses and napkins. I never thought about it but you are probably right, it cannot be pretty. (May I just try it once to see how it looks?) . . ."

" . . . Oh, darling, I am so sorry that I frightened you. It is true, the matches looked as if they had been used. The chemistry professor in the seminar only gave us the little sticks and made us mix the sulfa, not colors to make them look beautiful. I thought you would be pleased that you will have such a clever wife who can make her own matches! There is no German custom sending burnt out matches to somebody you do not love any longer. (And they are *not* burnt out! They give a crackling flame, just try it!)"

" . . . Guess what, my love? I got one hundred Marks for a poem I made about Pestalozzi. It is not very good; I wrote it for my children so it had to be simple. But now they will print it in the new readers for the schools and they paid me for it. I gave the money to a friend who knows

everything about the black market. She bought me a pound of sugar for it
. . ."

" . . . I, too, am sad that you were not sent to Berlin with those papers.
Don't they know that you would be the fastest carrier in the world? Perhaps soon they will have more papers and chose you to carry them to Berlin. We shall just keep hoping. By now we must be very good at it, we have
had such long practice."

Writing a letter every day between work, subway, and home, the careful phrasing fell by the wayside. I wrote whatever came into my mind at
the moment and slowly it sank into that dear, dense head of my lieutenant
that we, possibly, might not have enough to eat.

When it comes to denseness in that department, I do not exempt myself.
More than anybody around me at the time I understood that what was perceived as callous or even vengeful by the population was nothing but
thoughtlessness. An American soldier, cheerfully sauntering down West
Berlin's avenues, could not conceive the life of the people who lived
alongside him in the same city but whose paths never crossed his.

I could see myself—less than three years before—walking through the
white, blistering streets of Athens, wondering at the strange Greek custom
of gulping down cold beans out of tin cans on street corners or door entrances at any time of the day. And I was not proud to remember my own ob-
tuseness.

The lieutenant began to send powdered milk and cans of cocoa. With
an ecstatic Dolfi at my elbow, supervising, half incredulous myself, I cooked
the first pot of hot chocolate. I soon discovered that if I thickened the liquid with flour it turned into a remarkable solid pudding that would feed
us for days.

Taking advantage of a mild weekend in February, I gathered my courage
for a trip to the village near Potsdam where my childhood friend Carola
still lived. She had three young children and there had been no possible
way for her to pack up and flee to the West as so many others had done.

The train to Potsdam was literally filled to the roof. People were
crouched outside on the buffers between the cars; others were sitting on
top of the roofs. I would have preferred the buffers, but the appalling idea
of a possible head-on collision cured me, temporarily, of my fear of heights;
I would take my chances on the roof. The roofs of the railroad cars were
smooth and rounded; it became obvious (once I managed to climb up
there) that without a hold of some kind one would, at the first curve, in-

evitably slide over the edge. Every hook seemed to be taken; half a dozen hands clung to the two ventilation pipes. If I could not find something—anything—to hold on to, I would have to jump off before the train started moving. Resigned to do just that and to forget about the whole trip, I suddenly noticed a hole, probably torn by a shell fragment, just big enough for a hand to reach inside. I rolled my scarf into a thick pad and with my right hand took a firm hold around the jagged edge of the hole. My left fist was clamped around the handle of an army canteen filled with my present specialty, chocolate pudding, my gift for the hostess.

This was my first trip on the roof of a train and I found myself watching with more than a little apprehension for sudden bridges and tunnels. Dolfi had told me of a frightening experience. At my mother's request, he had ventured into the occupied east provinces where she had left a box with my father's books—for safekeeping, as she had thought at the time. The roof of the train was crowded with travelers when a marauding soldier made his way over the rooftops from car to car. Brandishing a pistol he took rings, watches, and money from his helpless victims, pistol whipping, in the course of it, a few who did not have much or whose face did not please him.

"I had only a broken comb on me," said Dolfi, "and I was not looking forward to my turn." The soldier had come from the front of the train and was facing backward . . . all the huddled people saw the bridge approaching but no warning cry was raised. There were only a few suppressed groans when the decapitated man rolled off the roof.

Carola, her children, and her mother were living in the former nursery of their old house, which had a woodburning stove. Her mother, skin and bones, with sunken, lusterless eyes, was bedridden after months of remorseless dysentery. All of them showed various symptoms of malnutrition. The children, aged two, three, and four, were kept in two cribs where they cried and played and slept through the day. The oldest one had bronchitis, the two younger ones suffered from a lingering infection that made them feverish and drained pus from their ears. Every morning Carola left to hunt for food. Every usable, movable item was carried, piece by piece, out of the house into the villages in exchange for a few potatoes, some grain or an egg or two. She rode her bicycle to Potsdam and joined the women who daily searched through the rubble of a grocery market for cans or other salvageable items. A village, thirteen kilometers in the opposite direction, had the only bakery that redeemed bread coupons. To get the children's skimmed milk ration she joined the line at another store. The wood for the stove had to be gathered ever deeper into the forest; the outskirts had long since been picked clean. It would be evening before she came home and the chore of washing the children and the sick woman, rinsing the sheets and feeding all of them would begin.

Carola was the one who could make everybody laugh when we were in the village school. She told me that when she was a youngster, she and her cousins had discovered a book, handed down from some lusty ancestor, about ancient sex customs of far away island tribes. I doubt that they read through it, but the illustrations left them round-eyed and giggly. They called it the "piggy book" and kept it well hidden from their elders. However, they were found out and their embarrassed parents had speedily confiscated it. Now, turning over every corner of the house for things to trade, Carola had once again come upon it. This deserved better than the village bumpkins. Carola rode her bicycle to Berlin — a seventy kilometer trip — to trade it at the grander black market there. It attracted more bidders, anxious to educate themselves on this interesting subject, than any oriental rug, and she came away with a bag full of cans and bread.

"Oh, it was pure gold, our piggy book," Carola said and then she laughed, the same mischievous, infectious laugh that I remembered from days long ago.

Chapter 27

Coming home from seminar on a Thursday afternoon in late March, I immediately noticed the white slip of paper that had been pushed through the mail slot onto the dark floor board. My heart, more attuned than my head, began to pound even before I had picked it up. It was just a scrap of paper, torn out of a notebook.

"Darling," it said, "why aren't you home when I come to see you? I shall be back at six."

What marvelous news! What terrible news! What was I going to do?! Where should I begin? This scrap of paper changed, within seconds, the entire perception of my surroundings. I had become so accustomed to its ugliness that I hardly saw it anymore. I suddenly looked at it with the eyes of a visitor. Mercilessly I took it all in: the wintry, uninviting room, the dark hall, the dismal kitchen where the dishes of the last two days were still stacked on the kitchen counter, the whole melancholy scene that was our everyday life. Where should I begin sprucing things up, make them look more cheerful, somehow? I had thirty-five minutes and the decision was made in ten seconds. If anything was to be repaired, polished, and spruced up, it would be me. Pritts would just have to forget about the bathroom for the next half hour.

I was rubbing my hair and my face with a dry towel when I heard Dolfi come in. Dolfi! I had forgotten about him. This was not to be a jolly get-together — this was only the most important meeting of my life and I didn't want anybody around, not even my staunchest supporter and comrade-in-arms, Dolfi.

Brushing my hair furiously, I opened the door and called out:

"Read the note on the table, Dolfi."

I heard him whistle softly in response. I stuck my head through the door, never missing a brush stroke.

"Listen. Make yourself a glass of milk, you know where the powder is. Go to Angelika and ask her to put you up. Take half the bread along for your supper, and take the rest of the cocoa can. Give Angelika the cocoa; she will give you something to put on your bread in exchange. Tell her I have a visitor, she will understand."

Not only would Angelika understand, she would jump to a dozen conclusions, eleven of them wrong. Angelika was a former classmate of mine, a chemist, who had been rehired by her old firm. She also was the single most astute black market entrepreneur west of the Kurfuerstendamm. In the course of the latter, she frequently entertained various international visitors. Angelika was neither a romantic nor a nymphomaniac, she only went to bed during a business deal when her visitor was reasonably clean but otherwise pigheaded. In consequence of her holding down two professions, her living standard was two or three notches higher than ours.

Dolfi complied without protest. I heard him rummaging around our room and he was gone when I emerged from the bathroom.

Three minutes later the bell rang; I flew to the door and pressed the buzzer and heard the lieutenant run up the stairs, two steps at a time.

I had not forgotten what he looked like, I remembered the full face, the thinning dark hair, the nice smile that showed strong, even teeth. I remembered the ridiculous steel-rimmed glasses and the large, mild, dark eyes behind them. But I had forgotten his voice and its deep resonance came as a shock. This was the man with whom I had exchanged almost a hundred letters during the last few months, whose every hour of day, every thought in his mind, was as familiar to me as my own. And yet, I had not even remembered his voice, and when we talked we would need the dictionary close at hand.

When I went into the kitchen he followed me. His eyes came to rest on the stacked dishes on the counter.

"That is not good," he said, "can't you make her wash them?" He thought they belonged to our tenant.

"No," I said sorrowfully, "I cannot make her do it."

Strictly speaking, this was the truth; Fräulein Pritts would rather be hung by her thumbs than rinse our plates for me, although I was gone ten hours a day and she sat in her room and read the stars. I was not about to enlighten my lieutenant on the finer points of this conversation.

What else do I remember of that evening? I remember the lieutenant lying on Dolfi's cot, his head in my lap; I take off those silly glasses and trace his closed eyes with my fingertips, telling him that those beautiful long, curled lashes are wasted on a man. Look at my short, stubby ones. I remember asking him to talk to me so I would never again forget the sound of his voice; requesting that he give my undying gratitude to his colonel who had sent him to Berlin on an errand that was not entirely necessary.

What I don't remember is being hungry or cold or thinking the room bleak and uninviting. And that evening, neither of us remembered to look at the clock and the lieutenant missed the last subway to his quarters.

The lieutenant stayed with a cousin in Berlin. This cousin worked for the military government and lived in an exquisite mansion in Dahlem, a suburb of Berlin. The lieutenant said that he would take me to his cousin's place the next day. He was surprised that I seemed jittery about the meeting; his cousin was an easy-going fellow, not a bit awesome, he assured me.

As it turned out, he also was a man of sense and sensibility (as Jane Austen would have put it). When we arrived he had disappeared. We found a note welcoming me and telling us to regard his place as our own. The lieutenant thought this was nice. I thought the world stopped turning. We simply did not expect such kindness from these quarters. I stood in the hall, looking around me (Americans always leave all the doors open—unthinkable in a German household), swept away by the pre-war atmosphere of large, airy rooms, elegantly furnished, of white glass curtains, freshly watered plants, lovely, subtly faded oriental rugs covering parquet floors, and heavenly warmth from invisible central heating.

While I was standing rooted in this pre-war wonderland, the lieutenant had been busy. Out of the pantry had come orange juice, bread, and cold cuts. He was now in the bathroom from where I could hear the splashing noise of two spigots turned on full force. He was drawing a bath for me. Whatever qualms I had about taking such liberties in a strange apartment melted at the sight of the oversized tub filled with steaming water, a huge cake of soap, and the two thick towels piled on the chair beside.

"Leave your shoes out here," said the lieutenant, and thinking nothing astonishing anymore I pushed them through the door and sank into the tub. The sensation of this, my first hot bath in three years, will be lingering in my memory as long as I shall command one. I am engulfed, to the tip of my nose, by the soft, caressing warmth. "Uralte Wasser steigen verjüngt um deine Hueften, Kind . . ." No, I won't translate that; it can only lose in translation. But I will say this: it's a mystical, sensuous line and that's what it felt like. Years and walls faded; I was floating in time-less enchantment. The conversation, however, which ensued through a crack of the door, was timely and down to earth.

The lieutenant as became evident to me, was sitting on a chair just outside the bathroom door, polishing my shoes. He rubbed oily brown boot paste onto the cracked leather and watched in amazement as it disappeared within seconds. His solution was to heap more paste onto it. Eventually, the shoes declared themselves saturated and he began to shine them. In the meantime he opened a conversation with the enchanted lady in the tub, necessitating her reentry into the world of sober realities. He had something on his mind and this was as good an opportunity as any to come out with it.

"I want to give you something." He had stopped brushing for a mo-ment and I could hear him clearly through the crack. "Something you want and need. You must tell me what you want most, anything at all, and I will get it for you."

Well, if the bath was not enough to make my head spin, this certain-ly was. At the same time I realized the horrendous dilemma it presented. Under ordinary circumstances, a man could ask this question of his wife, his mother, or beloved, and she might answer—thinking of herself as she was meant to do—a suede handbag, a pair of onyx earrings, a bottle of French perfume. But this was no ordinary circumstance. People whom I loved were in dire need; and *need* was everything that made life possible; *want* was anything that made it more bearable. The more I thought about it the more disturbed I became.

"What do you want most?" the lieutenant asked again, puzzled by the silence.

What I wanted was to shout: "This is stupid, stupid! Leave me alone. Don't ask me such a question." But he would not have understood. I closed my eyes and tried to think calmly. I would have to say something.

"An umbrella," I said. "I would like an umbrella."

Now the ominous silence was on the other side of the door.

"An umbrella?" the lieutenant finally said, incredulous.

By now I had regained my equilibrium and giggled into the warm steam. Here was my hero, my knight from distant shores, offering to pluck the moon from the sky and being asked instead for an umbrella.

"Do you really want an umbrella?"

I surrendered.

"Shoes," I said, not very loudly. But he heard me and this time, holding the wreckage of my footwear in his lap, he believed me. Good, shoes it would be.

He would send the request to his sister, he told me; she would know about shoes for young women. However, the sizes in America were numbered differently from German sizes, we would have to draw the outline of my foot on a piece of paper. This would be our very next project. Dried, warmly steaming, and dressed but still barefoot, he had me put my foot on a large piece of paper and pulled out a pencil.

"Let me do it," I said, filled suddenly with stark misgivings. I took the pencil out of his hand. "Don't watch."

So the lieutenant went into the kitchen to see what other contributions toward a meal the pantry might render while I bent down and drew the outline of my foot. When I picked up the paper, my worst fears were realized. I knew I had big feet, but what I was gazing at was not a human foot but the cave imprint of a flat-footed Neanderthal specimen. I would rather go barefoot for the rest of my life than let him send this awful drawing to his family in America.

"Are you done?" the lieutenant asked.

"No, the pencil slipped, I'll have to do it again," I called back. I put the paper on a table and began to erase the lines on both sides, redesigning them, pulling them closer together and thinning the middle where the arch was supposed to be. Then I shortened the whole thing the tiniest bit, gave the curve from the big toe to the little toe a more elegant slant, and decided, with a sigh that this would have to do. This finished product with all the aesthetic improvements had little resemblance to the original but that could not be helped. I would just have to give the shoes—if they ever arrived—to someone with more maidenly feet.

The lieutenant stayed for four days. As a chronicler of events that happened more than four decades ago, and striving to achieve a certain degree of objectivity, I have to note that our endeavors at entertainment beyond each other's company were not an unqualified success. Just being with each other was all we had hoped and wished for. But we were not an island unto ourselves; there was my brother and the lieutenant's cousin, there was Berlin and my role as hostess, and there were cool, clear, sunny March days outside.

The program of our first outing with the cousin was left to me. This was not as easy as it might sound. It was too early in the year for a boat ride across the lakes around Berlin. Many of the nicer spots in the city were off limits for Germans and they could not very well check me at the cloakroom. I finally decided on a walk through the zoo which I remembered as a great tourist attraction before the war. This turned out to be an unfortunate choice. The walks had been cleared of debris, but the animals were gone, shot by their keepers, either to keep them from starving or to prevent the hungry beasts from roaming the streets after being freed by an air raid. (As recently as last year, a silver-haired little lady in Berlin told me, while calmly eating a piece of marzipan torte, how she and her husband had run out of the burning building during an air raid only to step on a large crocodile at their doorstep. Luckily, the crocodile was even more stunned by the situation than they were.) We finally found one single cage occupied by an assortment of monkeys. In my relief to produce, at long last, something alive, I stepped too close and a large male reached through the grate and caught a strand of my hair. This caused a great deal of merriment between the gentlemen while I was having a ghastly time being a good sport about it. It took my companions a minute — during which the wretched beast nearly pulled part of my scalp off — to realize that I was in considerable trouble, and it took both of them to free my hair out of that devilish claw. So much for a dignified first impression on a member of the family. The cousin, a jovial, middle-aged, garrulous bachelor, was bound to give the folks at home a complete report of our first meeting. I was nursing a sore scalp as well as my bruised vanity and the thought of his description of our visit to the zoo was not exactly elating. I knew what a good story I would have made of it if it would have happened to him instead of me.

The next part of the program was up to the lieutenant who told me to close my eyes and joyfully whipped out two concert tickets. This, clearly, was not a good time to let him know that I am tone deaf. So, off we went to the concert hall. My feeble hopes that it might be off limits for natives were squashed at the door. One look at the printed program in my hand told me that it would be a long afternoon. It would now be a matter of either finding something to occupy my mind or suffering the most excruciating boredom since my mother dragged me to Lohengrin ten years earlier.

The first thing I did was to count the pieces to be played. The list was disheartening. I decided to time the first piece and multiply the time by the number of pieces printed on the program; it might give me an idea of how long an ordeal I was facing. I would be able to tell the end of the first piece by the applause. It was endless, and when the applause finally came and I began to multiply, I could see that we would still be sitting there four hours later. This brought me to a degree of despair that only the truly tone deaf can comprehend. For the secret and awful truth is that not only do we fail to be entranced by music, we feel greatly put upon since it is invariably connected with noise.

There was a piece called "Night on Bald Mountain." I resolved to make one more concerted effort to visualize what the composer had in mind when he wrote those notes. As far as I could make out, he thought it rather a lark; anyway the musicians seemed to have a jolly time of it. When the applause broke, I moved my finger to the next piece on the program. The lieutenant glanced over, shook his head and moved my finger three pieces lower. It seemed that we had been listening to something called "The Moldau" which had nothing at all to do with Bald Mountain. What had thrown me off were all the sub-movements listed under each number at the end of which one apparently did not applaud. This was good news, indeed, and would take a hefty chunk off the four hours. I tried to estimate how many people were in the audience: count the row ahead of us and multiply it by the entire number of rows. That did not work because I would have to do a lot of squirming; besides, I could not multiply that high. Next, I spent some time trying to figure out the ration cards of the orchestra. It would be grossly unfair, I felt, to issue all of them the same rations since the fiddlers worked at least ten times as hard as the man in the background who every once in a long while hit some metal sticks together or slammed a large lid on top of another one. At long last I closed my eyes, concentrated, tuned out, and recited all the poems I had ever learned from first grade up, some of them, happily, having eight verses or more. After that I went through the lyrics of all the songs I knew. I was deep into the *Wanderlieder* of my BDM time when tumultuous applause signaled the end of the concert.

The lieutenant was shiny-eyed and talkative and I only nodded once in a while in amicable agreement to keep him from inquiring about my own sentiments. I was afraid if I would overdo it our weekend would turn into one catastrophic succession of musical events and that was more than I could face.

The following day, at my suggestion, we went to the cinema. It was an American film, an engrossing drama. It was well written, well directed, and superbly acted. I loved it. It was many months before I discovered that the lieutenant loathed movies; just about as long, I would say, as it took him to find out that I was tone deaf.

We had none of those problems when we were alone. Lovers are the most self-centered people in the world. There was never a moment of boredom. Much of our time, now, was taken up with planning for the future. The lieutenant had written to his family—father, aunts, and lone uncle—that he had met a German girl and that he was going to marry her. The family answered by return mail. That was grand, they wrote, but why did he not come home first and rest up a bit; obviously the last years had been stressful and things always looked a little different after a good rest. I could have told them that this approach would not work. Anybody whose favorite German word was "doch" would only get more stubborn. He wrote back that he wasn't a bit stressed and that he simply would go on reenlisting until we were permitted to get married. This greatly alarmed everybody at home and there was some sort of family council to coordinate future efforts and procedure in that matter. It was about at this point that the lieutenant came to Berlin.

Our own plans began to take shape in the form of three goals: I would move to Wiesbaden where the lieutenant was stationed. We would marry at the first opportunity. And I would return to Thuringia in order to fetch Bertel. When the lieutenant left on the fifth day, we were both resolved to reach the first goal as speedily as possible, which meant that I had to obtain, somehow, the all-but-impossible "Zuzugsgenehmigung"—the permission to live in West Germany.

PART VII

1946-1947

Wiesbaden, West Germany

". . . and each beginning holds its own enchantment . . ."*

*". . .und jedem Anfang wohnt ein Zauber inne . . ."

Hesse

Chapter 28

About the middle of January my mother forwarded a letter from Kristin to me in Berlin. This was the first news I had from her in almost a year and I had thought of her with deep uneasiness. News from friends and relatives had been scarce, reaching us, if at all, only through notes trusted haphazardly to returning refugees. When our correspondence ceased, Kristin had been in a precarious position. She was still in Sofia, staying at the navy headquarters which were rapidly disbanding. Between her and her country lay the vast mountain ranges of the Balkan spewing forth thousands of guerrillas waylaying the retreating German soldiers with relentless fury.

Kristin had made it back safely. The navy, unhampered as yet by any rules calling for equal treatment of the sexes, had given priority to their female personnel. In some of their last available planes they were flown into Austria. There, without any further orders or instructions, they were left to their own devices.

Kristin had joined a small group of girls who had gathered around a navy supply sergeant. This was a wise decision. Through thousands of years of punishing wars, the remarkable fact has emerged that supply sergeants seldom perish. This one was no exception. He was not about to wither away, and neither were the young women who trusted their fate to his resourcefulness. By mysterious means he provided food and shelter; out of an empty hat he pulled his rabbits, conjured up bread and blankets and a place to lay their head at night. They had lived in a loft for some months until it became possible for them to attempt the journey home to their families. Kristin could not go back to East Prussia, now annexed by Russia. She had no news of her family. However, few problems were insolvable to the sergeant. He unearthed a cousin who lived in Wiesbaden in the

American zone, and she consented to give Kristin a room. This cousin and her little boy preferred to stay with her mother in the country and Kristin was now sharing the apartment with another refugee family. That was the situation when Kristin wrote to me.

The lieutenant, who was stationed in Wiesbaden at the time, went to see Kristin and reported to me on his visit. Kristin urged me to come to Wiesbaden, where she offered to share her room with me. Even after the lieutenant was transferred to Frankfurt, an hour's drive from Kristin's apartment, it was decided that I should try to get to Wiesbaden, since I would have a place there waiting for me. But getting a permit to live in the American zone was about as likely as getting an invitation to High Tea from the Kremlin.

Each one of the three western zones had to take its quota of refugees, people who had been driven out of the provinces given to Poland and Russia in the Yalta agreement. Villages and towns in the West that had been spared bombing and destruction often had to take in a number of homeless equal to the number of inhabitants, thus within weeks doubling their original population. The refugees, who arrived with nothing more than a suitcase and a few bundles, were deposited in hastily erected tin barracks just outside the town limits. In addition to this flood of the dispossessed, "treks" began to arrive.

Landowners in East Germany had found their own means of escape: long wagon trains drawn by horse or ox teams and loaded with their families, tenant farmers, and as many of their household goods as the wagons would hold. They were heading toward areas in the west where friends or relatives of the squires had their own large farms.

At some point each of the three zones declared themselves filled to capacity and placed stringent restrictions on any further influx of people. Travelers from then on would be admitted only if they were in possession of a "Zuzugsgenehmigung," an explicit entry permission issued by the mayor of a town or village, stating that they had living quarters waiting for them and would be allowed to remain there.

A great deal of influence was needed to obtain such a permit. Kristin, a refugee herself with no friends or ties anywhere, could do nothing but offer a place to stay. The lieutenant looked around his own limited connections and decided on a friend and fellow officer who had landed the job of town commandant of a forgotten little spa in the midst of the Taunus Forest, a beautiful mountain range above the Rhine. At the first possible opportunity the lieutenant drove up to see him. He found his friend comfortably settled in his office in the ancient town house. The windows of the panelled little room opened toward the slopes of the Taunus meadows where snowdrops, lilies of the valleys, and violets were already in full bloom. The commandant, his stockinged feet resting on a rather dusty desk, was immersed in a pile of old German school books. He had mastered the German language in record time and was now studying the native tongue. His goal, he explained to the lieutenant, was to converse with the mayor in the local dialect about the town's Roman ruins, its history, and the more current merits of Mosel versus Rhine wines. He saw no need to interfere otherwise with the town's business which the mayor seemed to be managing very nicely. He was on excellent terms with the natives, bore the burden of his august position with magnanimity and intended to re-enlist indefinitely.

Asking for a Zuzugsgenehmigung, however, would require a series of delicate negotiations. The mayor could not issue such permit without the consent of the town council, and the council, as well as the rest of the town, had only recently declared themselves up to their ears in shelters and refugees and, henceforth, hermetically closed to all newcomers. The commandant told the lieutenant he was quite sure that, eventually, he might wear the council down but nothing would be gained by pressuring those people too hard or too hurriedly. The lieutenant explained to his friend that all that was needed was the permit and that the person in question had no intentions of actually settling down in the area. The commandant, in return, assured the lieutenant that there wasn't a soul in town who would believe this.

My only other hope was an old friend of mine who was a prominent figure in one of the larger cities in the English zone. His prominence had been achieved through his artistic talents. He was a professor of music and a first-rate organist. The bishop of the city was an ardent music lover and, although he sadly suspected the professor of being an atheist, he took comfort in the thought that nobody who played Bach like the master himself could be entirely Godless. Often when the professor, who had access to the city's best instruments, stormed through the registers of a towering organ, the bishop would sit quietly in a pew, his eyes closed, letting the sounds that transcended all earthly doubts carry him into heavenly spheres. It was after such a performance that my friend approached the still entranced bishop and asked him to intervene with the mayor of the city half. This was Catholic country and a bishop's word was weighed in gold; within two weeks my organist friend sent me the permit to his city. Half the battle was won.

I did not want to go to the bishop's city or even live in the English zone. This permit would get me out of Berlin and to the west but not into Wiesbaden. More prudent planning was necessary. I decided to take my now well-advanced case to our neighbor, the man who lived in the apartment adjacent to ours. He was a poet and a writer and the only human being I personally knew who had spent some time in a concentration camp. He had been sent there (by our late minister for "Kultur and Propaganda") in order to reconsider some of his more forthright printed efforts. After contemplating my dilemma for a while, the poet told me to leave my identification card with him overnight. This card gave my original residence as the obscure town of "S. . . ." in the province of "Thuringia" which, as everybody knew, lay in the Russian zone. When I returned to him the next morning he handed me my card on which the town of "S. . . . ." had been unceremoniously relocated in the province of "Hesse" which, as everybody knew, was in the American zone. It was the neatest piece of amateur forgery imaginable and almost, but not completely, foolproof.

After having obtained the bishop's saintly permit to enter the west in general and my less saintly proof of residency in the American zone more specifically, days of feverish activities followed. I gave notice of my leaving to the school, washed and mended my clothes, wrote to my mother and Kristin, and, skipping school one morning, I went to Berlin's refugee center. If I wanted to get to West Germany, I would either have to go to a regular refugee camp or walk across the border at night, risking getting shot or, at least, taken prisoner by the Russian border guards.

While waiting in line for my turn at the admission desk of the camp I kept rehearsing my tale: I had fled my native East Prussia, had stayed with relatives in Berlin, and, being now in possession of a permit, wanted to settle in West Germany. If challenged, I was prepared to give a few colorful details of the town at the Russian border where I had spent a month with Kristin's parents.

There was only one admission desk and the camp director was sitting behind it. A large, elderly man, he was slumped so motionless into a chair that only his eyes showed some life. The expression of his face was daunting; past disillusionment, past despair even, it was one of utter resignation. It would be difficult to lie to such a face. The thought occurred to me that he himself with his low, broad forehead, wide-spaced eyes, and strong cheekbones, might be a native and refugee of East Prussia, and my story seemed suddenly threadbare and unworthy. I had not counted on facing a man like this. But there was no choice and I plunged into my speech not daring to stammer or look backward.

The slumped man listened quietly, playing with the pencil in his hand. When I had finished he lifted his eyes to meet mine.

"Not in a million years have you come from East Prussia."

Not accusing, not judging, just stating a fact. With those deepset, unfathomable eyes resting on me it was impossible to insist on my story. My eyes fell; there was nothing I could say.

"Let me see your permit."

He studied it for a moment, then wrote my name on a piece of paper, stamped it and handed paper and permit to me. I stepped aside to let the person behind me move forward. The paper in my hand said "Admitted."

* * * * * * * * * * * * *

The announcements to my little school girls that I was going to join the lieutenant met with delighted approval, although I had the unhappy feeling that they were certain I would be back the following Monday. I took polite leave of the Baroness (who clearly equaled my departure with the abandonment of a troubled ship) and a friendlier leave of my colleagues. I packed my suitcase and stuffed a tin box with tea in my coat pocket. I gave Dolfi a last bear hug, pushed an American candy bar through the mail slot in the door of my fellow conspirator, the poet, and set out to the refugee center.

The camp was on the outskirts of Berlin, encompassing numerous one-story barracks that housed the dormitories, kitchen, dining hall, and administrative offices. Here the surviving populations of whole eastern villages spent their weeks and months numbly waiting to be settled in the West. From the registration office I was sent to the de-lousing barrack, where white powder was shot up my sleeves, in my hair and down the front of my dress, after which my wrist was stamped and I was given the number of my dormitory barrack. My bed was in a row of twenty-four and featured two folded army blankets and a straw mattress, matted and molded by the weight and size of innumerable previous occupants.

On the third day my name was posted for departure and before dawn the next morning we were taken to a station where we boarded a freight train, about twenty to a boxcar. We had been told that our destination was Hannover in the English zone. (I had an English zone permit.) Designated officially as refugee transport, we crossed the border without incident, and toward noon our train pulled into the city's terminal. For a short time, the platform was teeming with refugees, their children, bundles, and parcels, but as the day wore on the crowd thinned and in the end I seemed to be the only one left. My train to Frankfurt was not due until evening. During the first hours I walked up and down the length of the platform, not daring to leave my suitcase out of eyesight. Toward late afternoon the station hall began to fill again and I pushed my suitcase close to the tracks and sat on it. The crowd grew steadily and by evening there was a solid wall of bodies, three and four deep, along the entire platform. It got darker; the train was late. When finally a voice over the loud speaker announced its immediate arrival, it was night.

"Arriving: the train to Frankfurt," crackled the voice above our heads. "Attention, please. The train is already filled. Do no attempt to board it. I repeat, do not attempt to board the train."

I could feel more than see the electrifying shock going through the human wall behind me. There was but a single thought in every person's mind: "I will get on!" I congratulated myself on my decision to sit tight in the front row for these long hours. The weariness of it would now pay off: I would be on the train.

What happened next was faster than can be written down. The train stopped, a tidal wave of human bodies surged forward, I felt something like a hard slap around my ribs and found myself between two cars under the train. My suitcase had broken my fall and I scrambled to my feet almost immediately. My first terrified thought was that the train, in order to prevent people from boarding, would start and run over me. I wanted to step on my suitcase making it quicker for me to get back onto the platform, but my second thought was that I would then be left with nothing at all. Everything I owned in this world was in that suitcase. I would have to save it first before climbing up myself. Cold sweat was breaking out on my scalp and the palms of my hands. Half crazed with fear, standing directly in front of one of those monstrous wheels, I picked up the case and heaved it onto the platform. Then, hanging on to the steps of the train door, I worked my way up, expecting with every beat of my heart the train to move and drag me along.

The train did not move. There was not a soul left on the platform. People were hanging out of windows and doors like bunches of grapes; everyone was on the train, everyone but me. My knees were like cotton wool; I sat down on my suitcase as I had sat all day, and my mind went simply blank.

It was not so much the recent shock or the bleak prospect of another twenty-four hours of waiting for the next train that filled me with numbing despair but rather the realization that I had no reason to assume that the same scene would not repeat itself over and over again. I had been so close to the incoming train, even in immediate proximity of two doors, and it had brought me nothing but terror and injury. All other people were travelling in groups and had been able to combine their efforts; I seemed to have been the only single traveler.

"Did you want to be on this train?"

The voice came directly from behind me; I turned around and only just made out the dark silhouette of a man; I could not see his face.

"Yes."

"Do you have anything?"

"I have some tea."

"Give it to me."

I pulled the tin box out of my coat pocket. It was dented but had not opened. I put it in the outstretched hand. The figure disappeared, swallowed up by the darkness. The tea was all I had and now it, too, was gone. I did not doubt the man, but I thought that he would be too late. The train was bound to leave before his return. Some minutes went by; the train did not move; neither did I.

"Come with me." The voice was behind me again.

"Give me your suitcase."

He walked beside me, his face still lost in the dark. But he spoke to me in slow, precise terms as somebody might do whose intention it is to say his piece once and not again.

"You will ride in the engine. Two men will be in there; they will take no notice of you. Do not try to talk to them, they cannot acknowledge your presence. You cannot enter the engine from the platform, it might be observed. You will have to climb in from the track side."

And so, for the second time within ten minutes, I found myself on the train tracks, this time not under the train, but directly in front of the engine. The man reached down and handed me my suitcase and I cautiously felt my way across the track ties to the other side of the engine. It was a steep climb from there. I first lifted my suitcase into the cab, then pulled myself up on the narrow iron steps. I could see the shadowy figures of two men; they had their backs turned to me, and, though my ascent was accompanied by a good deal of noise, neither of them turned around or threw as much as a glance at me. And so it remained the entire trip. I had pushed my suitcase into the one corner that I hoped was out of the way of both men. The engineer was standing at the controls at the front window of the cab and I pressed myself to the opposite wall. The fireman, a large shovel in his hand, stood a few feet back of us between the furnace and a coal heap that filled the entire fourth corner. The men spoke rarely to each other and not a single word to me. They would have testified — under oath, if necessary — that they never noticed my presence, that it was dark, that they were busy, that they saw me neither coming nor going.

I have often wondered through the years who my rescuer might have been. His face remained in the dark, I could discern neither his features nor his age. Ruling out the bodily manifestation of angels, I have come to the conclusion — barely less incredible — that it must have been a railroad official. Who else could it have been? He was a man of some authority. He had not wanted to board the train himself. He had taken the tea but had not vanished with it. He knew about engines and engineers and evidently had not been afraid to approach them with his proposition. It is possible that throughout the day he had noticed my lone vigil and, walking the length of the train before its departure, he was amazed to find me still sitting, desolately, on the same suitcase at the same spot. Something must have stirred in him, something of the patent unfairness of the situation must have moved him; perhaps he thought that, every rule in the book having been broken anyway, one more would make no difference. And so he got me onto the train that night and perhaps ever after erased all memory from his mind that at one time he, a sworn official, had acted impulsively, unprofessionally, and compassionately.

Very little of those years has been erased from my mind, and there were times since when I have hurried past a forlorn stranger and then retraced my steps and offered help, remembering that night and the faceless man.

The train roared through the darkness. The sleeping country flew by through the open door to my right. I had always believed that once the furnace of an engine was packed to capacity with coal before the train's departure, that load would keep it in steam until its destination. This optimistic assumption was speedily set straight. Stoking the furnace turned out to be an awesome and interminable task. Like an insatiable monster, it had to be constantly appeased. Every few minutes the fireman would open the door, exposing a yawning hole that spewed flames and searing heat into our faces, and with ferocious precision, he would hurl a few shovelfuls of coal into it. The coal pile in the corner was never allowed to settle. The engineer, his face turned toward the front, was spared most of it, but the stoker and I were permanently engulfed in a cloud of black dust.

At midnight, the train pulled into a tiny country station, alive with American uniforms. The station was halfway between two small villages that at one time had shared a church, whose sons and daughters, very likely, had intermarried for centuries, and whose cows had grazed on the pastures in between. Now a forbidding border ran between them which could not be crossed without official permit.

"*Raus!*" said the engineer, turning to me for the first time. It was the only word he ever spoke to me.

I climbed out onto the platform and so did all the other passengers. American soldiers were walking through the train, emptying compartment after compartment. Dazed men and women carrying bundles, baskets, and sleeping children filled the sandy stretch alongside the train. Soldiers stationed themselves in front of the train doors, flashlight in hand, and any traveler wanting to re-enter the train had to produce an entrance permit or proof of residency in the American zone. If they could show neither, they were turned back on the spot.

Here now was the acid test of my poet's multi-talents. The flashlight glared down on my identification card: my residential proof looked impeccable. If the soldier had held my card against a light rather than under it, he undoubtedly would have noticed the erasure. How often in those days were we made aware that it took both luck and nerve to simply get on with our lives. The soldier, reading the "Hesse," was satisfied and motioned me into the train. Not everybody was so fortunate, and when the train moved out of the station, forlorn little groups of people and bundles were left behind in no-man's land. I found a seat and, huddled in my corner, overwrought, sore, and grimy, I spent the rest of the trip between tremulous elation and uneasy sleep.

* * * * * * * * * * * * *

We arrived in Frankfurt at ten in the morning. My first destination was the station's washroom. After a trip like this, extensive repairs would be necessary. However, the image staring back at me out of the tarnished mirror was beyond repair. My face, neck, hair, and clothes were covered with coal dust. I looked no different from the stoker, who had looked very dirty indeed. No wonder the people on the train had shot me curious glances. Even amidst the hungry and unwashed I had achieved a kind of distinction.

The spigot offered a thin trickle of cold water. I dampened my handkerchief and began to rub my face and presently got my second lesson of the day: coal dust is greasy and therefore immune to cold water; it only spread the black layer more evenly over my face. How could I present myself like this to a government agency, asking for an American officer? I kept rubbing with a vengeance and when my handkerchief turned black I opened my suitcase, took out a clean piece of underwear, and continued to rub. Gradually my face lightened into a kind of dusky hue. I combed my hair, removing the top layer of coal. There was nothing I could do about my neck, ears and fingernails. Oh, damn it, damn it . . . this would just have to do. I picked up my suitcase and began the search for the postal administration building.

A lucky break: it was no more than three blocks from the station. A curious stare from the guard at the door: The lieutenant's office was two flights up.

This was not exactly your average bridal entrance. I had been on the road for thirty-six hours with neither food nor drink. I had been pushed under a train and hurt my ribs. I had sat five hours in the cab of a train engine between a shifting coal heap and a roaring fire. Every pore of my skin was suffused with coal dust; the inside of my nose, ears, and fingernails were black. I was itching all over. My suitcase was filthy and showed a long tear. My shoes were cracked. I wore my brother's old air force coat without the insignias; it had been blue before the ride in the engine.

I knocked at the lieutenant's office door and a female voice answered. The room was airy and bright. The larger desk was unoccupied. Behind a smaller table with a typewriter sat a young woman. She had turned away from the table; her feet were resting on the windowsill. Her hair was blond and freshly permed, she wore a fashionable American blouse, and she was buffing her fingernails. I hated her on sight. I hated her fluffy hair, her thin, nylon clad legs, and her pink nail polish. She was a German girl — how come she sat there, looking like this, wiggling her toes in the April sun and admiring her rosy fingertips? Didn't anybody tell her that there had been a war on out there?

She swiveled her chair around and stared at me; her face showed incredulous amazement.

"Is the lieutenant not here?" Even my vocal cords were covered with coal dust.

"No. No, he left a few minutes ago for a meeting. He won't be back until after lunch." She was too astonished to show curiosity or contempt.

This was the last straw. "I'll come back, then." I was out of the door before I had time to dissolve into tears.

Ten minutes later the lieutenant returned; he had forgotten some of his notes.

"There was a girl here," said the secretary, "a girl with a suitcase, asking for you."

The lieutenant whirled around: "What? Where is she now?"

"I don't know. I told her you would be back after lunch. She . . ."

The lieutenant rarely ever shouted, but he was shouting now.

"Why did you let her go?! Why didn't you keep her here?"

"How was I to know that . . ." The girl was completely nonplussed. But the lieutenant had already stormed out of the office.

I was slowly making my way back to the station where I would find a bench and wait for the next four hours. He might be back by two o'clock. There were no restaurants to have a meal, no washrooms with warm water. It was too cold to sit in the park. I was walking very slowly; the suitcase by now seemed to be filled with rocks and I put it down every few minutes to catch my breath. I was in no hurry to get anywhere. It was during such a rest that I heard the frantic blowing of a horn. A jeep was tearing down the street, hitting the curb beside me, and the lieutenant jumped out and ran toward me.

He had said to me once that men are not beautiful. Let him think that, I know better. When he jumped out of that jeep and ran toward me, he was the most beautiful sight I had ever beheld in my life. I had no illusions about my own appearance, but the lieutenant's face when he saw me showed nothing but unmitigated happiness. When he touched my hand and took hold of my suitcase it was as if I surrendered to him along with that wearisome burden all my cares, perplexities, and sufferings from that moment on to all eternity.

* * * * * * * * * * * * *

He drove me to his quarters, a handsome villa in a suburb of Frankfurt where his German housekeeper received us. She was a diminutive woman in her thirties, blond, jolly, and energetic, who watched over her four American officers like a mother hen. To communicate with her charges she had arrived at a language all of her own.

"You bee the Fräulein he talks von immer und immer! Achdulieber-gott, you look so bad. Reise was no good, eh? You geh, geh," she said to the lieutenant. "You be spaet for vork. Ich fix it, all O.K., you see. You geh vork now."

The housekeeper's name was Frieda. She was simple, warm-hearted, and practical. She adopted all the German fräuleins that her officers brought home at times. The officers' quarters were off-limits for women and Frieda loved the intrigue of it. This morning we were safe, she told me; the house had been inspected the day before; there would be no trouble today. The major's young lady, next door, had slept in yesterday and Frieda had been forced to push her into the closet. She had the key taken out of the closet door, she said, and had stood with her back to it while the two quarter-master inspectors were combing the room for telltale signs of illegal visitors. She had never lost a visitor yet, she proudly said; she always threw everything that did not belong to her officer in the closet with the girl; nobody could say that she was careless about such things. I learned to love Frieda over the next months and, like all of us who went in and out of this house, came to depend on and admire her keen instinct for danger. She was always one step ahead of all army regulations. On this, my first morning, she had me in a warm shower, fed, and in bed in no time at all. When the lieutenant came home from work that afternoon, I felt wonderful and certainly looked a great deal better. I even felt kindly toward his secretary whose new perm and rosy nails had, evidently, been lost on the lieutenant.

The following day we drove to Wiesbaden, where I would make my home with Kristin. She lived in a first-floor apartment in a dark side street. The front rooms were taken by the refugee family. Kristin's room consisted of a windowless kitchen, gloomy in summer and dank and uninhabitable in winter, and a large back room which had two high, narrow windows that permitted sunlight for a few hours every day. It was furnished with two sofas, a table, two straight chairs and a large, stiff armchair, a corner stand with a large mirror, a bookshelf fastened to the wall, and a woodburning iron stove with two cooking holes covered with iron rings. Along the wall beside the stove stood a kitchen bench with a water bucket. This was the warmest place in the apartment and was often occupied by Kristin, who was even more easily chilled than I. It was not an unfriendly room; it was bright in summer and cozy in winter and would be my home now for an indeterminate time. But before I could take stock of my new surroundings, one more unexpected and woeful bridge had to be crossed.

"This coal dust has really affected me," I complained to Kristin. "Look at these little red spots; they itch like crazy and there seem to be more of them all the time."

Kristin, solemn faced as always, examined my stomach and legs, her pale eyebrows lifting a hundredth of an inch.

"This is not coal dust, Evchen. This is scabies."

"*SCABIES*?!"

Scabies was the affliction of the homeless, the dispossessed. Scabies was never even mentioned in whispers. Scabies were tiny parasites that made their way under the skin, digging thin, straight tunnels that could be followed from one little red dot to the next. They were itchy, revolting, and widely contagious. People like us did not get scabies.

I furiously charged Kristin.

"How would I get scabies?"

"Did you sleep in the refugee camp?

"Yes, three nights."

"On a used mattress?"

I saw the matted gray sack with the deep human imprints before me and groaned.

"There's your answer," said Kristin. "Now, don't panic. That's one thing they have medication for. We'll get it this morning."

The pharmacist showed no surprise when he handed us the large glass jar. He had a whole row of them behind him.

"This is a sulfa salve. Don't just cover the visible spots and streaks with it. They will only emerge at another part. Have your friend cover your entire body with the salve and leave it on for thirty-six hours. Then wash it off. If you follow the directions I can guarantee you that you will be cured."

As soon as we were home I stripped to the skin and Kristin opened the jar. Immediately a whiff of foul air escaped. This was no mellow, cosmetically enhanced ointment; this was raw, yellow sulfur paste. Kristin began to rub it on my back, starting at the neck under the hair line. The odor became stronger, pervading the room. "This stinks, Kristin. I can't bear it."

"Turn around." She had finished my back and started on my neck, under the chin. The nauseating stench clung to my nostrils: "Not up there! Not all the way! Not thirty-six hours! That's inhuman."

"Hold still." She was painting my stomach. "You want to get rid of it, don't you?"

I was standing in the middle of the room, all but immobilized now by a thick coat of yellow grease whose secret ingredient had to be about a hundred rotten eggs. Kristin produced a large sheet and began to roll it around me.

"Lie down and stop hollering. Thirty-six hours is not that long."

Thirty-six hours were interminable. I was only permitted to go to the bathroom, after which visits she slapped some more paste on me and rewrapped me. The room smelled like Dante's Inferno, the bottom circle. Kristin did not bat an eyelash. True, she could leave the room if it became unbearable, but she would have to eat and sleep in it.

That afternoon, while I was lying on the sofa like an oversized, greasy eggroll, Kristin rushed into the room.

"George is here."

"Don't let him in," I whispered furiously. "If you let him in I shall never speak to you again."

"And he has a friend with him whom he wants you to meet."

"Kristin!" I shrieked, but the lieutenant and his friend were already in the door.

"Please excuse me . . ." I had pulled the sheet up to my ears.

"It's all right," said the lieutenant comforting. "Kristin told us that you are not feeling well."

He stepped closer and peered into my face.

"You do look a little peeked," he said concerned.

"I'll be fine tomorrow," I mumbled, sinking deeper under the sheet. I never in my life had wanted so much to hurl something at somebody as at this moment.

"This is my friend Ralph." The lieutenant was doing the honors. "He is originally from England."

"I say . . . hello, there," said the young man gamely. He was trying not to breathe through his nose. "So sorry you are a bit under the weather."

"Hello . . . Ralph? Ja, I don't feel so good today." (How would you two gentlemen like a jar of rotten eggs in your faces?) "I am sorry I cannot shake your hand."

"I better go," said Ralph, retreating toward the door. "Well, it was certainly a pleasure meeting you."

I had never heard this phrase before and this was not a good time to introduce me to it. It left me speechless with consternation.

The lieutenant looked disappointed.

"You will like him when you know him better," he said. "He is only eighteen and most of the time he is homesick."

"Yes," I said, "yes, I shall certainly like him. Next week. Please, darling, no more visitors until I am up again. Promise!"

The pharmacist had been right. After two soap and water scrubbings the spots faded and no new ones appeared. The lieutenant began commuting between Frankfurt and Wiesbaden. His German was good enough to communicate with Kristin, who spoke no English. He started to reorganize our room, pushing the sofas at a more convenient angle, piling the wood neater and closer to the stove, placing the table near the brighter of the two windows. In between he stood and absent-mindedly scratched his arms and chest.

"George, let me see your chest!"

The scratching stopped immediately. "There is nothing wrong with my chest. The shirt is scratchy."

It was worse at the next visit. On the third evening he sank down on the foot end of my sofa. Looking, at once, wounded and rather heroic, his eyes mournfully searched the room.

"Okay, where is the gook?"

By now his chest showed numerous spots and streaks. I covered his upper body and arms with the sulfa paste; that was all he would let me do. He put his army shirt over it and drove back to Frankfurt. And so he went to his office the next morning. Reeking to high heaven, his shirt sticking to the salve, he sat at his desk and dictated letters to his appalled secretary; he inspected facilities, went to meetings, and ate at officers' mess. Faced with such stoicism, the scabies gave up and disappeared.

Chapter 29

Herrengarten — "Squires Garden" — was the name of our street. It might have been that at one time but there was little left of its former grandeur. It was a dark and shabby thoroughfare but there was not a trace of trash on the narrow sidewalk. Once a week the steps and entrances of each house had to be washed down by the tenants; the landlords saw to that. The poorer you are, the more important cleanliness becomes; we all knew this. Kristin and I, living on the first floor, had only a few stairs to scrub, but the weekly sweeping of the cobblestone entrance also fell to our share.

The front rooms were occupied by a refugee family. The long corridor leading to the back of the apartment was narrow and dark; one toilet for all parties. The kitchen was useless, but our room in the back was cheerful enough. The iron stove was used for both heating and cooking, and as the sun grew in strength we often had the windows open all day.

Every evening the lieutenant appeared, punctually like the church tower clock. The few times that the car was unavailable he hitched the 70 kilometer ride with a passing army vehicle. On Saturdays I would return with him to Frankfurt and Frieda's comforting and watchful care.

We could have settled into an agreeable and pleasant routine, but we did not. Not yet. I had to return to the Russian zone to fetch Bertel, and Kristin was anxious to find her parents. She only had awaited my arrival to set her plan in motion.

Through relatives in Berlin she had succeeded in getting in touch with her family. Her father had been drafted during the last months of the war. Her mother, sister, and two-year-old niece had stayed on in their East Prussian town until the last possible moment, then packed a few things and fled west. Kristin's sister was seven months' pregnant and it was a miracle that all three had survived the flight. They got no further than a basement room in Berlin. The baby was born in the midst of bombs and artillery shelling and had died a few days later. Eventually, the two women and the child were sent to a small farm north of Berlin where Kristin's father found them. None of the hardships seemed to matter when Kristin's younger brother, their only son, appeared at their doorstep one day—scraggly, his uniform tattered, his feet wrapped in rags, but otherwise cheerful and unharmed.

They did what was possible with the little piece of farm land, but seed was scarce that spring and fields looked unpromising. One evening the young man took a shotgun he had found in the attic of the farmhouse and went into the woods. That night they had rabbit stew for dinner which his mother would stretch to more than one meal. But two mornings later a Russian patrol appeared, confiscated the shotgun and led the young man away in handcuffs. They never saw him again.

Then Kristin knew that she had to conquer her obsessive fear of the Russians and go and see her parents.

Both Kristin and I were resigned to go "black" over the border, which meant an illegal crossing in Germany. But the lieutenant all but ordered us to wait. There had to be a legal way to do so, he thought. Let's look at the facts here, he said: two young women who wanted to cross into the Russian zone, who would demand neither shelter nor food stamps, whose presence was unpolitical and, in any way, unthreatening—one desiring a short visit with her parents and the other wanting to fetch her two-year-old child. All reason and logic pointed to a legal permission. We told him that reason and logic had nothing to do with it; they had played no part in our survival so far and were not likely to do so in the near future. But this was inconceivable to him. He enlisted the help of his fellow officers and, eventually, even of his superiors. They began canvassing other military government agencies. Night after night the lieutenant appeared, answering our questioning looks with a stubborn look of his own:

"There has to be a way . . ."

It was early summer when he finally declared defeat. Sitting in the armchair in the corner of the room, looking disgusted and glum, he suddenly said:

"All right. How do you want to go about it?"

The lieutenant's world, so far, had been built on reason, logic, and justice. While Kristin and I expected nothing from those quarters, the lieutenant had trusted implicitly in their prevalence and his faith had received a painful blow. From now on he quietly and unhappily acquiesced, offering no more resistance to our plans. We needed something to bribe, we knew, something that could be hidden. We could take no bundles or boxes. On the advice of a German friend we decided on a bottle of whiskey that could be strapped, along with a small bag, around the waist under our clothes.

On a cool, clear morning the lieutenant drove us to the last village in the American zone. Our whiskey advisor, who had gone the same route some months before, had given us certain instructions which we were careful to follow. We kissed our gloomy friend and chauffeur goodbye but dared not turn around to wave for fear of drawing attention. In the last house of the village we found the toothless old woman we had been told to see. Wordless and unsmiling, she brought a glass jar into which we filled one third of our whiskey. She hid the jar in a stove pipe, locked the house and headed into the woods. Gathering her long, black skirt and petticoats, she quickly limped ahead of us over a barely visible path for a quarter of an hour until we came to a fork of the way. There she stopped, planted her feet on the ground and spoke to us for the first time.

"You'll have to take the path to the right. Keep to the edge of the woods. You will be safe for about two kilometers. After that the path will run along an open field. You'll see the Russian watchtowers to your right. Take care. From then on they will be able to see you, too. Go to the end of the field. You'll have to cross it somehow, there is no other way. Keep low. You'll see the village. If you make it, go into the first house. They might help you from there."

Without a goodbye or God's speed, she turned and hastened back. Kristin and I were on our own.

The only times in my life I have felt some kind of desperate bravura were in the company of somebody who was more frightened than I. There was no doubt that Kristin was scared out of her wits. She had never even seen a Russian soldier. Burnt into her mind, also, was her brother's fate. I had seen plenty of Russian soldiers, but I cannot say that this fact was particularly reassuring. I did not think that we were in danger of being shot, but I knew that being caught and deported was a much stronger possibility than either Kristin or the lieutenant were aware. Stalin's orders had been explicit on that point.

"Well, Kristin? You ready? This will be something to tell our grandchildren about."

And Kristin, whose face was white and pinched, took hold of my hand for a second and nodded. We walked the two kilometers in silence and stopped when the tree line to our right thinned and we could see the field. At regular distances, like windmills without arms, tall, dark structures were rising from the ground.

"The watchtowers," whispered Kristin.

We stopped to consult. Within a few steps the trees to our right would disappear entirely; we would have to go down on our hands and knees now. We strapped the bags and bottle more securely around the waist, stuffed the hems of our dresses under the belts and crouched down in the high grass. In single file we moved forward, keeping the movements of the weeds to a minimum. Once in a while we stopped completely. We could make out the silhouette of the soldier on top of the nearest tower. He had a pair of binoculars with which he periodically scanned the edge of the woods and the distant fields. His motions were bored, he often would not even finish the whole turn. Cautiously, snakelike, we moved ahead. A new formidable obstacle appeared: a dirt road had to be crossed, unprotected by any kind of growth. The deep wagon-wheel furrows were muddy from the last rain. By now we could see the outline of the soldier more plainly and when he turned his back to us we moved across with lightning speed, mud splashing on our arms and legs. Across the road, the village came into clear view, but it meant turning our backs to the watch tower, more stops and terrified looks over our shoulder.

We were within two hundred yards of the village now. Cautiously, first I got up and then Kristin. Forcing ourselves to walk slowly and without glancing backward, we made our way to the house that would save us.

We knocked on the door; it was opened immediately by an elderly woman, her face tight with anger. She must have seen our approach through the window.

"Lord Almighty, get in here! Do you want us all shot? Get that mud off you!" She led the way to the kitchen where she gave us some rags and water and, muttering furiously, watched us getting rid of the worst of the dirt.

"Your shoes, too. All they need is to see your muddy shoes. There ain't such mud in the village."

We produced the whiskey. "We can't give you all of it," I said timidly into the rage of the woman, "just a third. We have to save some for the rest of the trip."

I was sorry now that we had given the old woman on the other side so much; she had risked nothing. This woman here was risking her and her husband's liberty for us.

"Where do you want to go?"

"To the nearest train station."

There would be the milk wagon going on its daily run to the station. Maybe the driver would take us and maybe not. We would have to do our own negotiating. Taking us into her house, giving us water and rags to wash off the mud, was all she was prepared to do.

The milk truck was still loading when we got there. We stood close to the husky young driver who kept swinging the heavy cans onto the truck bed, ignoring us.

"Will you take us to the train station?" No answer.

"All we want is to get to the nearest train station."

The cans thudded onto the truck. He was deaf and dumb. I pulled the bottle neck out of my dress and wiggled it a little. A quick, sidelong glance; he kept on working.

"Just to the station?" At least, he had found his tongue. "I have to go through a check point. Sometimes they stop me, sometimes they don't. If they do, I'll tell them that you lied to me. Is that understood?"

"Yes. Yes, we promise." I did all the talking; Kristin was in a fog. We climbed into the cab; the bottle with the rest of the whiskey disappeared into a sack under the driver's seat; we were on our way.

A minute or two out of the village we could see a barrier lowered across the road. Half a dozen Russian soldiers were milling around, laughing and talking. I could feel Kristin go rigid beside me.

We had no luggage. Kristin and I wore scarfs knotted around our heads and our dresses were faded and mended. The milk truck slowed down and came to a full stop. One of the soldiers detached himself from the group and walked toward us. He had a rifle slung over his shoulder but otherwise seemed anything but fearsome. He was very young, fair-haired, and apple-cheeked; he looked, in fact, more pleasant than our driver. However, Kristin, who was sitting nearest to the window, spared him no glance. She was staring straight ahead; her face was bloodless, her hands in her lap, white knuckled and slightly trembling, were mangling her handkerchief. A saint would have grown suspicious beholding this study in terror.

A frantic impulse made me get hold of a strand of her hair, literally yanking her out of her fatal stupor.

"Ouch! What's the . . ." Surprise made her voice sound almost normal.

"Got you!" I cried, laughing, and: "Talk to me, you idiot. Move. Smile," I mumbled under my breath. "We are supposed to be two village wenches who see those guys every day, remember?"

The soldier had stepped closer and was peering through the window. At long last Kristin seemed to comprehend but all she managed was a feeble shove at me whereupon I cheerfully slapped her arm.

If the pounding of a heart had been audible, how many more times would we have come to grief!

The soldier tapped at the glass and winked at the driver who grinned and shrugged his shoulder in response. The soldier waved him on, the barrier creaked open and we were back on the road.

At the station, Kristin and I parted. I knew where I was going and what would be awaiting me. Kristin went into bleak uncertainty.

* * * * * * * * * * * * *

Once again the Rock Cellar was enfolded by the dark green leaves of the old oak tree. The bushes were blooming and the grass on the hill behind the house was ankle-deep. The windmill across the dale dipped its old arms at me in solemn welcome.

"How can I hand Bertel over to you if he does not know you anymore?" My mother looked doubtful and unhappy.

"I will stay until he does," I promised, remembering how quickly he had responded to me at our Christmas visit.

Wolfgang had returned to the city. Agatha was still swaying the sheets and studying the newspaper squares in the outhouse but the little goat was gone and I did not inquire about her. My mother was working now. Having one way or another gotten rid of all her tenants, she had to find a new source of income. Reviewing her options — training, location, circumstances, and opportunities — anybody but a woman of her caliber might have grown faint-hearted. Far from despairing, my mother decided she would teach ballroom dancing. Aware that a prophet has no honor in his own country, she prudently made no attempt to persuade her own town but pedalled her bike to the nearest village and looked up the local burgess.

"Dancing lessons?!" the old farmer exclaimed. "Why, those youngsters have to help in the fields. They don't hardly have shoes fit to walk in. They are glad if they have a solid meal in their stomach each day."

"That's precisely why they should learn how to dance!" said my mother firmly. Not surprisingly, this remained unchallenged. Nobody ever got a handle on my mother's brand of logic.

"All I want from you is permission to post the announcement and rent the town hall one afternoon a week."

The next village was run by a dyed-in-the-wool communist who wasn't sure of the Party line concerning dancing lessons. He eyed my mother suspiciously.

"Do you know how?"

"Of course I know how," said my mother, who had never given a dancing lesson in her life. "Would I be here if I didn't?" She was quite offended.

When she returned that night, she had posted her lessons in three villages, had rented three rooms for an afternoon each week and had acquired the temporary use of a gramophone. All that was left to do was to find somebody who would show her how to teach those lessons until the following weekend. For this she took a train to a larger town where she consulted an old telephone book for the address of pre-war dance studios. After a tenacious search she located a dispirited, shrunken little man who was sixty and looked eighty. My mother made him an offer: a suit of clothes (a pre-war, outgrown one of my brother) and a bag of cream of wheat for three days of dancing lessons and loan of some of his records. When I arrived at the Rock Cellar, business was booming. After five grim years, these weekly hours of music and dancing seemed heaven on earth to the village youngsters and there was no lack of pupils.

Bertel had begun to follow me around like my shadow; even my mother was satisfied. After two weeks we were ready to leave. I packed his clothes and the rest of my summer things; it did not make a large bundle but there was also the bag with blankets and food and I would have to carry Bertel once in a while. There was no question now of crawling through muddy fields on hands and knees. Once again I would have to try to go through a camp.

We went by train to a refugee center near the Russian-American border. My mother left us at the entrance of the camp. Again we were sprayed from top to bottom with disinfectant but no stamp was placed on the back of my hand. We were not admitted. "You have no valid papers," I was told. "Try Barrack B." We waited in Barrack B for an hour and were told that we had no valid papers. "Try Barrack 6A." After sitting on the steps of Barrack 6A for two hours we were told that, since we were not bona fide refugees, we would have to leave the camp. I asked for the camp director. "Barrack 12," I was told, "but he will tell you the same thing."

It was evening when Bertel and I finally sat on the single, hard straight-backed chair in the director's office and pleaded our case. This man, a large ruddy-faced East German, was no weary philosopher as the director in Berlin had been. During the entire interview he never sat down but kept pacing the room with long, angry steps, shouting and throwing threatening looks at us. "How did you get here?" he demanded, stopping and staring ferociously at me, "just tell me how you got here!"

"I came to fetch my little boy," I said, much intimidated by such hostility.

"I didn't ask you why you came, I asked you how you came!" he shouted, continuing his stomping about. "I tell you how you came," he answered his own question, dripping sarcasm now, "You had a friend—probably an American, right? He helped you across the border and now you want us to take care of you. Right?" Since this, unfortunately, was the truth, I had no answer.

"I'll tell you what you'll do," he said, stopping again and glaring at me. "You are going back the way you came, that's what you are going to do."

"But I can't," I said, aghast, "I have my little boy with me now."

"Well, you should have thought of that before. We are not permitted to take care of you. There are penalties, you understand? They'll close us down." More stomping, a furious kick against the metal wastepaper basket. "You are border hoppers, that's what you are. And every week you come here by the dozens and want us to get you back home. But *WE ARE NOT PERMITTED TO DO THAT*! Do I make myself clear?"

During all this tongue lashing Bertel had hidden his face against my shoulder. Now he looked up and saw that I was crying. Very much frightened by this he pressed closer and started sobbing. The director ceased his stomping and for a minute or two glowered at us in silence. Then he continued his pacing, his voice plaintive now instead of angry.

"For Christ's sake, stop that! Stop sniffling, both of you. This is not to be tolerated. Keep that child quiet. Why do I always have to clear up your irresponsible messes?!" He sank into his chair behind the desk and began scribbling.

"Take this and get out!" I clutched the paper, picked up my bundles and Bertel and fled. The paper entitled us to a meal, a bed, and transportation across the border.

At the dormitory I closely inspected our straw mattress, although I knew that scabies don't crawl or jump about like fleas or lice and could not possibly be seen in the folds of the gray sack cloth. Besides, what were a few measly little parasites compared to the victory we had just won? But when I laid down that night, with Bertel on a blanket beside me, I could not suppress a faint shiver of disgust before falling asleep.

In the late afternoon of the next day we were loaded into boxcars. The straw covering the floor was clean and the day was warm. This trip would be luxurious compared to the last one. However, an unexpected difficulty arose: I knew that Bertel no longer wore diapers, but I had no warning as to the extent and rigidity of his toilet training. Toward evening he became restless, he wanted to go to the potty. The boxcar had no toilet; there were erratic stops along the way when people would jump out and run behind the nearest bushes to relieve themselves, never losing the train out of eyesight. Sometimes these stops were as long as three quarters of an hour, other times they were no longer than a minute or two. At all times one had to be prepared to jump up and run for it. The people in the car usually managed to pull the unfortunate latecomer back inside before the train gathered speed. To take such a chance with a twenty-months-old baby was out of the question. By nightfall Bertel was crying. I pleaded with him to do what he had to do but he just clung to me, sobbing. I should have known that my mother did nothing by half. Bertel would burst before he would wet himself. By now furtive glances were shot at us from all direction; people guessed the child's trouble and avoided looking at us. At long last I got up, not caring any more what anybody thought, and carried the trembling child into a far corner of the car, where I crouched down with him. Bertel had buried his face into my neck, my shirt collar was moist with perspiration and tears. I quickly gathered some straw and shaped it into a little circle.

"Look Schaetzchen," I whispered, turning his puffed face around and away from me. "This is a straw train." I pointed to all the straw around us. "And straw trains always have straw potties."

The little boy stopped crying and stared at the hole in the straw. Smiling lightly and trying to appear quite matter-of-fact, I was holding my breath when I saw his face suddenly relax. His last hard, dry sob sounded more like a sigh; he slipped off my lap and started pulling at his clothes; it made sense to him.

Picking him up again I defiantly turned around to face the car, only to meet with quick smiles and friendly nods; some people even pulled their legs up to make it easier for us to reach our place.

"I know how he felt," said an old man, nodding and moving his knapsack out of our way. "It's hell."

By now it was quite dark. The car had no electricity and all the light we had came from the night sky through a crack in the door. There was not room enough for all of us to stretch out in a space of our own. The adjustment was instinctive and peaceful. Bertel was asleep; his head rested on my stomach, my right arm was thrown across his body—I did not want to take the chance of his waking in the night and wandering around in the darkness. My own head rested on the stomach of a fellow traveler; I had put it there because it was the only place left and there was no objection. All around me was the even breathing of sleeping human beings; a gentle snoring from a corner came and went; some rustling of straw as someone tried for a more comfortable position. I felt the rhythmic rising and falling of the man's chest under my head before I finally dozed off myself. It was not the worst night I ever spent.

With early daylight, the train came to a final stop. The conductor walked alongside the boxcars shouting for everybody to get out. We had arrived at our destination, the first town across the Russian-American zone border. Disheveled travelers, straw clinging to their clothes and hair, tumbled out of the cars and blinked into the bright light. There was no station house or platform; we had stopped in an open field. The station, the conductor shouted, was about a quarter of a mile ahead. Nobody asked for the reason; few things ever made sense to us.

People picked up their bundles, suitcases, and children and started walking between the tracks toward the distant station. It quickly became clear that Bertel could not walk unaided over the rough stones between the railroad ties. I told him that I would take the bags a little way ahead, drop them, and come back for him; but at the prospect of being left behind the child, terrified, clung to my skirt and would not let go. I then tried the reverse approach and to this he acquiesced. I would leave the bags behind and carry him a few hundred feet toward the station, then put him down on some grassy spot and walk back to retrieve our luggage, waving and calling out to him as I did so. It was a slow process, and we arrived at the terminal a long time after everybody else had disappeared. A man came out of the building, picked up the bags and led us into a room where a plate of warm porridge was served to each traveler. We ate gratefully, Bertel humming while he ate as he had done since his infant days. When we finished, the man had gone, the kitchen window was closed, and none of the travelers were around anymore. With Bertel holding on to my skirt, I picked up the bags to find a telephone. The lieutenant had been on steady alert throughout the last days; I was to call him the moment I arrived in the west.

"You mean, you folks don't know that we had a storm here last night?" said the station master. "You are only the hundredth person to ask for a telephone. All the wires are down around here. There is no phone and won't be for a couple days."

"How about a telegram?" I asked, apprehension closing in like brown fog.

"Same thing," said the station master, "not before tomorrow, at the earliest." The window snapped shut and Bertel, the bags, and myself were once again thrown onto our own devices.

Outside the station house the sky was blue and clear, a bright sun was shining down on large, broken branches which showed little blossoms between the fresh green leaves that soon now would be dead. Street signs had tumbled down; a large wire wastepaper basket had fallen over and the trash was strewn all through the little park across the street. Everywhere one looked were signs of the storm and the air was raw in spite of the bright sun.

Bertel's eyes were searching my face. With uncanny accuracy the child had learned to take all his cues from my own response to each new situation. I could not let on how completely at a loss I was again; there could be no panic, no tears, not with Bertel's eyes glued to my face.

All right, then, it was a matter of getting through the next thirty hours in a strange town that presented little else but closed shutters and locked doors. The town itself seemed in size and character not unlike our little town of Thuringia. Where would I turn to if I had been in a similar help-less situation back there? I suddenly thought of our pharmacist, this bluster-ing, generous man, and his anxious, kind-hearted wife.

We found our way to the town's pharmacy and they took us in. I won't say that they were not taken aback, slow to react, disconcerted by my puz-zling faith in them; but they took us in and gave us a meal and a bed and the next day they put our call through to Frankfurt. And when the lieutenant appeared four hours later, and Bertel and I and the bags were safely stored away in the little green car, they waved us off like dear house guests whose stay they had certainly enjoyed.

Chapter 30

Things were easier in Wiesbaden than they had been in Berlin. We settled into a routine that, temporary as it was, almost resembled a normal life. Shortly after Kristin's safe return from the east I began working for the Department of Price Control. It was dry, unimaginative work, but my supervisor, a retired old German police sergeant, livened up my days with wistful reminiscences of baffling murders, carnival pickpockets, and the elusive art of suicide. Kristin, who had been a court stenographer before joining the navy, declared herself happy if she never saw a steno pad again; she kept house, took Bertel to the park, and doggedly read her way through the bookshelf in our room.

Once a week, Kristin and I went to the cinema. I would go to the first show and when it was over, Kristin would be standing in line for the second show, holding Bertel by the hand. She would pass him to me under the dividing chain and while she sat through the late show, I would take Bertel for an evening stroll and put him to bed. Once a month we had to pick up our wood and coal rations. For this we borrowed a handwagon and walked about three quarters of an hour to the distribution center in another part of town. On those trips we could not take Bertel along and needed the help and goodwill of Frau Lemke.

The Lemkes were the refugee family who shared the apartment with us. They occupied the front room next to the house entrance with a window toward the street which featured — from spring to fall — a greasy cushion to rest Frau Lemke's elbows more easily during her long hours of vigil.

A second smaller, windowless room in the back served as a bedroom. Frau Lemke was a short-legged, spongy-looking woman with stringy, dark hair and unhealthy skin who was known to trade her soap coupons for sweets and cigarettes. However, we were careful to keep those speculations to ourselves, since it was this lady we had to ask to watch Bertel once in a while. Also, she was in possession of a one-eyed, emaciated teddy bear with which Bertel had fallen in love on sight and without which life had become unthinkable for him. She let him keep it, only discreetly reminding us from time to time that it was *her* teddy bear and could be repatriated, at will, into the windowless, unaired back room from where she had originally produced it.

Not only the lieutenant was passing now regularly through the entrance door under Frau Lemke's watchful raisin eyes. Kristin, too, had a caller.

Returning from the east she had been stranded for some hours at a country station and had approached a young man in uniform to ask him about the possible arrival time of the train. At the end of the war most German uniforms had been condemned and done away with and new ones created so rapidly that nobody knew anymore who was representing what. Unruffled, the tall young man explained that he was not a railroad official but a ranger at the Department of Forestry and that he had no more information about the trains' arrivals and departures than anybody else. Kristin, embarrassed, apologized and withdrew; but when the train finally arrived, the young man suddenly appeared at her side and helped her with her suitcase.

"He said he might come and see me," Kristin said, when she told me about it, "but I doubt it. He did not even write down our address."

It seemed, though, that the young man had a better memory than she gave him credit for. He remembered the street and the house number and — interviewed and directed by the tireless Frau Lemke — appeared at our doorstep one evening. He took Kristin out dancing, and when she returned her eyes were shining and there was a pink glow on her usually pale cheeks. The young man's name was Bernhard and he became as frequent a visitor as the lieutenant, with whom he now began to share the tasks of splitting wood, entertaining Bertel, and moving our furniture about.

* * * * * * * * * * * * *

Our first two goals — my move to the west and Bertel's joining us — had been achieved, though it has been a great deal easier to write it all down forty-three years later than to accomplish it in 1946. We would now concentrate on our marriage plans.

Neither the lieutenant nor I were sure how to go about it. The non-fraternization rules had been considerably relaxed—having proven to be next to impossible to enforce—but no American military personnel, man or woman, were permitted to marry Germans. We decided that our best hope lay within the conscience of a stout-hearted German minister whose faith in Christian ethics was stronger than his fear of occupation regulations. After attending services for some weeks, we believed that in the pastor of a large Protestant church near our living quarters we had found the right person. The lieutenant and I went to see him.

He was an elderly gentleman who had been plump at one time (and would be plump again in years to come) with a kind face and blue, slightly crossed eyes. The constant effort of focusing them on the same object gave him an expression of permanent puzzlement, underlined still by his hesitant way of speaking. Here was a man who wanted to do the right thing in a world that seemed to have lost all landmarks between sin and virtue.

I told him that it would have to be a church wedding only.

"The lieutenant will not be able to get permission to marry a German until he is discharged from the army," I explained, "and he won't be discharged until he is back in America. And I am not permitted to go to America."

The puzzled frown deepened; he was trying to focus both worried eyes on my face.

"But such a marriage would not be valid in Germany!"

"It won't be valid in America, either," the lieutenant consoled him.

One mild blue eye wandered around and came, chagrined, to rest on the lieutenant's face.

"It is not legal, then," the pastor said sadly. Kicking the lieutenant's leg under the chair to prevent further comfort from that quarter, I caught those worried eyes and for a moment they both focused on my face, reading and comprehending my quick smile. This wordless communication was between him and me and left the lieutenant out entirely. The pastor and I would have been hard put to remember all the illegal acts we had committed during the last dozen years. He knew as well as I did that this was no argument.

"Don't you think it would be better to have a Christian marriage than none at all?" I asked gently. "You know that we shall legalize it at the first possible chance."

Here was the rare occasion when no bribe could be offered. It would only have compounded the old gentleman's agonizing.

"Yes," he said, after a long silence, "yes, I shall marry you as long as you realize that you will have to go through a civil ceremony some time in the future." This was a courageous decision. I wanted to jump up and plant a kiss on his dear, bald, sorrowful forehead. But all I could do was beam at him.

"And, at the same time, we would like you to baptize my little boy."

The pastor's face brightened with pleasure; an unexpected gift had been offered to him. The relief was tangible. It was as if the solid making of a little Christian would make up for the performing of a not-so-solid marriage ceremony.

And so, on a rather hot and humid Saturday in July, in the presence of three splendid uniforms—the lieutenant's, Kristin's ranger, and the city fireman who lived next door to us—the marriage and baptism took place in the old Frankish church, and for many years after Bertel darkly connected weddings with cold water being inexplicably dripped upon one's unsuspecting head.

* * * * * * * * * * * * *

The lieutenant promptly reported the news to his family back home. It seemed to me that he awaited their reaction with a good deal of complacency. I felt anything but complacent. The family's attitude so far had wavered between a hopeful "This, too, will pass," and "We'll cross that bridge when we get to it." It had not passed. Fourteen months earlier the lieutenant had crossed that bridge. He had walked to the last house on the other side and he had never looked back since that day.

We did not have to wait long for an answer. The lieutenant appeared with not one but two letters, written by his father and addressed to me.

"They both say pretty much the same thing," he said, handing them to me. "My father wrote a letter to you and took it to the aunts for their approval. They thought that at one point he had used too strong a word so he rewrote it using another one."

It seemed that he, then, sent both letters to the lieutenant asking him to give me the one he thought more suitable. The lieutenant, who never in his life made up other people's minds for them, just handed me both letters, suggesting that I keep the one I liked better.

While he was roughhousing on the floor with Bertel, I sat at the table and concentrated on studying what I considered one of the most important letters of my life.

"When we learned," the first letter said, "that George married a girl with whose country we so recently had been at war, we were shocked, but we have decided to trust his judgment and to welcome you wholeheartedly into our family . . ."

The second letter was the exact copy of the first one except for the word "shocked" which had been replaced by "surprised." The rest of the letter was warm-hearted and cheerful and when I had finished, I sat there with a big lump in my throat. I answered it the same evening; that is, I began an answer. It took me a few days to compose such a letter, refusing the lieutenant's offer to help.

"I do not want you to believe that my English is better than it is," I wrote, and "I, too, was shocked to love an American . . ."

After this initial contact, the lieutenant's family adopted Bertel and me without conditions or reservations. The first parcel to arrive contained a pair of trim-looking walking shoes and I thought of it as a minor miracle that my feet slipped into them without permanently crippling my toes, considering all the improvements the drawing had undergone. Other parcels followed, clothes for Bertel and me, lovingly selected and packed by the aunts.

If my future family had accepted me, the occupation government had certainly not. My weekend visits at the lieutenant's living quarters in Frankfurt remained as precarious as ever, and more than once I spent a quarter of an hour in the lieutenant's closet while a beaming Frieda drove an inspection party to early flight with her exuberant cooperation and her terrible English.

The American officers whom I met during these visits were without exceptions easy-going, likable men, united in their fondness for German wine, women, and song, and in their dislike of officiousness, powdered eggs, and Spam. It was one of these fellow officers who introduced me to the mystical American drink called whiskey. Of course, I had heard about whiskey in all those cowboy and Indian books we read as children, but Kristin and I had not tasted as much as a drop of the precious bottle we had taken across the border.

On that memorable Saturday noon, the lieutenant had to keep an appointment and trusted me to this captain for entertainment and companionship. The captain, taking his host duties seriously, immediately offered me a whiskey, which I delightedly accepted.

"Water? Soda?" said the captain over his shoulder, getting hold of bottle and glasses.

"Water?" I asked, perplexed. I never heard of water being poured into beer, wine or brandy, those being all the drinks I was familiar with. And soda was something we washed dishes in.

"No, of course not."

The captain raised his eyebrows, shrugged his shoulders and, in true American live-and-let-live fashion, handed me a glass filled about one-third with a lovely, amber-colored liquid. We settled down to an amiable conversation, all about dogs as I recall. I was enlightening my host about the difference between a terrier and a German dachshund; a terrier was easier to train, but would give his affection to anybody who was fleetingly nice to him, while a dachshund never listened to anybody but fastens his affection on one single person and might lie down on the grave of that person, not to be dislodged by rain, hunger, or human kindness. Which reminded me of my grandfather, who, as I explained to the increasingly concerned looking captain, had insisted on standing bareheaded on a terrible November day at the graveside of somebody or other, and, I might add, with the direst of consequences . . . At this point I felt the chair under me, for inexplicable reasons, tilt forward and sideways at the same time which forced me to shift my weight rather suddenly. And that is, honestly, the last thing I remember of that amiable social hour. The next picture in my mind is the lieutenant standing beside me and holding me rather forcefully in an upright position in the same unreliable chair, while the captain, with guilty glances at the two of us, was hastily brewing coffee over a spirit flame.

This remained my only encounter with whiskey for a number of years. On Saturdays, in the officers' club to which German girls were now admitted (largely to avoid the yawning emptiness of the clubrooms that had existed while the off-limit rules were still enforced) we drank champagne that had been liberated in great quantities from German cellars along the

Rhine. Usually we shared one small bottle with the single exception of one night, when the party at our table had been particularly lively and we somehow lost track of all the little bottles in front of us. When we left at midnight the lieutenant suggested that we take a dip in the swimming pool behind the general's villa next door. Since the night was warm and the club rooms had been stifling, I thought this very clever of him. The fence proved no obstacle and in no time at all we were splashing around without a stitch of clothing, frolicking in the sun-warmed water under the ink-blue starry sky and not a thought of the slumbering general above us crossing our cloudless minds. When we finally climbed out and were drying ourselves with the lieutenant's green army undershirt we felt that the evening had been an unmitigated success, although I had lost one of my clip-on earrings and the lieutenant had dived into the pool with his watch still on his wrist.

* * * * * * * * * * * * *

Kristin and her ranger had become quite inseparable. Bernhard lived in a tiny attic room with no cooking or heating facilities and he had fallen into the habit of spending most of his spare time at our place. There was talk about marriage but Bernhard, who hailed from the northeast of Germany, was restless about his parents and before anything was settled he wanted to look them up and reassure himself that they were all right. Bernhard's younger brother, Klaus, also had been discharged to Wiesbaden and the two brothers decided to undertake the trip into the Russian zone together. These were two tall, strong young men who had come through the war unscathed and neither of them was unduly worried about a little black peacetime border crossing.

Kristin dreaded their going, the uncertainty of their success, and the long weeks of silence that lay ahead of her. It was a warm, humid summer and often on weekends the lieutenant would drive Kristin, Bertel, and me into the Taunus mountains for long walks. We carefully avoided mentioning Bernhard's name, nor did Kristin instigate any such conversation. As it had been the case so often before, I could not tell what went on behind the pallor of that inscrutable face.

Ah, but I do remember the day and the hour when we were sitting at the table eating dinner and the door opened and the long, emaciated, sunburned figure stood in the door frame. There were broad, fresh scratches on his face and a dark bruise above his jaw. This was not the jaunty young fellow who had taken Kristin out dancing until the wee hours of the morning. His eyes were deep in their sockets and there was a wild and haunted look about him. He was hungry, dirty, bone weary, and his talk was disjointed. Only slowly during the following days did we piece together what had happened.

All had gone well in the beginning. They had made their way across the border, found shelter in a village during their first day and hiked on toward their destination. Eventually they had reached their parents' farm which now belonged to a collective and was shared with other families. The parents were overjoyed at the appearance of both their sons and the young men stayed on for a few weeks, not having the heart to turn around and leave them so soon again. They had helped around the farm but there were two more mouths to feed and after a while some resentment began to stir in the collective. It was time to go. They had hiked to the Russian-American border without much trouble and waited for nightfall to cross the woods that separated the zones. After making their way cautiously through the darkness for an hour they had stumbled upon an armed Russian guard who had shouted at them to halt. The soldier ordered them to turn around and head back. His gun pointed, he was walking close behind them and every time one of the young men would stumble over a root the guard would hit him in the back or around the legs with the butt of his gun . Oddly enough, it was not the realization of their desperate position as much as this wanton beating that set the fuse off in the younger man.

"Don't do that!" said Klaus, temper flaring, after he had been knocked again sharply in the back with the gun butt. In response, the soldier gave him a second, even sharper blow across the shoulder blades. Neither Bernhard nor the soldier expected what was coming; I doubt that even Klaus knew what he was about to do. Within a split second he turned around and gave the guard such a powerful shove that the man fell to the ground.

"Run," Klaus shouted to his brother, "Run, run!"

And Bernhard ran. Instinctively, the two men chose different routes. The soldier jumped up and began shooting. The shots attracted other guards and soon the woods were filled with shouts and gunshots. Bernhard ran blindly with wild, uncertain jumps over roots and stones and ditches, branches tearing at his clothes and scratching his face, always heading west. He did not stop until he had reached the end of the forest, the end of no-man's land, and knew he was on the western side where he fell into the grass, choking, gasping for air, listening over the thumping of his heart for his brother's footsteps. The shouting and gunshots had ceased. Dawn came up through the trees behind him. The forest stood quietly, awaiting the day. There were no rustling of leaves, no footsteps. He had lost his brother. It was a story like a hundred others and we let it wash over us in numb resignation. We grieved for the plucky youngster who had saved his older brother's life but done himself immeasurable harm in the process. Bernhard, shaken by guilt and grief, remained nevertheless approachable and did not reject our efforts to help him over the inevitable depression. After some weeks, the wedding plans were revived and Kristin and Bernhard were married in the same church, by the same minister, and this time the lieutenant and I were standing at their side as witnesses.

Many months later, when the autumn winds had already swept the streets clean of most of the leaves and the last fall flowers in the park had succumbed to the night frost, another young man, stubby and frazzled, with clothes that were obviously not his own, stood in the same door frame, pleased as a child with our stunned surprise.

One of the shots had hit him in the groin, Klaus told us, and felled him on the spot. The soldiers had gathered around him, turned him over, poked at him, and seeing his blood soaked clothes and no sign of life, had left him for dead. He had pressed moss and stones against the wound and in the morning crawled onto a dirt road where a farm wagon had picked him up and taken him to a country hospital. It was a miracle that nobody ever inquired into his identity or the origin of his wound. The farmer, doctors, and nurses probably had quite a good idea but kept their guesses to themselves and no soldiers ever showed up to search the premises. These were lawless, violent times, but even then the guards might not have been too sure that they could kill and abandon a man at will and entirely without consequences, and possibly no official report had been made.

There had been a heavy loss of blood and Klaus's recovery was slow. It took months to regain some of his old strength but once he felt in control of his legs again, no lurking fear or terrifying memories kept him from trying again. And this time he found his way through the dank, dark autumn woods to the other side of the border without so much as stirring up a rabbit.

* * * * * * * * * * * * *

Kristin now spent her nights with her husband in his small, unheated attic room. Every morning she appeared at the door and rushed wordlessly to the little iron stove in the corner of our room, stretching out her hands, bending her whole body over it, soaking up the warmth which streamed from its surface. Only then, when she had reentered the land of the warm-blooded mammals, did she say good morning and resume the day's activities.

Many evenings and weekends during late summer and fall, the lieutenant, who had temporarily exchanged his little green Opal for a jeep, had driven us out into the woods to gather sticks, bark, and broken branches. We were a strange sight returning home after these excursions. I would sit, with Bertel on my lap, in front beside the lieutenant who was driving over the country roads and around city curves with extreme caution. The back of the jeep would be piled high with our wooden load and on top of it, holding the load down and at the same time hanging on for dear life, sat Kristin in her white raincoat, unsmiling, her blond hair flying in the wind, blue eyes looking grimly ahead, like a pouting prom queen who had expected more of her royal ride through town. Eventually she did protest, but by that time our supplementary winter supply had been sawed, cut, and stacked neatly under our window by the combined efforts of Bernhard and the lieutenant, and neither Kristin nor I were in condition to sit on a wiggly pile of sticks in the back of an open jeep.

It turned cold and parcels arrived from across the ocean with a snow-suit for Bertie and three maternity dresses for me. Kristin and I shared the dresses, both of us carried new life within us. In December, I said goodbye to my old sergeant at the Price Control and quit my job.

With Christmas approaching we were at a loss for presents to give to the lieutenant. The return of the Christmas market with its Lebkuchen and Gluehwein and hot sausages, its toys, candles, and hand-knitted woolens was still years away. No festive crowds strolled through the streets on December nights; the market place was abandoned and the store windows were glum, showing at best a dusty ornament or two that were not for sale. The two men went into the woods and cut down a little pine tree. We had no decorations and for a few days it looked as if the tree alone would have to do. But on the afternoon of Christmas Eve the lieutenant arrived carrying a box of small pretzels, a handful of candles, and, miraculously, a dozen red apples. At the mess hall that day they had received an apple with their rations and some of the lieutenant's fellow officers had donated theirs to the tree of a little boy in Wiesbaden. Bernhard fastened the candles with wires to the branches. We polished the apples until they gleamed and wrapped strings around their stems and hung them, along with the white-speckled brown pretzels, on the tree. There have been many beautiful Christmas trees throughout my life, but that is the one I remember best. It was lovely, really; a child's tree, with a charm all its own. There were toys from overseas for Bertel and presents for all of us from the lieutenant; and right then and there, with the candles shimmering and the smell of pine needles and apples and the wood stove in the air, none of us was empty-handed when we wished the lieutenant a Merry Christmas. I had found and bargained for an original pencil drawing by a talented young artist; Kristin had a plateful of finely decorated cookies for him, and Bernhard, with a happy and expectant grin, produced a wrapped parcel out of nowhere that revealed a pencil and a yellow writing pad. Kristin, mortified, gave him a quick poke in the ribs when she thought nobody was looking; but the lieutenant shook his hand warmly, saying that was just what he needed and of which there never was a sufficient supply, and Bernhard shot Kristin a pleased and triumphant look.

Chapter 31

Toward the end of 1946, besieged by letters and requests from military personnel, the U.S. government yielded: marriage between German women and American soldiers would be permitted after the soldiers were repatriated and discharged from military service. The young women would then receive immigration visas, provided they met a long list of stringent requirements. The first step was an application submitted by the soldier, followed by the young woman's birth certificate which had to be accompanied by the testimony of three trustworthy individuals declaring that the person in question had never committed any act harmful to the United States. This part was easy. The lieutenant filled out the forms, I dug out my birth certificate, and every one of the lieutenant's trusty army buddies was willing to swear that I never even harbored an evil thought toward their country. Those papers would then be evaluated and, if judged up to that point satisfactory, my name would be submitted to all four occupation powers to be checked against their list of wanted war criminals. This, we were told, might mean months of waiting. The lieutenant's time of military service was coming to an end. Unless he reenlisted, he would be sent back to the States and discharged with the rank of a captain. Reenlistment meant another twelve months in Germany. His family was anxious for his return; my visa might be issued within a shorter time than expected and we wanted our child to be born in America. So, it was best, then, for the lieutenant to go home.

It was a difficult decision and left us frightened and heavy hearted. We clung to the plan that, if my papers had not been processed by late spring of the next year, he would try for a civilian job in the occupation government in Germany, by no means a certainty.

When January 1947 came, my lieutenant was gone. Gone across the sea to be made a captain and, subsequently, a civilian; to join his family and begin a life that had, as yet, nothing to do with me and of which I knew very little.

"Suppose," I had said to him during one of our last evenings together, keeping my voice as light as I could manage, "just suppose that my papers have not come through in time; that April comes and even May and I could not travel anymore, and you would not yet have a job in Germany—you would have to send things for the baby to wear, clothes and diapers, a blanket, towels, and soap. And a bucket, oh don't forget a bucket. Summer things first, and later warm little sweaters . . . I shall write down a list and if I am not coming . . . if it looks as if I might not make it in time, you must send all those things as quickly as possible."

"We'll be together long before that, you'll see," the lieutenant had said, but he had folded the list very carefully and put it between his army papers in a leather folder.

* * * * * * * * * * * * *

"*Evchen, was soll nur werden?*" (Little Eva, what's to become of you?) Kristin said in the soft sing-song dialect of her homeland. She had gone to look for mail and once again come back with a letter from the lieutenant and no word from the government.

I had entered my own no-man's land. Kristin, who loved me dearly and would have given me the shirt off her back, longed to have our room for herself and her husband. More than once I had caught her looking wistfully at Bertel's crib where her own baby would sleep one day. "I think, I shall paint a flower basket at the headboard," she once said. When Bertel is gone, I thought.

I did not want the crib anymore, and I did not want to go on living in this room that was wanted and needed for Kristin's young family. I spent many hours sitting in the large chair that used to be the lieutenant's place, Bertel on my lap, rocking him gently back and forth and rubbing my cheek against his soft, blond hair. And Bertel, who was attuned to his mother as only the blind and the very young can be to the person nearest to them, Bertel would ask: "When will we go to America, Mamma?"

"Soon," I would answer as the weeks went by, "very soon now." At night, when he said his prayers, he began to add all on his own: "And please, God, let us go to America soon." I don't know what he thought America was; he only knew that it would make his mother happy to go there whatever it might be and so he earnestly prayed for it every night.

"When will you be coming?" the lieutenant wrote anxiously, the long list before him on his desk. "Have you heard yet? Will you be here in time? Are things moving?"

And then, suddenly, without fanfare or warning, things did begin to move. The fireman's mother-in-law, who was our landlady, an invalid, a bitter old woman who lived two floors above us, got a surprising visit one morning.

"Two army officers," her daughters confided to me, "they asked about your reputation. Mother had quite a conversation with them!"

"Well, I have no complaints as far as that goes," the old woman had said, elated by her unexpected importance, "she washes down the steps and entrance every week as she is supposed to do. And she keeps her child clean and quiet. But I would be amiss," said the old dragon meaningfully, "if I would not tell you that until a short time ago an American officer came to see her at least four nights a week."

The two men exchanged a quick look, thanked her politely, and departed. A few days later, during the afternoon hours when Kristin was out grocery shopping, I opened the door to another visitor. It was a man in major's uniform, neither young nor old, and his was the most non-committal face I had ever seen, not excluding my friend Kristin.

"May I have a few minutes of your time?" he asked.

He was a doctor, an army psychologist, and he wanted me to answer some questions. I led him into the back room and we faced each other across the table. I held Bertel on my lap; he would remain still and content that way. The major had a notebook and pencil; he did not bother with small talk. His questions were neither friendly nor unfriendly; they were polite and matter-of-fact; the answers were noted down swiftly and dispassionately. There seemed to be no right or wrong way to answer those questions.

The lieutenant's name? My own?

How long had I know him? Ten months.

What about my family; any siblings? Three brothers; one was killed in the war.

Had I been angry when my brother was killed? Angry? I don't know. Refusing to accept it. Terribly sad.

Was my mother strict? Too strict, maybe? Yes, I often thought so.

My relationship to my father? I loved him with all my heart.

What about the lieutenant's family? Had there been any direct contact? Oh, yes. "They sent this" I pointed to Bertel's sweater, "and the dress I am wearing. And very nice letters."

Did I hate Americans? No, no; I almost laughed, thinking of my whiskey friend and of the red apples at Christmas and the jolly signatures on my application.

What about the time when my brother was shot down by them? (So he knew about it!) How did I feel then? I hated the war. I always did.

Did the lieutenant have a job waiting for him? Yes, he already started.

Was he an educated man? Did I know what college he had attended? I thought for a moment. I had seen it mentioned in his papers.

"Some college named Harvard," I said.

For the first time the pencil hesitated, stopped; the major shot me a quick, questioning glance. He doesn't know how to spell it, I thought, and tactfully busied myself straightening Bertel's sweater. I wasn't too sure myself if it ended with a "d" or "t" (this being pronounced the same way in German). Just then the major apparently decided to take a stab at it and the pencil scribbled it down. Harvard. Ah, perhaps it was a "d" then.

Had I worked? Yes, in the navy during the war, and later taught school in Berlin.

Would I consider a visa that did not include the child? No, not ever. This was the first question that upset me. It also was the last one.

"All right," said the major politely. "Thank you for your cooperation." I took him to the door; a slight nod, a shadow of a smile, and he was gone.

There was a steady stream now of government communications. An appointment date was made for me for a chest x-ray in an army clinic. We were nine girls that morning, leaning against the sickly green wall of the hospital corridor, nervously awaiting our turn, and I saw three of them leaving in tears before my name was called. Dark shadows had been found on their lungs, they were told; they were to go on to more extensive tests, possibly a sanitarium for a while, before returning for another examination. They knew of no sanitarium that would take them. Only three of us passed this first day. TB, as I have mentioned before, was rampant and many carried it in the first stages without knowing it.

A week later I was scheduled for a complete physical examination. It was done by an American woman doctor with hard hands and nothing to say to us. She checked ears, nose, and throat, kneaded the abdomen and listened to our breathing, asking few questions and avoiding our eyes.

While I was slipping back into my clothes she sat down behind her desk, filling out her forms.

"What month?" she said, without looking up.

The icy voice was like a physical blow.

Leave my baby out of this, I wanted to shout, fiercely defensive. Your quarrel is with me, not with my child.

"Sixth," I said, instead, trying to match her coldness.

Unmarried American women serving in the armed forces in Germany usually looked through us as if we did not exist. We were invisible to them. But this airy treatment sometimes hid real anger. There had been a drawing, a cartoon, in the army newspaper sometime earlier which had not helped our mutual relationship.

A young girl was perched on the desk of an American general, holding a German dictionary. The general, sitting behind his desk in full uniform, looked puzzled and frowning. "But, Daddy," said the young girl plaintively, "I simply HAVE to wear civilian clothes and learn German or I will never get a date."

In fairness, it must be said that the decks were stacked in our favor. It wasn't just that there were more of us. There were other, more significant factors. The young German women, many of them war widows, were starved for tenderness, for the attention and touch of a man. They met those cheerful, healthy young Americans more than half way. In some cases more affection might have been shown than felt. But even then, the sudden sparkle of pleasure, the joyful exclamation being presented with a handful of candy bars, half a pack of cigarettes (invaluable for exchange purposes) or a pair of nylons was entirely unfaked. The American soldier was a king who could bestow genuine happiness with very little effort on his part. What hope had an American girl in Germany or Japan to compete with this?

Before he left, the lieutenant had trusted me to the friendship of an older major whose wife and children had come over a few months before. They lived in a pretty villa just outside of Frankfurt and they began looking after me conscientiously. The major's wife was a short, rotund, dark-haired woman with rosy cheeks, who loved her pretty new home, adored being spoiled by her German maids, and who treated me like a frail younger sister who needed kindness and care.

And when one gray, cold March day a thin, official letter arrived (looking not much different from all the others I had received) holding Bertel's and my entrance visa to the States and a short announcement of our departure date and time, I turned to them for help. They would send the telegram to the lieutenant, they would see to it that all necessary preparations were made, and they would take us to the airport in their car. I sent telegrams to my mother and brothers, gathered our belongings and tried to spruce up my two old, long-suffering suitcases. In between I would stop and hug Bertel over and over. We are going to America, oh Schaetzchen, we are really, truly going to America!

Many more things happened during that last week. Loving farewell telegrams arrived from my brothers. Wolfgang had a young wife now and a baby was on the way. I packed one last parcel for them and one for the eternally hungry Dolfi in Berlin. A hurried, urgent letter arrived from my mother: "*PLEASE*, wear a hat! I implore you not to arrive at your new family without hat and gloves, looking like . . ." Yes, I knew, like a maid on her day off. Wailing, furious, guilty, I scrounged around for a hat and found an old painter lady who was willing to part with her majestic, black, pre-war beret for a pack of cigarettes. Gloves had been sent to me in one of the parcels from America, solid, woolen ones, not exactly the kind my mother had in mind.

Bertel suddenly developed a temperature and blisters inside his mouth. I took him to our doctor who diagnosed it as a deficiency disease. "Not enough vitamins," he said, "we don't have medication for it yet. But he'll soon have all the vegetable and fruit he needs."

I began negotiations with Frau Lemke for the emaciated, one-eyed teddy bear. She was ready for me. A pair of stockings, four candy bars, and a jar of powdered milk, a king's ransom for that dilapidated toy, but leaving it behind was unthinkable. Everything I did not need immediately was left for Kristin, including two of the maternity dresses. The third one I would travel in.

The major and his wife invited me for a farewell dinner. It was a grand meal, served with solemn dignity by Frieda and her sister who both winked at me when nobody was looking. The major's wife had brought their little dog over from America and all through the meal the puppy kept pulling and worrying my shoe under the table in spite of the unobtrusive little kicks I aimed at him from time to time.

"Is the dog bothering you, dear?" asked my hostess, and I assured her, not at all, he was just being playful and not the least bit bothersome.

That night, after my host had taken me home, Kristin, always fashion conscious even when there were no fashions, exclaimed: "For heaven's sake, what happened to your shoe?" The wretched pup, I discovered, had chewed a piece out of the top of my right shoe about the size of a nickel.

"What will you do?" Kristin said aghast.

"What can I do? Wear them, of course. Don't be a daft," I said. My nerves were getting a bit frayed. Between Bertel's blisters, the stupid hat, and my chewed up shoe, our American entrance wasn't shaping up quite as planned.

Chapter 32

In the gray fog of our departure day in March, 1947, a long, sleek, black car stopped in front of our house; the major jumped out to help me with our suitcases, one of them discreetly held together with a rope; the other one, black and old-fashioned, still wore on its shiny surface the faded pictures of exotic places and countries that my parents had visited many years ago. Behind the first floor window Frau Lemke's unlovely countenance was visible, surrounded by a multitude of other figures; she must have hurriedly invited most of the neighborhood over. Kristin, looking pale and forlorn, was standing on the sidewalk, an empty milk can in her hand; she would be going on to the dairy shop to get her daily quota of skimmed milk. People across the street stopped and stared. I put Bertel into the car and climbed in after him, turned toward Krstin, who looked dazed, climbed out again and embraced her one more time before hurrying back into the car. The major closed the door, jumped behind the wheel and we drove off. Ten miles out of town, Bertel began to look frantically around the seat. We had left his teddy bear behind.

There were more than forty girls standing on the air field beside the large, four-propeller American plane. All were dressed in their best outfits, but none wore as splendid a headgear as mine. I was holding Bertel, my pocketbook and a carry-on bag; my hands were full and for the time being there was nothing I could do about it. The sky was overcast; a sharp March wind went straight through our coats. The girls shivered, smiling nervously at each other. Three or four of them carried lined baskets presumably with a very small baby under the pink or blue brand new American blankets that covered them.

Newsmen with large cameras appeared, getting in position, hollering at us. "Here, Fraulein, over here! Smile. Come on, stand together, closer . . . that's it. Smile!" For the first time I heard the expression "war brides." I did not want to appear in any pictures with that idiot hat, so Bertel and I stayed in the background. Eventually, we were seated and I immediately stuffed the hat behind me. More than half the plane was occupied by the young women; the rest were military personnel going home.

Suddenly we were airborne. Ecstatically I squeezed Bertel's hand; taking once again his cue from me, he tried to look joyful. He was not at all sure that he liked any of it. Night fell quickly outside the cabin window. Bertel was asleep. I closed my eyes and thought of my last plane ride, three years ago. Then, too, I was carrying a child inside my body, huddled on the narrow bench in the cavernous icy bowels of the transport plane, flying over the Balkan mountains; my only companion the sullen, silent girl across from me, and the pilot's words humming in my head like poisonous wasps: "Remember, the air space is not ours anymore . . . we are slow . . . we might be attacked at any moment."

This plane was warm and bright and when we descended over Amsterdam, the city beneath us was bathed in light. Beside me, Bertel awakened and made a retching sound; he was ash-white. Hastily I searched for the seasickness bag but by that time the wheels bumped onto the ground and Bertel's breathing returned to normal. Our stop in Amsterdam was short and soon the plane headed across the channel toward Ireland. When we began to descend over Shannon, Bertel gagged again and I quickly stretched him out over my lap. It was almost midnight now and a steady rain beat against the cabin window.

"You will be served a meal here. Please debark," said the stewardess. Slowly the plane emptied. I saw men in uniform standing outside the plane door, holding large umbrellas. The girl in front of me was carrying a baby basket. Quickly a man lifted it out of her hand, holding it close under his umbrella and a second man held an umbrella over the girl. A third man picked up Bertel and another one, returning from the lighted barrack across the runway, was taking me under his wing. Long tables were set up in the barrack and swiftly and efficiently a warm meal was served to us. Why do I recall all that so clearly . . . the umbrellas, the meal? I have a long memory for kindness but particularly and distinctly for kindnesses that came our way during those years from sources that we had learned to regard as alien

and hurtful and of which we expected, at best, indifference to our circumstances and existence.

When we left Shannon, the continent fell behind us, and with it a world
and a life that, for better or worse, we knew and of which we had taken
the measure and survived. Through the dark night sky we now were rushing toward another continent of which we knew little; one that had sent
for many months helmeted and goggled warriors over the ocean who rained
death and destruction on us. When those airborne warriors, at long last,
descended to earth to meet us, they had turned into loose-limbed, sociable
young men, remarkably untroubled, who smelled of soap and spearmint,
kicked their shoes and helmets about, and carried half a dozen family snapshots in their back pockets. One of these young men I had come to know
and love and that one was waiting for me now on the shore of this endless, mysterious continent, and all my hopes and fears rested with him.

We flew with the night and it seemed that this night would never end.
When the plane began its descent over Newfoundland to refuel, gray morning light appeared at the horizon. I saw nothing of the land beneath us.
This time the small child beside me, who had been sleeping, threw up so
quickly that I could not get the bag out in time. All of the midnight meal
surged up toward daylight and the one-hour stay at the airport was spent
in the washroom cleaning Bertel and his clothes. Most of the girls swarmed
through the halls, wide-eyed, mesmerized by the window displays of the
few diminutive shops. We had been told that we were not permitted to
have any currency with us and so the dollars which the lieutenant had sent
for our travel had remained with Kristin.

For the rest of the trip, Bertel slept like dead lying across my lap.
When we climbed out of the plane at La Guardia on this dismal March
morning it had been twenty-five hours since we had left Germany. I held
Bertel by the hand; he had gagged again coming down but the bag had
been ready this time and his stomach was just about empty. The little boy
kept close to me. White-faced, pinched with cold, his clothes still damp
from the cleaning, he looked around the raw, bleak airfield and pressed
harder against me.

"Where is America, Mama?" he said disconsolately.

Again there were men with flopping raincoats and large cameras milling around us and cries of "Hey, Fräulein, smile!" and "Over here, Fräulein!"
came from all sides. They wanted us to form a group . . . "The young ladies
with the baby baskets in front, please," but most of the girls looked hol-

low-eyed and tousled (Bertel was not the only one who had been airsick), and nobody wanted to be in front.

"Who are they?" I heard a man, passing by, ask one of the cameramen.

"They are the first war brides from Germany" was the answer.

"Good Lord!" said the man and shot an incredulous look back over his shoulder.

We were taken to a large room and told to wait for our names to be called. There were four or five desks with immigration officials behind them. When my name was called I went to the desk and sat down on the chair facing the officer. One glance told me that I was dealing with an enemy. He did not look at me or Bertel; his questions were abrupt, he took no notes; the answers were already right there on the papers in front of him.

"You will have to pay seven dollars airport tax," he said, at length, turning his fish eyes on me for the first time.

"We were not permitted to bring any money," I said, puzzled. He shrugged his shoulders and leaned back in his chair, his whole demeanor indicating that, in that case, I would have to go back where I came from. His manner made me uneasy; I was not certain anymore that we had met all the imperative requirements. Observing me out of the corner of his eye, he seemed pleased and I suddenly thought of my Latin teacher. Do people like that pull wings off little flies when they are bored? Having satisfied himself that I was scared, he picked up a phone and called the page phone. "Will Mr. George . . ." Mister! It came as a shock. I had never thought of him that way. All the Americans I knew wore uniforms.

Like a beam of daylight breaking through an ugly nightmare, George appeared beside the desk. He wore a camel hair coat over a white shirt and tie and through the rush of relief I felt, I found myself thinking: ah, that's what he looks like in civilian clothes! He sat down, taking Bertel on his lap who joyfully clung to him.

The immigration officer now was all courtesy and concern. George paid the seven dollars, signed some papers and asked if we were free to go.

"Just a moment," said my immigration friend. He scribbled something on a piece of paper, turned it upside down, and pushed it toward George, who read it, smiled, and nodded. The officer shrugged, looked resigned, and dismissed us with a wave of his hand.

Carrying Bertel on one arm and both suitcases with the other, George led the way toward the exit and the waiting car.

"What was on the paper?" I asked, curiosity killing me. George put Bertel down to open the car door, a grin on his face. He fished the paper out of his pocket and while he stowed away the cases, I read the immigration officer's parting message:

"Do you know that this woman is pregnant?"

"The old crocodile," I said indignant, and George laughed. And then he said: "Welcome to America, darling." He had a blue car, not new, but wonderfully large and comfortable and the first thing I saw was a brand new teddy bear sitting on the back seat.

George had taken a hotel room outside of New York. Bertel was running a fever now; the blistering around his mouth was getting worse. I longed to put him to bed but George wanted to show me at least a sample of the city. The skyscrapers whose tops I could not see through the car windows, the multitude of well-dressed people, the traffic in the streets were breathtaking. But it was the sight of the grocery stores that stunned me. Out of the open shop doors, onto hidden tables underneath, huge, golden oranges seemed to flow, blue and green grapes were draped around mountains of shiny apples and speckled grapefruits; bunches of yellow and green bananas looked as if they had been picked off the tree that morning.

"This is Fifth Avenue," George said, ". . . and this is Macy's. And this is 34th Street and this is the Empire State Building!"

"Look at the fruit, darling," I murmured into Bertel's hair. "Oh, darling, look at the fruit!"

We drove out of the city to New Brunswick, where George's brother-in-law was a student. Kathrin, his sister, a finely boned, graceful young woman, was expecting their first child within the week. (My instincts had been right, Kathrin had tiny feet and so did all seven unmarried aunts when I met them.) Her husband was a tall, balding young man with affable manners and a quick wit. A dog, about as big as his mistress, jumped ecstatically around us.

We could not take Bertel with us the next day; he was ill. George left to attend to some necessary legalities and my sister-in-law took me shopping: a light blue wool coat, two maternity dresses, a dark blue pillbox hat, a blue cardigan and a pair of shoes. Jack, George's brother-in-law, was entrusted with the babysitting. He knew no German outside of *Kindergarten*, *Gesundheit*, and *kaputt*, and Bertel spoke no English.

The wealth of clothes from which to choose almost made me forget Bertel for a while, but on the way home my conscience greatly bothered me and the hotel elevator did not rise fast enough to the fifth floor. I wondered how I could have left the sick child with a man he did not know and with whom he could not communicate. The hall was quiet; at least he was not crying. When I opened the door to our room I was struck dumb for a second. In bed, on top of the blanket, sat a small figure which I recognized by the pajama pants as my son. The rest of him was covered with an enormous paper bag into which two holes had been cut for the eyes and a slit for the mouth. On the chair beside the bed sat a similar figure, paper bag and all, only considerably larger. I ran toward the bed.

"How are you, Schaetzchen?"

"I am not *Schaetzchen*," a hollow voice from inside the paper bag said reproachfully. "I am a *SPACE* man. We are both spacemen."

"How did you manage that?" I asked in wonder, and the big fellow just grinned and shrugged his shoulders. "Nothing to it."

On the third morning, a police judge who looked as if he had slept in his clothes and had not been refreshed by it, mumbled the obligatory words and set his seal on the marriage certificate. Through the half open door I could see the unmade bed in the next room.

We gathered Bertel and our luggage at the hotel and got ready for the last leg of our journey.

"You take the dog along home," said Jack. "We can't have this monster and a baby in our small apartment. Your Dad knows," he added, and cutting Kathrin's tearful goodbye to the animal short, he shoved it firmly into the back of our car.

It was the longest car ride I had ever taken in my life. We stopped once to eat and walk the dog. Bertel, his forehead very warm now and blisters all around his mouth, slept fitfully, his head on my lap and his feet on George's knees. Both arms were clasped tightly around his new teddy bear.

"Dad moved into the guest room," George told me. "We have the big bedroom, and the nursery is right next door. We'll have a doctor for Bertel tomorrow; he'll get penicillin. It's supposed to work wonders, they say." I shifted positions gingerly; whenever Bertel got awake he threatened to be carsick.

It got dark; large, wet snowflakes began to splash against the windshield. The car rocked a bit in the rising wind and the dog in the back began to whimper. We stopped at a booth for a ticket and entered an autobahn.

"The Pennsylvania Turnpike," George said proudly, "it won't be long now." The snow came faster now, denser, less wet; the ground looked white and treacherous. When the car rounded the first mountain curves, the dog threw up on the floor behind us. George pulled to the side of the road and scooped up a handful of snow in an attempt to clean up the mess but the dog frantically tried to get past him and he had to give up. Twenty more minutes into the storm the car started to sputter and slow down. George shifted to second, then to first gear. The car moved on, unwilling but steadier.

"We'll have to find a garage at the next exit," George said. "Something is definitely wrong."

We crept through a sleeping town until we found an all-night garage. The garage was heated but a biting wind came through the open doors. I sat on an empty crate, holding Bertel with one hand; with the other hand I held on to the dog who showed every indication of wanting to head back east at the first possible opportunity. George went to telephone his father that we would be late. It might be midnight before we would reach home.

After an hour the mechanic declared that this was as much as he could do for the moment; it would make the last forty miles, he thought, and we headed back to the turnpike. The storm was really howling now; snowflakes were dancing frenzied in the beam of the headlights and George kept his eyes glued to the road.

And then, suddenly, we turned into an exit again, stopped, paid a man huddled in a booth, and drove slowly through a dark little town, lit only by an occasional street lamp.

"This is our court house," my "lieutenant" said, his voice hardly suppressing his excitement, "this is our street. Over there is Aunt Mabel's house, and across the white one, Aunt Natalie's. And here is our house!"

The two story brick house was the only one with all the downstairs windows lighted. The wind was whipping a large maple tree in front of it; the rigid old branches were straining toward the roof as if to look for shelter. Somebody in the house had been watching and listening and had heard the car stop over the howling of the wind. The front door opened and a man stepped onto the threshold. The dog jumped out of the car and greedily began eating the snow. George lifted Bertel off my lap and I stiffly climbed out of my seat. My legs were numb under me and I was afraid of falling on the snow-covered walk. Against the pale yellow light coming from the hall behind I saw the slight figure of a man standing in the doorway, his sparse, gray hair was standing straight up in the wind. As I walked toward him, he stretched out both his hands.

"Welcome," he said, "Welcome, welcome!"

EPILOG

1988

Berlin

My mother died on the second day of March, 1988, in her 93rd year. Since no known member of her family had ever reached this venerable age, she had seen no reason to leave so vital a concern in the hands of chance and untrustworthy genes. Sometime during the ninth decade of her life she had consulted and advised one or more specialists in almost every field of medicine and was able to speak with authority of the weaknesses and advantages of a dozen of Berlin's larger hospitals. Years ago she had decided that in a case of emergency, a call to the firemen was greatly to be preferred to a regular ambulance. They appeared quicker at the scene and were less given to taking blood pressure and temperature and asking a lot of unnecessary questions. They simply turned to the task at hand which seemed to them, as well as to my mother, to get her to a hospital as quickly as possible. My mother, in turn, cooperated gallantly by gaining consciousness long enough to direct them toward her handbag, slippers, and reading glasses and to provide them with the name and address of the hospital to which she wished to be taken.

Unfortunately, her faith in the sound judgment of those good men was cruelly shaken only a few months before her death. Concerned friends had a callbox installed in her apartment that was directly connected to a Red Cross Center and through which my mother signed off every evening before going to bed. Whenever she forgot to do so, the little box emitted a great deal of noise: loud beepings, interrupted intermittently by an urgent voice calling my mother's name until, half exasperated, half apologetic, she would rouse herself and respond. On this particular evening, when no answer could be elicited, the Red Cross worker, following procedure, called a neighbor, who put on her robe and shuffled across the hall to ring the bell and pound on the apartment door. When this, too, proved fruitless, the Red Cross alerted the fire department, which promptly went into action. Two astute fighters climbed to the second floor kitchen window and forced it open, smashing in the process every one of the ancient cactus plants on the windowsill. The men then located the bedroom and wakened my mother, who had been sound asleep and showed a deplorable lack of gratitude on this occasion. The next day she ordered bars installed across the kitchen window, prohibiting any further rescue attempts of this kind.

With the aid of the callbox, two cleaning women, the telephone, and something she called her "rhythm" (meaning a strict adherence to a daily routine), she managed quite well, although her children and friends began to worry about her rapidly failing sight, her imperfect hearing, and her frequent lightheadedness. She still went out at times, she held her subscription seat at the concert hall, and she still gathered occasionally a few friends for a tea party at her home.

The old ladies and gentlemen arrived, singly and slowly, and their panting up the one flight of stairs could be heard before they themselves came into sight. They came with their umbrellas and canes, their eyedrops and heart medication, and were seated around the table in carefully arranged order. (My mother would rather have forgotten the date of a party than to leave a seating arrangement to chance.) Two or three lamps shed their soft light through the room, causing the polished old furniture to gleam. The gold-stamped words on the rows of books and the solemn, white faces in the portraits shimmered through the darkness of the background.

The table was covered with a white lace cloth, stained faintly yellow in spots, which would be noticed neither by my mother nor her guests. They ate small fruit-covered cakes, using ornate silver forks, and they drank tea out of paper thin cups whose bottoms showed the same ancient yellow stains as the table cloth. None of these people were in good health; illness and death hovered behind each one of them like an unloved and unlovely companion who was nevertheless quietly acknowledged and accepted.

I never heard them discuss their ailments, pains, or fears. Theater, books, passionate opinions on politics and philosophies, were aired on these occasions, often until long past supper time. Then my mother would be left, sinking, at long last, into the cushions of the stiff little Victorian sofa, exhausted, exhilarated, and complaining: "Ach, how could they stay so long? Why did they not leave earlier? I was so afraid that they might expect sandwiches. Do you think they had a good time?"

"They had a wonderful time, Mutti," I would say. "Why else would they have stayed so long?"

"Do you think so? Ach, do you really think so?" my mother would say, enormously pleased but trying to look doubtful. "What did you think of Frau L.? She has such strong opinions about the pope. And you know, Frau M. is Catholic, though not extremely so; that's why I always put Dr. R. between them. He is very diplomatic in such cases; did you hear him say ..." and off she was, her exhaustion forgotten, reliving every incident of the afternoon. The success of such a party was her sustenance, her lifeline, the reaffirmation of herself as a person and hostess of consequence.

There was an unusual fact about the two cleaning women who appeared once a week and, pleasantly but haphazardly, kept the little household going: neither one knew of the existence of the other. My mother was convinced that by keeping the two women in ignorance of each other, she had hit on an unbeatable system. They would take much better care of her, she explained to me, if each one thought she was the only one responsible for keeping her old employer happy and comfortable. As soon as they learned of their competition, their interest would flag, their work ethic would suffer, and, furthermore said my mother, they would forever be blaming each other for cracked dishes and poorly washed woolens.

Incredible as it seems, this system worked for many years, though not without its moments of excitement. The inevitable crisis occurred one warm summer morning when suddenly the system seemed doomed and exposure imminent. However, my mother once again rose to the occasion. She woke that morning with a start and a feeling of impending disaster. It took her a few minutes to concentrate on the day's program and, with a shock, she realized that both women would appear *at her doorstep* within little more than an hour. By an appalling coincidence, each one, that week, had begged off her regular time and had been rescheduled by my mother for the same day. Neither one, at this point, could be reached by phone. Realizing this and stumbling out of bed was one and the same thing. With fumbling, flying fingers, she pulled on her clothes. Waiving all the niceties like water and soap, hairbrush and earrings, she gathered her purse and gloves, set her white straw hat adrift on her head, and rushed out of the door heading toward the subway. The older of the two women would arrive there half an hour before the younger one, who had to take a child to school.

She was standing at the top of the exit, breathing hard and holding on to the low cement wall beside her when the woman appeared coming up the steps.

"Frau Kamper! Ach, dear Frau Kamper," cried my mother, hurling herself at the astonished woman. "Something unexpected has come up. I have been invited for the day...yes, for the whole day. To Lake Wannsee. A boat trip and dinner, you know. In fact, I am on my way there right now. I am so sorry I could not reach you by phone," said my mother, who was very sorry indeed about this last failure. "Of course, I shall pay your subway fare..."

"That's perfectly all right, my dear," said the woman, laying a comforting hand on my mother's sleeve. She could not help noticing her old employer's agitation. "How lovely for you. What a nice day for such an outing. Now don't you worry about me. You just go and have a good time."

And then Frau Kamper, who had a kind and generous heart, took hold of my mother's arm and gently and firmly guided her down the subway steps and straight into the train to Lake Wannsee. All my mother's protests that she was to look after her own return trip were answered reasonably and cheerfully that she now had all day to do so and she stood there and waved and nodded to my mother until the train had pulled out of the station. My mother, who had feebly waved back, got out at the next stop and took the first train back home, where she arrived three minutes before the second woman rang the bell. She then took to her bed, put cold compresses over the region of her heart, and for the rest of the day concentrated on regaining her rhythm.

As the years wore on and the ranks of the old faithful thinned, her efforts to remain in control became ever more determined. Passing her kitchen door one day, I heard her speaking to an elderly house guest. "Dear Friedrich," she was saying in her clear, decisive voice, "since neither you nor I have any intention of entering an old folks home in the near future, I suggest that you remember where you put things."

In the end it was her circulatory system, marshalled along so energetically through so many years with long hikes and bruising cold rubdowns, that failed her. A hearing aid had to be obtained, regarded by her as an outrage and treated as such. When the thickest lenses refused to decipher her beloved books, she resorted to tapes. Although her walk became a slow and unsteady process, alarmingly resembling a rudderless ship on the high sea, she never consented to use a cane. A cane meant surrender, and this she was not yet prepared to do.

Her "rhythm" now was everything to her. Visits by her great grandchildren, notorious interrupters of routine and rhythm, were prohibited. Grandchildren's visits were curtailed and programmed to the smallest detail. Her children from overseas had to appear before evening or spend the night at a hotel. When George and I, who were staying with her for a week, returned from a visit with friends at the rhythm-threatening hour of a quarter to ten P.M., she had put the chain on the door and locked us out. A young woman now appeared every morning for three hours, tending to her wishes and needs and filling the role of chauffeur, nurse and companion. When the woman left for her yearly vacation with her family, my mother sulked for days. She severely scrutinized all replacements and thereafter suffered them with irritable resignation.

The only tolerated deviations from her rhythm were those that had her consent and would place her at the center of attention. On those rare moments, the years would fall off her as so many wilted leaves, and once again she was the indestructible, commanding figure she used to be. When, on her 90th birthday, she entered the large lobby of East Berlin's most luxurious hotel, her waiting family rose in awe to greet the small, elegant woman who approached them slowly and serenely on the arm of her oldest son.

"It is a great honor for me," said the young East German hostess, caught in the grace and spirit of this ancient lady, "to help you celebrate this day." And my mother inclined her head in a gracious and unsurprised acknowledgement of this tribute.

There were nights now when she was frightened and in pain and neighbors had to call for an ambulance. Her hospital stays became more frequent and lasted longer. On the whole, she rather liked those stays. She always had a private room. The few times some poor, misguided admissions employee put her in a double room, my mother would either fall violently ill or else raise such a ruckus that the error was hastily corrected. She praised brusque or indifferent nurses for their kindness, giving them no choice but to become kinder and more attentive. She soon knew all about their varicose veins and their difficult teenagers at home. And she always was a little in love with the chief of the medical staff, the "Herr Professor." When this man trifled with her affection, when he forfeited this love, she went home and took his hospital off her list.

During one of these hospital stays in the summer of 1986, I spent some time alone in my mother's apartment. Every morning I took the subway for the hour-long trip to the other side of the city. The hospital was a massive, bleak building surrounded by a spacious park with shade trees, flower beds and grass plots sprinkled with wooden benches. This park was by no means thought of as only decorative; many wan and wrinkled figures in ill-fitting, washed-out hospital robes shuffled along the pebbled walks or rested on the benches, feeding the birds with crumbs saved from their breakfast.

The hospital halls were sober and uncompromising, but my mother's room, though small, was cheerful enough. I always found her propped up by an assortment of cushions, seated at the table beside the large window that gave her view into the branches of a tree and a bit of lawn beneath it. When I entered the room she turned her head toward the door. If her face lit up and she stretched her arms out toward me, I knew that we were off to a good start. Whenever something had offended her during my previous visit, or when she considered me late (which was not so much measured by the clock but by the time she had been waiting for me), she would say good morning in a distant voice and politely inquire about my health and my rest that night. I frequently spent the time walking between the subway station and the hospital going over various details of my visit the day before and rehearsing how much of my own phone conversations and encounters I should report to her. Her thin, veined hands reached eagerly for the mail I had brought. Peering through her thick spectacles, which always seemed much too heavy for the frail face, and holding a large magnifying glass over the paper, she would study the handwriting on the envelopes and the signatures on the cards.

"*Ach, die gute Charlotte,*" she would say, "I wonder if she is still upset over her daughter's wedding. This one is from Frau S. Look at the fine hand! She still goes every summer to the lecture series in Heidelberg." My mother's respect and admiration for learning would remain with her to the last day of her life.

For a minute she studied intently the handwriting on the next envelope; then, with a short, imperious motion, she pushed the letter aside without comment. I knew the woman who wrote it. A few years earlier she had committed the unforgivable sin of phoning my mother after a long period of silence when I happened to be in town. My mother did not consider that a coincidence, and I knew that she would neither answer nor read the letter.

It was a good morning and my mother was full of talk of the nurses, the young residents, and, of course, her beloved professor.

"But you know," she said sadly, "I don't think he is giving me the right kind of medicine. It does not seem to help. It takes my appetite, it makes me dizzy. And around midnight last night I hardly had any pulse at all."
"How do you know that, Mutti?" I asked.

"Well, of course by counting it," she said impatiently. "I often take my pulse in the night."

"You must tell the professor about this. He might want to change your medication."

"Yes, of course, I will, some time," she said. "But he is so very busy; I shall have to wait for a good opportunity. In the meantime I am taking my old medicine again."

"What do you mean: your old medicine?"

"Look in my handbag," said my mother.

I opened the heavy black purse which lay at the bottom of the bed and stared aghast at half a dozen pill boxes and little brown bottles. "You take that stuff, too, along with the medication here?"

"Yes," said my mother, very pleased with her foresight, "I brought it with me just in case the new medication would not work."

After a while she grew restless. She asked for her brush and pulled it through her dry gray hair. Then she arranged her cushions and straightened her robe. Her answers became distracted. "What time is it?" she asked. She had taken off her heavy spectacles and now, fumbling a bit and fingering her ear, she pulled out her hearing aid. "What time is it?" she asked again. Just then I could hear a quick step in the hall. With one swift motion my mother pushed her hearing aid under the pile of letters on the table and the professor entered the room, a good looking man in his mid-forties, a little balding, with fresh color and a jovial manner. He was alone and he sat down on the edge of the bed as one might do for a friendly little social call.

"How are we today," he said, smiling at his patient. It was not a question. "Your mother is a very exceptional person," he said, still looking and smiling at her. "She is coming along just fine. We are all very fond of her. In another week or two she might be well enough to go home again. We will certainly miss her."

I looked at my mother. Her cheeks were flushed and there was a sparkle in her eyes that seemed to break through the milky veil that usually covered them. She was smiling at him, completely unselfconscious, with the shy, adoring expression of a young girl in love for the first time. And the man in the short, white, unbuttoned coat, sitting casually with crossed legs at the bottom of the bed, responded to it just as unconsciously. I decided that this was not the time to bring up the black handbag and its sinister contents.

The entire visit did not take longer than three or four minutes. After the door closed behind him, my mother turned to me, beaming.

"What do you think?" she said. She was automatically pushing her hearing aid back into place. "Did you like him? Did you truly like him? Isn't he wonderful? Tell me what he said!"

I am sorry to report that this love affair, too, came to an abrupt end. On one of the professor's visits, my mother's pretty nurse-companion was with her. After a minute or two, the professor's attention strayed, and for the rest of the visit he addressed himself with some warmth to the young woman, right over his patient's head. His patient did not forget this. The next time she went to a hospital, it was a different one in another part of town, and she never consented to see him again.

When her circulatory system became too weak to sustain her legs any longer, my mother entered a hospital for the last time. While the doctors consulted and talked about life-saving operations, of taking her left leg, my mother, at long last, came to terms with death. She did it alone, consulting no one, as she had made every decision alone for half a century. One more time this ninety-two-year-old woman, debilitated by medication, riddled by pain, exhausted by age and illness, mustered all her formidable strength and willpower and pitted it against her surrounding world. Without a doctor's signature, over the nurses' protest, she discharged herself from the hospital, ordered an ambulance, and was taken to a place where there was no talk of knives, where pain was dealt with effectively, and death was an acceptable alternative.

And so she spent the last days of her life in peaceful half-slumber, reminiscing in her conscious moments, and holding her son's hand and her eyes resting softly on her daughter-in-law as they had not done in bygone years. Her rhythm intact, she died in her sleep, as she had planned all along.

* * * * * * * * * * * * *

I did not know the minister who spoke with affection and knowledge at my mother's memorial service, but this did not surprise me. Although on the darker side of the agnostic herself, my mother had always counted at least one clergyman among her more intimate friends. These men were, by no means, clones of each other, but they all shared certain traits: they were no strangers to worldly habits, and were endowed with a good sense of humor. They were philosophers as well as theologians who liked their Rhine wine, a pretty face, and a lively discussion. But as the century grew older, so did they; one by one they faded into illness and death and left a vacancy increasingly hard to fill. My mother's own growing frailness made it more unlikely to meet new people and her requirements for this position were stringent.

Through friends she made the acquaintance of an older minister, a sardonic-looking man who qualified well in the Rhine wine department, but who seemed to have more doubts than she herself in religious matters which, she felt, was both unbecoming and alarming.

The second possibility, a young pastor of ruddy complexion and healthy opinions, came to grief over bad timing. During one of his visits, believing my mother to be occupied for a while with the teapot, he attended to his nose; but my mother, never to be second-guessed, turned around unexpectedly and this candidate, too, was speedily excused.

She confided her frustration to an old friend, a scientist, who upon his retirement had joined a religious community in the south of Germany. His response was immediate and ecstatic: "Jesus was ready to redeem her with his blood and receive her with open arms into his flock." My mother's answer to this joyful news was not all he had hoped for. Anymore such nonsense, she wrote, and she would be obliged to end their otherwise enjoyable friendship. This letter was read with some melancholy by the old gentleman and no more spiritual advice was dispatched from those quarters.

* * * * * * * * * * * * * *

And now we were seated in a half circle in the dimly lit chapel and listened to this stranger, this tall, bespectacled man, with his friendly, round face and his black robe, talking earnestly of the deceased. He told us about the last two years of friendship and trust with which this remarkable lady had honored him. He, himself, he said, would sorely miss their inspired discussions and her noble and good advice. There was nothing routine about his talk; he was both eloquent and moving and he genuinely grieved for her.

Truly, we had lost a remarkable woman. Her children had not known her very well, but the minister did not say this. Possibly, he was not aware of it.